KW-326-482

Arab and Islamic Laws Series

The Islamic Law of Personal Status

Third Edition

Jamal J. Nasir, CVO, BA (Hons), PhD (Lond)

Barrister (of Lincoln's Inn)
Former Minister of Justice and Senator of Jordan
Senior Counsel on all questions of International,
Arab and African Laws
Member of the Jordan Bar and entitled to
practise before other Arab Bars
Member of the Nigerian Bar
Counsel on Islamic Law
One time Lecturer on International Law
Advocate

KLUWER LAW INTERNATIONAL
THE HAGUE / LONDON / NEW YORK

Published by:
Kluwer Law International
P.O. Box 85889, 2508 CN The Hague, The Netherlands
sales@kli.wkap.nl
http://www.kluwerlaw.com

Sold and Distributed in North, Central and South America by:
Kluwer Law International
101 Philip Drive, Norwell, MA 02061, USA
kluwerlaw@wkap.com

Sold and Distributed in all other countries by:
Kluwer Law International
Distribution Centre, P.O. Box 322, 3300 AH Dordrecht, The Netherlands

Library of Congress Cataloging-in-Publication Data is available

Printed on acid-free paper.

ISBN 90-411-1661-3
© 2002 Kluwer Law International

Kluwer Law International incorporates the publishing programmes
of Graham & Trotman Ltd, Kluwer Law and Taxation Publishers
and Martinus Nijhoff Publishers

This publication is protected by international copyright law.
All rights reserved. No part of this publication may be reproduced, stored in a retrieval
system, or transmitted in any form or by any means, electronic, mechanical,
photocopying, recording or otherwise, without the prior permission of the publisher.

Printed and bound in Great Britain by Antony Rowe Limited.

Dedicated in gratitude and affection to my late father Jamil, as all his friends knew him, to my son, Khaled, in recognition of his distinguished academic and professional achievements, and to my family

Table of Contents

Foreword

It was with diffidence that I agreed to write this brief Foreword to Dr. Jamal Jamil Nasir's learned work on *The Islamic Law of Personal Status.* Although as a comparatist I have, of course, an interest in Islamic law, my knowledge of the great legal tradition embodied in the Sharia is both limited and superficial. Accordingly, I can only discuss in general terms Dr. Nasir's valuable work.

Dr. Nasir writes with the practitioner particularly in mind. The very nature of the Islamic legal tradition requires that the contemporary law of personal status found in Arabic countries be presented against the background of the Quran and the Sunna as explicated by the several Juristic Schools. The Sharia – resting on Allah's commands for Muslim society – was, and remains, a divine law.

Accordingly, Dr Nasir begins with an Introduction which treats the historical development of Islamic Jurisprudence, the Islamic Schools of Law, and the Methodology used by Islamic Jurists. Turning then to particular topics such as marriage, dower, dissolution of marriage, inheritance, and wills, he begins the discussion in each instance with a consideration of the subject in Sharia law. The legislation and contemporary views of particular Arabic countries are then presented for each topic.

This approach emphasizes the continuity of the Islamic law respecting personal status; at every point, the influence of the Sharia on contemporary practices and solutions is evident. This is not to say that contemporary legislation and practices exhibit no differences from the Sharia. However, at least to a non-Muslim, the differences seem, by and large, to take the form of evolutionary developments from – rather than sharp breaks with – the Sharia tradition.

The task Dr. Nasir set for himself being the presentation of the personal law of various Arabic countries to practitioners, he does not pursue the question of how faithful this contemporary legislation is to Islamic tradition. Doubtless no simple answer can be given, although the issue is one of considerable cultural and political importance in many parts of the Middle East.

For a variety of reasons, in the past the presentation of Islamic law to Western lawyers has been to a considerable extent through the writings of non-Muslims. These writers have, for the most part, been deeply learned in the Arabic language and in Islamic culture and history. However, a non-Muslim's perception and understanding of an area such as personal status is informed by a sensibility that is different from that of a Muslim.

Accordingly, a treatment of *The Islamic Law of Personal Status* by an Arab with Dr. Nasir's distinguished credentials is particularly welcome. Member of the Jordan Bar and former Minister of Justice of that country, he practised before the Federal Supreme Court of Nigeria and appeared before International Tribunals. His present practice at the English Bar includes questions of Islamic law. His book is an important contribution. Although intended primarily for the practitioner, it contributes as well to general understanding of an area of law that is of special significance in Arabic society.

Arthur Taylor von Mehren
Story Professor of Law
Harvard University

Preface

This new and complete third edition, like its predecessors, is a systematic account of the Islamic personal status provisions under both the traditional Sharia Law and modern enactments of Middle Eastern and North African states. Indeed this work is the first of its kind, both in the Arabic and English languages.

Since the first and second editions of this book were published, an enactment of personal status provisions has occurred in Kuwait, the Yemen and Sudan. These new provisions have been given adequate coverage in the relevant chapters of this third edition in order to complete the chain of modern enactments in the Islamic states. What is equally important is that this new edition has adapted into the English language, probably for the first time, the original works of the Shiite and Jaafari schools. At the same time, the analysis of the legal aspects of each of these schools has been carried out possibly more thoroughly than ever before.

The encouraging reception of the first two editions by the Courts, legal practitioners and those concerned with the development of Islamic Law (especially among Muslim communities abroad), has been an incentive to respond to the requests of so many to undertake a revision, taking account of these recent enactments, and to include all the substantial amendments and additions that have taken place since the publication of those first two editions.

It is my hope that the publication of this third edition, after many months of research and investigation, may offer direct access based on up-to-date developments, particularly to courts and practitioners, as well as to universities and other institutions and their students, and to others interested in this most important subject.

These editions contribute to a general understanding of an area of law that is of specific significance to the lives of many millions of people of the Islamic faith throughout the world.

I feel it is now appropriate to explain that Islamic fanaticism is alien to Islamic teachings. It is not in the Islamic tradition or way of thinking. Equally, fundamentalism is just one way of understanding the Quran and the *Sunna*, and no fundamentalist has the right to impose his opinions as the ultimate truth. Fundamentalism, when it is synonymous with fanaticism, wherever it occurs, in whatever religion or doctrine, is a disease that must be rooted out.

Introduction
Origins and Development of Islamic Jurisprudence

1. Definition

What is Islam? The Arabic word is a derivative of the Arabic radical *Salam* from which many other words are formed, such as *Salaam* meaning peace,[1] *Salaama* meaning safety, *Saleem* meaning healthy, safe, sound, etc.

The word 'Islam' itself is the noun form of the verb *aslama* which means to surrender. Juristically, Islam is man's submission and resignation to and acceptance of God's Commands and Will. This was fundamentally the message revealed to every prophet to deliver to his own people throughout the history of mankind.

In this sense, Islam and its derivatives are used in many verses of the Quran. Ibrahim [Abraham], the common ancestor of the Arabs and Jews, is described as 'a faithful Muslim'. (3:67)

> '"Or were ye witnesses when Jacob, approaching his death" quoth he to his sons "What will ye worship after me?" Quoth they, "We shall worship thy God and the God of thy fathers, of Ibrahim, Ismail and Isaac. One God to whom we submit"' [we are Muslims] (2:13)
> 'Said the Disciples [of Jesus], "We are the partisans of God, we believe in God and bear thee witness we are Muslims."' (3:52)
> 'Verily we have revealed the Torah; therein is guidance and light; thereby the Jews are judged by the prophets who submitted [to God] "Aslamu."' (5:44)

More specifically, Islam is the religious faith proclaimed by the Prophet Muhammad from 610 AD to his death in 632 AD. This is the meaning of the word in later '*Suras*' (chapters or sections of the Quran). 'Today I have perfected your religion for you and completed My Grace upon you and have chosen for you Islam as your religion.' (5:13)[2]

---

[1] Cf. Darus-Salam, *Haven of Peace*, a description of Baghdad at its golden age as the capital of the Abbasid Empire. It is also the name of the capital, spelt as Dares-Salam, of the United Republic of Tanzania, and forms part of the name of the Sultanate of Brunei Darussalam.
[2] This fifth *Sura* of the Quran "Al-Maida", was revealed in Medina, during the last pilgrimage rite "*Hijjatul-Wadaa*", performed by the Prophet shortly before his death.

1

Within a century of the Prophet's death, early generations of Muslims of the Arabian Peninsula, the birth-place of Islam, could spread, through conquest, the system of values of their nascent religion over a great part of the then known world. The boundaries of the new Islamic empire reached from Spain to India, through Central Asia.

Today, there are about one billion Muslims,[3] one fifth of the world's present population, drawn from a vast variety of races and cultures, extending west from the heart-land of Islam to the shores of the Atlantic, and east to the shores of the Pacific, bound by a common faith and a sense of belonging to a single community (*Umma*), a bond which dates back to the very beginnings of Islam.

There are two main Muslim Schools,[4] the Sunnis (*Ahlus-Sunnati Wal Jamaa*) usually meaning the community at large, (*Al Jumhoor*) who constitute nine tenths of the *Umma*, and the Shias who comprise the balance. However, they all believe in One Universal Just God, in the mission of His Apostle Muhammad, the seal of all prophets, and in the mission of all the other apostles and prophets before him, including Jesus Christ, Moses, Ibrahim and Adam, and in the Teachings and Books revealed to them, in the Unseen (*Ghaib*), in the Resurrection (*Baath*) and in the Life Hereafter (*al-Aakhira*), 'When anyone who has done an atom's weight of good shall see it and anyone who has done an atom of evil shall see it.' (91:7–8)

2. Early Legislation: The Era of the Prophet (10 BH–12 AH, 610–632 AD)

From the days of the Prophet, Islam was not just a religion but a complete code for living, combining the spiritual and the secular, and seeking to regulate not only the individual's relationship with God, but all human social relationships.

The Prophet was at the same time a religious mentor, military commander, social reformer and political leader. Muslims believe that the Quran, the Word of God, was revealed to His Messenger for the guidance of mankind, to provide the heart of the Islamic faith and to lay the foundations of Islamic Law and social order.

Islamic legislation, or the 'Sharia', can be traced back to the migration (*hijrah*) of the Prophet and his followers from Mecca to Medina, where the nucleus of the Islamic state was formed in 622 AD which became year zero of the Hijrah.[5]

During the previous twelve years, Revelation received by the Prophet in

---

[3] *The Illustrated Encyclopaedia of World Religion* – Great Britain, 1997, p. 150. *The Lexicon Universal Encyclopaedia* (1993) gives three estimates of the world Muslim population: between 1.2 bn. and 750 m., with a likely medium of 950 m.

[4] Professors Goldziher and Fyzee have used the word 'schools' instead of 'sects' to translate the Arabic term *madh-hahib* (plural of *madh-hab*) because the difference between Sunnis and Shias, apart from the doctrine of Imamat, is not great enough to make them into two sects. The word 'schools' is adopted in this work for the same reason. See Fyzee *Outline*, p. 36.

[5] The Muslim calendar is dated not from the first Revelation, nor from the birth of the Prophet, but from his arrival in Medina on Friday, 1 July 622 AD, which was ordered, during the reign of the Second Caliph, Omar, to be dated as the first day of the first month "*Muharram*" of the first year of the Hijrah. The Hijrah year is lunar, alternately 30 days and 29 days long (to be exact: 29.5306 days). The Hijrah calendar is official in Saudi Arabia, Yemen and the Gulf Emirates. Egypt, Syria, Jordan and Morocco use both the Muslim and Christian (Gregorian) calendars. In all Muslim countries people use the Muslim era privately.

Mecca dealt mainly with theological and ethical questions. *Suras* revealed in Medina laid down the legal foundations of the new state. Provisions were revealed concerning the life of the individual and the community, and the relations of the new polity with its neighbours, such as worship rites (*ibadaat*), holy war (*jihad*), penalties (*hudood*) for sins, marriage and its effects in terms of maintenance and parentage etc., dissolution of marriage, rules of succession and rules for peace and war. Civil obligations were also regulated.

The sole source of legislation during this period was divine Revelation, 'The command is for none but "God."' (12.:40) Revelation was not confined to the Holy Quran, but included also the authentic rulings and deeds of the Prophet, known as the '*Sunna*' or '*Hadeeth*' (Tradition), which three expressions are used synonymously. The Quran says about the Prophet that 'His words are not his own devising' (53:3) The ultimate legislator is God Himself, not the Prophet who is just the messenger. 'The Apostle's duty is solely to proclaim.' (5:102) Where the Quran sets down general commands, it is the duty of the Prophet to explain them in detail. 'And we have sent down unto thee the Message that thou mayest explain clearly to men what is sent for them.' (16:44)

The ritual prayers are ordered and timed generally in the Quranic verse 'And perform ritual prayers at the two ends of the day and at parts of the night.' (11:114) It was the Prophet who taught his Companions (*Sahaaba*) 'Perform prayers as you see me do.' showing them the positions, exact times and all other details. The religious tax (*az-zakaat*) is a Quranic obligation under various verses (e.g. 22:78, 24:56). It was left to the Prophet to quantify it saying 'Give away a quarter of a tenth of your property.'

If there was no Revelation in either form, the Prophet would say so and wait for divine inspiration. For example, a woman complained to him that her husband, using a pre-Islamic formula called *zihar*, likened her to the back of his mother, and she asked the Prophet for an Islamic ruling. The Prophet said he had not been told the divine ruling on this but thought she became unlawful to her husband. She prayed for a Revelation which was duly received by the Prophet (58:1–4) and which commanded such husbands to perform some specific expiation before they could resume marital relations with such of their wives.

These two forms of Revelation – the rehearsed, (the Quran) and the unrehearsed, (the *Sunna*) – are the ultimate source, and proof, of Sharia rulings (i.e. Islamic legislation). As we shall see, they are, in the final analysis, the sole authorities acceptable to the Shia jurists. But Sunni jurisprudence accepts two other proofs or sources: namely *ijmaa* (consensus) and *ijtihaad*,[6] (independent reasoning when there is no higher authority). This last source raises a problem: was there any *ijtihaad* at this time of the Prophet's life? Did he ever practice it and was he ever wrong?

Some Sunni jurists answer these questions in the affirmative. Professor Shalabi cites the above case of *zihar* as an example of the Prophet's *ijtihaad*, an error later corrected by the Quran. Another example is when the Prophet consulted his two senior Companions about the prisoners of war of Badr. Abu Bakr, the future successor of the Prophet, suggested releasing them on the payment of a ransom, and Omar, Abu Bakr's successor, advised that they should be killed as

---

[6]The Shias accept *ijmaa* and *ijtihaad*, but in a different connotation more akin to their principle of authority. Refer to the section on the Shia.

ruthless enemies of the faith in order to protect Muslims. The Prophet chose ransom and release, and was reprimanded for that choice: 'No prophet may have prisoners of war until he has thoroughly subdued the land. You look for transient goods of this life while God looketh for the Hereafter.' (8:67)[7]

Professor Shalabi even sees a compelling justification for this error. It is a recognition of the need of the *Umma* to have *ijtihaad* and its outcome: an opinion which may be right or wrong. The Apostle's error is a consolation for those jurists who err. It urges people to respect the jurists' opinions without scandalising them over their mistakes, and impresses on jurists themselves the fact that they should not fanatically insist on their opinions, which always must be kept under review.[8]

Professor Qasim deals reluctantly with the subject, but stresses emphatically that whilst Revelation is available, there is no room, or need, for *ijtihaad*. He cites the Quran's description of the Prophet: 'His words are not his devising.' (53:3) As a receiver of divine Revelation, the Apostle must be infallible, a position held firmly by the Shia. Professor Qasim denies that the Prophet made a mistake in the case of the Badr prisoners of war, which, whilst there was no explicit text to cover it, demanded an urgent decision. All the Prophet did was to apply another Quranic text, in praise of those who 'conduct their affairs through mutual consultation.' (42:38)[9]

But the Sunni jurists are unanimous that the Prophet encouraged his Companions to use reasoning and to try hard to reach an opinion if there were no textual authorities. If they were wrong, they would be rewarded, and if they were right, their divine reward would be double.[10] A famous *Hadeeth* records that the Prophet sent Muadh ibn Jabal to Yemen as a judge and asked him how he would rule when a question arose. Muadh answered that he would rule according to the Book of God; failing to find the answer there, he would turn to the *Sunna* of his Apostle; finding nothing he would try his best to reach an opinion. The Prophet was delighted and thanked God for guiding the apostle of His Apostle to please God and His Apostle.[11]

However, it must be stressed that opinions given under *ijtihaad* during the Prophet's lifetime were always subject to confirmation or amendment through Revelation, the sole legislative authority then.

With the death of the Prophet, (*Rabia* I, 11 AH, June 632 AD), this era of laying the foundation for Islamic Sharia came to a close. There was no controversy, there having been only one source for rules, divine Revelation, and one ultimate judge, the Prophet without whose confirmation no ruling could become binding. Apart from the Quran, which was written down by order of the Prophet, no juristic authority was written down then because the Apostle forbade any of his judgments (*Sunna*) to be written down for fear of confusion with Quranic texts. Written works were yet to come.

---

[7] Shalabi, *Introduction*, 1985, pp. 99–100 (in Arabic).
[8] *Ibid.* p. 103.
[9] Qasim, *Principles*, 1983 p. 78 (in Arabic).
[10] Sarakhsi, *Mabsut*, vol. 16, p. 70 (in Arabic).
[11] Ibn Qayyim al-Jouzia, *Aalaam*, v. 1 p. 202.

3. The Era of the Patriarchal Caliphs (*Al-Khulafa-ur-Rashidoon*) (11–41 AH, 632–661 AD)

The death of the Prophet led to the first disagreement in the *Umma* (Nation) of Islam, which later gave rise to the main two important factions, the Sunnis and the Shias. It was over the succession of the spiritual and political leadership of the Nation (the Imamat). The majority believed it should be up to the people to choose the successor of the Prophet under the Quranic verse '... and who conduct their affairs through mutual consultations'. (42:38) A minority believed that the Prophet had designated his cousin-cum-son-in-law Ali ibn Abi Talib to succeed him as the first Imam, quoting and interpreting certain texts. The former group, (the majority), later came to be known as the Sunnis, the latter becoming the precursors of the Shia. The majority won the day, and thus began the reign of the Patriarchal Caliphs. Their reign of thirty years marked the heroic age of Islamic conquests, bringing the Muslim Arabs into contact with people of other races and cultures, thus posing questions to which no answers had previously been devised or sought. From personal status to international level, questions arose concerning private matters of the family, contracts and obligations, and matters of public interest, whether political or administrative.

The reigning Caliph, being the Prophet's successor, retained both spiritual and secular authority over the *Umma*. With no Revelation available after the passing away of the Prophet, the Caliph, sitting as a judge, had first to consult the Book of God, seeking a divine ruling to apply in the case, failing which he would try to find the answer in a reliable Tradition of the Prophet known to him or other Companions of the Prophet. If he failed again, he would seek the advice of the learned and pious leaders and apply their unanimous opinion.[12]

The same approach was closely followed by Omar,[13] the Second Caliph, who was the first to adopt the title of '*Ameerul-Moemeneen*', the Commander of the Faithful.

Here again the same principle of authority of the Quran and the *Sunna* was closely observed, with the addition of *ijmaa* (consensus), the unanimous opinion of the learned and the pious, based on the authority of the Prophet's Tradition 'My community shall not agree in error'. This new source became needed for the first time because the Prophet, deemed infallible even by the orthodox Sunni jurist, Ibn Qayyim al-Jouzia,[14] was not available to give the final ruling.

A fourth source of authority for judgment appeared in this period: namely opinion (*ar-raay*), arrived at through the *ijtihaad* explained above. Judge Shuraih recalled that Omar instructed him to apply in court the judgments of the Apostle known to him, failing which, the rulings he knew of the eminent enlightened scholars. If he could not find them, he ought to do his best to reach his opinion seeking the advice of people of wisdom and piety.[15] Later the Caliph wrote to him 'If you are trying a matter that must be decided upon, look in the Book of God for a ruling to apply: if you find nothing then apply the Prophet's judgment, failing which the findings by the good people and righteous leaders, failing which

---

[12] *Ibid.* p. 62.
[13] *loc. cit.*
[14] *Ibid.* p. 5.
[15] *Ibid.* p. 84.

you then have the choice: if you like to try hard to reach your own opinion, then go ahead, or if you wish, discuss the matter with me, which I believe is the right course for you.'[16]

An important feature of the *ijtihaad* (reasoned opinion) in this period was its empiricism. The pious Companions, conscious of the burden of responsibility involved in making legal judgments on any but factual questions, left aside all hypothetical issues. Omar was quoted as forbidding people to ask about matters that had not happened.[17] A leading early Kufi jurist, Ibn Abi Leila, (Kufa being part of Iraq) is quoted as saying 'I met one hundred and twenty of the Prophet's Companions, and each one of them who recited a saying of the Prophet wished that another Companion (*Sahabi*) had recited it, and each of them who gave an opinion wished that it had been given by another.'[18]

Opinion was not held to be an authority or a final say, and was used sparingly and only when it had to be made. It was always accepted as potentially incorrect and, unlike the Quran or the *Sunna*, it could be accepted or rejected. A clerk once wrote of an opinion of the Caliph Omar 'This is God's judgment and Omar's opinion.' The Caliph reprimanded and corrected him, 'This is Omar's opinion: if it is right, then it is by God's Grace, if it is wrong, it is Omar's fault.' Another *Sahabi*, Abdullah ibn Masud, was asked about a wife whose husband died before consummation and without having specified her dower. He answered 'She deserves the dower of an equal. If that is right, it is by the Grace of God, if it is wrong it is due to me and to the devil.'[19]

Yet many rulings of the period remain valid and applicable according to many Sunni schools. An example of such rulings is that a repudiated pronouncement by a husband implying the number three verbally or by a gesture should be irrevocable. This was ordered by Omar, contrary to a reported ruling by the Prophet that such a repudiation should be counted as a single one, and thereby would be revocable in certain circumstances. The four Sunni Schools still hold Omar's rulings. However, contemporary legislators in Arab Islamic countries have gone back to the reported Prophet's Traditions.

The era of the pious four Patriarchal Caliphs came to a close with the death of their last Commander of the Faithful, Imam Ali, in the year 41 AH, 661 AD. It left a single written-down legal authority, the Holy Quran. It was compiled by order of the First Caliph, Abu Bakr, urged by his eventual successor, Omar, following the martydom of many Reciters (people who had learned the Quran by heart) in the battle of Yamama, and for fear that parts of it would subsequently be lost if it was left unwritten for too long. It was compiled again under the Third Caliph, Othman. Again, the Prophet's *Hadeeth* was left unwritten for the same reason as before: fear of confusion with the Book of God.

The same reason prevented the writing down of the rulings and *ijtihaad* of the Caliphs and the *Sahaaba*, which were learned by heart by their followers. One exception is noteworthy; the letter sent by Caliph Omar to his judge, Abu Musa al-Ashaari, who left it under a will to a custodian. The document lays down rules for trying cases, a method of finding legal authorities in the absence

---

[16] *loc. cit.*
[17] *Ibid.* p. 69.
[18] *Ibid.* p. 34.
[19] *Ibid.* p. 63.

of authentic texts, rules of evidence and conduct of the judge and the disputing parties. It was highly praised and respected by Ibn Qayyim who devoted two thirds of the first volume of his '*I'laamul Muwaqqeen*' to a commentary thereon and who strongly urged scholars, judges and jurists to study it carefully as indispensable reference material. In fact he used it to present his whole doctrine on the roots or principles of jurisprudence (*usulul-fiqh*). Nevertheless, Goldziher doubts the authenticity of this letter of Omar to Abu Musa, especially as it uses the term '*qiyas*', which was not known until later.[20] In fact, Ibn Qayyim himself expresses, by implication, some doubt. Apart from some words about which the narrator was not certain, the latter records that the person who first told him about the matter said also that there was no chain of authority, the only test of authenticity at the time.[21]

4. The Umayyad Empire (41–132 AH, 661–750 AD)

Throughout the first Islamic polity, the fundamental unity between the spiritual and the secular in the city state of Medina remained unscathed under the Patriarchal Caliphs, just as it had been under the Prophet. However, the advent of the Umayyads, the first royal dynasty in Islam, saw the first distinction between the religious and the secular. The Caliphate, although retaining its spiritual title, with the ruler remaining the Commander of the Faithful, gave way to the empire state. The Umayyad rulers became too concerned with politics and power to be accepted by the religious scholars who avoided them,[22] and as a result, consultation between rulers and scholars lost its former prominent place in the laying down of legal precepts.

The new secular sovereigns introduced hereditary systems instead of the democratic election of their ruler by the *Umma*. Muawiya ibn Abi Sufian, the founder of the dynasty, defied the Islamic prohibition of adoption by acknowledging as a brother an erstwhile foe in order to gain his political support.[23]

They antagonized the pious scholars and the surviving Companions of the Prophet by overruling judgments attributed to him. They violated the Islamic sanctuaries of Medina and Mecca.

Further events affected juristic developments in this epoch and beyond it. The controversy over Imamat and the choice of the right leader of the *Umma* reached a peak, and resulted in the emergence of three opposing groups, the Kharijis, the Shia, and the moderate people of the Sunna and Jamaa. (1) The Kharijis, 'the dissidents', were against Ali, and also against Muawiya whom they considered a usurper, and they believed that the Imam should be freely elected by the

---

[20] Quoted in Al-Mussawli, *Al-Ijtihaad*, pp. 58/9.
[21] *Aalaam*, v.1, p. 86
[22] The notable exception was Caliph Omar ubnu Abdil Aziz, (reigned 99–101 AH, 719–721 AD), a pious, scholarly and righteous ruler. His mother was the granddaughter of his namesake Omar ubnul-Khattab, the Second Patriarchal Caliph.
[23] This is the famous Ziyaad, historically known as ibn Abeeh, i.e. 'the son of his father' an Arabic euphemism for a bastard. He was the illegitimate son of Ubaid ar-Rumi. Muawiya, on the evidence of the notoriously unreliable Abi Mariam, acknowledged Ziyaad as a brother, calling him Ziyaad ibn Abi Sufian, contrary to the Quranic verse banning adoption "Call them by the names of their fathers, that is justice in the sight of God." (5:33). Accepting and adhering to Muawiya's acknowledgement, knowing it was false, Ziyaad ignored the Prophet's Tradition "Hell is set for whoever denies

rank and file of Muslims without any restriction of race or tribe, and that he must be obeyed as long as he abided by the Commandments of God and His Apostle, and would be dismissed on failing to do so. As for legal and religious authority, they accepted the Quran and acknowledged only the Prophet's Tradition transmitted by one of their own number. (2) The Shia held that Imamat was the exclusive right of Imam Ali and his descendants born of Fatima, the Prophet's daughter. They constitute the house of the Prophet under divine texts of the Quran and Tradition. Only the Imams, due to their divine authority, are trusted by the Shia to transmit authentic *Hadeeth*. (3) The moderate people of the Sunna and Jamaa believed that the Imam must be elected from among the eligible members of the Quraish clan, according to a Tradition to that effect. They accepted all *Hadeeth* authenticated through a chain of authority.

Unlike the previous two phases when difference of opinion was at a minimum and it was much easier to reach consensus within the tiny polity, no such consensus was available after the emigration of a number of the Prophet's Companions and their followers (*Tabi-oon*) from Medina to new centres of the expanding empire. Juristic answers and methods to solve identical questions were bound to differ, thereby reflecting the difference of cultural and intellectual climates. Two differing courses became discernible:

The first was centred in Medina, where life was simple and uneventful, with plenty of rulings by Abu Bakr and Omar still vividly remembered and many transmitters of the Prophet's Traditions still alive. The followers of this trend closely observed the literal manifest meaning of the Quranic verses or the Prophet's *Hadeeth*, for which they were called 'The People of Hadeeth' (*Ahlul-Hadeeth*). They remained faithful to the empirical and factual traits of the previous period, considering only actual events, and never daring to over-step the limits of what was known under the authority of the Book of God and the *Sunna* of His Apostle, heeding the Quranic prohibition 'Pursue not that of which thou hast no knowledge.' (17:36).

The second trend was pioneered by the scholars of Kufa, Iraq, where there was a different cultural environment. Life there was much more complicated and eventful. There were far fewer transmitters of the Prophet's Traditions. Therefore there was a much greater need to rely on reasoning by analogy (which became known as *qiyas*) and individual opinion, (*ra-ay*), hence their description as 'The People of Opinion (*Ahlul-Ra-ay*). They would not refrain from hypothetical cases and used them so often that their opponents called them '*Al-ara-Aytiya*', 'The Let us assume-ists'.

It must be stressed, however, that (a) there were some scholars in Medina who tried to go beyond the manifest meaning of the text and venture an independent opinion and vice-versa in Kufa: (b) no opinion was ever given while there was a textual authority; and (c) these two opposing tendencies have permeated Islamic thought throughout the ages and in all spheres, including jurisprudence. As for consensus, it was much harder to attain than in the previous phase.

The Umayyad era came to an end with the fall of that dynasty and the advent of a new dynasty, the Abbassids.

Again we have no written juristic text from this period apart from the already written Quran. The Prophet's *Sunna* was yet to be recorded in writing. The

_____

his real father.".

pious Caliph Omar ubnu-Abdil Aziz had instructed his Medina judge in 100 AH to compile the *Sunna* out of concern over 'Scholars passing away and erudition becoming extinct, and to guard the Prophet's Tradition against fraud.' But Omar died a year later before any recording had even begun.

5. Period of Islamic Jurisprudence (*fiqh*) as a Discipline in Its Own Right (132–350 AH, 750–960 AD)

Islamic juristic thought reached its peak during this period, starting with the death of the last Companion in the last days of the Umayyad dynasty and spanning the whole of the golden Abbassi era (from the second to the fourth centuries AH, the eighth to the tenth centuries AD). Islamic jurists devoted their lives to recording the general discursive rules and codifying the various juristic doctrines, based either on political grounds, or on scholarly research. Their rulings were derived from the texts of the Quran, the *Sunna* of the Prophet and from the specific circumstances of their regional environments.

Thriving juristic thought in this period went hand in hand with the development of other disciplines: the exegesis of the Quran arranged and collected in a single book (the *Mus-haf*); the Sunni compilation of the Prophet's Traditions under stringent rules to sort out the authentic from the forged (whilst the Shia applied different rules as explained later); and the Arabic translations of Greek major texts on philosophy and logic.

The hostility between the rulers and the scholars that marked the later stage of the Umayyad reign was over. The Abbassids had campaigned, in the name of religion, for their state to restore the Caliphate to the House of the Prophet, a nephew of Abbas their ancestor. They sponsored the religious scholars and treated them with respect. They granted jurists full freedom of thought on all matters except those related to the questions of the Caliphate and politics. When on the authority of a *Hadeeth*, Imam Malik ruled that a repudiation made under coercion was void, (a ruling which has been adopted in modern Islamic legislation, as we shall see in the section on divorce), the second Abbassi Caliph, Abu-Jaafar al-Mansur, ordered him not to tell it to the public. This was because his subjects' pledge of allegiance to him (*baia*) was secured with the subject making an oath that his wife be divorced from him should his pledge be breached. This security would be without effect if there was coercion and the people gave the pledge against their free will. When Malik refused to obey, he was whipped.[24]

In order to conform with Islamic principles, jurists were asked to give Sharia rulings on a variety of questions all over the vastly extended Islamic State with its many different customs and ideas. Many centres of legal learning appeared in all parts of the empire: in Medina and Mecca of the Hijaz Province, in Kufa and Basra of Iraq, in Damascus of Syria and al-Fustaat of Egypt. Tours by scholars of those centres enhanced dialogue and rapprochement and enriched fertile interaction among schools of juristic thought.

Various schools of Islamic juristic thought flourished, producing systematic doctrines which differed from one another according to their interpretation and

---

[24]Abu Zahra, *Malik*, p. 61.

knowledge of texts, their customs, social environments and their political allegiances.

The oldest school is the Shia, traced back by the commentator of Imam Ali's masterpiece *'Nahjul Balaagha'* to the immediate aftermath of the Prophet's death, but set as a system by the sixth Imam Jaafar-as-Sadiq (80–140 AH, 699–765 AD) after whom the doctrine was named and who was the teacher of the two oldest Sunni Imams, Abu Hanifa of Kufa (80–150 AH, 699–767 AD) and Malik ibn Anas of Medina (93–179 AH, 712–795 AD). The third Sunni Imam, Muhammad ibn ash-Shafii (150–204 AH, 767–820 AD) was a disciple of Malik and stayed close to him until his death. The fourth major Sunni Imam Ahmad ibn-Hanbal (164–241 AH, 780–850 AD) was the brightest and most favourite student of ash-Shafii. More will follow about these five Imams whose authority is still referred to in contemporary Sharia statutes.

There were other minor schools, like the Kharijis previously mentioned, the Zahiries, etc., which are now of only historical importance. Others, still surviving, are the Abadis, named after Abdullah ibn Abad (1st century AH), in Oman, Zanzibar and North Africa (where the name becomes 'Ibadis').[25] One of the last expontents of their doctrine is the Morrocan scholar Muhamad ibn Youssof Atfeesh, in his ten volume treatise *'Sharhun-Neel'*. Many Sunni commentators and some orientalists describe the Abadis as Kharijis, a description which they detest and strongly reject.[26] In fact there is little difference between them and the mainstream of Sunni schools. The same is true of the Zaidis, named after Imam Zaid (killed in battle in 121 AH, 740 AD), to whom is attributed *'Majmu-ul-Fiqh'*, the oldest surviving written treatise on Muslim Law. Sunni scholars describe the Zaidis as 'a moderate Shia group'. They are centred in Yemen.

This period saw the first written down manuals on Islamic Jurisprudence and the Sharia, long after the writing down of the Quran. The master, from Imam Jaafar as-Sadiq to Imam Ahmad ibn-Hanbal, would personally dictate his teachings to his pupils, or one of them would record the master's commentary and later read it back to him. As said above, the first such manual was Zaid's *'Majmu'*, the second being Imam Malik's *'Muwat-taa'*, a compendium of *Hadeeth* of the Prophet, precedents made by the Prophet's Companions, and jurisprudence. Malik's pupil Imam ash-Shafii described it as 'The most authentic book that appeared on the earth after the Book of God.' The second Abbasi Caliph, Abu Jaafar al-Mansur, was so impressed by it that he wanted to make it the written constitution of the new State. It took Malik forty years to finish.

The first book on the Shia Jurisprudence was written by the seventh Imam, Musal Khazhim, son of Imam Jaafar. His book *'Al-Halal Wal-Haram'* ('The Permissible and the Forbidden'), was written in order to reply to questions put to him.

Imam Abu Hanifa did not write down his own teachings himself, but was said to have asked his disciples to do so. Of these, two stand out: Judges Abu Youssof (112–183 AH, 730–800 AD) and Muhammad ash-Shaibani (131–189 AH, 748–806 AD)[27] The only remaining work by Abu Youssof is *'Al-Kharaj'* ('Land

---

[25] Judge as-Siyali, *"Izalat"*, Cairo, 1979, p. 5.
[26] Judge as-Siyali, *"Al-Haqiqa"*, Muscat, 1980, pp. 11
[27] In the classical Islamic Sharia manuals Abu Hanifa and Abu Yousof are called *"Ash-Shaikhaan"* (the two masters), Abu Youssof and Muhammad *"As-Saahibaan"* (the two friends), and Abu Hanifa and Muhammad *"At-Tarafaan"* (the two ends).

Tax') written by order of Abbasid Caliph Harun ar-Rasheed. Muhammad ash-Shaibani is credited with having had the Hanafi doctrine recorded and preserved. Amongst the books writers have ascribed to him is the important anthology of six manuals which is definitely authentic '*Kutubu Zahirur Riwaya*' which consists of '*Mabsut*', '*al-Jami-us-Sagheer*', '*al-Jami-ul-Kabeer*', '*az-Ziyadaat*' and two works on international law: '*as-Siyarus Sagheer*' and '*as-Siyarul Kabeer*'. There were also other books less authoritatively attributed to him.

Imam ash-Shafii left his great work '*al-Umm*' ('The Main Source') which he dictated to his Egyptian pupil, Rabia ibn Sulaiman al-Muradi (174–270 AH). '*Al-Umm*' is entirely devoted to pure jurisprudence. Unlike Malik's '*Muwat-taa*', it is much more than a compilation of the Prophet's *Hadeeth* and the Companions' precedents. It cites those texts only to prove the legal point being made. As an introduction thereto, he wrote '*ar-Risaala*' ('The Epistle') dealing with the methodology and sources of jurisprudence (*usul ul-Fiqh*).

Imam Ahmad ibn-Hanbal was a prolific author, but his greatest work is definitely '*Al-Musnad*' in which he compiled more than forty thousand *Hadeeth*, meticulously authenticated by him and arranged according to the Companions on whose authority they had been recorded. Considered by scholars as the best and most authentic work of the genre, he had to sort out one hundred and fifty thousand *Hadeeth* to select those which he judged to be beyond doubt.

The Sunni jurists of the day relied in their reasoning on the Book of God and the *Sunna* of the Prophet under strict rules of the Science of Tradition (*Usulul-Hadeeth*), on precedents on which the Companions agreed or differed, roughly corresponding to the principle of consensus (*ijmaa*), on analogical deduction (*qiyas*),[28] on consideration of public interest and pragmatism, and finally on the various local customs all over the expanding Islamic empire.

On the other hand, sticking to the principle of divine authority, the Shia jurists accepted definitively the Book of God and the *Sunna* which meant to them the Prophet's report related by the Imam. *Ijmaa* likewise must be approved by an Imam. There is no room for *qiyas*. The *mujtahid*, an independent jurist, acts on behalf of the absent Imam from whom he derives his authority and the validity of his opinion. This will be discussed later.

The extensive growth of juristic literature and resources did certainly contribute to legal knowledge and research flourishing and expanding, and made life easy for the Muslim lawyers of the day. It went further, to the point where jurists, especially of the Hanafi persuasion, did not confine themselves to real events and factual problems. They went beyond them to the realm of hypothetical research, assuming problems that might arise and anticipating solutions for them. This hypothetical jurisprudence, first pioneered by the Hanafis, became so popular that the Shafiis and Malikis joined in and went to the extreme, posing hypothetical cases that were unlikely, if not impossible, to occur.

Life became too easy for judges and jurists. With ready-made solutions they had no more use of *ijtihaad*, no more need to exert themselves to the utmost degree to form their original judgment in a case or as a rule of law. At the end of the period there was no more incentive for independent *mujtahideen* as viceroys

---

[28] *Qiyas* as used by Islamic jurists means reasoning by analogy: i.e. inference that if two things are similar to one another in some respects they will probably be similar in other respects. As a logical concept '*qiyas*' is the Arabic translation of 'syllogism'.

(*walies*), and judges were no longer chosen from among scholars known for their scholarship and piety, but from among the followers of the school favoured by the state. This was started, ironically, by the most daring school of reasoning and opinion, the Hanafis, and first of all by Abu Youssof when he was the Chief Justice of the state, and who set the tradition of the Hanafi monopoly of judicial offices.Thus was ushered in the next stage of Islamic juristic development.

6. The Age of *Taqleed* (Imitation) and *Jumud* (Stagnation) from 350–1200 AH, 10th–19th Centuries AD

Taqleed is defined juristically as the acceptance by a person, the *muqallid*, of a judgment, and/or the acting thereupon, without a binding authority, as in the case of a layman accepting or acting upon a statement by another layman, or even a *mujtahid*, accepting or acting upon an opinion of another *mujtahid*. If there is a binding authority warranting such acceptance of, and/or the acting upon a judgment, this is not *taqleed*. Such is the case of a layman accepting the advice of an authoratitive jurisconsultant (*mufti*), or a judge giving a ruling on the evidence of a reliable witness. In both events there is an authority or a proof to justify the acceptance, and therefore there is no *taqleed*.

In this sense, *taqleed* is deemed by some jurists to be an obligation on the layman under the Quranic verse 'If you do not know, ask the people who are versed in Scriptures.'(*ahludh dhikr*) (21:7). But if it is fanatical blind following, *taqleed* is forbidden for the qualified learned '*faqih*' or '*mujtahid*', who is capable of exerting himself to the utmost to reach an independent interpretation of law.

But the full development of juristic schools in the previous period led to followers who attached themselves to a given school with the consequent reluctance to follow the path of independent research, and jurist disciples campaigning for their respective schools, writing books praising their Imams and issuing legal opinions (*fatwa*) banning the departure of any follower of a given doctrine to another.

Jurists of the Sunni schools abandoned the primary sources of Sharia, the Book of God and the Prophet's *Sunna*, and centred on the study of the works of their Imams to the point of mistaking these works for the whole Sharia.

It must be stressed that the Imams themselves strongly prohibited people from imitating them, and never considered their own opinions any more than plausible and non-binding, not to be followed blindly or fanatically, and recognized the existence of other equally valid interpretations. Imam Abu Hanifa is reported to have said 'Nobody who has not known my proof shall advise according to my opinion.' Whenever he gave any opinion he used to say "This is what an-Numan ibn Thabit (meaning himself, Abu Hanifa) thinks, the best he could, and anyone who can propose a better opinion is worthier to be right.' Malik said 'There is no person whose opinion cannot be debated and refuted, apart from the Apostle of God.' According to ash-Shafii 'If you find my judgment contrary to the *Hadeeth*, follow the *Hadeeth* and throw away my judgment.' Imam Ahmad ibn Hanbal said to one of his followers 'Don't imitate me or Malik or any other, but go to the source of their teachings; the Book and the *Sunna*. No one should give an opinion unless he is knowledgable of the rulings of Sharia scholars and their doctrines.'

The period of *taqleed* falls into two phases: the first of consolidation of schools stretches for about three centuries from the mid-fourth century of the Hijra, the tenth of the Christian era; and the second phase of stagnation and the 'closure of the door of *ijtihadd*', begins from 656 AH, 1,258 AD, the year of the Mongol devastation of Baghdad.

The first phase retained a measure of *ijtihaad*, when the jurists made a magnificent contribution complementing the work of the Imam founders of the Sharia Sunni Schools.

(1) They set the reasoning for the provisions transmitted from their Imams in order to deduce more particular opinions based on them.
(2) Each group established the juristic rules implied by their respective Imam, thereby bringing to completion the Science of *Usulul Fiqh*, the methodology of Muslim Jurisprudence. The only drawback was the concomitant fanaticism which sometimes rendered those rules biased and twisted.
(3) They compared the various opinions attributed to one and the same school, due to the different narrations of the disciples reflecting the Imam's changing judgment. Those opinions were meticulously researched and set in order of priority on the strength of their respective proofs.[29]

While this contribution was given within the inner circle of a given school, another contribution transcended these confines through debates between followers of different schools which were mainly aimed at defeating the opponent, but were also productive in restricting an absolute judgment or narrowing a universal statement. Most of these debates were between the Hanafis and Shafiis, and the latter and the Hanbalis. The Malikis stayed away.[30]

In the second phase, extending to the end of the twelfth century of the Hijra, the nineteenth of the Christian era, 'the door of *ijtihaad* was closed.' As recently as the early twentieth century, the great jurist Ali Haidar, President of the Ottoman Court of Cassation, Chief Jurisconsult, Minister of Justice, Professor of Civil Law in Instanbul University, in his now classic commentary of the Mijalla, defends such closure on the ground that the existing four Sunni schools have provided enough material to stop any further research by later jurists, and that the aim is to avoid too much discordance. He also notes that the Shia have not closed that door.[31] There is more to follow about the Mijalla.

Another contemporary jurist, Professor Shalabi, sympathises with the religious scholars who were startled by the deteriorating state of Islamic Jurisprudence and Court judgments, when some jurists and judges were not qualified or trusted enough to rely on their wisdom. Whereupon, at the end of the fourth century of the Hijra, the eminent Sharia scholars declared the end of *ijtihaad*, and restriction of judges and jurists to the opinions of the past Imams who founded the Sunni Schools. The judges and jurists then became imitators, *(muqallideen)* and no longer interpreters of the law *(mujtahideen)*.[32]

The jurists then devoted their efforts to writing books on their respective Schools, only rarely resorting to independent interpretation or reasoning.

[29] Shalabi: '*Madkhal*', p. 139.
[30] *Ibid.* p. 140.
[31] Ali Haidar, '*Commentary on Mijallat-el-Ahkaam*'. For more information on the Mijalla see the end of this section.
[32] Shalabi, *opt. cit.* p. 137.

Those books, to start with, were easy to understand. Then, through lack of interest or enthusiasm, were abridged to overcome the reluctance of students to read lengthy treatises. Abridgment went on to the point of rendering the books too enigmatic and difficult to understand. They required commentaries by scholars, which needed further elucidation by others and clarification of that elucidation. That left us with a variety of books of various styles and forms, known as '*Mutoon*' (Texts), '*Shurooh*' (Interpretations), '*Hawaashi*' (Margins for Explanations) '*Taqreeraat*' (Paraphrasing) and '*Taaleeqaat*' (Commentaries).[33] Too many of these were wasted on terms and words, without any due attention to the intentions and reasoning of their Imams.

There were, during this phase, jurists or legal reformers who still urged their colleagues to abandon *taqleed* and go back to *ijtihaad* from the prime sources of Sharia, the Quran and the *Sunna*. Standing out among those reformers were Ibn Taymiyya and his disciple Ibn Qayyim al-Jouzia, both of the eighth century of the Hijra. They endured persecution for their campaign.[34]

7. Modern Renaissance: Beginning early 13th Century AH, late 19th Century AD

Eventually the door of *ijtihaad* was re-opened during the thirteenth century AH, the late nineteenth century AD, as the impact of the West was felt in Muslim society. The traditionalists of the previous phase were regarded as being out of touch with the times. Modern juristic Sunni thinkers such as Jamal-ud-din Al-Afghani (1249–1315 AH, 1838–1897 AD) and his Egyptian disciple Muhammad Abduh (1260–1322 AH, 1844–1905 AD) rebelled against stagnation and called for social and legal reforms. They disputed any paramount or exclusive authority of the basic doctrine of *taqleed* as embodied in the law recorded in the medieval manuals, and purported to represent the interpretation placed by the early jurists upon the Quran and the *Sunna* of the Prophet. Contemporary jurists claimed the right to an independent interpretation of the original divine texts in the light of modern social circumstance. They criticised the traditionalists for misunderstanding some texts as implying moral exhortation, e.g. the verse 'Marry women of your choice two or three or four.' (4:3) The modern reformers held that such provisions must be interpreted in their historical and social context. Muhammad Abduh, known affectionately to his disciples as 'The Imam', reached the highest religious judicial office in Egypt, the '*Mufti*', i.e. the Chief Interpreter of Islamic Law. He was a fervent believer in the compatibility of Faith and Science, which after all owes a great deal to Islamic contributions for its development in the West. Abduh called for a purified Islam, going back to the original sources, to early Islamic rationalism, free from obsolete medieval prejudices. He urged the Muslims to embrace modern knowledge to avoid being condemned to backwardness. The disciples of the Imam influenced the shaping of modern Islamic personal status laws in Egypt, and consequently in all parts of the Arab Islamic world. They could steer a course between the changing circumstances of modern life and what was once held to be the immutable Islamic Law. They contributed

---

[33] *Ibid.* p. 140.
[34] *loc. cit.*

to the development of a new pluralistic, eclectic juristic stream which made it possible for the political authority to choose from among the various schools of jurisprudence, the *Madhaahib*, the opinion deemed best to suit the needs and circumstances of modern Islamic society. This approach bore fruit in some newly introduced legal provisions, such as the doctrine of the mandatory will and compensation for arbitrarily divorced women, discussed later in relevant chapters.

What the Imam and his disciples managed to achieve in the modern Arab Islamic Personal Status legislation of the twentieth century had been earlier achieved in the late nineteenth century (1876) in the Ottoman Mijalla, (the Ottoman Civil Code) derived from the Islamic Sharia. Made up of 1,851 articles, it was based in principle on the Hanafi Juristic School. It was not, however, restricted to that doctrine since it adopted provisions from the other schools which were deemed best suited to the people's interests and the spirit of modern times. It remained until recently, the written Civil Code of Syria, Jordan and Iraq.[35] Even with the enactment of new civil codes in these countries, the merit of the Mijalla lies in its concentrating, into 99 articles, the essence of Islamic Jurisprudence. These articles will be discussed in a later section.

Although the Islamic law courts, known as the Sharia Courts, have been abolished as a separate entity in Egypt and Tunisia, the original Islamic Law, known simply as Sharia, is still applicable in its entirety in parts of the Arabian Peninsula. It is Sharia Law which is still in force in matters of personal law, including the law of succession and religious endowment (*waqf*) in all states with Muslim majorities except Turkey. New penal and civil codes based on European models have replaced the Sharia, which remains, nevertheless, a source of guidance to the secular courts in the absence of any specific legal provisions. In the constitutions of the overwhelming majority of Arabic and Islamic states, it is provided that the Sharia is an important source of legislation. Such a provision was included in Egypt for the first time in the 1971 Constitution to the effect that the Sharia principles were 'a main source of legislation', a phrase which has been amended in 1980, in a national referendum, into '*the* main source of legislation'. We find similar provisions in the constitutions of the State of Kuwait 1962, Syria 1973, Iraq 1964, Somalia 1960, Indonesia 1956, Pakistan 1973, etc. The Egyptian Supreme Constitution Court has ruled on 10th May 1985, that obligation on the Egyptian law-maker to treat the Sharia as the main source of legislation extends only to the laws promulgated after the date of that amendment.[36]

---

[35] In his '*Outlines of Muhammadan Law*', Oxford 1949, p. 25 Professor Fyzee holds that this period of *taqleed* strictly extends to 1924, the abolition of the Ottoman Caliphate. This is definitely convenient, as it follows the rule of dating each period with a major historical event, while admitting that such dating is arbitrary and realizing that the development process continues. But then the *taqleed* period stopped with the introduction of reformed laws, first in Egypt in 1920, and even before then with scholars becoming more original and eclectic. Also we must not forget that there is still a 'Caliph', a recognized head of the Sunni Maliki rite in the person of the King of Morocco, who holds supreme religious authority in his capacity of *Ameer-el-Muminin*, i.e. Commander of the Faithful. This title of the Ottoman Sultan was never recognized in Morocco.

[36] Jordan was the last Arab State to replace the Mijalla with a Civil Code, Provisional Law No. 43 of 1976 which came into force on 1.1.1977. Even then, under Article 1448/1 thereof, only the Mijalla provisions that are contrary to the new Code are abrogated. Likewise the Iraqi Civil Law No. 40 of 1951, abrogating the Mijalla provisions under Article 1381, retains Book 14 on Proceedings and

8. The Scope of This Book

Islam, as we have seen, regulates both the spiritual and secular aspects of human life. Islamic jurisprudence, '*fiqh*', 'consists of a knowledge of the precepts of the Divine Legislator in their relation to human affairs' (Mijalla Article 1); human matters related to life hereafter (*al-aakhira*) which are called '*ibadaat*' (worship rituals); and matters related to this world which are classified into marital questions '*munakahaat*', civil transactions '*muamalaat*' and penal code '*hudood*'.

Ibadaat are held to be perennial, immutable and valid for all times and places. They include the Five Pillars of Islam (*Arkaan-ul-Islam*), namely the declaration of faith (*ash-Shihadah*), the five congregational daily prayers (*as-Salawaat*), the payment of religious tax (*az-Zakaat*), the fast of Ramadan (*as-Saoum*), and the once in a life time pilgrimage to Mecca (*al-Hajj*) for those who are physically and financially able to perform it. The Shia add a sixth: *Jihad*, i.e. Holy War.[37]

The major Islamic jurisprudence works, both classical and modern, Sunni and Shia, invariably start with the *ibadaat*, followed by the other branches of Islamic Law in a variable order, treated on an equal footing and considered the most important and comprehensive concepts of Islamic Law in everyday life.

However, in this book, addressed mainly to the legal practitioner in the field of what is known as personal status, or family matters, there is no room for *ibadaat*, without belittling in any manner their indisputable importance to Muslims. No room either for civil transactions, even less the penal codes, as the provisions of Islamic Law on these two realms have been superseded by new civil and criminal laws derived from European sources in the vast majority of contemporary Islamic states.

That leaves what Islamic classical jurists used to call '*munakahaat*' marital matters, i.e. marriage and issues related thereto, namely divorce, parentage, guardianship and the like. Closely linked to these matters are succession and bequests. All these subjects are still governed by the Islamic Sharia, both in modern secular Islamic states (except in Turkey), and in the conservative religious states of the Arabian Peninsula and others. These topics constitute the subject-matter of this book.

Prior to the detailed treatment of these subjects, and as a further part of this introduction, it is necessary to give a glimpse of the Islamic schools of law and their methodology as a *sui generis* system of legal thought.

Book 16 on Courts and Judges.
[37] The Egyptian Official Gazette No. 20 of 16 May 1985.

CHAPTER 1

Islamic Schools of Law and General Sharia Maxims

1. The Main Division: Shia and Sunnis

During the lifetime of the Prophet, no controversy arose over general principles or detailed particulars. Every question was decided through Revelation either in the Quran, the Word of God, or the *Sunna*, (the Prophet's acts or sayings) believed to be of divine origin under the Quranic verse 'His words are not his own devising.' (53:4).

The Quran and the *Sunna* were then, and remain for ever, the paramount authorities of the Sharia, the Divine Islamic Law. No school disputes this. That explains why, on matters of principle, the resemblance between the various Muslim schools of law is 'most striking';[1] and why Goldziher and Fyzee do not talk about Islamic 'sects', but about 'schools'.[2] Differences do exist though, and not only on details, of which there are many, even within the same group of schools: the Sunni and the Shii. The reason is that although they accept the absolute authority of the Quran and the *Hadeeth*, they differ on their interpretation of the Holy Scriptures and their assessment of the reliability of, and the meaning they attach to the reported *Hadeeth*.

But the fundamental difference between the two groups, the Sunni and the Imami Shia, is the latter's doctrine of Imamat which sets them apart in their respective theories of government, their vision of the substantive Sharia Law (*fiqh*) and its theoretical bases (*usulul-fiqh*). This doctrine explains what is usually described as the Shii idealism and transcendentalism as contradistinct from the Sunni basic pragmatism.

The Imamat doctrine provides a systematic approach to the main themes of the Sunni and Shii positions:

A. The Sunni Position

The Sunni is an abbreviation of *Ahlus-Sunnati Wal Jamaat*, 'People of Tradition and Community.' They constitute 90% of Muslims all over the world, hence the reference to them in Sharia manuals as *Al-Jumhoor*, 'the public at large', the Arabic word originally meaning 'the overwhelming majority' (*Lisanul* Arab Dictionary). The definition of the phrase is 'a Sharia term used to denote the

---

[1] David & Brierly, *Major Legal Systems*, London, 1968, p. 390.
[2] Fyzee, *op. cit.* p. 36.

general public of Muslims who have not been affected by political differences and stayed away from the divisions amongst various sects and parties.'[3] Shia authors, e.g. Qadi an-Numan, the author of the Ismaili manual *'Daaim ul Islam'* refers to the Sunnis as *al-Aamma*, the laity or commonality (as distinct from *al-Khaassa*, the elite, namely the Shia).[4]

They are the traditional or orthodox Muslims and represent the mainstream of Islamic theology and jurisprudence. They believe they are the exponents of the original and unadulterated Islamic orthodoxy as revealed in the Quran and in the Traditions and precedents set by the Prophet and his Companions, and as elaborated by the great early Islamic thinkers. Under this broad paradigm, two trends have been referred to above, namely the early schools of manifest content (*ahlul Hadeeth*) and reasoned opinion (*Ahlul-Ra-ay*).

When they talk about 'Imams' they do not mean the word in the Shii sense; i.e. a religious and secular leader of the *Umma*, but the founding fathers of the four surviving Sunni schools of law, the *Madhaahib* (singular *Madh-hab*). The ruler is usually called 'the Caliph', i.e. successor of the Prophet, or *Ameerul-Moemeneen*, i.e. the Commander of the Faithful. As shown in the historical survey, he was elected by the people to uphold the rule of the Sharia and conduct the affairs of the *Umma*. We have seen how the first two Patriachal Caliphs exercised both political and religious leadership. But they were aware of their shortcomings when they had to interpret the Sharia, and admitted their opinions were their own: if right, then it was by the Grace of God, if wrong, they alone were to blame.

The same pious and self effacing attitude was adopted, as we have seen, by the four great Sunni Imams, in the Sunni sense of the term: Abu Hanifa, Malik ash-Shafii and Ahmad ibn-Hanbal. Their schools, named respectively after them, can be summed up as follows:

(1) The Hanafi doctrine spread during the Abbasid Dynasty and was the official doctrine under the Ottoman Empire, and thereafter in Egypt, Syria, Jordan, Palestine, Lebanon and Sudan. It is followed now by the Muslim population of Turkey, Albania, the Balkans, Caucasus, Afghanistan, Pakistan, China, India and Iraq.

Imam Abu Hanifa was meticulous about ascertaining the authenticity of any Tradition attributed to the Prophet, making ample use of *qiyas* (analogical reasoning) and *'istihsan'*, i.e. giving preference to a rule other than the one reached by the more obvious form of analogy. His juristic research was not confined to factual questions, but included hypothetical cases. 'Legalistic devices' (*hiyal shariya*) are an essential characteristic of his doctrine used in an attempt to compromise between the legal, the ideal and the real, to bridge the gap between jurisprudence and reality, stressing the fundamental pragmatism of his own doctrine and that of the Sunni doctrines in general.

Imam Abu Hanifa refused the highest judicial office in spite of tremendous pressure from the Caliphs. But his closest disciple, Abu Yusuf Yaqub bin Ibrahim al-Ansari (113–183 AH, circa 730–798 AD) reached the office of Chief Justice and amalgamated the Hanafi School of Opinion and the Hijazi School of Tradition, his judicial experience providing the link between theory and practice,

---

[3] Qasim, *op. cit.* pp. 113 and 129ff.
[4] *Daaim ul Islam*, vol. 1, pp. 76/7.

and helping to propagate the Hanafi doctrine within the judicial offices, until then almost exclusively monopolized by Hanafi jurists.

(2) The Maliki doctrine is the official rite of the Moroccan Kingdom and the State of Kuwait as provided in their Personal Status Laws. It is widespread in Egypt, Sudan, North and West Africa and the eastern central part of Arabia. At one time it was followed in the Andalusian region of Spain, due to the fact that most of Maliki's disciples were Egyptian scholars who attended his lessons in Medina, and after returning to Egypt, moved later to North Africa and then to Spain.

Although Medina lost its political importance when the seat of government moved first to Damascus and later to Baghdad, it retained its predominance as a seat of learning since it was the original domicile of the Prophet's Companions, Ansar and Muhajireen, and the dwelling place of the Traditionists (the narrators of the Prophet's Tradition) of whom the most eminent were Aisha, the Prophet's widow, and his Companions Abdullah ibn Abbas, Abdullah ibn Omar and Zaid ibn Thabit.

The sources of the doctrine were the Quran, the Prophet's Traditions, consensus (*ijmaa*) and analogy. The Malikis' conception of consensus differed from that of the Hanafis in that they construed it as the consensus of the community represented by the people of Medina. Above the precedents set by the Medinites, they held the single source Traditions and analogy, to which they also preferred the ruling of whichever Companion was deemed to be the authority on the subject.

Malik made extensive use of *Hadeeth*, and did not assign to analogy the status accorded thereto by the Hanafis, often deriving his rulings from the principle of public interest (*istislah*), the Hanafi "*istihsan*", and a strong pragmatism. Maliki reasoned opinion was not, therefore, confined to analogy.

The difference between the doctrine of the Malikis and the Hanafis is one of degree, not of nature. They both used Tradition and reasoned opinion, but with variable stress and to differeing extents. Both schools tolerated divergence of opinion within their doctrines.

(3) The Shafi doctrine of Imam ash-Shafii was the first juristic system to be based on clear principles and distinct methods. It represents a middle course between those renouncing personal opinion and those who follow in blindly, with a slight preference for the Tradition. It spread in Jordan, Palestine, Syria, Lebanon and Yemen and has a large following in Egypt, Indonesia, the Philippines, Brunei Darussalam, Singapore, Malaysia, Thailand, Sri Lanka and the Maldives.

Ash-Shafii, a pupil of Malik, wrote the first book ever on the principles of Islamic Jurisprudence called 'Ar-Risala' ('The Epistle'). To him, the paramount sources are the Quran and the *Sunna*, failing which it is analogy thereon. Should a Tradition of the Apostle of God be narrated as authentic by generation after generation, then it is the conclusive ruling. Consensus overrules a Tradition narrated by a single authority. A Tradition shall have its manifest meaning attributed to it, and if liable to multiple interpretation, the nearest to its manifest purpose shall prevail. Of conflicting Traditions of apparently equal validity, the most authentically attributed shall prevail.

(4) The Hanbali doctrine was not considered as a juristic system according to some historians who described Imam Ahmad Ibn-Hanbal as a Traditionist.

Yet, considering the answers he gave to juristic questions put to him, compiled in a book entitled '*Masail*' ('Questions'), these do reveal a juristic doctrine with an independent method and original principles.

Although fundamentalist to the extreme in its rigidity in matters of ritual, this doctrine is equally noted for its tolerant approach to transactions, advocating allowance or non-prohibition in the absence of any text to the contrary.

The Hanbali School did not enjoy the popularity of the preceding three Sunni doctrines for a combination of reasons, among them the exclusion of its exponents from power and judicial office, a reluctance to give personal opinion, a rejection of analogy (which they only used as a last resort when all other sources failed) and their fanatic intolerance towards other doctrines.

Later some Hanbali leaders, such as Ibn-Taymiyya (died 728 AH, circa 1328 AD) and his disciple Ibn Qayyim Al-Jouzia (died 751 AH, circa 1350 AD), did exhibit tolerance and gave personal opinion. They made Hanbali teachings known to the people, especially in matters of transactions.

During the twelfth century AH, nineteenth century AD, Muhammad Ibn-Abdul Wahhab revived the Hanbali doctrine in Najd and spread it in Hijaz in the Arabian Peninsula. The Hanbali teachings are today the official doctrine of the Kingdom of Saudi Arabia.

Hanbalism derives its provisions from the Quran and the *Sunna*, which prevail over any consensus, opinion or inference. It acknowledges without question an opinion given by a Companion of the Prophet if there is no dissention, otherwise the opinion of a Companion nearest to that of the Quran or the *Sunna* prevails. Quite often, the Hanbalis do not indicate a preference where there were conflicting rulings by the Companions, but declare them all potentially valid. Traditions of the Prophet, according to the Hanbalis, are either valid or exhibit varying weaknesses which are nevertheless acknowledged.

The era of the great Sunni Imams was followed, as shown above, by an era of imitation (*taqleed*) in which later scholars followed the methods laid down by the founding father and built upon them, without any individual jurist even claiming the status of the earlier Imams, the only authorities entitled to interpret the Divine Law, after whom the 'gate of interpretation' was declared closed.

Although that 'gate' was re-opened over a century ago, and recourse to the basic sources of the sacred Scripture and the Prophet's *Hadeeth* was resumed, there remained the same pragmatic realism of attempting to accommodate the exigencies of modern ages and development. There is a new spirit of eclecticism without surrendering entirely to a single school or doctrine. The basic dominating belief is that the law had been completed before the Prophet's departure from this world: 'This day I have perfected for you your religion and completed upon you my grace and have chosen for you Islam as your religion.' (5:3) Mankind can work on this foundation through reason to find answers to all questions: if wrong there is one reward for trying hard (*ijtihaad*), if right, there are two.

B. The Shia Position

With the Imami Shia we move to an entirely different world vision: They have been the minority of the Islamic *Umma* from the days of the Umayyad Empire. They developed an ethos which sustained them for centuries, aptly described by a modern scholar as 'an attitude of mind which refuses to admit that majority opinion is necessarily true or right, and – which is its converse – a rationalised defence of the moral excellence of an embattled minority.'[5]

This ethos revolves round the doctrine of Imamat. They believe that God in His infinite compassion and justice towards His creation would never leave them without a guiding authority (*hujja*) who is a prophet or testamentary vicegerent (*wassey*) or Imam, whether visible and known or concealed, to instruct and lead them. Unlike the selected Caliph, who is only a political and military leader and applies the Sharia, the Divine Law, the Shia Imam is chosen by God as He pleases, as He chooses His Prophets and Apostles as He pleases: 'Thy Lord doth create and choose as He pleases. No choice have they ... .' (28:68) 'No believer, man or woman, may have an option in a matter decided upon by God and His Apostle.' (33:36) The Imam is below a Prophet in perfection and above the ordinary human being. He is the divinely inspired, impeccable and infallible, '*masoom*', (free from sin and error) spiritual and secular leader of the *Umma* and the final interpreter of the Divine Law. Those who can be either right or wrong in giving a Sharia ruling cannot be the right leaders of the nation.[6] One main difference between the Prophet and the Imam is that the former receives Revelation from God and gives the message to the people, while the latter receives and gives the word from the Prophet.[7] The Imami Twelvers, the 'Ithna-Ashari', count twelve Imams.[8] The twelfth Imam, Muhammad al-Mahdi is believed to be still alive, in the major Occultation '*al-ghaibat ul-Kubra*' from which he will re-appear at the end of time '... to fill the world with justice and fairness as it was filled with oppression and tyranny' according to a Tradition of the Prophet. During the Occultation, the Shia's *Mujtahidoon* (plural of *mujtahid* – eminent religious scholar) under the Imam's putative guidance, act on his behalf as the recognized interpreters of the law, in accordance with the canonical Traditions. In so doing, they differ from their Sunni opposite numbers. D.B. Macdonald puts it brilliantly thus:

'The Shiites still have *mujtahids* who are not bound to the words of a Master, but can give decisions on their own responsibility. These seem to have in their hands the teaching power which strictly belongs to the Hidden Imam. They thus represent the principle of authority which is the governing conception of the Shia.'[9]

The Imamis quote the Quranic verse 'And when Ibrahim was tried by his Lord to perform some obligations which he fulfilled to perfection, He [God]

---

[5] Hamid Enayat, *Modern Islamic Political Thought*, London 1982, p. 19 quoted by David Waines, '*An Introduction to Islam*', Cambridge 1998, p. 46.

[6] Qadi abu Hanifa an-Numan at-Tameemi, author of *Daaim ul Islam*, comments on Omar, the second Patriachal Caliph, admitting that an ordinary woman understood Sharia better than he did. The Qadi is surprised at such an admission being considered a virtue when it should have disqualified Omar as a leader. See *Daaim ul Islam*, vol. 1, pp. 125/6.

[7] Al Kashiful Ghataa, *op. cit.* pp.210/11.

[8] The twelve Imams of the Shia Ithna-Ashari (dates of death shown in both Hijra and Christian Era Calendars) were: (1) Ali ibn Abi Talib al Murtada (40/661); (2) al-Hassan ibn Ali al-Mujtaba (49/669); (3) al-Hussayn ibn Ali ash-Shaheed (61/680); (4) Ali ibn-ul-Hussayn (Zainul Abideen) (95/714); (5) Muhammad al-Baqir (115/733); (6) Jaafar as-Sadiq (148/765); (7) Musa al-Kadhim (183/799); (8) Ali ar-Rida (203/818); (9) Muhammad ul-Jawad at-Taqi (220/835); (10) Ali an-Naqi (254/868); (11) Al-Hassan ul-Askari (260/874); (12) Muhammad ul-Mahdi al Hujja (the Authority) al Qaim bi amril-laah (Upholder of the Divine Command) Sahibuz-Zaman (Master of Time) (entered major occulation in 329/940).

[9] Macdonald, *Muslim Theology*, p. 116, quoted by Fyzee, *Outlines*, p. 35.

said "I will make thee an Imam to mankind." He [Ibrahim], pleaded "And of my descendants." He [God] said "My promise will not be granted to the sinful".' (2:124) Their jurists interpret it as confirming that the Imam must be sinless as God denies the sinful His Promise, which is the Imamat. They also infer that the Imamat is distinct from Prophethood, as Ibrahim was already a Prophet and was granted the Imamat as a reward for having perfectly performed his obligations.

God is believed by the Imamis to make His choice of the Imam known to His Prophet who should announce it to the *Umma* by specific designation (*bin-nuss*). They believe that this was how the Prophet came to appoint Ali ibn Abi Talib, his cousin-cum-son-in-law, as his vicegerent (*wassey*), having been strongly urged to do so by God according to their interpretation of the verse 'O Apostle proclaim what hath been revealed to thee from thy God and if thou didst not thou wouldst not have conveyed His message and God will protect thee from people.' (5:67) Whereupon the Prophet, on his way back from his last pilgrimage, called the people to attend a large meeting, three months before his death, at Ghadeer Khamm, a brook between Mecca and Medina. There, before the whole gathering, he held Ali's hand and said 'He of whom I am the *maoula* (patron) of him Ali is also the *maoula*. O God, be the friend of him who is his friend and the enemy of him who is his enemy.'[10]

On another occasion, during an expedition, the Prophet said to Ali 'To me you are what Aaron was to Moses, except that there will be no Prophet after me.' According to the Ismaili Chief Justice, Qadi Abu Hanifa an-Numan at-Tameemi, this could only mean that Ali should be the Prophet's successor to lead the *Umma*, on the authority of the Quranic verse 'And Moses said to his brother Aaron "Take my place amongst my people."' (7:142).[11]

Shortly before his death, the Prophet declared 'I am leaving you after me the two momentous authorities[12] if you cleave to which you will never go astray: the Book of God and my nearest kin (*itrati*).

The same procedure of appointment by explicit designation (*bin-nuss*) is repeated, with every predecessor nominating his testamentary successor. Thus Ali nominated his eldest son al-Hassan, who nominated his brother al-Hussayn and so on to the last twelfth Imam of the Ithna-Ashari Imamis. The Ismaili Imamis part way from the Ithna-Asharis at the Seventh Imam whom they believe to be Ismail, the eldest son of Imam Jaafar as-Sadiq.

The Imamis believe that the Prophet was the repository of all Divine Laws which God revealed to him (the Prophet proclaimed them relevant when needed). The remaining undisclosed doctrines and teachings of Islam, he imparted to his successor designate Ali, who imparted them in his turn to the second Imam, his

[10] Al Kashiful Ghataa, *op. cit.* p. 221.
[11] Qadi an-Numan, *Daaim ul-Islam*, vol. 1, p. 57.
[12] Thus we translate '*ath-thaqalain*', dual form of *thaqal*, defined in the *Lisan* Arabic Dictionary as everything that is rare, precious and well protected. This Arabic grammar form for 'two' occurs once in the Quran (55:31) to mean the Jinns and the Humans, being the two species privileged by God with reason and discretion as explained in the Arabic Dictionary *Lisan*. The Tradition reads slightly differently in Sunni reports: 'I am leaving you two matters which will save you from going astray: the Book of God and my Sunna' (or the Sunna of His Prophet) instead of '*itrati*'. The Shia version appears as well in *Musnad Ahmad* by the Sunni Imam Ahmad ibn-Hanbal.

eldest son al-Hassan, and so on to the twelfth, the Mahdi who is awaited. Hence the sacred nature and source of the Imam's knowledge.

Iman and Islam: Faith in the Imam makes the Imamis '*Moemeneen*', that is to say 'believers'; derived from the word 'Iman', meaning 'belief' or 'faith', as distinct from the general public, the '*Muslimeen*', derived from the word 'Islam'. This distinction is rooted in the Quran: 'And the Bedouin Arabs said "We have believed" (*aamanna*)." Tell them: You have not believed, rather say "We have surrendered (*aslamna*)" without belief having entered your hearts.' (49:14) The next verse explains further what 'Iman' is. 'The believers are solely those who have believed in God and His Apostles, then have never doubted but have striven with their property and persons in the cause of God. Those are the sincere ones.' (49:15). On this, Al Kashiful Ghataa defines Iman as 'Declaration of faith, certainty and action.'[13] Stressing the action element of Iman, he quotes Imam Jaafar's definition 'Iman is belief in the heart, declaration by the tongue and performance of the worship pillars' (*arkaan*).[14] He is careful to point out that this is Iman in the narrower sense. In a wider sense it is synonymous with Islam and means the belief in God's Oneness, His Apostle's Prophethood and the Day of Reckoning.[15]

Qadi an-Numan is more precise and strict. He devotes a whole chapter to Iman, followed by another on how it differs from Islam. Having described it as that 'without which no action is accepted by God',[16] he links it with faith in the Imam, 'Iman is the confession of the faith that there is no God but God: One, without a partner, and that Muhammad is His Servant and Apostle, that Paradise is true, Hell is true and Resurrection is true, that the Hour shall come without any doubt, the firm faith in God's Prophets and Apostles, the knowledge of the Imam of the time, trusting and believing in him and submitting to his commands, performance and fulfillment of the obligations imposed by the Almighty upon His servants, heeding all His prohibitions and obedience to the Imam and abiding by his orders.'[17]

Qadi an-Numan then quotes the fifth Imam, Muhammad ibn Ali on the difference between Iman and Islam, 'Iman is in the hearts and Islam is that according to which marriages are concluded, estates are inherited and bloodshed is prevented.' adding that Iman is an inner circle within the wider circle of Islam[18] a point akin to Al Kashiful Ghataa's general and more specific connotations.[19]

---

[13] Al Kashiful Ghataa, *op. cit.* p. 211.
[14] See Sect. 8 Introduction.
[15] Al Kashiful Ghataa, p. 210.
[16] *Daaim ul Islam*, vol. 1, p. 38 (13).
[17] *ibid.* p. 40.
[18] *ibid.* p. 49.
[19] Does this make a *Mumin* (a believer) higher than a mere Muslim? Fyzee reports an interesting case of an Ithna-Ashari woman applying for divorce from her Sunni husband on the ground that while a man may marry a woman of an inferior faith, a woman can only marry an equal (*kufa*), contending that a *Mumin* woman cannot marry anyone but a *Mumin* man. Mr. Justice Sulaiman of Allahabad Court, disallowed it and held that such a marriage was perfectly valid under the Shia law, although the pious may deem it undesirable (*mukruh*). Fyzee notes that the reverse case does not exist as the Sunnis make no distinction between Iman and Islam and quotes Mulla, *Mohammedan Law*, S.199A, asserting that the marriage of a Sunnite woman with a Shiite man is valid beyond dispute before Indian Courts. Refer Fyzee, *op. cit* p. 34.

How does the belief in the Imam affect the Shia *Fiqh*? Professor Ahmed aptly remarks that although the Shia Imam doctrine, as distinct from the Sunni concept of Caliphate, may seem unimportant and puzzling to a non-Muslim, it has led to major political consequences.[20] To this must be added: firstly that the main political impact has occurred specifically under Ithna-Ashari Imamology and precisely in Iran; and secondly that the doctrine's consequences are far more important in the Imami jurisprudence theory '*Usul*'.

Starting with the political dimension, the Imam is the ultimate authority on matters sacred and secular, chosen by God, not by the people, and divinely guided. The Utopian state of the Ithna-Ashari Imamis is not a democratic republic or kingdom but a theocracy. The only legitimate political authority is the Imam's. As early as the third century AH (ninth AD), the Shii historian Abul Abbas al-Yaaqubi uses the word 'Caliphate' for the period of Ali's rule, simply describing the 'days' of his three Patriarchal predecessors, Abu Bakr, Omar and Othman.[21] Likewise, Shii authors, ancient and modern, use the title '*Ameerul Moemeneen*', the Commander of the Faithful, exclusively for Ali.

While the ideal state of things, from the Shii Ithna-Ashari point of view, when the Imam holds both political and religious (legislative) power, was achieved only once, under the reign of the first Imam, Ali, the power of interpreting and promulgating the law remains the Imam's solely. While the Imams lived among people, there was no problem in knowing or understanding the Sharia. But with the twelfth and last being in protective concealment until his return at the end of time, there arose the practical problem: who could fulfill his legislative and interpretive function and guide the Community in the interval? The answer, as we have seen above, is the *Mujtahid* or *Mujtahidoon* who are the representatives of the Hidden Imam. But there seems to be a trend calling for them to assume political authority as well, and this is what looks to be happening since the revolution in Iran.

The turning point in the political history of the Ithna-Ashari Shiism is the emergence at the turn of the ninth/tenth century AH (17th/16th AD), in Iran, of a new dynasty, the Safavids, with a strong religious character, who proclaimed the doctrine as the state religion of the realm which they created in the form which, with some modifications, has survived to the present day.[22]

The Safavid Shahs claimed descent from the Imams, a claim acknowledged but later subtly dropped. Still they continued to project themselves 'as the sole legitimate representatives and agents of the Hidden Imam, giving them a religious aura which no subsequent ruler in Iran would possess.'[23] They created political structures for the protection and encouragement of the Twelver Shia tradition. For more than two centuries, they attracted scholars from other areas, notably Jabal Aamil in South Lebanon and Bahrain, to erect Shia religious culture on firm foundations. Their era saw the Shia '*Ulamaa*' ('Scholars') consolidate the new Shia society which, Waines suggests, in retrospect 'may be regarded as the beginning of the long gestation of a twentieth-century revolution.'[24]

To start with, in the Shia polity of the Safavid Shahs, the Shah and the

---

[20] Akbar S. Ahmed, *Living Islam*, p. 48.
[21] Waines; *op. cit.* p. 46.
[22] Bernard Lewis, *The World of Islam*, p. 16.
[23] Waines, *op. cit.* p. 192.
[24] *ibid.* p. 172.

Scholars served each other's interests. The second Safavid Shah, Tahmasp (d. 984/1576) appointed a Shia Scholar, Ali al-Karaki (d. 940/1534) from Jabal Aamil in South Lebanon, as his deputy, to manage the expenditure of the taxes raised on behalf of the Hidden Imam.

His successor, Shah Abbas, assumed the Scholars' authority, but still served the religious cause by creating a *waqf* for the benefit of the twelve Imams and making bequests to religious institutions from his private treasury.[25]

Still, the Scholars debated the idea that the leading religious scholar among their ranks, the *mujtahid*, could be acknowledged as the Imam's representative on earth, an idea which would imply, if pursued to its logical conclusion, a challenge to the legitimacy of any secular power which claimed the right to rule Iran.[26]

The twelfth AH (18th AD) century saw the emergence of movements of religious renewal. Shia religious leaders defended their financial independence against all transient rulers and managed to emancipate their community from any essential link with the Iranian monarchial institution.

There was a conflict between the Akhbaris of the Iraqi Shia centres of learning of Najaf and Karbala and Usulis of Iran over the exercise by the *mujtahid* of fresh independent judgment on all matters of religious practice and the nature of religious authority in the absence of the Imam.

The Akhbaris held the only legitimate sources of legal knowledge to be the Quran and the Traditions of the Prophet and the Imams. Since the community must continue to submit to the Imams' guidance, however remote in time that was, Traditions were the best guide to their true intentions. As to the other sources of law allowed for in Sunni legal thought, the Akhbaris dismissed *imjaa* as irrelevant and *qiyas* as Satan's tool. Implicit in their position was the view that the Imams had dealt with all major questions in their Traditions which might in future arise. On the other hand, Usulis claimed for the *mujtahid* a key role in the interpretation of law and doctrine in order to deal with changing socio-historical conditions. As an expert in the Traditions as well as other branches of knowledge, the *mujtahid* was distinguished by the independent use of reason applied to the sources. The *mujtahid* claimed to achieve only probable knowledge of the Imams' intentions, in contrast with the Akhbari, who claimed a near, albeit not absolute, degree of certainty as to the detail of the Imams' teachings. Since *mujtahid* decisions were fallible, differences of opinion were allowed and decisions could be reversed.

The Usulis rejected the Akhbari principle of *taqlid al-mayyit*, that is, adhering solely to the views of deceased religious leaders, and insisted that all believers must choose and follow a living *mujtahid* and abide strictly by his decisions, a doctrine which had several important implications. One was that every new generation required its own *mujtahid* to interpret the law; second, it gave the *mujtahid* authority in the community beyond anything Sunni *Ulamaa* could claim for themselves, and third, it gave their judgments a status above even the decrees of state.

Victory of the Usulis over the Akhbaris by the end of the century led to the idea of a collective leadership of *mujtahid* and the development of a hierachy

---

[25] *ibid.* p. 193.
[26] *ibid.* p. 248.

within the religious class. The head of the hierachy was selected and acknowledged by the leading qualified *mujtahid* from among themselves. Each in theory
was a source for imitation (*marj at-taqlid*) by others, who were bound to accept
the *mujtahid's* judgment without question. In effect, the *mujtahid* had appropriated
the prerogatives of the Hidden Imam, and the basis of their authority was now
independent of state patronage as it had not been under the Safavids.[27]

These ideas paved the way to the *mujtahids'* opposition to all secular power,
even to a government which professed Shia loyalty. Ultimately it led to the 20th
century claim by Ayatullah al-Uzma Ruhullah Khomayni, that the scholars
could rule directly.

In his "*Wilayatul Faqeeh*" ("Guardianship by the Juriconsult") in 1970, Imam
Khomayni called for an Islamic State headed by pious and righteous scholars
of Sharia. He urged scholars to teach that religion cannot be divorced from
politics and that men of religious learning have much more to do than just study
menstruation and puerperium.[28] They must explain to the people, besides the
matters related to worship rituals, the Islamic teachings on politics, rights, crimes,
economy and society.[29] Scholars are the vicegerents of the Prophet, after the
Imams, during the major occulation. They must perform the duties of the Imam
on his behalf, without being elevated thereby to the status of the Prophet or
the Imam.[30]

He established a case for qualified *ulamaha* as the authoritative interpreters
of the sacred law in the absence of the Hidden Imam, to assume the right to
rule. The theory was in place: only the opportunity to put it into practice was
required. The moment was, indeed, fast approaching, for the end of the 1970s
marked the beginning of the fifteenth Islamic century, the moment in traditional
Islamic thought for the appearance of a great figure of renewal (*mujaddid*).
Against the background of growing popular fury toward the Shah's regime,
religious symbols were a potent means of mass mobilization. In December 1978,
the commemoration of the martyrdom of Imam Hussayn was the occasion for
massive public demonstrations against the Shah, who four weeks later, finally
departed Iran, a sick and broken man.[31]

On 12th February 1979, Iran was proclaimed an Islamic republic. A new
constitution was approved at the end of the year, establishing a parliamentary
form of government with an elected president, a single-chamber consultative
assembly, the Sharia as the basis of the legal systems, and a council of guardians
dominated by religious leaders. The Constitution vests supreme authority in a
faqeeh with Imam Khomayni appointed for life.

Thus has the dream of '*Wilayatul Faqeeh*' become a reality.

I turn now to the effect of Imamology on the Shia *usul*, principles of
jurisprudence.

Based on the principle of authority, the Imamis admit only the two fundamental sources of the Sharia, both traced to Revelation: the Quran and the Sunna.

Al Kashiful Ghataa begins a resumé of Shia tenets saying 'Muslims agree
unanimously that the proofs of Sharia precepts consist exclusively of the Book,

---

[27] *ibid.* pp. 203/4.
[28] Ayatullah al-Uzma Khomayni, *The Islamic Government* (in Arabic) p. 20.
[29] *ibid.* p. 120.
[30] *ibid.* p. 75.
[31] Waines, *op. cit.* p. 252.

the *Sunna*, Reason (Ijtihaad) and Consensus (Ijmaa): In that respect, there is no difference whatsoever between the Imamis and other Muslim groups.'[32] But on closer examination, an enormous gap appears.

Of course the Holy Quran is accepted by all. But when it comes to exegis, the readings differ. The only interpretation acceptable to Shiis is that given by the Imams.

As for the *Sunna*, the *Hadeeth*, (the Traditions attributed to the Prophet), they accept the *Hadeeth* only from the members of the House of the Prophet, discarding 'all other reciters from Bukhara, Merv or Nishapur', not because they are against such reciters, but because they are too zealous to safeguard the religious tenets and observe the Prophet's precepts to accept *Hadeeth* from any source other than the infallible descendants of the Prophet.[33]

Al Kashiful Ghataa argues likewise. 'The only *Hadeeth* to carry weight [for the Imamis] are those transmitted by the Members of the House [of the Prophet] through generations from their grandfather, God's Blessing be on him, and his house, i.e. what is reported by as-Sadiq, from his father, Al-Baqir, from his father Zainul Abideen, from his father, the Prophet's grandson (*subt*) al-Hussayn, from his father the Commander of the Faithful, from the Apostle of God, God's Peace be upon all of them.'[34] He goes on to dismiss other reciters, 'As for the reports related by such men as Abi Huraira, Samra ibn Judub, Marwan ibnil Hakam, Amr ibnil Aas and their like, they are worth nothing to the Shii.'[35]

Introducing his erudite book on the *Fiqh* of Imam Jaafar as-Sadiq, Chief Jaafari Justice Maghniya explains his plan:

'I took every care to rely for source on the text as reported from the Imams, as this is the surest way to learn about God's precepts and the Sharia of their Grandfather, the Apostle of God, according to the Quran "And if they refer it back to the Apostle and those in authority among them, it would become known to those of them who investigate." (4:83) If I failed to find the text of the Book or the Imams I referred to a rule approved by their scholars who trace every rule back to the Holy Quran and infallible Imams.'[36]

As for *Ijmaa*, it is not an authority *per se* but derives its value from being approved by an Imam or his representative.

Apart from those sources shared by both Schools, there are definite Sunni procedures that the Shia dismiss outright; above all the *qiyas*, deduction by analogy. The Imamis, both Ithna-Ashari and Ismaili, quote a famous debate between the sixth Imam, Jaafar as-Sadiq, the founder of the School and his disciple, the Sunni Imam Abu Hanifa. Imam Abu Hanifa called on Imam Jaafar who asked him what authority would he seek if he failed to find it on a given matter. Imam Abu Hanifa replied that he would draw analogous conclusions from a similar matter on which there was an authority. Imam Jaafar reminded him that Satan was the first to use deduction by analogy and that was a sin;

---

[32] Al Kashsiful Ghataa, *op. cit.* p. 235.
[33] Muhammad al-Khalisi: *Rays from the Life of as-Sadiq* (in Arabic) *Najafy*, n.d pp. 61/62.
[34] Al Kashiful Gataa, *op. cit.* p.236.
[35] *loc. cit.*
[36] Muhammad Jawad Maghniya *Fiqhul Imam as-Sadiq*, vol. 1, p. 6.

when God ordered him to prostrate himself before Adam to which Satan replied: 'I am better than he is as you have created me of fire and created him of clay and fire is a nobler element than clay.' for which he was to suffer eternal humiliating torture. To prove to Imam Abu Hanifa that deduction cannot apprehend the wisdom of God, Imam Jaafar asked him, in the eyes of God which is the more monstrous sin, adultery or murder. Abu Hanifa answered: murder, to which Jaafar wondered why two witnesses were required under Sharia evidence law for murder, while four were required for adultery, when logical deduction would have the witnesses the other way around. Finally Imam Jaafar warned Imam Abu Hanifa 'Fear God, O Numan, and stop using deduction by analogy. On the Day of Final Judgment, we shall be standing, we and those who think differently, before God and He shall ask us about what we said and you about what you said. We shall answer "We have said, God said and the Apostle of God said" and you and your friends will say "We had the opinion that ... and we made deduction by analogy". And God shall do to us and to you what he likes.'[37]

The Shia Imams have been persistently reported to affirm that 'If Sharia rulings are based on deduction by analogy, the faith would be destroyed'.[38]

So far we have been dealing mainly with the Ithna-Ashari branch of Shiism, but have also shown the identity of opinion between it and the Ismaili branch especially on the authority of Imams and even their representatives, the *mujtahid*, although the Ismailis call them '*daiees*' ('missionary heralds'). They both regard Imam Jaafar as-Sadiq as the chief transmitter of Sharia decisions (hence the description of Ithna-Ashari doctrine as 'Jaafarism'). They agree to the Imams until Imam Jaafar, and then part ways, with the Ithna-Ashari adopting Musa and his descendants to the twelfth Imam, and the Ismaili minority following his elder brother Ismail.

The Great Fatimid Imams, in North Africa, were descendants of Ismail. Established in Tunis early in the third AH/10th AD century, the Dynasty, a few decades later, spread into a great empire which ruled in Egypt for more than two centuries. There, they built the capital Cairo, and founded in it, over a thousand years ago, al-Azhar University, named after Fatima az-Zahraa, the Prophet's daughter and considered to be the oldest university and the greatest Islamic seat of learning in the world. Late in the fourth AH/11th AD century, the Ismailis split into Mustaalis who supported al-Mustaali as the ninth Fatmid Imam, and the Nizaris who supported his brother Nizar.

Like the Ithna-Ashari, the Ismailis add *Jihad* (Holy War) to the worship ritual obligations and add also *wilaya*, i.e. belief in the Imam. Unlike the Ithna-Asharis, it is an article of Ismaili faith to accept the two principles of 'the manifest' (*az-Zahir*) and 'the hidden' (*al-Batin*) The manifest is concerned with prophethood and the observance of the Prophet's religious teachings, precepts and laws according to their literal meaning. The hidden is the deepest meaning and interpretation of the Divine Scriptures.[39] For example, the manifest obligation of fasting is to abstain from food and drink and intercourse, while the hidden

---

[37] Qadi an-Numan at-Tameemi, *Daaim ul Islam*, vol. 1, p. 132.
[38] Al Kashiful Ghataa, *op. cit.* p. 236, quoting al-Kaafi.
[39] *Daaim ul Islam*, vol. 1, p. 34.

duty is to abstain from committing sins, dishonest acts and to stick to truth and wisdom.[40]

When they interpret the Quran, the Ismailis distinguish between what is meant for the public and what is confined exclusively to the initiated. A parallel distinction exists in the Ismaili hierarchy between the imam, the only person endowed with perfect knowledge, and the *dais*, his representatives on the one hand, and the common believers on the other, with various degrees of knowledge and insight.

The main Ismaili legal text is *Daaimul Islam* (Pillars of Islam) by the afore-mentioned Qadi Abu Hanifa an-Numan ibn Muhammad at-Tameemi al-Maghrabi (d. 363 AH/995 AD) who held the office of Chief Justice in the reign of the Ismaili Imam al-Muiz Ledeenillah, the Fatimid Caliph who invaded Egypt, established an empire comprising half of the world's Muslims then, built al-Kahira (Cairo) as its capital, and erected al-Azhar as a mosque college for the instruction of Muslim youths in the precepts of Shii Ismailism.

The Arabic text of Daaim ul Islam remained in manuscripts[41] until 1995 when it was published in print in Beirut, verified, compared to two manuscripts annotated and with an introduction by the Ismaili scholar Dr. Arif Tamir. He traces *Daaim* back to the earliest book on Islamic Jurisprudence which is, according to him, *Imam Ali's Precedents*, passed to his great grandson Imam Muhammad al-Baqir who transmitted it in turn to Imam Jaafar as-Sadiq. Dr. Tamir stresses that the ultimate source is the Imam's holy grandfather, the Apostle of God, as the prime authority on Sharia, Revelation and the precepts of the science of the 'Manifest'. The interpretation of these precepts is, according to Dr. Tamir, summed up in *Daaim ul Islam*.

In spite of the source being the same, some Ismaili provisions on marriage and succession are more akin to the Sunnis. The book falls into two volumes: (1) on the worship rituals, *ibadaat*, of which there are seven: belief, ritual purity, prayers, religious tax, fasting, *hajj* and *jihad*: (2) on transactions of which the relevant parts here are marriage, gifts, wills and inheritance.

2. Universal Juristic Maxims

Apart from the *Usul*, the basis from which Islamic law is inferred, Muslim jurists compiled a number of universal rules of jurisprudence (*al qaw aid al-kullia al-fiqhiyya*), from which particular legal provisions may be deduced. The earliest Hanafis compiled seventeen such rules, which were subsequently increased to thirty-seven by al-Karkhi, who died in 340 AH (951 AD); then to eighty-six by

---

[40] *ibid.* p.29.

[41] That is why I wrongly complained, in the earlier editions of the present book, of 'a peculiar dearth of Ismaili legal texts available, and refrained from dealing with the Ismaili practices there (p. 15), for which I apologise. Tyahji in his *Muhammadan Law*, 3rd ed., 1940, p. 26 remarked that 'the law of the Ismaili Shias ... is less easy to discover. Some of their texts have been printed and published and translated, if at all, only recently.' He considered himself lucky to have had access to notes from *Daaim ul Islam* for the 2nd edition, and been assisted for the 3rd by Fyzee unifying the references to *Daaim* which was not printed then. Professor Fyzee was still saying, in 1948, that *Daaim* was being edited and translated by him. Incidentally, Dr. Tamir, the editor of the Arabic text, refers to him as his friend when he visited Syria in 1951 to look at the manuscripts of *Daaim ul Islam*, with a variable degree of success, while he was the Indian Ambassador in the Middle East. *Daaim ul Islam* p. 35.

ad-Dabbousi who died in 430 AH (1038 AD). The Egyptian Hanafi jurist, Ibn-Nujaim, who died in 910 AH (1563 AD) reduced all universal legal rules to 6 fundamental maxims.

In order to provide the newly created tribunals with an authoritative statement of the Islamic law in matters of contracts and obligations, the *Mijallat ul Ahkam al-Adliyya,* that is the Compendium of Legal Provisions, referred to for brevity as the Mijalla, was codified in 1293 AH (1876 AD) as the Ottoman Civil Code. In the Explanatory Memorandum, the Drafting Commission, citing Ibn-Nujaim, but remarking that his work was not followed up by later Islamic jurists and that many of the universal Islamic maxims were scattered in the various Islamic legal texts and often mixed with particular provisions of law, decided to compile the most general legal maxims by way of an Introduction to the Code. The Mijalla contains ninety-nine such maxims of Islamic jurisprudence.

These maxims must be distinguished from general theories. They are simply yardsticks for the deduction of particular precepts within the general theories, such as those dealing with contract, ownership, obligations and the like, which were not treated by the ancient Islamic jurists but are now the subject of research by contemporary scholars.

Although the Mijalla has been superseded by the national civil codes of Syria, Iraq and Jordan, the general legal maxims constituting Articles 2–100 inclusive of the Mijalla are mostly included in their new civil codes and recently the UAE's. Some of these rules are also provided in Article 6 of the Sudanese Personal Status Law for Muslims/1991. We shall now deal with the most important of these maxims in the Mijalla, avoiding their overlapping, and showing, where applicable, when they appear in the respective civil codes. They can be grouped under five headings:

(1) Intention
(2) Proof
(3) Flexibility
(4) Injury
(5) Custom

(1) Intention

A matter is determined according to intention, that is to say, the effect to be given to any particular transaction must conform to the object of such transaction (Art. 2).[42] This is based on an authentic Tradition that: "Deeds are judged by intentions and each shall get what he intends." It follows that should there be a discrepancy between the intention and the appearance, intention, if known, shall prevail. A particular application of this rule is Article 3 (Art. 155 Iraqi, 214 Jordanian): "*In contracts, effect is given to intention and meaning and not to words and phrases.*" The Mijalla cites the example that a contract for sale and subject to the right of redemption shall have the force of a pledge.

(2) Proof

Certainty is not dispelled by doubt (Art. 4). This is the general principle of proof and becomes Article 74 of the Jordanian, 445/1 of the Iraqi, and 35 of the UAE.

---

[42] Mijalla. In this section the first Article in brackets refers to the Mijalla.

From this general rule the Islamic jurists derived the principle of *istis-hab* whereby "*A state of affairs known to have once existed is regarded as having persisted unless the contrary can be proven*" (Art. 10; Arts. 4, 75, Jordanian, 447, Iraqi and 36 UAE).

Other articles related to the same rule are: "*Freedom from obligation shall be deemed the original state of things*" (Art. 8; Arts. 73, Jordanian, 444, Iraqi and 37 UAE). This fundamental principle finds a specific application in an authentic saying of the Prophet: "*Evidence is for him who affirms; the oath for him who denies*", a provision which forms Article 76 of the Mijalla (Arts. 77, Jordanian and 448/1, Iraqi). This principle is further elaborated in Article 77: "*The object of evidence is to prove what is contrary to appearance; the — object of the oath is to ensure the continuance of the original state*" (Arts. 78, Jordanian and 448/2 Iraqi).

Under the same rule of certainty fall several other provisions:

"*No attention shall be paid to inferences in the face of obvious facts*" (Art. 13);

"*Where the text is clear, there is no room for interpretation*" (Art. 14; Arts. 215, Jordanian and 2, Iraqi).[43]

"*One legal interpretation shall not destroy another*" (Art. 16);

"*No statement is imputed to a man who keeps silence, but silence is tantamount to a statement where there is an absolute necessity for speech*" (Art. 67; Arts. 95, Jordanian; 81, Iraqi; and 44/1 Kuwaiti);

"*No weight is given to mere supposition*" (Art. 74), supposition (*tawahhum*) being deemed weaker than doubt (Art. 60 UAE).

(3) Flexibility

Difficulty begets facility (Art. 17). The same rule is worded differently as "*Latitude should be afforded in the case of difficulty*" (Art. 18). The basic provision is derived from the Quran in various verses, e.g. "God intends every facility for you; He does not want to put you to difficulties" (2:185).

Several rules are inferred from this basic one:

"*Necessity renders prohibited things permissible*" (Art. 21; Arts. 222, Jordanian, 212, Iraqi and 43 UAE);

"*Necessity is estimated by the extent thereof*" (Arts. 22; Art. 212, Iraqi);

"*Necessity does not invalidate the right of another*" (Art. 33; Arts. 63, Jordanian, 213/1, Iraqi and 45 UAE); e.g. if a hungry person eats bread belonging to another, such a person must later pay the value thereof on being able so to do.

"*An act allowed by law cannot be made the subject of a claim to compensation*" (Art. 91; Arts. 3, Syrian; 61, Jordanian; 6, Iraqi; 4, Egyptian; and 4, Libyan).

Schacht describes this tendency as the "concerted action of interested parties", which is, according to the sociology of law, a primary source of law. While respecting the orthodox Sharia, it bestows on it a greater flexibility and adaptability and supplements it in many respects. It allowed the use of *hawala*, or bill of exchange, and in general the *hiyal*, or legal devices, which is the use of legal

---

[43] The same principle is adopted, albeit in a different form, in the Civil Codes of Egypt, Syria, Libya, Kuwait and Algeria (Article Nos. 150, 151, 152, 193, 111, respectively) reading as follows: "When the wording of a contract is clear, it cannot be deviated from in order to ascertain by means of interpretation the intention of the parties."

means for extra legal ends that could not be achieved directly with the means provided by the Sharia.[44]

(4) Injury

"*No injury shall be committed nor shall be met by injury*" (Art. 19). This is an authentic saying of the Prophet explaining the Quranic ruling "The recompense for an injury is an injury equal thereto, but if the person forgives and makes reconciliation, his reward is due from God." (42:40) Ideally there should be no injury, but should any injury be committed, it shall entail compensation equal in degree to the injury suffered. This is adopted in the Iraqi Civil Code (Art. 216) and the Jordanian Civil Code (Art. 62). From this general rule, many others follow:

"*Injury is removed*" (Art. 20; Art. 62, Jordanian);

"*An injury cannot be removed by the commission of a similar injury*" (Art. 25);

"*A private injury is tolerated in order to ward off a public injury ...*" (Art. 26);

"*Severe injury is removed by lesser injury ...*" (Art. 27; Arts. 65, Jordanian, 213/1 and 214/1, Iraqi);

"*Repelling an evil is preferable to securing a benefit*" (Art. 30; Arts. 64, Jordanian, 6, Iraqi and 44 UAE).

A particular application of this provision is that "*When prohibition and necessity conflict, preference is given to the prohibition*" (Art. 46; Art. 4/1, Iraqi).

This is the basis of the whole concept of *Maslaha* which is defined as "the procurement of benefit and the avoidance of injury within the spirit of the Sharia", and sets concern for human welfare high above the logic of formal principles of deduction.

(5) Custom

Custom is an arbitrator (Art. 369, 46 UAE). By custom here is meant current usage among people in their transactions. It is acknowledged by the Sharia, and jurists allow conventional conditions in contracts, even if they were not explicitly mentioned, provided that the custom in question does not conflict with the Sharia. This rule is cited in the explanatory memorandum of the Jordanian Civil Code, in comment on Article 2/3 dealing with custom and guideline to be followed by courts in the absence of a legal text and a Sharia enunciation. Several rules follow:

"*Public usage is conclusive evidence which must be observed in action*" (Art. 38);

"*No doubt that judgments shall vary with the change in the times*" (Art. 39; Art. 5, Iraqi);

"*In the presence of custom no regard is paid to the literal meaning of a thing*" (Art. 40);

"*Effect is only given to custom where it is of regular occurrence or when universally prevailing*" (Art. 41);

"*Effect is given to what is of common occurrence, not to what happens infrequently*" (Art. 42);

"*A matter recognized by custom is regarded as though it were a contractual*

---

[44]Schacht, J. *An Introduction to Islamic Law* (Oxford, 1979), p. 210.

obligation" (Art. 43; Arts. 100, Jordanian; 186, Iraqi; 95, Egyptian and Libyan; and 96, Syrian);

"*Matter recognized by merchants is regarded as being a contractual obligation between them*" (Art. 44);

"*A matter established by custom is like a matter established by law*" (Art. 45).

CHAPTER 2

Personal Status Laws in the Arab States

1. What is Personal Status?

Personal Status, *Al-Ahwaal Ash-Shakhsiya*, is a recent legal term in Arabic, unknown to the classical Islamic jurists, and non-existent in all classical texts of Islamic jurisprudence. As recently as 1880, when the first version of the Sharia Courts Bill was issued, the Egyptian legislator used the phrase "matters of the Sharia", *Al-Mawaad-dul-Shariyya*, to refer to questions of personal status.

In fact, the very concept seems to have been unknown to the early Islamic jurists to whom the Sharia consists of two major divisions, beliefs on theology and human acts. The latter was divided again into worship rituals and transactions to regulate acts between persons, such as contracts, marriage and kindred institutions, or acts dealing with property, e.g. sale and rent. The Shafiis make marriage and matters related thereto a category in its own right, alongside three other categories: worship rituals, transactions and penology.[1]

The term was first known in Egypt in the 1890s in the title of a book *Sharia Provisions on Personal Status* by Muhammad Qadri Pasha, then an Egyptian Minister of Justice who had earlier compiled two other books on civil transactions and the questions of *waqf* (see Glossary and Chapter 14), all three books based on the Hanafi doctrine. It was first used in Iraq in the Courts Bill of 28 November 1917, then in the Sharia Courts Act 1923 and the Basic Iraqi Law (Constitution under the Monarchy).[2]

The first definition of personal status was given on 21 June 1934 by the Egyptian Court of Cassation as follows:

"Personal Status is the sum total of the physical or family descriptions of a known person which distinguish him from the others, and gives legal effects under the law in his social life, such as being male or female, married, widowed or divorced, a parent or a legitimate child, being of full legal capacity or defective capacity due to minority, imbecility or insanity, being of absolute or limited legal capacity.

As for matters related to property, they are all by nature real status questions. But the Egyptian legislator, finding that *waqf*, gift and will, all

---

[1] Imam ash-Shafii, *Al Umm*, Vol. 5, *The Book of Marriage* (Cairo).
[2] M. Naji, *Sharh Qanoon ilAhwal-ish-Shakhsiyya* (Baghdad, 1962), pp. 10–22; A. Karam, *Al Ahwal-ush-Shakhsiyya* (Baghdad, 1979), p. 5.

being contracts without consideration, are based on the religious concept of charity, and includes them in the personal status issues. ..."[3]

The verdict seems to defeat its own purpose for setting an objective criterion to distinguish personal from real status matters. It also fails to distinguish the status and the legal capacity, which is in fact a consequence of the status.

The Iraqi legislator refrained from any definition of personal status, and instead enumerated the questions related there in a limitative way. Inductively these questions are:

(i) the *waqf*: conditions; beneficiaries of their allocation; administration; and the guardian;
(ii) status, including being alive, dead, missing or absent;
(iii) legal capacity and the accidents thereto;
(iv) betrothal, marriage, prohibited degrees, registration and proof;
(v) marital rights and duties, dower and maintenance;
(vi) repudiation of marriage;
(vii) parentage and degrees of kinship;
(viii) custody and fostering;
(ix) maintenance of descendants, ascendants and other kin;
(x) guardianship, wills, acts taking effect after death and questions of inheritance.[4]

Many legislative provisions on the above (e.g. inheritance) are left to the classical Sharia texts.

The Tunisian Presidential Decree of 26/11/1376 AH, 26/6/1957 AD, Raid 51-57-19, enumerates personal status questions as follows:

"Personal Status shall include disputes over the status of the persons and their legal capacity, marriage, property dispositions between spouses, mutual rights and duties of the spouses, divorce, repudiation and judicial separation, parentage, acknowledgement or disavowal of paternity, family and descendants' relationships, maintenance duties among relatives and others, rectification of parentage, adoption, tutelage, guardianship, interdiction, attainment of majority, gifts, inheritance, wills and other acts taking effect subsequent to death, the absent person and the declaration of a missing person to be dead" (Art. 2).

2. The Present State of Legislation on Personal Status in the Arab States

In the majority of modern Arab Islamic states, there is as yet no legislative enactment on personal status. The Sharia Law as compiled in the traditional legal manuals, is still formally applied in its entirety in most Arab Gulf States, Saudi Arabia, Yemen, Libya and Sudan. I shall come back to that after a brief outline of the state of legislation in the rest of the Arab world.

In Egypt, as previously mentioned, the eminent jurist Muhammad Qadri

---

[3] Civil Cassation on 21/6/1934, Appeal No. 40J. Year 3, Published in *Al Muhamat*, year 13, p. 87.
[4] M. Naji, *op. cit.* pp. 27–28.

Pasha compiled in 1893 *The Sharia Provisions on Personal Status*, a book of 646 Articles on marriage, divorce, gift, interdiction, wills and inheritance, all based on the Hanafi doctrine. For a long time the book was the standard textbook for Egyptian Islamic Law students and a manual for the Sharia Courts, although it did not acquire the official acknowledgement of the State. A commission of Islamic Law scholars published in 1916–1917 a draft code on marriage and divorce which met with a strong opposition and was shelved. Two decrees were promulgated: 26/1920 and 25/1929, which parted from the then adopted Hanafi Law and adopted the rulings of other doctrines on some questions related to maintenance, *iddat*, divorce and separation on grounds of insolvency, absence of the husband and injury to the wife. A Presidential Decree No. 44/1979 was issued introducing new rulings on divorce, polygyny, maintenance, arbitration between the spouses, custody and guardianship of the children, thus giving the woman improved rights to divorce and maintenance. The Constitutional Court on 4 May 1985 declared that the said decree was unlawful on the grounds that the State President had no lawful power to issue such a decree since there was no urgency to enact it. The People's Assembly, therefore, promulgated Act No. 100/1985 to take effect on the same date of publication of the Constitutional Court ruling of the non-constitutionality of Decree No. 44/1979, with only minor changes thereto. For some years now, the People's Assembly has been considering a draft law on marriage and divorce, but no decision has been taken yet.

In the Lebanon, with its complicated sectarian structure, each denomination has been accorded an autonomous juristic personality. Article 9 of the Lebanese constitution asserts:

"The freedom of belief is absolute. The State, while paying homage to the Almighty God, shall respect all religions and doctrines, shall guarantee the freedom to conduct religious rites under the State's protection provided it shall not contravene the public order, and shall also safeguard for the citizens of whatever religion or sect, due respect of their Personal Status Code and their spiritual interests."[5]

The Lebanese Law recognizes the three major religions and their subdivisions. The Islamic sects include the Sunnis, the Shia Jaafari, the Shia Alawites, the Ismailis and the Druzes. Of these, only the Druzes have a Codified Personal Status Act of 1948 amended in 1959. For the Sunni and Jaafari sects Decree No. 241 of 4/11/1942 regulated the constitution, the procedures and the judiciary of the Sharia Courts. One Article, 111, of the decree specified the relevant applicable law as follows:

"The Sunni judge shall give judgement according to the most authoritative opinion of the Hanafi Doctrine except in those cases specified in the Family Rights Act, promulgated on the 8th of Muharram 1336 AH, the 25th of October 1917, in which case the rulings of the said Act shall be applied by the Sunni judge. The Jaafari judge shall give judgement in accordance with the Jaafari Doctrine, and the relevant provisions thereto of the Family Rights Act."

---

[5] Quoted by Baylani, *Personal Status Laws in the Lebanon*, p. 12, n. 1.

This latter Act had been promulgated by the Ottoman Sultan Muhammad Rashad on 25 October 1917, shortly before the collapse and the termination of sovereignty of the Ottoman Empire in the Arab countries and was never, therefore, enforced. Article 111 was thus a revival thereof. Although the above-mentioned decree of 1942 was subsequently amended and then abrogated, the latest Act of 16 July 1962 retained the full text of Article 111 in a new Article 242.[6]

In Syria, a compendium of personal status provisions was promulgated under the Presidential Decree No. 59 on 17/9/1953. According to the Explanatory Memorandum thereof, the new legislation derived from five sources:

(i)   the Customary Family Rights Law, on which court rulings were based;
(ii) the Egyptian Law modified to suit the local conventions;
(iii) Qadri Pasha's *Sharia Provisions of Personal Status Questions*;
(iv) an eclectic adoption by the Legislative Committee of rulings under doctrines other than the Hanafi;
(v)   A Personal Status Law Draft by the Damascus Judge.

The Presidential Decree No. 59/1953 covered the subjects of marriage, divorce, parentage, custody, legal capacity, wills and inheritance. It was amended by Law 34 on 31 December 1975 in respect of polygny, the dower, fostering, custody, maintenance and guardianship. The said Laws apply to all Syrians except the Druzes (Art. 307), and the Christian and Jewish Communities who shall apply their own religious provisions governing betrothal, marriage conditions and effects, wife's obedience, wife's maintenance, minor's maintenance, declaration of voidance and dissolution of marriage, dower and custody (Art. 308).

In Iraq the Sharia remained the general law of the land without any distinction between the personal status and the civil cases, until the last days of the Ottoman Empire, with the promulgation of the Mijalla, the Civil Code which separated civil from personal status although it remained subject to the Sharia and especially the Hanafi School. Personal status matters were defined for the first time in the Provisional Sharia Procedures Act of 1336 AH (1917 AD) which made them the subject of the exclusive jurisdiction of the Sharia courts, to be decided according to the Sharia provisions. In 1917, a Declaration by the C-in-C of the British Army of Occupation, later amended in 1921, put personal status matters for the Jaafaris under the jurisdiction of the civil courts to be decided on according to the Jaafari doctrine, while retaining the jurisdiction of the Sharia courts for the personal status cases of the Sunnis, again applying the Hanafi teachings.

In 1923 the personal status matters of the Jaafaris were referred to the jurisdiction of the newly formed Jaafari Sharia courts, applying the Jaafari Doctrine.[7]

On 30 December 1959, the Personal Status Act No. 188/1959 was promulgated as the Universal Personal Law for all the Iraqis, except those for whom special legislation was made, the exceptions being the Christians and the Jews for whom special religious courts were established under the Religious Courts for the Christian and Mosaic Denominations Act No. 32/1947.

In the Explanatory Memorandum for the 1959 Act, it was noted that:

[6] Ibid. pp. 17–18.
[7] M. Naji, *op. cit.*, pp. 14–15.

"The Sharia Provisions of Personal Status have never been compiled in a single code, selecting from the jurists' opinions those most acceptable and convenient for the times, with the Sharia judiciary basing their judgments on the classical jurisprudence texts, inferred opinions on controversial issues and the decisions of the Courts in Islamic States."

This attitude was retained in the first Article of Act No. 188, asserting that:

2. "In the absence of any legislative provision to be applied, judgment shall be given under the principles of the Islamic Sharia most suitable to the provisions of this Act.
3. The Courts shall be guided by the rulings established by the judiciary and Islamic Jurisprudence in Iraq and the other Islamic States whose laws are akin to the Iraqi laws."

Act No. 188/1959 has since been amended by Acts No. 11/1963 and No. 21/1978.

In Jordan, the Personal Status Law was promulgated on 5 September 1976 as Provisional Law No. 61/1976 abrogating the previous Jordanian Law of Family Rights No. 92/1951 (Art. 186/1). It is provisional in the sense that it was issued under Article 31 of the Constitution in the absence of the National Assembly.

It refers to the most authoritative Hanafi opinion for recourse in matters not covered in the said Law (Art. 183). It deals with marriage and betrothal, marriage contract, the dower, repudiation, dissolution by order of the Court, *iddat*, parentage, fosterage, custody, maintenance for kin, and provisions concerning the missing person and the mandatory will. It leaves the details of inheritance provisions to the classical texts.

In Morocco, a Royal Commission was briefed in August 1957, to elaborate a Code of Islamic Law. The Commission decided unanimously to present a project of such a Code which was promulgated by a number of Royal Decrees, issuing a series of books dealing with personal status, the whole of which would constitute "The Code of Personal Status and Succession". The first two books on marriage (Arts. 1–43) and the dissolution of marriage (Arts. 44–82) were issued under Decree No. 1/57/343 of 22 November 1957, to take effect as from 1 January 1958. The same date was set for the application of the provisions of Book III on parentage and the consequences thereof, namely custody, fosterage and maintenance both for the wife and the relatives (Arts. 83–132) under Decree No. 1/57/379, followed by Book IV on legal capacity and proxy under Decree No. 1/58/019 of 25 January 1958, Book V on Wills (Arts. 173–216) under Decree No. 1/58/073 on 20 February 1958, and finally, Book VI on Succession (Arts. 217–297 under Decree No. 1/58/112 of 3 April 1958. These provisions apply throughout the Kingdom of Morocco, to the exclusion of any other rulings. Recourse is ordered to the most authoritative or best known and widest applied opinion of the Maliki rite in all cases which are not covered by the Code.

Amendments, additions and abrogations were made under Decree No. 1/93/347 of 10 September 1993 in respect of guardianship in marriage, divorce, polygyny and custody of children.

In Tunisia, personal status questions are governed by the Personal Status

Mijalla promulgated on 6/1/1376 AH, 13/8/1956 AD, Raid 66-56, amended by Law No. 40 of 2/3/1377 AH, 27/9/1957 AD, Raid 19, to abrogate a separate personal status law for Jewish and non-Muslim Tunisians who are now subject to the same legislation. It deals with marriage (later amended by Act 1/1964), divorce (with additions under Act 41/1962 and 7/1981), *iddat*, maintenance, custody (as amended under Acts 49/1966 and 7/1981), parentage, the missing person, inheritance, majority and interdiction (as amended under Act 7/1981), wills (added under Act 77/1959), and gifts (added by Act 17/1964). Further amendments of provisions on marriage, divorce, maintenance and custody of children were made under Law No. 74/199 of 12 July 1993.

A decree of 20/12/1376 AH, 18/7/1957 AD, regulates the administration of estates. Act No. 27 of 12/8/1377 AH, 4/3/1958 AD, was issued in respect of public guardianship, sponsorship and adoption, and was later amended by Act No. 69/1959.

In Algeria, the Family Law No. 84/1984 was promulgated on 9 June 1984 dealing with marriage, maintenance, guardianship, inheritance, wills, gifts and *waqf*. It applies to all Algerian citizens and those residents in Algeria subject to the provisions of the Civil Code relating to conflict of laws (Art. 221).

Four weeks later, on 7 July 1984, in Kuwait, Law No. 51/1984 in the matter of Personal Status was promulgated by the Emir. Before that, the courts in the State of Kuwait used to apply the provisions of the Maliki doctrine in cases of personal status. The new Law is divided into three main parts: marriage (Arts. 1–212), wills (Arts. 213–287) and succession (Arts. 288–336). Under Article 343, recourse should be made to the most authoritative opinion of the Maliki doctrine in the absence of any provision, then to the general principles thereof. It applies to those who were governed by the doctrine of Imam Malik and to the non-Muslims of different religions or denominations, non-Maliki Muslims being subject to their respective doctrines (Art. 346).

In the Republic of Sudan, the Personal Status Law for Muslims was promulgated on 24 July 1991, to apply to all cases still before the Court, and abrogating the previous legal instruments of Sharia circulars, judicial memoranda and other court instructions. It comprises five books on Marriage, Provisions and Effects, Dissolution of Marriage, Legal Capacity and Guardianship of the Person and the Property, Gifts, Wills and *Waqf*, and finally, Inheritance. It empowers the Supreme Court, Personal Status Division, to issue rules to explain or interpret the provisions of the Law having recourse to the historical sources from which this Law is derived (Art. 5, 1/2).

In the Yemeni Republic, the Presidential Council promulgated Law No. 20/1992 on Personal Status on 29 March 1992. It comprises six books dealing with Betrothal and Marriage Contract; Provisions on Marriage Dissolution, Provisions on Kinship, Gifts and Like Matters, Wills and finally Inheritance. It is mainly eclectic, and provides recourse to the most authoritative Sharia provision on matters for which there is no ruling in it, and abrogates all other legal texts contrary to it.

In the Sultanate of Oman, the Personal Status Law was issued under Royal Decree No. 32/97 on 4 June 1997. It consists of five books regulating Marriage, Dissolution of Marriage, Legal Capacity and Guardianship, Wills and lastly, Inheritance. In the absence of any specific text on any matters, it provides for recourse to the Sharia rules that are most in concordance with the provisions of the Law. It does not apply to non-Muslims unless they ask for it to apply.

In the remaining States where no personal status legislation has been enacted, the predominant rite prevails. For example, in Saudi Arabia it is the Hanbali rite that applies, and in the Great Socialist People's Libyan Arab Jamafiriyya, Sharia courts apply the Maliki doctrine, although a Personal Status Law, said to be in the making, is thought to be eclectic.

Since as early as 1977, endeavours have been made to codify a united Personal Status Law for all the members of the League of Arab States. After several congresses and committee meetings of the Arab Ministers of Justice, a draft Unified Personal Status Law for all the member States was worked out as a first step to promulgate it as a law by the individual States. It is mainly based on the Sunni, especially the Hanafi doctrine, with some additions in line with the latest legislations, especially in the matter of the mandatory will.

3. Conflict of Laws

Apart from Tunisia, conflict of laws in personal status matters is dealt with in the Civil Codes of Arab States which have modern Personal Status Laws.

The Tunisian Legislative Order of 26/11/1376 AH, 24/6/1957 AD, Raid 51-57-19 as amended by Law No. 40 of 2/3/1377 AH, 27/9/1957 AD, Raid 19 rules under Article 1 that "Foreigners shall be governed by their National Law in matters of personal status". Under Article 4, it specifies the applicable law to settle a dispute between two litigants of different nationalities according to the subject matter in the following manner:

(i) The respective personal status law of each party in matters of status, legal capacity and conditions of marriage.

(ii) The personal status law of the husband at the time of marriage in matters of mutual rights and duties of the spouses, property dispositions between spouses, divorce, repudiation and judicial separation.

(iii) The personal status law of the person liable for payment in matters of payment of maintenance.

(iv) The personal status law of the minor or person placed under interdiction in matters of tutelage, guardianship, interdiction and majority.

(v) The personal status law of the father in matters of parentage, rectification of parentage, acknowledgement or disavowal of paternity.

(vi) The personal status law of the adopter and adoptee in matters of adoption.

(vii) The personal status law of the adopter in matters of effects of adoption.

(viii) The personal status law of the deceased, the donor and the testator in matters of inheritance, gifts, wills and other acts taking effect subsequent to death.

(ix) The personal status law of the absent person or missing person deemed to be dead, in the matter of absence and the missing deemed tantamount to death.

Egyptian, Syrian, Iraqi, Jordanian, Libyan and Algerian Civil Codes, and the Kuwaiti Law No. 5/1961 in respect of Legal Relations Containing a Foreign Element, contain identical provisions, similar to the Tunisian, as to the applicable law in any case of conflict in the following fashion:

(i) The fundamental conditions relating to the validity of marriage are governed by the national law of each of the two spouses (Arts. 12, Egyptian; 13, Syrian; 19, Iraqi; 13/1, Jordanian; 12, Libyan; 11, Algerian). However, both the Iraqi and Jordanian Civil Codes (Articles 19/1 and 13/2 respectively) add that a marriage between two foreigners or a foreigner and a native citizen shall be deemed valid in form if it is concluded according to the law of the country where it is made or the laws of each of the two spouses. This provision has been adopted from Articles 6 and 7 of the Hague Convention of 13 June 1902.[8] The Kuwaiti law distinguishes between the material conditions for the validity of marriage, e.g. the legal capacity, the validity of consent and the conditions of freedom from any marriage impediments, which shall be governed by the national law of the spouses if they are of the same domicile, otherwise by their respective national law (Art. 36) and the formal conditions for marriage, such as solemnization and religious rites, which are governed by the law of the country where marriage was contracted, or by the national law of each spouse (Art. 37). The same Article adds that the said national law must be observed in respect of notice or publication of marriage, although the absence of such a notice or publication shall not render the marriage void in countries other than those whose regulations have been violated.

(ii) The effects of marriage, including its effects upon the property of the spouses are regulated by the law of the country to which the husband belongs at the time of the conclusion of the marriage (Arts. 31/1, Egyptian; 14/1, Syrian; 19/2, Iraqi; 14/1, Jordanian; 13/1, Libyan; 12, Algerian; 36, Kuwaiti).

(iii) Repudiation of marriage is governed by the law of the country to which the husband belongs at the time of repudiation, whereas divorce and separation are governed by the law of the country to which the husband belongs at the time of commencement of the legal proceedings (Arts. 13/2, Egyptian; 14/2, Syrian; 14/2, Jordanian; 13/2, Libyan; 12, Algerian). Iraqi Article 19/3 makes repudiation, divorce and separation subject to the law of the country to which the husband belongs either at the time of repudiation, or of commencement of the legal proceedings. Under Kuwaiti Article 40/5/1961, divorce is governed by the latest common nationality of both spouses during marriage and before divorce or separation action; otherwise, the husband's national law at the time of marriage shall prevail.

(iv) Notwithstanding the above provisions, the national law alone shall apply if one of the two spouses is a native citizen (Arts. 14, Egyptian; 15, Syrian; 19/5, Iraqi; 15, Jordanian; 14, Libyan; 13, Algerian; 36, Kuwaiti).

(v) Obligations as regards payment of maintenance to relatives are governed by the national law of the person liable for such payment (Arts. 15, Egyptian; 16, Syrian; 21, Iraqi; 16, Jordanian; 15, Libyan; 14, Algerian). Kuwaiti Article 45 adds that the Kuwaiti law shall govern temporary maintenance to such relatives.

(vi) The national law of a person who is to be protected shall apply in respect of all fundamental matters relating to natural and legal guardianships, receiverships, and other forms of guardianship of persons without legal

---

[8] Explanatory Notes to the Jordanian Civil Code, p. 45.

capacity and of absent persons (Arts. 16, Egyptian; 17, Syrian; 20, Iraqi; 17, Jordanian; 16, Libyan; 15, Algerian; 46, Kuwaiti).

(vii) Inheritances, wills and other dispositions taking effect after death are governed by the national law of the deceased (the propositus), the testator, or the person disposing of property at death (Arts. 17/1, Egyptian; 18/1, Syrian; 18/1, Jordanian; 17/1, Libyan; 16, Algerian). Articles 47 and 48 of the relevant Kuwaiti Act concur, adding that the form of the will and other dispositions taking effect after death shall be governed by the law of the disposer at the time of disposition or of the country where it occurred. The same ruling applies to the gift (Art. 49). Iraqi Articles 22 and 23, while ruling that the law of the deceased or the propositus at the time of his death shall apply to the questions of inheritance and wills, make the following provisos:

(a) Difference of nationality shall not bar inheritance of movable and real property but no foreigner shall inherit from an Iraqi unless the foreign law allows an Iraqi to inherit from him.

(b) A foreigner who leaves no heir shall have his property in Iraq devolved to the Iraqi State notwithstanding any provision to the contrary under the law of the foreigner (Art. 22).

(c) The Iraqi law shall apply as to the validity of the will for and succession to the immovable property situated in Iraq and owned by a deceased foreigner (Art. 23).

(viii) As for legal capacity and status, the laws of all the above-mentioned Arab States are unanimous that it shall be governed without any exception by the law of the country to which the persons belong by reason of their nationality (Arts. 11/1, Egyptian; 12/1, Syrian; 18/1, Iraqi; 12/1, Jordanian; 11/1, Libyan; 10, Algerian; 36, Kuwaiti). This provision is valid even for the legal capacity for marriage, notwithstanding the case when one spouse is a native citizen as under (iv) above.

(ix) Under the Sharia, betrothal is not a binding contract between the two parties, it being only a promise to marry. This attitude is adopted by all Arab States except Kuwait, where Article 35 of Act No. 5/1961 reads as follows:

> "Betrothal shall be considered a matter of personal status, and shall be governed in terms of validity by the domicile law of the male suitor, in terms of effects by the domicile law of the suitor at the time of betrothal, and in terms of cancellation by the domicile law of the suitor at the time of cancellation".

4. The Method Followed in this Work

It is quite clear from the above that the Sharia Law has not been abrogated even in those states which introduced recent legislative enactments. These recent texts sometimes referred to Sharia rules, e.g. on inheritance under the Iraqi Law. In other instances they selected the rules of a specific Sharia doctrine, e.g. the Hanafi in Syria and the Malikis in Morocco. Even in certain innovations, e.g. the prohibition of polygyny in Tunisia, some Sharia texts were quoted in support. The majority of Arab Islamic States still apply the Sharia Law in its entirety.

Therefore in the following chapters I shall deal with the basic Sharia rulings and cite the relevant legislative enactment where appropriate. In the light of the definition and enumeration of personal status questions, I shall cover the following subjects even if some are relegated in some countries to the respective Civil Codes:

Marriage, Dower, Maintenance, Dissolution of Marriage, The *Iddat*, Parentage, Rights of Children, Maintenance for Descendants, Ascendants and Collaterals, Guardianship, Rules of Inheritance, Wills, the Religious Endowment (*waqf*) and Gifts (*hiba*), in that order.

CHAPTER 3

Marriage

1. Definition

Marriage, according to the classical juristic definition, is a contract prescribed by the legislator, and it denotes the lawful entitlement of each of the parties thereto to enjoy the other in the lawful manner.[1]

The Tunisian Code omits the definition altogether. The Syrian, Iraqi and Jordanian Codes Arts. 1, 3/1 and 2, respectively[2] give an almost identical definition:

"Marriage is a contract between a man and a woman who is lawfully eligible to be his wife with the objective of joint life and procreation."

The Sudanese Law also gives an almost identical definition, but stresses the intention that it is to last for ever (Art. 11).

The Moroccan Decree elaborates more on the definition:

"Marriage is a legal pact of association and solidarity between a man and a woman, meant to last, the objective thereof being to maintain chastity and lawful wedlock, multiplying the nation through founding a family under the patronage of the husband, on solid grounds, to ensure for the contracting parties the discharge of the responsibilities related thereto in security, peace, love and respect" (Art. 1).

The Kuwait Law No. 51/1984 defines marriage as "A contract between a man and a woman who can lawfully be wed to him, to the end of tranquillity, chastity and the strength of the nation" (Art. 1). In a similar vein, Algerian Article 4 reads "Marriage is a contract lawfully concluded between a man and a woman, the ends of which are, *inter alia*, the formation of a family based on love, compassion, co-operation, chastity of the two spouses and the preservation of legitimate lineage". In Yemen, marriage is "an association between two spouses under a legal (Sharia) pact whereby the wife shall be lawfully available to the husband, the objective being to build a family based on good companionship" (Art. 6).

In the Omani Law, "Marriage is a lawful contract between a man and a woman, the objective thereof being chastity and the creation of a stable family,

---

[1] Abu Zahra, *On Marriage*, p. 17; Abdullah, *Personal Status*, p. 23.
[2] Unless otherwise stated, all Articles mentioned refer to the Arab Codes of Personal Status described in the previous chapter.

under the guardianship of the husband, on bases to guarantee for them the discharge of the burdens thereof with affection and compassion" (Art. 4).

Marriage is therefore a civil contract, without the Christian notion of sacrament.[3] Still, it is a unique contract in that:

(i) the rights and obligations which derive from it are dictated by the legislator, and shall not be subject to any agreement to the contrary between the parties; and

(ii) in spite of their civil character, marriage contracts are mostly regulated under religious jurisdiction to impart upon their effects a character of sanctity.

There are substantial differences in the provisions of marriage between the two major streams of Islamic jurisprudence, the Sunna and the Shia, which will be pointed out as the various headings are dealt with.

2. Preliminaries of Marriage

The prelude to the marriage contract is the betrothal (*khutba*), which is the request by the man for the hand of a certain woman in marriage, and the approach to her, or to her kin, with a view to describing his status, and to negotiating with them the subject of the contract and their respective demands in that connection.[4] For the betrothal to be valid, both parties should be aware of the circumstances of the other, and should know the potential spouse's character and behaviour in order that the contract may be valid, and the union it establishes be viable; the means of obtaining this information is through enquiries, investigations, consultations, and the meeting of the couple, provided that it is within the presence of a chaperon.

If the man's offer is accepted by the woman, or those who are legally entitled to act on her behalf, the betrothal shall take place, and would be a reciprocated promise of the man and the woman to marry in the future. Once betrothal has taken place, no other man shall be allowed to approach the woman with a view to betrothal knowing that the woman has already been betrothed. This restriction is lifted should the previous betrothal be cancelled.

A. Conditions of Betrothal

Since the betrothal is a preliminary to a marriage contract, no betrothal shall be valid unless the woman is eligible forthwith for marriage. Therefore no

---

[3] Art. 1 of the Oriental Church Act 1949 for Syria and Lebanon reads as follows: "Marriage is a contract raised by The Lord Jesus to the sublime status of a sacrament. Therefore a valid marriage between two baptized persons is both a contract and a sacrament." An eminent Roman Orthodox Jurist Ibn-ul-Assal, wrote, "A marriage contract shall not be made or solemnized except with the presence of a Priest, his prayers for the two parties thereof, and his bestowing Eucharist upon them at the time of the Nuptial Service whereby they are united and become one body. Otherwise it shall not be marriage. It is the prayer which renders women lawful for men and men for women ..." *Al-Majmuu As-Safawi*, p. 40.

[4] Betrothal is used in preference to the word engagement because it is a more conventional arrangement and, unlike the latter, does not entail, *per se*, damages on the breach thereof as will be explained in more detail later in the text.

betrothal of a married woman can take place, as it will then constitute the violation of the husband's rights. The woman revocably divorced cannot be betrothed explicitly or implicitly as her married status still holds, and the husband has the right during the *iddat*[5] period to return to the marriage at any time without her consent.

The widow, during her period of *iddat*, may be betrothed implicitly but not explicitly. An explicit request of betrothal is a phrase like "I would like to marry you" or "I request you to be my wife". An implicit request of betrothal is such a phrase as "I would like to marry a good or a beautiful woman" or "I intend to marry (or I wish to find) a suitable wife for me." The irrevocably divorced woman cannot be engaged implicitly or explicitly until the end of the *iddat*. Any other impediment of marriage, as we shall see later, shall also prohibit any betrothal. Such impediment could be permanent, as in the case of a prohibited degree, or temporary, such as the betrothal of a sister while the man still has her sister as his wife. We shall deal later with the subject of the prohibited degrees.

It should be pointed out that a forbidden betrothal is considered a religious sin, but if a man asks a woman who is already betrothed, or is still in her *iddat*, to marry him, and their marriage takes place after the *iddat*, such a marriage shall be deemed legally valid and binding if it fulfils all the legal requirements.

B. Breach of Betrothal

Betrothal, like other marriage preliminaries, is merely a mutual promise of marriage between the two parties. It does not constitute a marriage contract, and therefore is not binding on either party. Classical Islamic jurists and modern legislators are unanimous that either party has an unquestionable right to break the betrothal, otherwise it would be entering, under coercion, into a contract meant ideally to be for a lifetime. There are explicit provisions to that effect in modern Personal Status Codes recently passed in Islamic countries, e.g. Tunisian Personal Status Mijalla of 60/1956, Article 1: "Every promise of marriage shall not be deemed marriage and shall not be binding."; Moroccan Article 2: "Betrothal and other customary preliminaries of marriage are a promise of marriage and do not constitute a marriage. ..."; Jordanian Article 3: "No marriage shall be solemnized by just a betrothal. ..."; Article 4: "Each party to the betrothal may break it." Article 2 of the Syrian Personal Status Code and Article 3 of the Iraqi Code read: "Betrothal, marriage promise, reading the *Fatihah* ... shall not constitute a marriage." The Syrian Legislator adds: "Each of the fiancé and fiancée may break the betrothal." The Sudanese Law defines betrothal as "a promise of marriage in the future and is equivalent to the reading of the *Fatiha*, ("the opening" which is the first *Sura* of the Quran, an essential part of every ritual prayer (*salaat*) in a traditional betrothal) the exchange of gifts and any other current custom considered lawful" (Art. 7). It comes to an end on (a) either or both of the parties withdrawing; (b) the death of either party; or (c) the occurrence of a marriage impediment (Art. 9). The Yemeni Law defines betrothal as a request for and promise of marriage, including the reading of the *Fatiha* and the exchange of gifts (Art. 4/1) The Omani Law defines it as "a request for and promise of marriage" (Art. 1).

---

[5] *Iddat* (literally "the counted period"): A period of continence following the dissolution of marriage by death, divorce or otherwise. See Chapter 7.

While the breach of betrothal is an unconditional right of each party according to the jurists and under the law, an injury may befall the party who has not committed the breach. Some Islamic jurists of all schools rule out any amends being made in such a case under the general Sharia rule that "An act allowed by law cannot be made the subject of a claim to compensation." Other modern Islamic jurists, e.g. Professor Abu Zahra of Egypt, relying on the general rule that "There shall be no injury, no injury shall be met with an injury, and injury shall be removed", maintain that the injured party shall be entitled to amends to make good a breach of betrothal on grounds other than betrothal *per se*, e.g. if furniture was bought or accommodation secured at the request of the declining party.[6]

The Egyptian Court of Cassation, the highest court of the land whose judgments are binding interpretations of the law, has ruled that:

"Betrothal is only a preliminary step towards a marriage contract, a mere promise that is not binding on either party who are lawfully free to end it at anytime, especially as in the marriage contract the two parties must enjoy absolute liberty to enter into it, in view of its paramount importance to society, which freedom of action shall be hindered if either party is under the threat of being liable to damages. However, if the promise to marry and the subsequent withdrawal therefrom are accompanied by other acts entirely independent thereof, of such a nature as to cause material or moral injury to one of the parties, such acts shall give rise to a lawful suit for damages against the party from whom they emanate on the ground that such acts, apart from the mere breach of promise, shall constitute tort that requires redress."[7]

The Jordanian Provisional Law No. 61/1976 does not contain any provisions in such a case. Following the Maliki School, Article 3 of the Moroccan Decree rules that the man may recover any gifts unless he is the party who committed the breach, a position also maintained by the Tunisian Act (Article 2) in the absence of any condition to the contrary. The Syrian Personal Status Act rules in Article 4 that:

"1. Should the fiancé pay dower in cash and the woman uses it to buy furniture and then the fiancé withdraws, the woman shall have the option either to refund the dower or hand over the furniture.
2. Should the woman break the betrothal, she shall return the dower or the equivalent thereof.
3. Presents shall be subject to the provision of gifts."[8]

The Sudanese Law provides that if either party withdraws for no reason, he or she shall recover nothing gifted to the other. If there is reason, the withdrawing party shall recover all gifts if they still exist, or the value thereof on the day of receipt if they have perished. (Art. 10) The Yemeni Law rules that any withdrawing party shall return the same gifts if existing, or their equivalent value on the day of receipt (4/3). No gifts shall be returned if betrothal is terminated on

---

[6]Abu Zahra, *On Marriage* (Cairo, 1950), p. 38; O. Abdullah, *Islamic Sharia Personal Status* (Alexandria, 1968), pp. 53–55.
[7]Cassation Hearing of 14/12/1939, Appeal No. 13, Year 9J., *Compendium of Legal Rules (Civil)*, Vol. 1, p. 118.
[8]See Chapter 15 on Gifts.

death, or for a cause over which no party has control, or due to a marriage impediment occurring (4/3). If the termination causes any injury, the party causing it shall be liable for damage (Art. 5).

The Omani Law gives similar rulings in Art. 3.

(a) Each of the parties to the betrothal may withdraw.
(b) The party who withdraws from the betrothal without reasonable excuse must return any gifts which still exist, or the like or the value thereof at the time they were given, unless custom dictates otherwise, or they are perishable by nature.
(c) No gift shall be returned if the betrothal is terminated by death, or is due to a cause over which neither party has any control, or to the occurrence of an impediment to the marriage.

The Shafiis rule that the gift shall be recovered under all circumstances; the Hanafis, whose opinion is generally upheld by the courts in most Islamic states, take the view that any betrothal gifts, like gifts in general, are recoverable as the donor is entitled to revoke such donations if they have not increased in value, been disposed of or destroyed.[9]

3. Pillars and Conditions of Marriage Contracts

A. Pillars

Like any other contract, a marriage contract can only be concluded through the two essentials or pillars (*arkan*) of offer and acceptance by the two principals or their proxies (Arts. 5, Syrian; 14, Jordanian; 4, Iraqi; 8, Kuwaiti; 4, Moroccan; 12, Sudanese and 7 Yemeni).

Jordanian Law stipulates that offer and acceptance shall be through explicit words of marriage, *inkah, tazweej* (Art. 15), a position adopted from the Shafii School. In other Arab countries, words denoting marriage linguistically or according to custom are allowed (Arts. 6, Syrian; 4, Iraqi; 4-1, Moroccan; 10, Algerian; and 9, Kuwaiti). This position derives from the Hanafis, who also admit metaphorical words, which may be:

(i) Words denoting taking possession instantly without consideration such as gift and charity, which are unanimously deemed by the Hanafis to mean an offer of marriage. This position is confirmed by the Quran and the Prophet's Tradition: e.g. "... and a believing woman if she give herself unto the Prophet and the Prophet desires to take her in marriage a privilege of Thee only not for the rest of believers", found in a verse beginning: "Oh, Prophet we have made lawful unto thee Thy wives unto whom thou has paid their dowries, and those whom thy right hand possesseth of those whom Allah hath given thee as spoils of war ..." (33:50)
(ii) Words that denote immediate ownership for a consideration like buying and selling. If the metaphor for marriage is corroborated, some Hanafi jurists accept such words as a valid offer of marriage. Others refuse it. But words denoting taking possession of the usufruct immediately are unanimously denied to constitute an offer of marriage.

---

[9] Abiani, *Commentary on the Sharia Provisions*, p. 9.

The three Imams, Abu Hanifa, Malik and Ahmad Ibn Hanbal agree that Islamic marriage can be solemnized in languages other than Arabic. But Imam ash-Shafii stipulates that an Islamic contract of marriage shall be concluded only in Arabic for those who know it, on the analogy with the prayers which can only be performed in Arabic.[10]

Marriage can also be concluded by the language of signs for those who cannot speak or write (Arts. 10, Syrian; 4/2, Moroccan). It may be in writing if one party is absent (Articles 7, Syrian; 6/2, Iraqi). Both rulings are included in Kuwaiti Article 9, Sudanese 14/f, Yemeni 8.

Offer and acceptance must occur at the same meeting. If the meeting is over after the offer and before the acceptance, the offer becomes void (Arts. 11, Syrian; 6/1a, Iraqi; 5/1, Moroccan; 14/b and c, Sudanese; 7, Yemeni).

The offer shall not be withdrawn by the offerer after it is accepted by the other party. But the offerer may withdraw before acceptance, in which case there is no contract nor any obligation, which can only result from the concordance of the two essentials of offer and acceptance (Syrian Art. 11/1).[11]

If the offer is made through a messenger or a written letter, the acceptance shall be required at the meeting where the message is delivered or the letter is read (Yemeni 8). An acceptance at a later meeting shall not be valid. Article 10, paragraph c. of the Kuwaiti Law No. 51/84 states: 'For acceptance to be legally valid ... (c) the contract session between the two parties to the contract, starts at the moment the offeree receives the written offer, or by hearing that by a messenger. In such a case, the contract session is deemed to continue for three days, during which acceptance will be held valid, unless the offer sets another adequate delay or the recipient indicates rejection.

Mutual hearing and understanding of the offer and acceptance are essential to establish a marriage contract, even if such understanding is only in broad outline and not necessarily in detail. Without hearing and understanding, there shall be no contract linking offer and acceptance (Arts. 11/1, Syrian; 15, Jordanian; 6/1b and c, Iraqi; 10/e, Kuwaiti; 14/e, Sudanese).

B. *Conditions of Legal Capacity*

(1) *Legal capacity*

Both parties must possess legal capacity. The contract shall be deemed void if either or both parties are devoid of legal capacity. Full legal incapacity of either party shall render the contract null. A person possessing partial legal capacity may act as a proxy for a third party in a marriage contract, while his own marriage shall be subject to the approval of the person possessing the power thereto. A person of full legal capacity can conclude a marriage contract as a principal or as a proxy. For the purposes of marriage, a wastrel is deemed of full legal capacity, as interdiction, if any, affects only his financial dispositions.[12]

---

[10]Imam ash-Shafii, *Al Umm*, Vol. 5, p. 33.

[11]The same principle is again expressed in the Civil Codes of Egypt, Syria, Libya and Algeria. In a case in which an offerer could not, by reason of the transaction, in accordance with commercial usage, or on account of other circumstances, have anticipated a formal acceptance, the contract is deemed to have been concluded if the offer is not refused within a reasonable time. Failure to reply is equivalent to acceptance when the offer relates to dealings already existing between the two parties or when the offer is solely in the interests of the offeree. (Egyptian 98; Syrian 99; Libyan 98; Algerian 68).

[12]Abu Zahra, *op. cit.* pp. 58–59; Abdullah, *op. cit.* pp. 97–98.

(2) Puberty and majority

The legal capacity for marriage is not always the same as full civil legal capacity. The Tunisian Law (Art. 5) stipulates that no marriage can be contracted between a man under 20 years of age and a woman under 17 without special court permission, which shall not be given unless there are serious grounds and it is unquestionably to the welfare of the two spouses. The same law sets the age of full civil capacity at 20 years for both sexes (Art. 157). The marriage of persons under the legal age is subject to the guardians' consent. The matter is referred to the court if such a consent is withheld, but the spouses-to-be persist (Art. 6).

In Egypt, all persons attaining majority in possession of their mental faculties and not under legal disability, have full legal capacity to exercise their civil rights. The majority of a person is fixed at 21 years completed, in accordance with the Gregorian calendar (Art. 44 of the Egyptian Civil Code No. 131/1948). Yet, the legal age of marriage is indirectly suggested under the Sharia Court Act No. 78/1931, Article 99 as amended by the Law No. 87/1951, which bars "the judicial consideration of any matrimonial suit if the wife's age is less than 16 lunar years or if the husband's age is below 18 lunar years without special permission."

In the Lebanon, there are different provisions for the Sunnis, the Shias and the Druzes. Article 4 of the Family Rights Act which governs the Sunni personal status stipulates, for the bridegroom to possess legal capacity for marriage that he be at least 18 years old, and the bride to be 17. Articles 5, 6 and 7 of the same Act give the court the power to sanction the marriage of adolescents below the set ages should their condition so warrant. The Jaafari doctrine requires puberty for the parties to be proven, provided that no marriage shall be allowed for a boy under 15 years or a girl under 9. Under the Druze Personal Status Act of 1948, the bridegroom shall possess legal capacity for marriage on reaching 18 years of age and the bride on reaching 17 years (Art. 1). The sectarian judge may give marriage permission to an adolescent boy who is over 16 years but below 18 years, should his condition so permit, subject to the consent of his guardian (Art. 2). The same licence may be given to an adolescent girl who is over 15 but under 17, subject to the same provisos (Art. 3). Without the guardian's consent, each adolescent may apply for the annulment of marriage within six months as from the date of reaching the age fixed in Article 1 (Art. 4). Any marriage of a boy under 16 or a girl under 15 is categorically prohibited (Art. 5).

The Moroccan Decree fixes the age of legal capacity for marriage at 18 for the boy and 15 for the girl (Art. 8) while allowing marriage for parties under the statutory age of majority subject to the consent of the guardians with the right of appeal to the court (Art. 9).

The Jordanian Law stipulates that the bridegroom shall have reached 16 years and the bride 15 years to possess the legal capacity for marriage (Art. 5), while fixing the age of majority at 18 years according to the Gregorian calendar (Civil Code Act 43-2).

The Syrian legislator requires the attainment of puberty as a pre-condition for the capacity of marriage (Art. 15-1) setting the respective age at 18 for the boy and 17 for the girl (Art. 16). The age of full legal capacity, or the age of majority, is 18 full calendar years (Art. 46 of the Syrian Civil Code). However, an adolescent boy having completed 15 years, or a girl having completed 13 years, claiming to have reached puberty, may apply to the judge for marriage, who shall grant them permission subject to the realization of their truthfulness and their physical capabilities (Personal Status Act, Art. 18/1).

The Iraqi Personal Status Act fixes the age of legal capacity for marriage at 18 years (Art. 7/1 as amended by Art. 1 of the Act 21/1978), which is the legal age of majority (Civil Code, Art. 106). A minor of 15 years may be granted permission by the court, subject to his proving physical ability and to his guardian's consent, which can be waived by the court if it is unreasonably withheld (Art. 8 of the Personal Status Act No. 188/1959 as amended by Art. 2 of Act No. 21/1978). The Kuwaiti Law simply stipulates sanity and puberty as conditions for marriage legal capacity (Art. 24a). The judge may allow the marriage of an insane or imbecile male or female, if a medical report certifies that such a marriage would help recovery, and the other party is agreeable (Art. 25b). It prohibits the notarization or the ratification of a marriage contract unless the girl has reached 15 and the boy 17 years of age at the time of notarization (Art. 26).[13] The Sudanese Law provides that every person is deemed of full legal capacity unless otherwise ruled by law, and the age of authority is 18. (Art. 214/215) Under the Yemeni Law, the man must be of legal capacity (*mukallaf*) and minors under the age of 15 are not allowed to marry. (Arts. 4 and 5). Under Omani Law, marriage capacity is achieved on reaching 18 years of age, and being of sound mind (Art. 7).

An innovation in the Syrian, Jordanian and Moroccan Codes regulates the age gap between the two spouses-to-be. Under the Syrian Article 19, if they are disproportionate in age, and no good is seen to be forthcoming, the judge may withhold permission for them to marry. The Jordanian Article 7 is more categorical and precise, ruling that "No marriage contract shall be solemnized for a woman under 18 years of age if the husband-to-be is over 20 years older than her, unless the judge makes sure of her consent and free choice, and that the marriage is in her interests." Article 15 of the Moroccan Personal Status Decree simply leaves the harmonious proportioning of the ages of the spouses to the discretion of the wife solely.

(3) Sanity

Legal capacity requires, besides age, being of sound mind (Arts. 15/1, Syrian; 5, Jordanian; 7/1, Iraqi; 6, Moroccan). However, the court may grant an insane person or an imbecile permission to marry on the strength of a medical report certifying that marriage would help the patient's recovery (Arts. 15/2, Syrian; 8, Jordanian; and 40, Sudanese). The Iraqi and Moroccan Laws add that this shall be subject to the other party's awareness of the fact and consent thereto (Arts. 7/2 and 7, respectively). Similar provisions are ruled in Articles 11 and 12/a/5 of the Yemeni law adding that any illness must not be hereditary. (12/6) Article 8 of the Omani Law provides as follows:

[13] An emotionally charged problem with which practitioners are frequently faced is the child marriage. As seen in my review, the minimum age for a wife-to-be is 15 years unless special permission is granted by the court. But it cannot be denied that various subterfuges are often used, especially in rural and bedouin areas, to present prospective brides to the authorities as being older than they really are. A case in point are two studies reported in the Article "Iranian Cultures" in the *Encyclopaedia Britannica*, Vol. 9, p. 865, revealing that the median age of women's marriage in four villages near Shiraz was between 13 and 15 years, and 80 per cent of working class wives of Ispahan were married between the ages of 9 and 16 years of age inclusive. Against this background, the Iranian law makes the marriage of any person under the minimum legal marriage age (of 15 years for women) an offence that renders the person responsible liable to six months' to two years' imprison-

(a) Marriage of the insane or imbecile shall only be contracted by the guardian thereof after the court issues permission to that effect.
(b) The judge shall only give permission for the marriage of the insane or imbecile after ascertaining that the following conditions have been complied with:
 i. the other party must be aware of the mental state of the insane or imbecile when accepting marriage thereto,
 ii. the mental condition is not such as to be hereditary,
 iii. the marriage will prove beneficial to the afflicted party.
The last two conditions must be the subject of investigation and confirmation by a competent committee.

Under the Sharia, a marriage contract shall be null and void if either party to the contract is insane, an indiscriminating imbecile or an indiscriminating minor, due to the absence in this case of the will and consent.[14] The Druze sect rules out the marriage of the insane under any circumstances.[15]

C. Guardianship in Marriage and Marriage by Proxy

(1) Guardianship

(a) Guardianship of persons and property is dealt with separately in a later chapter, following the Islamic Sharia and legislation. At this stage I shall only treat guardianship in marriage.

Guardianship in marriage falls under two categories in respect of the ward, according to the classical Sharia tenets:

(i) Guardianship with the right of compulsion (*wilayat-ul-ijbar*) is exercised over a person of limited or no legal capacity wherein the guardian may conclude a marriage contract which is valid and takes effect without the consent or acceptance of the ward;
(ii) Guardianship without the right of compulsion (*wilayat-un-nadb*) is exercised when the woman, whether a virgin or previously married, possesses full legal capacity, but in deference to social customs and traditions, delegates the conclusion of her marriage to a guardian. In fact, this is more of an authorization of agent than guardianship. Some Islamic jurists call it joint guardianship when the woman has been previously married.

Nevertheless, the general consensus of jurists is that the woman shall not conduct her own marriage contract, whether she is a virgin or previously married, even when she possesses full legal capacity. Only the Hanafis do not require a guardian to conclude the contract on behalf of the woman unless she is of limited or no legal capacity.

According to the Sunni Schools, marriage guardians shall be agnates[16] in the following order:

---

ment, rising to two to three years' if the girl is below 13. However, permission may be granted by the court for the marriage of a girl of 13 years.
[14] Abdullah, *op. cit.* p. 71.
[15] Lebanon Druze Personal Status Act, Art. 5.
[16] Agnate (*asaba*): person whose relationship to the ward can be traced without the intervention of female links. See also the chapters on Guardianship of the Person and Inheritance.

(i)   descendants, i.e. the son and the son's son how-low-soever;
(ii)   ascendants, i.e. the father and the true[17] grandfather, how-high-soever;
(iii) the full brothers and the agnate brothers and their male descendants, how-low-soever;
(iv) the agnate uncles and their sons.

In the absence of agnates, guardianship shall be vested in relatives according to proximity; otherwise it shall be vested in the Head of State and his delegate, notably the judge.

According to the Shia Ithna-Asharis, the guardian is indispensable in order for the marriage of minors and majors of defective or no legal capacity to be valid. The guardian is always the father or the agnatic grandfather how-high-soever, failing which the legal guardian, otherwise the judge. Marriage guardianship shall never pass to the mother, the father's mother, any agnate or cognate in the absence of a father, an agnatic grandfather or a legal guardian, but shall be vested in the judge. Only the judge shall have the power to act as the marriage guardian for an adult who has reached the age of majority in a sane state, then later becomes insane.[18] The Ismailis maintain that the Prophet ruled "No (valid) marriage shall be concluded without a guardian and two righteous witnesses", and that Imam Jaafar declared "Marriage to a woman without a guardian is void."[19]

These are the general Sharia rules on marriage guardianship. Recent legislations adopt most of them. The order of guardians is strictly followed in Jordan (Art. 9), in Morocco (Art. 11), in Tunisia (Art. 8), and in Syria (Art. 21). The judge is declared the guardian for whoever has no guardian (Arts. 24, Syrian; 12, Jordanian; 8, Tunisian). The same rule is specified under Article 11 of the Algerian Personal Status Law which rules that the marriage of a woman shall be conducted by her guardian who is her father, failing which a close agnate relative of hers, and under Article 29 of the Kuwaiti law which briefly adopts the order of inheritance, as does Sudanese Law, Art. 32. Under Yemeni Article 16, the marriage guardian is the closest agnate relative, then the next, beginning with the father, how-high-soever, then son how-low-soever, then brothers, then their sons, then paternal uncles, then their sons, and so on. The Omani provisions on marriage guardianship run as follows:

Art. 11 (a) The marriage guardian is the agnate in his own right (*asib bi-nafsih*) in the order of inheritance. Should two guardians be at the same degree of proximity of relationship, either of them, on his own terms, may act as marriage guardian, preference being given to the one agreed to by the betrothed woman.

     (b) The guardian must be a male adult, of sound mind, and under no restrictions due to pilgrimage or *umra*, and if his ward is Muslim, must himself be Muslim.

Art. 12 If the nearest guardian is too often absent, of unknown address, out of reach or does not accept guardianship, guardianship shall pass, by permission of the judge, to the next in line.

Art. 13 The judge becomes the guardian of anyone who has no guardian.

---

[17] The agnatic grandfather. See also chapter on Inheritance.
[18] Al-Hilli, *Jaafari Personal Status Provisions*, p. 10.
[19] Qadi an-Numan, *Daaim ul Islam*, Vol. 2, p. 172.

Art. 14 The judge shall not contract the marriage of his own ward to himself, nor to any ascendant or descendant of his own. [the judge's]

However, guardianship with the right of compulsion is expressly prohibited in Morocco under Article 12/4 which reads:

"The guardian, even if he is the father, shall not compel his daughter who has reached puberty, even if she is a virgin, to marry without her permission and consent unless temptation is feared, in which case the judge shall have the right to compel her to marry in order that she may be under the protection of an equal husband who will take care of her."

In a similar vein, Articles 12 and 13 of the Algerian Law rule that no guardian can stop his ward from marrying if she so wishes, and if it is in her interests. Should he prevent her from doing so, the judge may give her permission without prejudice to the provisions of Article 9 aforesaid. However, the father may prevent his virgin daughter from marrying if that prevention is in her interests. But no guardian, whether a father or otherwise, can compel his ward to marry, nor can he get her to marry against her consent.

The Iraqi legislation goes even further, ruling, under Article 9 as amended by Article 3 of Law No. 21/1978 that:

"No kin or stranger may compel any person whether male or female to marry against his/her consent. A marriage contract under compulsion is void if no consummation has occurred. Similarly no kin or stranger may prevent the marriage of anyone who has the legal capacity for marriage under this Law."

The Kuwaiti legislator steers a middle course – a virgin between puberty and 25 years of age needs a marriage guardian, who shall be an agnate in his own right (*asaba bin-nafs*) in order of inheritance, failing whom, the judge (Art. 29); the previously married or the female of 25 or over, has the choice in marrying, but shall delegate the act of entering into the contract to her guardian (Art. 30).

In the Lebanon, the Sunnis distinguish between the male and female minors. The boy does not need the consent of his guardian, but permission by the court is to be granted only on his proving that he has reached puberty and can afford to marry. Under no circumstances may a boy under 17 years of age be made or allowed to marry (Art. 7 of the Family Rights Act). No girl may be married under 9 years of age. Between 9 and 17 she may marry by court permission, which may be granted if she claims to have attained puberty, is of a condition suitable for marriage and she obtains the consent of her guardian. Above 17 years of age her guardian's consent shall still be required for a minor to marry, but the judge may allow her to forego this consent if the guardian's refusal is unfounded.

Guardianship with the right of compulsion was practised by the Lebanese Sunnis observing the Hanafi law until the coming into force of the Family Rights Act, which prohibited the marriage of the minor in all but a few exceptional cases, and confined the exercise of the right of compulsion to the marriage of the insane (male or female), provided that such marriage is necessary for them and is permitted by the Sharia judge (Arts. 4–7).

However, this right is retained by the Lebanese Jaafaris. The guardian may make the minor marry regardless of his consent. But the minor may choose between continuing the marriage or applying for its annulment on reaching majority, should he deem such a marriage to his disadvantage. The Jaafari Doctrine makes no distinction between male and female minors who both need the consent of the guardian and the judge's permission for their marriage. On the other hand, if the father or the grandfather refuses to give the minor in marriage, no other relative or judge may do so, regardless of the grounds for the father's or grandfather's refusal. Should the minor be given away in marriage by a judge, the marriage shall be subject to his/her approval on reaching majority.[20] The Ismaili rule that no woman shall marry without her permission, citing a Tradition of the Prophet and a ruling by Imam Ali.[21]

For the Lebanese Druzes, refer to paragraph 3.B.(2) above (Puberty and Majority).

In Syria, Jordan and Morocco, all forms of compulsion to marry are excluded. The guardian still retains the right to object to the marriage of his ward, but can be overruled by the judge.

(2) Marriage by proxy

A person of full legal capacity, whether a man or a woman, may authorize another person to conduct the marriage on his or her behalf. Likewise, a marriage guardian may appoint an agent for that purpose. Such authorization may be given orally or in writing, and it shall not require evidence, although this is desirable.

The authorization shall be effective and binding on the principal if it conforms with the principal's instructions, otherwise it shall be subject to the principal's consent.

The marriage proxy is merely acting on behalf of the principal in respect of concluding the marriage contract, and his mission shall be deemed accomplished once the marriage contract is made. Therefore, the husband cannot require the wife's proxy to enforce his wife's obedience, nor can the wife demand that the husband's proxy, as such, should pay her the dower unless he has guaranteed it, in which case he shall be liable to pay it to her, by virtue of the guarantee, not of the marriage proxy.

These are the general rules of Sharia on proxy which generally apply in Muslim states with certain restrictions. The Moroccan Law restricts the power to appoint a proxy for marriage to the guardian in respect of his female ward, and the husband-to-be (Art. 10/1); a judge shall not solemnize his own marriage or that of any of his ancestors or descendants to his ward (Act. 10/2). Under the Syrian Law (Art. 8/2) a proxy may not marry his female principal unless he is explicitly empowered to do so in his power of attorney, a ruling similarly adopted by the Kuwaiti Law, Article 27/b. While not requiring any conditions to be fulfilled in the marriage proxy, the Tunisian Law (Art. 10) rules that the proxy shall not appoint any other agent without permission of his male or female principal. It also stipulates that the authorization of agents shall be through a legal document to include expressly the designation of both spouses, otherwise it would be void. The Jordanian and Iraqi Laws simply allow offer and acceptance to be made either by the principals or their proxy or proxies (Arts. 14 and 4, respectively).

[20] Al-Hilli, *op. cit.* p. 11.
[21] Qadi an-Numan, *Daaim ul Islam*, Vol. 2, p. 172.

4. Conditions of Validity of the Marriage Contract

Apart from complying with the provisions regarding offer and acceptance, marriage capacity and sanity, etc., the marriage contract has to fulfil other requirements to be valid according to Sharia and/or modern laws. These relate to witnesses, eligibility of the woman, and form of contract.

A. Witnesses

Sunni jurists throughout the ages are unanimous that the presence of witnesses is essential to ensure publicity which makes the division between lawful wedlock and fornication. They rely on proven Traditions of the Prophet: "Publicize marriage even with timbals", "There is no marriage without witnesses." Aisha, the wife and narrator of the Prophet, quotes him also as saying: "There can be no marriage without a guardian and two honest witnesses. If there is any dispute between them, the ruler is the guardian of the person who has no guardian." The first Patriarchal Caliph, Abu Bakr, is reported as saying: "Marriage in secret is not allowed until it is publicized and witnessed."

The witnesses must be two men or a man and two women, adult, sane and free. They must hear and understand offer and acceptance. If both parties of the marriage are Muslim, the witnesses must be Muslim. If the wife-to-be is a *Kitabi* (a believer in Christianity or Judaism, literally a member of the people of Scriptures), the jurists Muhammad, Zafar, Shafei and Ahmad do not accept that the witnesses be *Kitabis*; Imam Abu Hanifa and Abu Yussof accept such witnesses. The Hanafi School does not stipulate that the witnesses must be righteous, arguing that the philanderer is as good for publicity purposes as the righteous, that he can enter into a marriage on his own or his ward's behalf and that he is eligible to hold public office, therefore, *a fortiori*, he must be acceptable as a witness. Shafei and Ahmad dissent, on the ground that, apart from publicity, a witness must also serve the purpose of proof in the event of a denial, and no philanderer's evidence is admissible.

The modern Arab laws observe these provisions collectively. In Syria, "It is a condition for the validity of a marriage contract that it be witnessed by two men, or a man and two women, who are Muslim, sane and adult and shall hear offer and acceptance and understand the intention thereof" (Art. 12). In Iraq, Article 6/1 reads: "No marriage contract shall be concluded if any of the following conditions for conclusion of validity is missing: ... d. The witness of the marriage contract by two witnesses possessing legal capacity." The Jordanian legislator virtually repeats (in Article 16, under the heading "Conditions for the valid conclusion of the marriage contract") the text of the Syrian Article 12 with the qualification that the witnesses must be Muslim if the spouses are, and adding that the witnesses of the contract may be the ancestors or descendants of the parties. In Morocco, "It is a condition for the validity of the marriage contract that it be witnessed by two righteous men who shall hear at the same meeting the offer and acceptance from the husband or his deputy and from the guardian, after the wife's consent and her authorization to him to act on her behalf" (Art. 5/1). The Tunisian Code simply requires for the validity of a marriage contract, the presence of two reputable witnesses (Art. 3). Article 9 of Algerian law reads as follows: "A marriage contract shall be concluded on the consent of the two spouses and in the presence of the wife's guardian and two witnesses, and on an agreed dower." Article 11 of the Kuwaiti law requires for the validity of the marriage "the presence of two Muslim witnesses who are male, adult and sane, who shall hear the speech of the contracting parties and understand the meaning thereof"; it also allows two *Kitabi* witnesses if the wife is a *Kitabi*. The Sudanese and Yemeni Laws require two male or one male and two female witnesses who are righteous, Muslim and of legal capacity (Arts. 26 and 9 respectively). The Omani Article 28 requires for the validity of the marriage contract, the presence of two Muslim adult men, of sound mind and trustworthy to hear and understand the statements of the contracting parties.

On the other hand, the Shia do not require the presence of two witnesses for the validity of a marriage contract. Their presence is not a condition of validity, but it is at best desirable (*marghub*) as a precaution against denial. It is preferable that the witnesses be in possession of the requirements for acceptability, but the contract shall remain valid even if they are libertines, and even if they lacked all other requirements for acceptability.[22] The Ismailis rely on a similar ruling by Imam Muhammad al-Baqir when asked about a marriage contract without witnesses: "God mentioned witnesses only in respect of divorce. If there were no witnesses present at the marriage, there is nothing to answer for before God. But he who brings in witnesses shall make his heirs secure and shall not fear punishment by the Authority. The presence of witnesses at a marriage adds to certainty, and must be the practice."[23]

The Druzes of Lebanon require the presence of witnesses who may be the ascendants or descendants of the two parties, provided that there shall be no less than four witnesses (Art. 14 of the Lebanese Law of 24/2/1948).

B. *The Eligibility of the Woman*

The woman who is the object of the marriage must be immediately eligible for marriage to the person who proposes. There must be no impediments on the grounds of kindred, affinity or fosterage, or on grounds of the social status (being already married, or during an *iddat*, or equality) or because of difference in religion. In view of the importance of the subject, I shall deal with this condition in a later section under the heading of "Marriage Impediments".

C. *The Form*

The Sharia jurists require that the marriage contract form shall have immediate effect, and shall not be suspended or deferred to the future. It may include conditions for either or both spouses which must be observed if they are advantageous to either party. Examples of such conditions are: that the woman retains the right to dissolve the marriage; that neither party may leave the town they agree to settle in; that the husband may not marry another.

Concurring with these provisions, the Shias do not allow any marriage which is conditional on a non-existent condition or a non-existing occurrence. But they acknowledge a marriage on an irregular condition, e.g. non-payment of dower, in which case the marriage is valid and the condition is void. They acknowledge for both parties *Khiyar-ush-shart*, i.e. the stipulated right of cancellation, e.g. if the wife

---

[22] Al-Hilli, *op. cit.* p. 5.
[23] Qadi an-Numan, *op. cit.* p. 173.

is not a virgin or not free from physical deformity.[24] The Ismailis hold that the only valid conditions of marriage are those that do not violate the Book and the *Sunna*. They quote a ruling by two Imams, Jaafar as-Sadiq and his father Mohammad al-Baqir, about a man who promised the family of his wife, as a marriage condition, that if he took a second wife or bought a slave girl, then the second wife should be divorced and the slave girl would be set free. They both said "God's conditions are above men's: if the man wishes he may keep his promise, and if he wishes he may marry a second wife or buy a slave girl, and the second wife shall not be divorced and the slave girl shall not be freed."[25]

The Hanafis, on the contrary, deem this last condition null and void while the contract remains valid.[26]

It seems that the Hanbalis adopt the fairest and closest doctrine to the Sharia spirit and the one most likely to serve the interests of both spouses. They maintain that any condition agreed between the parties, orally or in writing, must be honoured and given effect, and any party who made that condition shall retain the right of cancellation if the condition is broken, unless there is a Sharia proof of its being void. They cite the Quranic verse "And fulfil every engagement for it will be enquired into (on the day of Reckoning)" (17:34), and the Prophet's Tradition "The worthiest conditions to be honoured are those that make women lawful for you." If any condition could be proven void under the Sharia, it should not be stipulated at all, and if made, must be deemed null and void, e.g. a condition by a wife to have a previous wife divorced.[27]

The Tunisian Code upholds the stipulated right of cancellation if an agreed condition is not honoured or is violated, without any liability if divorce takes place before consummation (Art. 11).

In Iraq, the legitimate conditions stipulated in a marriage contract must be honoured (Art. 6/3). The wife is granted the right to apply for cancellation if the husband does not comply with any such condition in the contract (Art. 6/4).

In Jordan, an advantageous condition for either party that does not conflict with the marriage aims, does not involve anything unlawful, and is recorded in the contract, shall be honoured according to the following guidelines:

(i)   If the wife stipulates a condition apt to secure her a lawful interest and not to infringe on a third party's right, e.g. not to be removed from her town, or to reserve to herself the right to divorce at will, or to live in a given locality, or for the husband not to marry another woman, the condition shall be valid and binding, and the failure to honour it shall give the wife the right to apply for cancellation without prejudice to any of her marital rights.

(ii) A condition by the husband that secures him a lawful advantage without infringing on a third party's right, e.g. for the woman not to work outside the matrimonial home, or for her to live with him at the town where he works, shall be valid and binding, and any violation thereof shall entitle the husband to apply for divorce and to be discharged of her deferred dower and *iddat* maintenance.

[24] Al-Hilli, *op. cit.*
[25] Qadi an-Numan, *op. cit.* Vol. 2, pp. 179–180.
[26] Al-Abiani, *Sharia Personal Provisions*, p. 17.
[27] Abul-Naja, *Hanbali Jurisprudence*, p. 60; Ibn Qayyim al-Jouzia, *Zaad-ul-Maad*, Vol. 4, p. 4, and *Ilam*, Vol. 2, p. 246.

(iii) A condition included in the contract that conflicts with its purpose or involves anything unlawful, e.g. a condition by one party that the other party shall not share the matrimonial home, shall not live as man and wife, shall drink alcohol or shall alienate a parent, shall be deemed void, but the contract shall remain valid (Art. 19/1/2/3).

Likewise, the Syrian Legislator deems any condition in the marriage contract that contravenes its legal order or intentions and involves any illegality, to be void without affecting the validity of the contract (Art. 14/1). A condition that secures the wife a lawful interest without jeopardizing the rights of a third party or restricting the husband's freedom in his lawful business shall be valid and binding (Art. 14/2). A condition that restricts such freedom of the husband or infringes on the rights of a third party shall be valid but not binding to the husband and shall entitle the wife making the condition, if the husband does not honour it, to apply for divorce (Art. 14/3). The Kuwaiti legislator (Art. 40), electively distinguishes between three kinds of marriage contract conditions: (a) a condition that violates the very roots of marriage, e.g. for the husband not to touch the wife, shall render the contract void; (b) a condition that runs against the implications of marriage without contravening its principles, e.g. that there will be no mutual inheritance between the spouses, shall be void while the contract remains valid; (c) a condition that contravenes neither the roots nor the implications of marriage and is not prohibited, e.g. for the wife to complete her studies, shall be binding and enforceable, under pain of the beneficiaries applying for rescission. Such a condition must be recorded in the marriage document (Art. 41). The right to apply for cancellation shall be lost if the beneficiaries thereof drop it expressly or implicitly (Art. 42). The Omani Law provides more elaborately on marriage conditions under Article 5 as follows:

Art. 5 (a) The spouses are bound by the conditions of their contract except for any condition that either imposes something unlawful, or forbids something lawful.

(b) If the contract is subject to a condition that runs against the objective or intention thereof, that condition shall be deemed void, but the contract shall remain valid.

(c) Only conditions stipulated expressly in the marriage contract need be honoured by either party.

(d) The spouse who suffers injury as a result of his or her partner's failure to observe a condition of the contract is entitled to ask for a divorce.

5. Permanent and Temporary Marriage

The Sunnis and Shia Ithna-Ashari part ways on the form of marriage contract dealing with the duration of marriage. The Shia Ismailis adopt the Sunni position.

The Sunni jurists are unanimous that the form of the marriage contract must not include or imply any time limit, in the belief that the aim of marriage is the establishment of a lawful and permanent partnership, the founding of a family and the caring for and bringing up of children, all being aims attainable only with a life-time contract dissolved only by death. On these grounds, they prohibit the form of timed marriage which was known in paganism and remained in the early days of Islam until it was firmly prohibited by the Prophet six times on six occasions. This is known as the *muta* (temporary) marriage. The Shia deny the abrogation of this form of marriage as explained below.

The Sunni jurists further argue that even under the Shia doctrine, *muta* marriage is not marriage proper since it established no maintenance nor inheritance rights for the woman.

While the *muta* is unanimously deemed null and void by the Sunnis, a Hanafi jurist, Zafar ibn ul-Hudhail stands alone in considering a temporary marriage a valid contract which remains effective and binding while the time limit is a void condition to be dropped. This argument is adopted by some other Sunni jurists in some forms of offer and acceptance. An example is when a man says to a woman: "I want to marry you on condition that I divorce you after a month" and she replies: "I accept". The marriage is valid but the condition is void, and the contract shall be permanent.[28]

Of all the modern Arab legislation on personal status, *muta* and temporary marriage are mentioned explicitly only in the Jordanian Law. Under Article 42 it is stated that neither a *muta* nor a temporary marriage shall have effect if the marriage was not consummated, and under Article 34/6 of the same law, it states that such a *muta* and temporary marriage, having no effect, is deemed irregular. 34/6 also establishes certain effects if consummation did take place (see 9. below "Effects of Marriage"). The Sharia (Sunni) provisions apply in other codes which fail to mention temporary or *muta* marriages. Both the Sudanese and Yemeni Laws (Arts. 11 and 7 respectively) stress that the intention must be to stay together for life, not temporarily.

The Shias maintain that the *muta* marriage has not been abrogated. They cite a verse of the Quran: "And those of whom you seek *consent*, give unto them their portions as a duty". (4:24)

A Shia male may contract a *muta* marriage with a Muslim, Christian, Jew or *magi* (fire-worshipping) woman, but not with a woman professing any other faith. A Shia woman shall not contract a *muta* marriage with a non-Muslim.[29]

For a *muta* marriage contract to be valid, two conditions must be met: the term of cohabitation should be fixed and may be a day, a month, a year or a number of years; and a dower should be specified.

If the term is fixed but the dower is not specified, the contract would be void. In the converse case, i.e. if the dower is specified but the term is omitted, the contract shall be void as a *muta*, but may operate as a permanent marriage.

No right of divorce is recognized in a *muta* marriage which is dissolved *ipso facto* by the expiry of the term. However, the husband may, at his will, terminate the contract verbally by "making a gift of the term to the wife" even before the completion of the term.

The wife is entitled to full dower if the *muta* marriage is consummated, even if the husband puts an end to the contract in the manner described above, but he is entitled to deduct a proportionate part of the dower if the wife leaves him before the expiry of the term. If the *muta* marriage is not consummated, the wife shall be entitled to half the dower.

A *muta* wife shall not be entitled to maintenance.

Although a *muta* marriage does not create mutual rights of inheritance between

---

[28] Abu Zahra, *op. cit.* p. 48.
[29] Al-Hilli, *op. cit.* p. 32.

the man and the woman, the children conceived while it exists are legitimate and entitled to inherit from both parents. Where the cohabitation of a man and a woman commences in a *muta* marriage, with no evidence as to the term for which the marriage was contracted, the proper inference would be, in absence of evidence to the contrary, that the *muta* continued during the whole period of cohabitation and the children conceived during that period are legitimate and entitled to inherit from their father. The Ismailis believe that the Prophet prohibited the *muta* marriage, and quote Imam Ali saying "There is no marriage without a guardian and two witnesses, and without one dirham or two and for one day or two. This is fornication and not a marriage condition." They report that Imam Jaafar was asked about the *muta* marriage. He asked the enquirer to describe it. He was told. "A man says to a woman 'Marry me for a dirham or two for a term of a day or two." The Imam declared, 'This is fornication, and can only be done by a libertine." Qadi an-Numan argues that the *muta* marriage is no marriage because there is no divorce, no mutual inheritance and no maintenance.[30]

6. Marriage Equality

Equality between the two spouses in certain matters is a condition for the validity of marriage according to the Hanafi doctrine applied in Egypt, or for the marriage contract to be binding in Syria (Art. 26), Jordan (Art. 20), Morocco (Art. 14/a) and Kuwait (Art. 34). It is a right to be exercised by the wife and the guardian, according to the Sharia and the laws of Syria (Art. 29), Morocco (Art. 14/a) and Kuwait (Art. 34).

Equality, which can be defined as parity of status, is considered by the Hanafis in six matters: lineage, Islam, freedom, property, trade or craft, and piety.

The Malikis consider equality in religious piety, freedom from defects, and lineage in that the husband should have a known father and should not be a foundling whose parents are unknown.

The Shafiis require for equality, freedom from defects, lineage, chastity, craft and solvency.

The Hanbalis consider religious piety, lineage, solvency and craft.

The Jordanian Law simply requires for the marriage contract to be binding that the man shall be equal to the woman in property, explaining that this means that the man is able to afford the advance dower and the wife's maintenance (Art. 20). Both the Syrian and the Moroccan Laws make equality a matter of convention and custom (Arts. 28, 14/b, respectively). Kuwaiti Article 35 sets religious piety as the criterion of equality; Article 36 grants the wife exclusively the right to decide on the age suitability.

Equality must be considered at the time of the marriage contract (Arts. 20, Jordanian; 14/6, Moroccan; 34, Kuwaiti).

The Syrian Law entitles the guardian to apply for the annulment of the marriage if the woman marries a person who is not her equal without the guardian's consent (Art. 27).

The Jordanian Law distinguishes between two cases: (i) if the guardian gives in marriage his ward, whether she is a virgin or previously married, with her

---

[30] Qadi an-Numan, *op. cit.* Vol. 2, p. 181.

consent, to a man whose equality is known to neither of them, and then it becomes known that he is not an equal, neither shall have the right to object; (ii) if equality is stipulated at the time of marriage or if the husband declares he is an equal and then it transpires that he is not, both the wife and the guardian may apply to the court for the dissolution of marriage (Art. 21), similar to Kuwaiti Art. 38.

This right shall not apply if the woman is pregnant (Arts. 30, Syrian; 23, Jordanian).

The Shia Ithna-Asharis also consider equality in marriage from the husband's side, who must be at least equal to the woman in lineage, Islam, property, piety and craft. All except Islam are considered the woman's rather than the guardian's right. They are considered at the time of the contract and are not a condition of validity. Islam of the husband is a condition for the marriage to be valid: no Muslim woman may marry a non-Muslim. Islam is considered for the husband himself regardless of his ancestors, and the prestige of learning is above that of lineage. For craft, the Shias also refer to custom. The right to apply for a separation is denied if the woman was fully aware of the facts prior to the contract and consented thereto, or on discovery of lack of equality after the contract.[31]

7. Marriage Impediments

It is an essential condition for the validity of marriage that the woman must be eligible forthwith to marry the man who proposes. In other words, there must be no impediment under the Sharia or the law against the marriage of a certain woman to a certain man.

Marriage impediments are either permanent or temporary. Permanent prohibition is based on three grounds: kindred, affinity and fosterage. Temporary prohibition is based on existing marriage, irrevocable divorce or difference of religion. Impediments are mostly temporary because once the impediment is removed, marriage can be solemnized. In this section, impediments are dealt with in the order stated above.

A. Permanent Prohibition

(1) On grounds of kindred

Permanent prohibited degrees for marriage on grounds of kindred are ordained in the Quranic verse "Prohibited to you are your mothers, daughters, sisters; father's sisters, mother's sisters, brother's daughters, sister's daughters." (4:23) These include directly or by implication the man's ancestors and descendants, the descendants of his first ascendants, and the first descendants of every ancestor how-high-soever (Art. 33, Syrian; 14/1, Iraqi; 25, Moroccan; 15, Tunisian; 13, Kuwaiti; 15, Sudanese; 24, Yemeni and 30, Omani). The Jordanian Law is much more specific: the prohibited degrees for marriage fall into four categories:

(i)   mothers and grandmothers;
(ii) daughters and granddaughters how-low-soever;

---

[31] Al-Hilli, *op. cit.* pp. 16–17.

(iii) sisters and sisters' and brothers' daughters how-low-soever;
(iv) paternal and maternal aunts (Art. 24).

The same prohibitions apply for the Jaafaris.[32]

(2) On grounds of affinity

There are four categories for these prohibited degrees:

(i) The wife of any ascendant how-high-soever, whether agnate, as the father's father, or consanguine as the mother's father, whether there is or is not consummation. This is ordained by the Quranic verse "And marry not women whom your fathers married; except what is past: it was shameful and odious and an abominable custom indeed." (4:22)
(ii) The wife of any descendant how-low-soever, *whether marriage thereto is consummated or not*, and whether an agnate, like the son's son, or consanguine like the daughter's son. This is ordained under the Quranic verse "... wives of your sons proceeding from your loins." (4:23)
(iii) Ascendants of the wife how-high-soever *regardless of consummation*, under the Quranic verse "Prohibited to you ... and your wives' mothers." (4:23)
(iv) Descendants of the wives how-low-soever, *provided that marriage is consummated*, under the Quranic verse "... and your step-daughters under your guardianship, born of your wives to whom you have gone in – No prohibition if you have not gone in." (4:23) The Jordanian law explicitly adds in this category the daughters of the wives' children, provided consummation has taken place (Art. 25/4).

These are the Sharia provisions according to the Malikis, Shafiis and Hanbalis, and to the Laws of Iraq (Art. 15), Jordan (Art. 25), Morocco (Art. 27), Tunisia (Art. 16), Algeria (Art. 26), Kuwait (Art. 14), the Druzes of Lebanon (Art. 13), and the Jaafaris and the Ismailis.

Following all the doctrines except the Shafii, the Syrian law includes in the prohibited degrees in this category, in addition to the wife of the ascendant or descendant or any woman with whom either had sexual intercourse, and in addition to the ascendants of the wife, the ascendants and descendants of any woman with whom the man had sexual intercourse (Art. 34/1–2). The same provisions are ruled in Arts. 15, Kuwaiti; 16, Sudanese; and 24, Yemeni.

The Shia Ithna-Asharis likewise add to the prohibited degrees in this section, the ascendants and descendants of a woman with whom a man committed adultery. The adulteress shall be a prohibited degree to his ascendants and descendants, but not her ascendants and descendants.[33]

The Ismailis hold that it is unlawful for a man to marry the natural or foster daughter or mother of a woman with whom he committed adultery, according to a ruling by Imam Muhammad al-Baqir.[34]

(3) On grounds of fosterage

The general rule is that any prohibited degree on grounds of kindred is also prohibited on grounds of fosterage (suckling), under the Quranic verse "... and

---

[32] Al-Hilli, *op. cit.* p. 8; Qadi an-Numan, *op. cit.* Vol. 2, p. 184.
[33] Al-Hilli, *op. cit.* p. 8.
[34] Qadi an-Numan, *op. cit.* Vol. 2, p. 187.

your foster mothers who gave you suck and your foster sisters" (4:23) and the
Prophet's saying "Fosterage shall create the same prohibited degrees as kindred",
a provision adopted by all schools and modern Arab legislation (Arts. 35/1,
Syrian; 26, Jordanian; 16, Iraqi; 28/1, Moroccan; 17, Tunisian; 27, Algerian; 16/a,
Kuwaiti).

However, there are exceptions to this general rule referred to in general in the
above-mentioned Articles of the Syrian, Iraqi and Jordanian Laws, save for
exceptions under the Hanafi Doctrine or enumerated in detail in Articles 17
(Tunisian), 28/2 (Moroccan) and 28 (Algerian). The last three Articles sum up
those exceptions, ruling that "only the suckling baby, excluding his brothers and
sisters, shall be deemed a child of the foster mother and her husband".

For fosterage to create a prohibited degree, suckling must take place in infancy
and reach a certain number. The jurists differ on both these points. The Hanafis,
followed by the Malakis, maintain that even one feed is enough. The Shafiis and
Hanbalis require five feeds for certain fosterage to be established, a position
adopted by the Laws of Syria (35/2), Morocco (28/3), Kuwait (17), Sudan (17),
Yemen (25), and Oman (33). No limit is set in Jordan, Iraq or Tunisia.

As for the length of fostering, the Hanafis make it thirty lunar months, on the
strength of the Quranic verse "In pain did his mother bear him and in pain did
she give him birth and his bearing to his weaning is thirty months". (46:15) The
Malikis, Shafiis and Hanbalis make it two lunar years, quoting two Quranic
verses, "The mothers shall give suck to their offspring for two whole years if the
father desires to complete the term" (2:233), and "In years twain was his weaning". (31:44) This is the position adopted in Syria (35/2), Tunisia (17) and
Morocco (28/3). Algerian Article 29 maintains that fostering shall create a
prohibited degree only if it occurs before weaning or during the first two years
of life, regardless of the quantity of the milk taken by the suckling child.

According to the Jaafari doctrine, for suckling to create prohibited degrees,
the following four conditions must be fulfilled:

(i)   that the woman's milk shall flow as a result of a legitimate birth;
(ii) that the baby shall suck from the woman's breast directly;
(iii) that it shall suck milk during the first two years of life;
(iv) that it shall suckle from the breast of the same woman for a day and a
      night or 15 sucklings without being separated by any other feed. The same
      Shia exceptions apply.[35]

The Ismailis adopt Imam Ali's ruling that one sucking from the breast is
enough to create a prohibited degree.[36]

There is no prohibited degree on the ground of fosterage for the Druzes of
Syria (Art. 307/c) nor Lebanon (Chapter 2, Druze Personal Status Law 1948).

B. Temporary Impediments

Temporary impediments to marriage are based on (i) existing marriage;
(ii) irrevocable divorce; (iii) religion. Except for a few cases due to divorce, these
impediments could theoretically be removed to allow for a valid marriage. I
shall deal with each in turn.

---

[35] Al-Hilli, *op. cit.* pp. 97–99.
[36] Qadi an-Numan, *op. cit.* p. 191.

(1) Existing marriage

An existing married status is an impediment to a valid marriage in three situations: (a) woman married or in her *iddat*; (b) unlawful conjunction; (c) polygyny. There is a fourth case, unique to the Kuwaiti law.

(a) A woman who is validly married or is observing her counting period (iddat) subsequent to a revocable or irrevocable divorce or death of the husband cannot marry another man until the marriage is lawfully dissolved or the *iddat* is over, under the Quranic verses "Prohibited to you ... women already married" (4:23–24) and "Divorced women shall wait concerning themselves for three monthly courses" (2:228) and "If any of you die and leave widows behind, they shall wait concerning themselves four months and ten days." (2:234) *Iddat* will be treated in a separate section.

Jurists are unanimous that such a marriage is irregular and the parties should separate of themselves or by a court order if no consummation occurred. But if it did, jurists differ: Hanbalis and Shafiis rule that the spouses should be separated, but the man can marry the woman again on completing her *iddat*. The Malikis maintain that they must be separated and that the woman shall be permanently prohibited to him.

This provision prohibiting the marriage to a married woman or a woman in her *iddat* is adopted in the laws of Syria (Art. 38), Jordan (Art. 27), Iraq (13), Morocco (29/6), Tunisia (Art. 20), Kuwait (Art. 19), Sudan (19c) and Yemen (26/3). The Jaafaris concur.[37]

A special case in this context is that of the absent or missing person. Under the most authoritative provisions of the Sharia adopted in the Egyptian Law No. 25/1929, such a person shall be deemed dead after four years of his going missing in circumstances which make it likely to presume his death. In all other circumstances, the court shall have the discretion, after ordering enquiries and investigations by all the possible means, to fix the time at which he shall be deemed dead (Art. 21). After the court's ruling in this manner, the wife shall observe the *iddat* of death (Art. 22). The same provisions are indicated in the Kuwaiti Articles 146 and 147.

The Jordanian Law follows closely those provisions. It elaborates on the circumstances which make it likely to presume death as follows; an earthquake disaster, an air raid, collapse of public security, commotion and the like, when the court shall rule on his death one year after his going missing. If he went missing in a known location and is likely to have perished, the court shall rule on his death four years later. Otherwise, the judge shall have the discretion to determine the time of the missing person's death after ordering all the necessary investigations to find out whether he is alive or dead (Art. 177), whereupon the missing person's wife shall observe the *iddat* of death (Art. 178).

If the missing person appears or is proven to be alive after a court ruling on his death in the above manner, the Egyptian legislation ordains that his wife shall be his unless she was married to a second husband unaware of the first husband's being alive, in which case she shall belong to the second husband unless the said *iddat* was not observed (Maintenance and some Personal Status

---

[37] Al-Hilli, *op. cit.* p. 9.

Provisions Act No. 25/1920, Art. 8). The same ruling is adopted in Kuwaiti Article 148. According to the Jordanian Article 179, the marriage to a second man of the woman whose husband was deemed dead and then appeared to be alive, shall remain valid if consummation had occurred; but it shall be annulled if there was no consummation. The same ruling is adopted in Sudan (Art. 266/6), Yemen (120/6), and Oman (197/2). The Tunisian Law simply requires the wife of the missing person to observe the *iddat* of death as from the date of the court order deeming her husband dead (Art. 36). The Jaafaris concur.[38]

In Syria, the missing person's definition is "every person of whom it is not known if he is alive or dead or who is known for sure to be alive but his whereabouts are unknown" (Art. 202). His being missing comes to an end on his return, or under a court ruling declaring him dead having reached eighty years of age, or four years after his going missing in war or similar cases listed in military laws in force (Art. 205).

(b) Unlawful conjunction. This is an impediment which forbids a Muslim to have two wives at the same time who are related to each other by kindred, affinity or fosterage, such that had either of them been a male, they would have been prohibited from marrying each other under the Quranic verse listing the prohibited degrees "... and two sisters in wedlock at one and the same time except for what is past". (4:23) This is supplemented by the authentic Tradition of the Prophet, "There shall be no marriage at the same time to a woman and her paternal or maternal aunt, nor a woman and her brother's or sister's daughter."

The Sunni and Shia Ithna-Ashari and Ismaili jurists are unanimous on this impediment with the exception of some Kharijis who allow simultaneous marriage to women so related apart from sisters, sticking to the literal text of the Quranic verse. Again, the jurists are unanimous that the prohibited degree in unlawful conjunction holds whether the ground is kindred, affinity or fosterage. The only exception is the two Hanbali scholars, Ibn Taymiyya and his disciple Ibn Qayyim, who allow such a conjunction between prohibited degrees on account of fosterage in the absence of a Quranic text on this impediment.

Unlawful conjunction is removed on one of the women being divorced, and after the lapse of her *iddat*.

The Jordanian, Iraqi, Syrian, Kuwaiti, Sudanese, Yemeni and Omani Laws adopt this impediment in its widest connotations (Arts. 31, 13, 39, 20, 19/a, 27 and 35/1 respectively).

The Moroccan Law includes an exception, allowing simultaneous marriage to a woman and her step-mother or step-daughter (Art. 29/1), contrary to the definition given above.

This impediment is unthinkable in the Tunisian, Syrian and Lebanese Druze Laws, where polygyny is forbidden, as I shall discuss in the next section.

(c) Polygyny. Under the Sharia, both according to the Sunnis and the Shias, a Muslim man can have up to four wives at the same time, subject to certain conditions, in accordance with the three major sources: The Quran, the Tradition and Concensus. The Quran rules "Marry women of your choice, two or three

---

[38] Al-Hilli, *op. cit.* p. 41.

or four; but if ye fear that ye shall not be able to deal justly then only one." (4:3) As for the Sunna, the Prophet on several occasions ordered the newly-converted to Islam who had many wives to keep four and discharge the rest. As for consensus (*ijmaa*), Muslims from the days of the Prophet until now have approved, both in words and in deeds, the simultaneous marriage to four wives.

This ruling has been strictly adhered to in the laws of Syria (Art. 37), Jordan (Art. 28), Iraq (Art. 13), Morocco (Art. 29/2), Kuwait (Art. 21) and Oman (Art. 35/2), under which no man can marry a fifth wife until one of the existing four is divorced and has completed her *iddat*.

Under the Tunisian Law, polygyny is forbidden, and constitutes a criminal offence, rendering a man who marries before his previous marriage is dissolved liable to a penalty of one year's imprisonment and/or a fine of 240,000 francs, even if the new marriage is unlawful (Art. 18). Polygyny is also prohibited among the Druzes of Lebanon (Act of 24/2/1948, Art. 10), and of Syria (Art. 307/6).

The controversy over polygyny started in the early 20th century, with Egypt and the Middle East opening to Europe. Modern religious reformers, led by Sheikh Muhammad Abdou (died 1905), advocated restrictions of polygyny, considering it an injustice to the woman. Other reformers argued that polygyny must be prohibited, quoting from the Quran verse 129 of *Sura* Nisaa, IV (the same *Sura* which allowed polygyny): "Ye shall not be able to deal in fairness and justice between women however much ye wish", in addition to the earlier verse "... but if ye fear that ye shall not be able to deal justly then only one" (verse 3).

The fundamentalists reacted strongly, arguing that such an interpretation would render the Quranic allowance for up to four wives absurd and inoperative, and that in order to honour it, a distinction must be made between justice in verse 3, which would mean equality between wives in material and tangible matters, and justice in verse 129 which would then mean inner feelings over which man has no control. They quoted Traditions of the Prophet to substantiate their opinion.[39] For a while, the fundamentalists in Egypt won their case, forcing legal reforms on the subject during the 1920s, 40s and early 50s to be shelved.

But the trend seems now to be in favour of restricted polygyny if not monogamy forthright.

In Iraq, marriage to more than one wife is allowed only by permission of the judge, who shall not give it until he makes sure of fulfilment of two conditions:

(i) that the husband is financially capable of supporting more than one wife;
(ii) that there is a legitimate interest (Art. 3, para. 4).

The judge has also the discretion to rule that wives would not be treated in fairness and equity, whereupon he shall not permit polygyny (*ibid*. para. 5). Any man who contravenes the two said paragraphs shall be liable to a penalty of one year's imprisonment and/or a fine of one hundred Iraqi dinars.

The Syrian legislation is less categorical while following the same course. The judge has the power to forbid a married man from taking another wife unless there is a legitimate justification, and the financial capability to support both wives is proven (Art. 17).

Although the Jordanian Law imposes no obvious restrictions on polygyny, it

---

[39] *Cf.* Abu Zahra, *op. cit.* pp. 89–96.

allows the wife to stipulate in the marriage contract that the husband shall not take another wife, and entitles the wife to sue for divorce if such a condition is not honoured (Art. 19/1).

The same allowance for the wife is repeated in the Moroccan Law (Art. 31). There is also a provision prohibiting polygyny if injustice among wives is feared (Art. 30/1). Marriage to a second wife is not allowed unless she is made aware of the fact that the husband is already married, and the first wife is entitled to apply to the court to assess any injury inflicted on her as a result of a second wife, even if there is no stipulation against it (Art. 30/2).

The Egyptian Act No. 100/1985 follows the same trend, adding to Act No. 25/1929 Article 11 *bis* which requires the husband to declare in the marriage document his social status, stating in his declaration the name of the wife or wives living with him in matrimony. The Notary Public is required under the law to notify her or them of the new marriage by registered mail with recorded delivery. The new law entitles the wife whose husband has married again to apply for divorce if she suffers a material or moral injury that renders continued marital life between them difficult, even if she has not stipulated in their marriage contract that he may not marry another. The judge shall try to effect a reconciliation, failing which he shall order an irrevocable divorce. The wife shall lose the right to apply for divorce on this ground on the lapse of one year from her knowledge of the marriage to another, unless she has consented thereto whether expressly or by implication. This right shall be renewed whenever the husband marries again. If the new wife does not know that her husband is already married until after her marriage to him, she may also apply for divorce. The Yemeni law follows the same trend in Article 12:

1. A man may have up to four wives if he is capable of dealing with them justly; if not, then one wife only.
2. If another wife is to be taken, the following conditions are met:
   (a) That there is a lawful benefit.
   (b) That the husband is financially capable of supporting more than one wife.
   (c) That the woman is aware that the man already has another wife.
   (d) That the present wife is notified of the fact that her husband wishes to take another wife.

(d) Kuwaiti Article 23. Article 23 of the Kuwaiti Personal Status Act No. 51/1984 prohibits the marriage of a man to a woman whom he stirred viciously against her husband, unless she is first remarried to her previous husband who then later repudiates her or dies, leaving her a widow. This provision, unique to the Kuwaiti law, is introduced to safeguard the family "rendering futile the action of those who try to break the union of the spouses, by inciting the wife to harm her husband or luring her by money or otherwise, in order to be able to marry those women who have been tricked by them", according to the Explanatory Memorandum to the Law. It derives from the Maliki doctrine which treated such incidents by prohibiting the second marriage and rescinding it if it was concluded. Some Malikis rule such a prohibition to be permanent. Others consider it to be only temporary, to be removed on the first husband divorcing the woman for the second time or leaving her a widow. The Kuwaiti law adopted the latter ruling, considered to be the most authoritative Maliki opinion, according to the Jurist Zarqani.

(2) Irrevocable repudiation

A specific form of irrevocable repudiation is meant here, namely a third pronouncement of repudiation following two previous ones. During a first or a second pronouncement, the husband may withdraw his pronouncement and the marriage continues without new dower or contract, or even without the woman's consent before the expiry of the *iddat* period. But after a third pronouncement, she becomes temporarily prohibited to him until she marries another husband after completing her *iddat* and is later duly separated from that second husband through death or divorce. The authority is two Quranic verses: "Divorce must be pronounced twice and then (a woman) must be retained in honour or released in kindness." (2:229) And a little later, "And if he hath divorced her (the third time), then she is not lawful unto him thereafter until she has wedded another husband." (2:23)

This is the universal Sharia provision, followed by both the Sunnis and the Shias. It has been included in all modern Arab legislations, except Tunisia (Arts. 36, Syrian; 30, Jordanian; 29, paras. 3 and 4, Moroccan; 13, Iraqi; 22, Kuwaiti; Sudanese 19/d; Yemeni 26/5).

In Tunisia, this becomes a permanent impediment. The husband is prohibited from marrying his divorcee after three pronouncements (Art. 19). Although the fundamentalists consider this is a violation of an honoured provision, the Tunisian commentator, Muhammad al-Tahir as-Senoussi bases it on a Tradition by the Prophet in which he cursed such a marriage, and a ruling by the Second Patriarchal Caliph, Omar, that "If a man is reported to me to have done that, I would stone him", both quoted by Ibn Qayyim, a Hanbali fundamentalist himself, who considered such an arrangement as a distorted Sharia which it is the duty of every Muslim, and especially those in power, to stop.[40]

Another form of irrevocable divorce, by mutual cursing (*mulaana* or *lian*) constitutes a permanent marriage impediment, unless the husband admits perjury.[41] Some Hanafi jurists, on the authority of a Tradition of the Prophet, rule that the impediment shall stay for ever.[42]

According to the Druzes, any divorce shall render the divorcee permanently prohibited to the husband (Lebanese Druze Personal Status Act/1948, Art. 11, Syrian Personal Status Act, Art. 307-G).

(3) Difference of religion

The Sharia makes a distinction between men and women in respect of the impediment of difference in religion. The Sunni and Shia jurists are unanimous that no Muslim woman can marry a non-Muslim under the two Quranic verses, "And give not your daughters in marriage to polytheists till they believe" (2:221) and "O ye who believe! When believing women come into you as fugitives, examine them. Allah is best aware of their faith. Then, if ye know them for true believers, send them not back unto the infidels. They are not lawful for the infidels nor are the infidels lawful for them." (40:10)

This universal prohibition shared by the Shia Ithna-Ashari and the Ismaili[43]

---

[40] Muhammad al-Tahir as-Senoussi, *Mijalla of Personal Status* (Tunis, 1958), pp. 28–29.
[41] Abu Zahra, pp. 98–99; Abdullah, pp. 403–404; Al-Hilli, pp. 86–86; Qadi an-Numan, pp. 228–231.
[42] Abu Zahra, p. 346.
[43] Al-Hilli, p. 16; Qadi an-Numan, *op. cit.* Vol. 2, pp. 199–201.

has been incorporated in the modern Personal Status Laws of Syria (Art. 48/2), Jordan (Art. 33/1), Iraq (Art. 17), Morocco (Art. 29/5), Kuwait (Art. 18/2), Yemen (Art. 29) and Oman (Art. 35/7). It also applies even where it is not explicitly mentioned. The marriage of a Muslim woman to a non-Muslim man shall be void unconditionally, regardless of being consummated or not. The two parties have to be separated.

As for Muslim men, they are prohibited from marrying a non-*Kitabi* woman. These include those who do not believe in any prophets or holy scriptures, the atheists, the idolaters and the worshippers of the sun or stars. A *magi* woman, i.e. a worshipper of fire, may marry a Muslim man according to the Shias, who consider her an equivalent to the "People of the Book", "*ahl-ul-kitab*", meaning the Jews and the Christians.[44] The Sunnis include the *magis* among the prohibited infidels. This provision is based on the Quranic verse "Wed not polytheists till they believe". (2:221) The authority allowing the Muslim man to marry a woman of the "People of the Book" is the Quranic verse:

> "This day are all good things made lawful to you. The food of those who have received the Scripture is lawful for you and your food is lawful for them. And so are the virtuous women of the believers and the virtuous women of those who received the Scripture before you (lawful to you) when you give them their marriage portion and live with them in honour, not in fornication, nor taking them as secret concubines." (5:5)

8. Marriage Formalities

Under the strict Sharia provisions, for both the Sunnis and the Shias, a marriage contract shall be valid, effective and binding if it fulfils all the previous requirements. The Sharia proper does not require either or both parties to be adults, since minors, having reached puberty may marry. It does not even stipulate that a marriage contract shall be written down in a formal or informal document, nor even to be written at all. This is the position held in all Islamic States where there is no codified legislation.

In Egypt, however, while the above position is not disputed, the legislator has laid down certain rules both to prove marriage and to hear matrimonial disputes before the courts. Under the Decree No. 78/1931 in respect of the regulation of the Sharia Courts, Article 99, paragraphs 4 and 5, two conditions are set for hearing a matrimonial case before the court:

(i) that matrimony be proven by a formal marriage certificate;
(ii) that the ages of the wife and the husband shall not be below 16 and 18 years of age respectively.

Nevertheless, it must be stressed again that the Egyptian Law did not dispute the validity, effectiveness or binding of a marriage contract concluded under the Sharia, but only prevented judges from hearing matrimonial cases in which the

---

[44] Al-Hilli, *op. cit.* p. 9.

parties have not reached the prescribed ages, and from hearing a matrimonial case when matrimony was denied if there was no written formal document.

Some formalities must be complied with in the case of marriage of an Egyptian Muslim man to a non-Muslim or foreign woman. Under Article 27 of the *Madhoon* Regulations of 1915, the *madhoon* (that is the public officer authorized to solemnize marriages) shall not conclude either the marriage of an orphan who has no guardian, nor contracts in which one party is a foreign citizen or is not a Muslim, as this shall be left to the courts. Moreover, the Egyptian Ministry of Justice has prepared a special document in Arabic, English and French containing the most important terms, rights and duties of marriage under the Islamic Sharia; namely, that the husband may marry more than one wife, that he may divorce his wife, that his children by a *Kitabi* wife shall be Muslim like the father, and that there shall be no inheritance between the spouses if they differ in religion.

In the Lebanon, according to the Family Rights Act and the Sunni and Jaafari Sharia Judiciary Act regulating the personal status of the Lebanese Sunni and Jaafari denominations, the Sharia Court of the jurisdiction of the domicile of either party has exclusively the power to solemnize marriage contracts for Muslims. Likewise, the Personal Status Officer can only record marriage contracts duly solemnized and bearing the authentication of the spiritual chief by whom a contract was solemnized. Again, these legal texts do not invalidate a Muslim marriage that does not observe these rules. But the civil and spiritual authorities would not recognize such a marriage unless the competent Sharia Court rules that it is proved.

As for the Druzes of Lebanon, it is a condition for the validity of a marriage contract to be solemnized by a *Sheikh Aql* (i.e. the local Druze religious chief), or the denominational judge or their duly delegated deputies (Art. 16 of the Lebanese Druze Personal Status Act of 1948).

For the Syrian Druzes, the judge must ascertain the legal capability of the parties, and the validity of marriage before the contract (Art. 307/a).

As far as the other Syrians are concerned, the law (Art. 40) lays down elaborate regulations:

(i) The marriage application shall be submitted to the district judge accompanied by the following documents:
   (a) a certificate of the local chief giving the names of the parties to be married, their ages, their domicile, the name(s) of the guardian(s), and a declaration that there is no legal impediment to the marriage;
   (b) a certified extract of the birth and personal status records of the parties;
   (c) a medical certificate by a physician chosen by the parties to the effect that they are free from contagious diseases or medical impediments to the marriage. The judge may confirm these particulars through a physician he appoints;
   (d) marriage permission for those of military and national service age;
   (e) the approval of the Public Security Directorate if either party is a foreigner.
(ii) No marriage concluded outside the court shall be confirmed before these formalities are complied with, without prejudice to any penal clause.

The judge shall forthwith allow the marriage contract to be solemnized once these documents are submitted. In the event of doubt he may order a delay of ten days to publicize the marriage in whatever way he deems suitable (Art. 41). If the contract is not concluded within six months, the court's permission shall be deemed void (Art. 42). The judge or any legal assistant authorized by him shall solemnize the contract (Art. 43). The marriage certificate shall include the following particulars:

(i)   the names of the two parties in full and their respective domiciles;
(ii)   solemnization of the contract and the date and the place thereof;
(iii) the names of the witnesses and agents and their respective addresses in full;
(iv)   the amounts of the prompt and deferred dowers and whether the prompt was received or not;
(v)   the signatures of the parties concerned, that of the *madhoon* and confirmation by the judge (Art. 44).

The court's assistant shall record the fact of the marriage in his special register, and shall send a copy thereof to the Civil Status Department within ten days of the marriage date, which copy shall spare the parties the notification of the marriage to the said department, with the court's assistant held liable for negligence should he fail to send the said copy (Art. 45). All these marriage formalities are free of any charge (Art. 46).

In Jordan (Art. 17) the following rules are laid down:

(a)   The man desirous to marry shall refer to the judge or his deputy to solemnize the contract.
(b)   The marriage contract shall be solemnized by the judge's *madhoon* as per a formal document. The judge shall perform this formality personally in exceptional cases on permission of the Chief Sharia Justice.
(c)   A marriage entered into without a formal document, shall render the person who makes it, the spouses and the witnesses, liable to the penalty set under the Jordanian Penal Code and to a fine of no more than one hundred dinars each.
(d)   Any *madhoon* who fails to record the contract in the official document after payment of the dues shall be liable to the two penalties of the previous paragraph, and shall be dismissed.
(e)   The Sharia judge shall appoint the marriage contract *madhoon*, on the approval of the Chief Sharia Judge who may issue whatever instructions he deems suitable to regulate the functions of the *madhoons*.
(f)   (sic) The Muslim consuls of the Hashemite Kingdom of Jordan abroad shall solemnize marriage contracts and hear the divorce pronouncements of Jordanian citizens abroad, and shall record these documents in special registers.
(g)   "Consuls" shall include the Hashemite Kingdom of Jordan Ministers, Plenipotentiaries, *Chargés d'Affaires*, Counsellors and their deputies.

In Iraq, Article 10 enumerates the formalities for the registration and proof of marriage contracts. The marriage contract must be registered with the competent court, free of charge, in a special register under the following conditions:

(i) Submission of a statement free of fiscal stamp, of the identity of the parties, their ages and the amount of dower, with a declaration that there is no legal impediment against marriage, the said statement being signed by the contracting parties and certified by the local chief or two dignitaries of the locality.

(ii) The enclosure of a medical report certifying that the spouses are free from epidemic diseases and other medical impediments, together with other documents stipulated by the law.

(iii) The contents of the statement shall be recorded in the register to be signed by the contracting parties, or stamped with their thumb prints in the presence of the judge who shall certify it, and give the spouses that marriage document which shall be valid without any further evidence, and enforceable in respect of the dower unless disputed before a competent court. Any man who contracts his marriage outside the court shall be liable to imprisonment for not less than six months and not more than a year, or to a fine of not less than three hundred and no more than a thousand dinars. The penalty shall be increased to no less than three years' and no more than five years' imprisonment in the event of the man contracting marriage outside the court while he is already married.

In Morocco under Article 41, the marriage contract shall require two honest witnesses, and must be preceded by filing three documents:

(i) a certificate by the representative of the administrative authority of the names of both parties, their ages, domicile and the name(s) of their guardian(s);

(ii) a statement of the husband's personal status; and

(iii) a proof of the dissolution of marriage where the woman has previously married to ascertain that she has completed her *iddat* and has no legal impediment.

The marriage certificate under Article 42 should include:

(i) The names of the spouses and their parents, their respective domiciles, ages, identification, e.g. nationality, and the name(s) of the guardian(s).

(ii) The fact of solemnization of the contract, its date and place, showing whether it is done by the spouses and the guardian(s).

(iii) A full statement of the status of the wife showing whether she is a virgin or previously married, an orphan, or has a father alive with or without a natural or a legal guardian appointed by the judge, and if she has been previously married, if she is divorced or widowed and the completion of her *iddat*.

(iv) Reference to the certificate by a representative of the administration authority quoting the number thereof.

(v) The amount of the dower specifying the prompt and the deferred parts thereof and whether it was received in hand or by admission.

(vi) The signature of two honest witnesses certified by the judge and under his seal.

Under Article 43, the text of the contract shall be recorded in the court marriage register and a copy thereof shall be sent to the Department of Civil Status, and the original shall be given to the wife or her representative within fifteen days from the date of the contract. The husband is entitled to a copy thereof.

In Tunisia, it is simply stated that only a formal document shall prove the marriage under a special law (Art. 4). The Civil Status Act No. 3/1377 AH (1957 AD) as amended by Acts Nos. 71/1958, 20/1962, 2/1964 and 12/1964, requires (Art. 31) that the marriage contract inside Tunisia shall be solemnized before the local religious Sheikhs or the Civil Status Officer, together with two honest witnesses.

The marriage of Tunisians abroad shall be solemnized before the Tunisian diplomats or consuls or according to the laws of the country in which it takes place.

Under Article 32 of the same Act, the marriage contract shall include the following particulars:

(i)   The spouses' names, family names, professions, ages, dates and places of birth, domicile and residence and nationality.
(ii) The names, family names, profession, domicile and nationalities of their parents.
(iii) A declaration by the witnesses that each spouse is free from any marriage commitment.
(iv) If applicable, names and family names of the previous spouse of each spouse, together with the date of death or divorce dissolving the previous marriage contract.
(v)   Where applicable, the consent or permission required under Article 3 of the "Personal Status Mijalla" and the specification of dower.

Under Article 33 the local Sheikhs must, within a month from the date of the contract, send to the Civil Status Officer of their area, a notification of the marriage before delivering a copy of the marriage contract to the parties concerned.

Under Article 34, the Civil Status Officer of the area where the contract was solemnized shall record the marriage notification in a special register immediately on being informed thereof, and shall inform the Civil Status Officer of the place of birth of the spouses, of the fact of marriage. The latter officer shall record on the marriage contract the particulars of the birth of each spouse (Art. 35).

Any marriage contracted contrary to the provisions of Article 31 above shall be deemed void (Art. 36), nevertheless giving the following three effects:

(i)   establishment of parentage;
(ii) the starting of the *iddat* from the date of the voidance declarations; and
(iii) the creation of prohibited degrees on grounds of affinity (Art. 36 *bis*).

The Tunisian spouses married abroad according to the laws of the country in which their marriage was solemnized shall record their marriage in the marriage register of the nearest Tunisian Consulate within three months (Art. 37).

Foreigners in Tunisia shall marry in accordance with the Tunisian Laws on the strength of a certificate by their Consul that they can marry. Two foreigners of the same nationality may marry before the diplomatic or consular representatives of their country in Tunisia, who shall inform the Civil Status Officer of the locality where marriage took place (Art. 38).

Article 14 of the Yemeni Law makes it a legal obligation on the writer of the contract, the husband and the wife's guardian to record the marriage contract document with the competent authority in the book set for that purpose, within a week of the contract date, or face a penalty. Such an obligation can be performed by any one of the three. The wedding document shall include the spouses' ages, their identity card numbers and the amount of the prompt and deferred dowers.

Omani Article 6 requires the marriage be formally authenticated by official document, but can be proven by evidence or mutual confirmation.

9. Effects of Marriage

The effects of marriage depend on the quality of the marriage contract. Classical Islamic jurists and some modern Islamic legislators classify the marriage contracts into valid, irregular and void. The Shias consider the irregular equivalent to the void.

The valid contract (*sahih*) is a contract which fulfils all its essentials and conditions of conclusion and validity. This is the Sharia definition, also adopted in Syria (Art. 47), Jordan (Art. 32), Morocco (Art. 32/1), Kuwait (Art. 43/b), Sudan (Art. 54) and Yemen (Art. 30). Under the Sharia, a valid contract may be either effective (*nafidh*) if both spouses possess full legal capacity, i.e. adult, sane and of discretion and act on their own, or suspended (*mauquf*) if either lacks full legal capacity or is represented by a voluntary agent (*foudouli*), in which case the contract shall be subject to the approval of the guardian or the principal. This distinction is retained in the Syrian Law, Article 52, and the Sudanese Article 58 which make the suspended marriage equivalent to an irregular marriage.

The irregular (or defective) marriage (*fasid*) is a contract which fulfils its essentials and conditions of conclusion but lacks a condition of validity, e.g. the presence of witnesses (for the Sunnis), or the marriage of a man to his foster sister without either of them knowing of the fact.

The Syrian Article 48/1 gives a similar definition of the irregular marriage as "every marriage which satisfies its essentials of offer and acceptance but lacks some conditions". Sudanese Article 62 and Omani Articles 39–41 are similar.

Rather than giving a definition, the Jordanian legislator enumerates inclusively the cases of irregular marriage as follows:

(i) if either or both parties lack conditions of marriage capacity at the time of the contract;
(ii) if there are no witnesses;
(iii) if the contract is entered into under coercion;
(iv) if the witnesses do not comply with the Sharia descriptions;
(v) the case of unlawful conjunction on grounds of affinity or fosterage; and
(vi) the *muta* and temporary marriage. (Art. 34).

The Tunisian Mijalla defines the irregular marriage as one which is subject to a condition that conflicts with the substance of the contract or which contravenes the conditions laid down earlier (Art. 21).

The void marriage (*batil*), under the Sharia, is a marriage defective in its essentials or in any condition of conclusion or of validity. The marriage contract shall be void if the formula does not denote its establishment, if a contracting party is lacking capacity, if acceptance does not conform with offer, and if the woman was a prohibited degree to the man who wants to marry her, and yet he proceeds to marry her fully aware at the time of contract that she is a prohibited degree. Some Hanafis maintain the distinction between irregular and void marriages on the ground of the good faith or semblance (*shubha*) in the irregular marriage although both categories are not valid. Other Hanafi jurists, e.g. Kamalud-Din Ibn al-Hammam, treat both contracts alike, maintaining that marriage could be only either valid or invalid.

The Syrian Law mentions expressly one case of void marriage, namely the marriage of a Muslim woman to a non-Muslim (Art. 48/2). But the understanding is clear that any marriage that does not comply with the conditions of validity and conclusion is void.

The Jordanian legislator enumerates expressly three cases where the marriage shall be deemed void; namely:

(i)   the marriage of a Muslim woman to a non-Muslim;
(ii) the marriage of a Muslim man to a non-*Kitabi*; and
(iii) the marriage of a man to a woman in a prohibited degree on grounds of kindred, affinity or fosterage (Art. 33).

The Kuwaiti legislator gives a succinct account of this classification in the following three Articles:

Article 43:
(i)   There are two kinds of marriage: valid or non-valid.
(ii) Valid marriage is one which fulfils its essentials and all conditions for validity according to the provisions of this Act. Any other marriage is non-valid, which is either void or irregular.

Article 44:
A valid marriage is either effective and binding, effective and non-binding, or not effective at all.

Article 45:
(i)   An effective and binding marriage is one which is not subject to any other person's permission, nor is rescindable, according to the provisions of this Act.
(ii) An effective but non-binding marriage is one which can be rescinded on a ground allowable under this Act.
(iii) A non-effective marriage is one contracted subject to the approval thereof by a person having authority to approve it.

Further, Article 49 rules a marriage to be void in the following events:

(i)   If such a defect in the formula or in the legal capacity of the contracting party occurs so as to bar the conclusion of the contract.
(ii) If the wife is a prohibited degree on grounds of kindred, fosterage or affinity, or is a wife of another man or counting her *iddat* from him, or is a three-time divorcée of the husband, or is a case of unlawful conjunction or does not believe in any divine religion.

(iii) If either spouse is apostate or if the husband is non-Muslim and the woman Muslim.

Provided, for paragraphs (ii) and (iii) that it is established that prohibition, and the grounds thereof, are known; no ignorance is a defence if it cannot reasonably be attributed to the sort of person who is alleging it. Every other invalid marriage, apart from these cases, shall be deemed irregular (Art. 50).

There seems to be no mention of void marriage in the other modern laws, presumably because it is not considered a marriage at all or is expressly prohibited by the competent authorized officers.

Yemeni Law admits only two kinds of marriage: valid, which is identical to the definition above, and void if any condition is missing. If there is no consummation of the marriage, it has no effect at all, and the parties should separate voluntarily or by order of the court. With consummation, the woman receives the lesser of the specific or proper dower, paternity of offspring is established, the woman observes her *iddat* following separation or death, a prohibited degree on the grounds of affinity is created, and there is no punishment if the party was unaware of the irregularity of the marriage. (Arts. 30–32).

Manek in his handbook *Mahomedan Law* (*Muslim Personal Law*) gives an easy-to-understand clue in order to distinguish between valid, *fasid*, (described here as irregular) and void marriages under the Sunni Law, based on the nature of the impediment to the marriage. If the impediment is an *absolute and permanent prohibition* the marriage is void. If it is only *relative or temporary or due to an accidental circumstance*, the marriage is invalid (irregular).[45]

The Shias and the Druzes alike do not recognize this distinction between void and irregular marriage, deeming every marriage in which the conditions for validity are not met to be utterly void. But this distinction is important for the Sunnis both under the Sharia and the modern laws. It makes it possible to retain some lawfulness of the marriage effects under an irregular contract before the discovery of the defect therein under certain conditions, and the correction thereof in certain cases. But nothing like that can be done for a void contract.

To start with, both irregular and invalid marriages prior to consummation shall have the same effect, that is to say no effect whatsoever, and the parties shall separate either of their own accord or by order of the court in a case for separation and annulment, which it is the duty of every Muslim to institute. This is the Sharia Law adopted also expressly by the Jordanian legislator (Arts. 41, 42 and 43) and honoured by all the other countries where the Sharia provisions are applied in absence of any specific legal text.

If there was consummation under an irregular marriage contract, the Muslim Sunni jurists and the modern legislators are unanimous that it shall create the woman's entitlement to dower, her observation of the *iddat*, the lawful parentage of the offspring and a prohibited degree on grounds of affinity. The Jordanian Law excludes other effects such as mutual inheritance and maintenance before and after the dissolution without specifying the dower (Art. 42). Notwithstanding the above ruling of the necessity of separation between the parties under an irregular contract, no action in respect of any irregular marriage on grounds of

---

[45] Manek, *Mahomedan Law (Muslim Personal Law)* (Bombay, 1948), p. 43.

minority shall be heard if the wife gives birth or is pregnant, or if the two parties at the time of the action possessed legal marriage capacity (Art. 43).

The Syrian Act is more specific. Under Article 51:

(i) An irregular marriage before consummation shall be deemed a void marriage.
(ii) Consummation shall bring about the following effects:
    (a) the wife shall receive the dower of the equal or the designated dower, whichever is less;
    (b) the parentage of the children is established under certain rules;
    (c) the creation of prohibited degrees on grounds of affinity;
    (d) the wife shall observe the *iddat* of divorce or death of the husband and shall receive the *iddat* maintenance, but without any mutual rights of inheritance between the two spouses;
    (e) the wife shall be entitled to matrimonial maintenance for as long as she remains unaware of the irregularity of marriage.

The same provisions apply to suspended marriage before the approval (Art. 52). The offspring shall be considered the husband's if born after one hundred and eighty days from the date of consummation, or if born between the minimum and maximum term of pregnancy, creating all the effects of parentage, including the prohibited degrees, rights of inheritance and kindred maintenance (Arts. 132 and 133).

The same provisions are set in Kuwaiti Articles 50 and 51.

Under the Moroccan Law, an irregular marriage on grounds of the contract *per se* shall be dissolved before consummation, but shall entitle the woman to a dower after consummation. If it is irregular on the grounds of the dower, it shall be dissolved prior to consummation without any dower, and shall entitle the woman, after consummation, to the dower of the equal. Every marriage unanimously considered irregular, such as a prohibited degree on the grounds of affinity, shall be dissolved without divorce prior to consummation and following it, but it shall create the necessity of *iddat* and the establishment of parentage, provided good faith is proved. A marriage where opinions differ on its irregularity shall be dissolved before or after consummation through divorce and shall create necessity for the observation of the *iddat*, the proven parentage, and mutual inheritance prior to dissolution (Art. 37 [1] and [2]).

Under the Tunisian Law (Art. 22), the irregular marriage shall be deemed of necessity void without divorce; the mere fact of the contract shall not create any effect, but the fact of consummation shall only create the following effects:

(i)   the entitlement of the woman to the dower agreed upon or a dower ordered by the judge;
(ii) the establishment of parentage;
(iii) the observation of *iddat* by the wife as from the date of separation;
(iv) a prohibited degree on grounds of affinity.

The same effects are ruled for the irregular marriage under Sudanese Article 64 and Omani Article 42.

The Ithna-Asharis maintain that any marriage contract that lacks any condition of validity shall be invalid, and shall create no effects. The parties shall leave one another or shall be compelled to separate. It shall create no prohibited degrees on ground of affinity if separation takes place prior to consummation, the parties shall not inherit from each other and the dower of the equal shall be payable only after but not before consummation, even if another dower was agreed upon.

The void marriage, both with or without consummation, shall have no effect whatsoever, the relationship being deemed illegitimate, and any offspring shall be likewise deemed illegitimate. This is the Sharia Law retained expressly in the Jordanian Code (Art. 41), in Kuwait (Art. 48), in Sudan (Art. 61) and in Oman (Art. 43). Only the Hanafis acknowledge one effect of consummation, which is the creation of the impediment of fornication which establishes, according to them, a prohibited degree on the grounds of affinity.

A valid and effective marriage contract shall create established legal effects in respect of the rights and duties for the wife, for the husband, and other rights and duties common to both of them (Moroccan, Art. 33). The Jordanian Code sums them up as dower and maintenance for the wife, and mutual right of inheritance for them both (Art. 35), adding certain conditions regarding the matrimonial home (Arts. 36, 37, 38 and 40). It also stresses good treatment of the wife by the husband, and her obedience to him in lawful matters (Art. 39). The Syrian law sums up the effects of valid and effective marriage as the dower and maintenance for the wife, her duty to follow her husband, the mutual rights of inheritance and family rights, such as the parentage of the offspring and the creation of prohibited degrees on the grounds of affinity (Art. 49). Both the Sudanese and Omani Laws refer to all the effects of legality (Arts. 57 and 40).

In view of the importance of the dower and maintenance, they will be dealt with in separate chapters. Here I shall deal with the other effects of the valid and effective marriage, under the Sharia and the modern laws where applicable.

(1) Under the Sharia

The first duty of the spouses is faithfulness and chastity in that the man and the wife should not enter into any extra-marital relationship. Failure to observe this duty constitutes adultery which can constitute a ground for divorce. This is based on the Quranic verses: "And who guard their modesty – save from their wives or the (slaves) that their right hands possess, for then they are not blameworthy. But whoso craveth beyond that, such are transgressors." (23:5, 6, 7)

The Moroccan Law makes it a right of the husband that the wife shall guard her chastity (Art. 36/1) as does Omani Law (Art. 36/2), and as does the Sudanese Law, which stresses that she "safeguards him in respect of herself and his property" (Art. 52/b).

(2) The common matrimonial home

It is the duty of the husband to provide, and the right of the wife to have, a suitable matrimonial home according to the Quranic verse: "Lodge them where ye dwell, according to your wealth, and harass them not so as to straiten life for them." (65:6)

The wife should follow the husband to the matrimonial home, provided that it complies with the Sharia requirements, that is, that it should be in accordance with the husband's financial standing; habitable, private and not occupied by others, even if they are the husband's kin; and provided that the husband is trustworthy towards her and her assets, and has paid her dower or the agreed prompt portion thereof. She shall not leave it without her husband's permission, but she can do so to perform a religious duty such as pilgrimage, accompanied by a member of kin of a prohibited degree. She may also visit a sick parent without the husband's permission, since the rights of parents, under the Sharia, are paramount to those of the husband. Otherwise her leaving it without his permission shall deprive her of her maintenance entitlement as she would then be rebellious (*nashiza*). This will be dealt with in the chapter on maintenance. This common life in a matrimonial home is stressed as a mutual right and a duty of the spouses under the Moroccan Decree, Article 34/1.

The matrimonial home is more elaborately dealt with in the Syrian law which makes it a duty of the husband to provide his wife with a home that is conventional for his equals (Art. 65), and makes it a duty of the wife to live with her husband after receiving the prompt instalment of her dower (Art. 66). The husband is not allowed to live with his wife and another wife at the same home without her consent (Art. 67). In the case of polygyny, the husband shall provide his wives with equal homes (Art. 68). The husband shall not bring any relatives of his to live with his wife (apart from his minor child under the age of discretion) if such relations maltreat her (Art. 69). The wife shall of necessity travel with her husband unless it is otherwise stipulated in the marriage contract, or unless the judge were to find an excuse for her not to travel (Art. 70).

According to the Jordanian Law, the husband shall provide a dwelling containing all the necessary appliances according to his means, and in the place where he lives and works (Art. 36). The wife, following the receipt of her prompt dower, shall obey and live in her husband's lawful home and shall, under pain of losing her right of maintenance, travel with him to any destination he wishes, even if it is abroad, provided her safety is secured and that the marriage contract does not stipulate otherwise (Art. 37). The husband shall not have his relatives or his child above the age of discretion (by another woman) live with him in the home he set up for his wife without her consent. The exception to this would be his poor disabled parents if he has no means to support them on their own, and has no alternative but to have them stay with him without their impeding matrimonial life. Likewise, the wife shall not have her children by another husband, or her relatives, to live with her without the consent of the husband (Art. 38). The husband married to more than one wife shall be equally fair to them, and shall not have them live in the same home without their consent (Art. 40).

Similar provisions are laid down in the Kuwaiti Law. The husband must accommodate his wife in a home worthy of his equals (Art. 84/a); he shall not, without her consent, accommodate her with another wife of his (Art. 85); he shall not let anyone share their home, except his children under the age of discretion and other children of his who need a home, and his parents, provided the wife will not be jeopardized thereby.

(3) The creation of prohibited degrees on the grounds of affinity

The respective ascendants and descendants of each spouse shall be prohibited degrees for either as explained in the section dealing with impediments of marriage. Unlawful conjunction shall also apply.

(4) Proven parentage of the offspring

Marriage establishes the husband's parentage of the offspring unless there is indisputable evidence to the contrary. The Hanafis maintain that even the very fact of the marriage contract, regardless of consummation, creates the parentage. Other jurists maintain that parentage is established on the ground of the contract with the possibility of consummation. I shall deal with this in more detail in the chapter on parentage.

(5) Mutual inheritance

Each spouse shall inherit from the other in the event of death while lawful matrimony exists in fact, or is deemed to be existing, unless there is an impediment to inheritance. This will be discussed in detail in the chapter on inheritance. Except for the Shia, consummation of marriage is not a condition of inheritance: if either spouse dies after the valid contract and prior to consummation, the other shall inherit. For the Shia ruling, see the chapter on inheritance.

Even though the *muta* marriage creates no mutual inheritance rights, a stipulation agreed upon by the two parties to that effect shall be lawful and effective.

(6) Decent treatment

It is the moral duty of each spouse to treat the other with respect and kindness and to live together in harmony and peace. This is a moral duty incumbent according to the Quranic verses: "And consort with them in kindness, for if ye hate them it may happen that ye hate a thing wherein Allah hath placed much good." (4:19) "And they (women) have rights similar to those (of men) over them in kindness." (2:228) "And of His signs in this: He created for you helpmeets from yourselves that ye might find rest in them, and He ordained between you love and mercy. Lo, herein indeed are portents for folk who reflect." (30:21)

The Moroccan Law makes "living together in harmony, mutual feelings of respect and kindness and concern for the welfare of the family" a mutual right and duty of the spouses (Art. 34/2).

The Jordanian Law provides that it is the duty of the husband to live decently with his wife and to treat her with kindness, and a duty of the wife to obey her husband in lawful matters (Art. 39). This duty of the wife to obey her husband is also asserted under the Moroccan Law (Art. 36/2).

Further, the Moroccan Law adds to the above, two rights of the woman, namely, to be allowed to visit her relatives and to invite them to visit her in kindness and according to decent custom; and her complete freedom to dispose of her property as she wishes, without any supervision or control by the husband, who has no right of guardianship in respect of his wife's property (Art. 35/3/4). It also adds, to the rights of the husband, that the wife shall suckle her offspring if she is able, shall supervise a household and put it in good shape, and shall honour her husband's parents and relatives in kindness and according to decent custom (Art. 36/3/4/5).

10. Mixed Marriages

Several references have been made in the previous sections to the subject of mixed marriages, e.g. in the context of marriage impediments and formalities.

Generally speaking, the same principles which govern valid marriage contracts in accordance with the Sharia and modern Islamic legislation apply to mixed marriages as well. However, in view of the importance of this subject with which the legal profession is confronted only too often in daily practice, it behoves me to compile in a brief form, the main rules which are dealt with in more detail in the previous sections in this chapter, and in the following chapters on dower, maintenance, dissolution of marriage, the rights of children, inheritance and wills.

The same conditions on the legality of the marriage contract apply to mixed marriages. The most important condition relates to religion. Under the Sharia and all modern Islamic laws, both for the Sunni and Shia schools, a marriage of a Muslim woman to a non-Muslim man is null and void, even if it is validly solemnized according to the laws of any given non-Muslim state. For such a marriage to be valid the man must have converted to Islam at the time of the contract.

On the other hand, a Muslim man cannot enter into a valid marriage, under the Sharia and the Islamic modern laws, to a non-Muslim woman who is not Christian or a Jewess (or a *magi* according to the Shias). It must be stressed that the impediment is restricted to religion, without anything to do with nationality.

A non-Muslim woman validly married to a Muslim enjoys the same rights as a Muslim wife in respect of retaining sole control of her property. In fact this right is extended even to foreign women married to non-Muslims in Arab states.

Although under the Sharia, and in the overwhelming majority of modern Islamic states, the Muslim man can have up to four wives at the same time, under certain conditions and restrictions, a non-Muslim wife can stipulate in her marriage contract that her Muslim husband shall not take another wife and can retain to herself the right to terminate the marriage on her own.

The dower is the legal right of the wife of a Muslim whether or not she is Muslim herself. During her marriage she has the inalienable right to be maintained by her husband regardless of any private means she may have. She is entitled also, under the laws of certain Arab states, to damages in the event of arbitrary divorce by her husband, over and above the maintenance due to her during her *iddat* which she must observe.

She has the right to custody of a male infant for the duration of breast feeding, according to the Shia, or until he reaches the age of discretion, according to the Sunnis, and of a female infant until she reaches puberty. In all cases she retains the right to access. The only restriction is that there should be no danger of her converting the child to a religion different from its father's.

A non-Muslim widow has no right to inheritance in the estate of her Muslim husband, since it is a condition for an heir to profess the same religion as the propositus. But she can be left a part of the estate, not exceeding one-third, by way of a will.

For details of these provisions, reference should be made to the relevant chapters.

CHAPTER 4

Dower

1. Definition and Juristic Qualification

The Dower (*Mahr, Sadaq* or *Oqr*, also referred to in the Quran as *Nehla, Ajr* and *Fareeda*-portion) is a sum of money or other property which becomes payable by the husband to the wife as an effect of marriage. The Quran ordains: "And give the women (on marriage) their dower as a free gift." (4:4) In another verse: "We know what We have appointed for them as to their wives." (33:50) It is an obligatory and fit gift by the man to win her heart and to honour marriage. The Moroccan legislator defines the dower as: "The property given by the husband to indicate his willingness to contract marriage, to establish a family and to lay the foundations for affection and companionship" (Art. 16).

Contrary to a widely held misconception in the West, dower is not a bride-price. In fact, it is expressly prohibited, under the Moroccan law, Article 19, for the guardian, be he a father or not, to receive anything for himself from the suitor in consideration for the marriage of his daughter or ward to the suitor. The same prohibition is stressed under Jordanian Article 62, for the wife's parents or relatives to receive money or anything else from the husband in consideration of getting her to marry him, or giving her away to him. The husband shall have the right to recover whatever he has so given, or the value thereof. According to the Hanafi jurist Al Kamal ibn ul Humam (died 861 AH), "Dower has been ordered to underline the prestige of the marriage contract and to stress its importance. ... It has not been enjoined as a consideration like a price or a wage, otherwise it would have been set as a prior condition."[1] This is the reason why dower is neither an essential nor a condition for the validity, binding or effectiveness of the marriage contract. It is not mentioned as such in any modern Islamic legislation. A marriage contract is deemed valid without any mention of dower. The classical jurists cite the authority of the Quranic verse, "It is no sin for you if ye divorce women while yet ye have not touched them nor appointed unto them a portion (dower)." (2:236) The jurists infer that since no sin is committed by those who divorce their wives before marriage consummation or agreement on dower, and since divorce can only occur after a valid marriage, therefore this verse proves that a marriage contract can be valid without any mention of dower.

---

[1] *Fat-hul Qadeer*, Vol. 3 (Cairo), pp. 143, 324. AI-Kassani, *AI-Badaia*, Vol.4 (Cairo), p. 43.

The qualification of dower as an effect or a consequence of the marriage contract rather than as an essential or a validity condition thereof, does not reduce or weaken in any way the wife's entitlement to it. In fact it is both an inalienable and imprescriptible right of the wife:

(i) It is *inalienable* in that it is taken for granted even if it is not expressly stated in the contract. The Shias maintain that if the husband makes a condition in the marriage contract that he shall pay no dower, this condition shall be null and void, but the contract shall remain valid.[2] The Ismailis, relying on a Tradition quoted by Imam Ali, believe that denying the wife her dower is an unforgivable sin.[3] They also hold Ali's ruling that there is no marriage without a dower.[4] Kuwaiti Article 52 provides that the dower shall be due to the wife by the very fact of a valid marriage contract. The Syrian Law adds to the same ruling that it shall be so, whether it is specified, not specified or ignored completely (Art. 53), and that the husband can only obtain discharge thereof by paying it to her (Art. 61). Dower of the equal shall apply in the event of failure to specify it or in an irregular specification thereof (Syrian, Art. 61/1; Iraqi, Art. 19). The Jordanian Law makes dower the property of the wife from which she cannot be compelled to buy furniture or domestic appliances (Art. 61). In Tunisia, it is the wife's exclusive property to dispose of in any way she likes (Art. 12). A similar provision to the last two applies under Moroccan Article 18. Sudanese Article 28 rules that the dower is the property of the woman, and any contrary stipulation shall be void. Yemeni Article 33/2 uses the same words, but adds "For her to dispose of as she likes."

(ii) It is *imprescriptible* in that the wife shall not lose her entitlement to it through prescription alone. This is a basic Sharia provision adopted expressly in the Syrian Law, "The deferred dower shall not be subject to prescription provisions even if a promissory note was made of it as long as the state of matrimony exists" (Art. 60/2). The same law also makes it "a privileged debt following immediately after the payable maintenance debt referred to under Article 1120 of the Civil Code" (Art. 54/3).[5]

The Moroccan and Tunisian Codes (Arts. 21 and 13, respectively) deny the husband any right to force the wife to connubial intercourse until he pays her her dower. However, if the wife allows consummation, she shall only retain the right to claim her dower as a debt due to her on her husband. His inability to repay it shall not be a valid ground for divorce.

2. Quality of Dower

According to Sunnis and Shias alike, the dower may consist of anything that can be valued in money, is useful and ritually clean. The Syrian, Moroccan and Omani Laws rule that "anything that can be the object of a lawfully valid

---

[2] Al-Hilli, *Jaafari Personal Status Provisions*, p. 6, Art. 12.
[3] Qadi an-Numan, *op. cit.* p. 174.
[4] *Ibid*, p. 175.
[5] Art 1120, para. 1C of the Civil Code: "The following claims are secured by a privilege over all the debtor's property, whether movable or immovable. ...... (c) alimony due by the debtor to members of his family and his kin.".

obligation is a valid dower" (Articles 54/2, 17-1 and 22, respectively). To this, Article 54 of the Kuwaiti Law adds: "be it a property, a service or a usufruct, provided it does not conflict with the husband's status of guardian". Sudanese Article 27 uses the same words but drops the condition. The Tunisian Law holds that "anything that is lawful and can be valued in money may be designated as a dower" (Art. 12).

Therefore, the dower may be immovable property, e.g. land and buildings, measurable movable property, e.g. cattle or crops, specific chattels or a usufruct with a pecuniary value. Wine and pigs are not valid dowers, being ritually unclean, even to a *Kitabi* wife. Nor is a non-pecuniary concession, such as not to take another wife or not to move the wife out of her town. The Explanatory Note to the Kuwaiti Law, in respect of the said Article 54, does not allow the husband becoming a servant to his wife as a dower, as it entails degradation of the husband, and runs against his being the guardian.

The property given as a dower must be reasonably specified for identification. The husband may designate a horse, a dress of certain material, or a weight of cotton, in which case he shall be bound to provide the article designated at an average value. But a vague dower, e.g. "an animal" or "a house" shall not be valid, without however invalidating the marriage contract itself, but the dower of the equal shall be due. According to an authentic Tradition of the Prophet, respected by the Shias, teaching the Quran can be a valid dower.[6]

3. Quantity of Dower

Classical jurists and modern law makers set no ceiling for the dower (Arts. 54/1, Syrian; 17/2, Moroccan; 12, Tunisian; 53, Kuwaiti). Tradition has it that the Second Patriarchal Caliph, Umar ibn-ul-Khattab, tried to limit excessive dowers, but was stopped by a woman quoting the Quranic verses, "And if ye wish to exchange one wife for another and ye have given unto one of them a sum of money (however great) take nothing from it. Would ye take it by way of calumny and open wrong? How can ye take it (back) after one of you hath gone into the other and they have taken a strong pledge from you?" (4: 20/21) The Ismailis follow Imam Ali's advice not to set too high a dower, which would breed animosity.[7]

But there is no such unanimity on the minimal dower. The Shafiis, Hanbalis and Shias maintain that there is no such limit. On the authority of the Quranic ruling, "... so that you seek them with your property in honest wedlock, not debauching" (*ibid.* 24) they argue that any property, regardless of quantity, is acceptable as dower. This position is expressly held in Syria (Art. 54/1), Morocco (Art. 17/2) and Kuwait (Art. 53). It is also implied in Iraqi Article 19/1 and Jordanian Article 44, which both rule that the wife shall be entitled to the dower specified in the contract, with the Jordanian adding "however small or large".

The Malikis set a quarter dinar of gold or three dirhams of silver[8] as the

---

[6] Al-Hilli, *op. cit.* p. 19 and *Saheeh-ul-Bukhari* and *Saheeh-u-Muslim*, *Fiqh al-Sunna* by Sayyid Sabiq (Cairo), p. 136. The Ismailis maintain Imam Jaafar's ruling that a man may marry a woman teaching her a Quranic *sura* (chapter) as a dower. Qadi Numan, *op. cit.* p. 175.
[7] Qadi an-Numan, *op. cit.* Vol. 2, p. 175.
[8] The Dirham is a silver coin weighing 2.97 grammes; see *Encyclopaedia of Islam*.

minimal dower, by analogy with the statutory (Sharia) limit for punishable theft. The Hanafi doctrine, applied in Egypt and among the Lebanese Sunnis (Family Rights Act) maintains that the minimal dower shall be ten dirhams, citing the authority of a Tradition of the Prophet to that effect, a Tradition whose authenticity is disputed by other schools.[9]

A similar position is held by the Tunisian legislator who rules that "dower shall not be insignificant (*tafih*)" (Art. 12).

4. Prompt and Deferred Dower

The dower, being a consequence of the marriage contract rather than an essential or a condition of it, shall be the right of the wife once the valid contract is made. However, it need not be paid in full at once, but may be split into two portions, prompt and deferred. This provision is retained from the Sharia in the modern Arab laws (Arts. 55, Syrian; 45, Jordanian; 20/1, Iraqi; 20/1, Moroccan; 53/a, Kuwaiti; 29/1, Sudanese; 34, Yemeni; and 24a, Omani). All these laws allow the whole or part of the dower to be deferred. However, Jordanian Law requires that any such agreement shall be recorded in writing, otherwise the whole dower shall be deemed prompt.

Iraqi, Syrian and Kuwaiti Laws rule that if no such arrangement was written down, then prevailing custom shall be followed. That is also in general the Sharia provision, applying the maxim that "A matter recognized by custom is regarded as though it was a contractual obligation." In Egypt, for example, the custom is to divide the dower into two equal shares.

The deferred dower shall become payable on the date agreed upon, otherwise it shall become payable immediately on the earlier of two events: divorce or death. The Iraqi Law makes any date for the payment of the deferred dower void in the event of divorce or death, when it becomes immediately payable (Art. 20/2). The Jordanian Law is more elaborate: under Article 46, if a date is set for the deferred dower, the wife shall not be entitled to claim it before the said date, even in the event of divorce. However, the Article continues, in the event of the death of the husband, that date will be void. Further, if the term is grossly indeterminate, like "till the time of affluence", or "on demand", the term shall be invalid, and all of the dower shall be deemed prompt. If no term was stipulated, the deferred dower shall be deemed payable on divorce or the death of either spouse.

5. Specified and Proper Dower
(Dower of those Equal to the Wife)

The dower may be specified (stipulated, designated, *musamma*) in the contract, in which case it shall be binding on the husband, provided that the contract is valid and subject to reservations by those who require a minimal value. If it is omitted, irregular, or if there is an invalid condition that no dower shall be payable, then the proper dower or the dower of the equal (*Mahr-ul-mithl*) shall

---

[9] *Cf. Fat-hul Qadeer*, Vol. 3, pp. 185, 206.

apply (Arts. 54 Jordanian, 55b Kuwaiti, 29/4 Sudanese and 33/1 Yemeni). According to the Sunni and Shia jurists, the equal to be considered is a woman who is an agnate relative of the wife-to-be, e.g. her sister, paternal aunt or cousin. If there is no woman equal to the wife among her agnate relations, the equal may be a woman belonging to a family equivalent to her father's but not her mother's family.[10] The Shafiis differ, maintaining that in the absence of an agnate, the equal shall be a consanguine relative, otherwise the nearest woman in terms of age, education, wealth, beauty, pedigree and virginity or previous marriage.[11]

Jordanian Article 44, while retaining that the equal shall be an agnate woman relative, rules that in the absence of such relative the equal shall be considered among the wife's peers of her townfolk. Aspects of equality, according to the jurists, include beauty, youth, social status, e.g. being a virgin, a divorcée or a widow, wealth, intelligence, piety, manners, being with or without children, etc.

The specified dower may be increased or reduced under certain conditions. The Sunnis and the Shias allow the husband, his father or grandfather if he lacks legal capacity, to add to the specified dower, on the authority of the Quranic verse "And there is no sin for you in what ye do by mutual agreement after a dower (*fareeda*) is prescribed." (4:24)[12] Provided that the husband is sane, major and under no interdiction due to imbecility or prodigality, he may add to the basic specified dower. Such an addition shall be the right of the wife to claim, together with the basic dower, with the difference that it cannot be halved, unlike the basic dower in the event of divorce before consummation, but shall be dropped altogether.[13] The addition shall be binding on the husband on three conditions:

(i)   That it is determinate. If a husband says to his wife, "I have added to your dower" without further specification, no addition shall be valid.
(ii) That it occurs while they are still actually or deemed to be linked by marriage, i.e. if they are not separated or during the *iddat* of a revocable divorce. Otherwise it is void.
(iii) That it is accepted at the same sitting where it has been offered by the wife, or her guardian if she lacks the legal capacity to accept. The idea is that such an increase is a gift whose essentials are offer by the donor and acceptance by the donee.

Likewise, a wife possessing full legal capacity may discharge her husband, subsequent to the marriage contract, of all or any part of her specified dower, it being exclusively hers to dispose of in any way she likes. The object of this discharge, which is tantamount to a reduction, is unidentifiable property, such as money, and measurable articles. It shall be valid if the husband accepts it or keeps silent, and shall be void if it is rejected. As for identifiable property, e.g. a specific piece of land, or a given house, provided that it is free of any debt, the wife may make it a gift to the husband who has to accept it for it to be valid. Unlike increase, no father, grandfather or guardian of the minor wife has the power to reduce her specified dower.[14]

[10] Al-Hilli, *op. cit.* p. 19; Abdullah, *Personal Status*, pp. 286, 287; Abu Zahra, *On Marriage*, p. 183.
[11] *Al Umm*, Vol. 5, p. 64.
[12] Al-Hilli, *op. cit.* p. 20; Abdullah, *op. cit.* pp. 294–298.
[13] *Loc. cit.*
[14] *Loc. cit.*

These Sharia provisions are included in the Jordanian Article 63 which reads: "The husband may increase the dower after the contract and the wife may reduce it provided that they possess full legal capacity of disposition. This shall be attached to the original contract if it is accepted by the other party at the sitting where the increase or reduction has been offered." A similar ruling is incorporated in Article 58 of the Kuwaiti Law.

An identical text to the Jordanian Article constituted Article 57 of the Syrian Decree No. 59/1953, but it was amended under Article 5 of Act 34/1975 to read as follows: "No increase or reduction of the dower nor any discharge thereof during the state of matrimony or the *iddat* of divorce shall be considered, and it shall be deemed void unless it is made before the judge. Any such disposition made before the judge shall be attached to the original contract if it is accepted by the other party." The reason given in the Explanatory Memorandum to the said Act No. 34/1975 is to stop any duress, moral or otherwise, that either spouse may be subject to during marital life to accept any increase, reduction or discharge of the dower.

In another amendment destined to safeguard the interests of both spouses against complicity or excessive amounts of specified dower, the Syrian legislator, under Article 4 of Act No. 34/1975, added paragraph 4 to Article 54 of Act No. 59/1953 reading as follows: "Any person who alleges complicity or artificiality of the specified dower shall be required to duly prove such an allegation. On proving either, the judge shall order the dower of the equal unless a designated dower shall prove genuine."

6. Entitlement to the Dower

Apart from a valid marriage contract which makes *per se* the dower an established right of the wife, consummation with the semblance of the right to have intercourse or under an irregular marriage contract shall also render the wife entitled to a dower. In the case of consummation with the semblance of the right, or under an irregular marriage contract, if the dower is validly specified, the lesser of the specified dower or the dower of the equal shall be due to the wife on separation. If the dower is irregularly specified the wife shall have the right to the dower of the equal.[15] While ignoring consummation with the semblance of the right to have intercourse, the modern Personal Status Laws of Iraq (Art. 22), Syria (Art. 63), Jordan (Art. 56), Kuwait (Art. 50a), Sudan (2 and 3), Yemen (35 and 36) and Oman (24/b) hold the previous Sharia provisions. Although the Shias treat an irregular marriage contract (*fasid*) as a void marriage to all intents and purposes, they maintain, nevertheless, that consummation under such a contract shall establish the woman's right, on separation, to the dower of the equal even if a specified dower has been agreed upon.[16]

Although the dower becomes an exclusive right of the wife under a valid marriage contract, the amount thereof due to her varies according to circumstances. She may be entitled to the whole dower, half of it, or may have no dower at all.

---

[15] Abu Zahra, *Personal Status*, p. 184.
[16] Al-Hilli, *op. cit.* pp. 7 and 21.

A. The Wife's Entitlement to the Whole Dower

It is unanimously agreed by the Sunnis that the whole dower shall become due to the wife on the occurrence of either of two events:

(i) the actual consummation of marriage;
(ii) the death of either spouse before consummation.

If it is the wife who dies, her heirs shall take the residue of her whole dower from the husband after deducting his share.[17] All the jurists agree that the whole dower shall be due to the wife in the event of the death of the husband, by natural causes, suicide or murder by a third party. It shall be also due on the husband killing his wife. Only Imam Abu Hanifa and his two Companions rule that this right of the wife shall not be lost if she killed her husband, a ruling honoured in Egypt. But the three other Imams, Malik, ash-Shafii and Ahmad Ibn-Hanbal and the Hanafi jurist Zufar, maintain that the wife shall lose her entitlement to any dower if she killed her husband before consummation, on the grounds that crime shall not pay, by analogy to her being then deprived of the inheritance, therefore, *a fortiori*, of dower. The Kuwaiti legislator codifies this ruling in Article 62 which reads as follows: "If the wife kills her husband in a case of murder that bars her from inheritance, before consummation of marriage, she shall repay any part she received of the dower, and shall lose her right to any balance thereof. If the murder was committed after consummation, she shall have no right to any balance". The former Hanafi position is held in Egypt and adopted by the Moroccan Law, Article 20/3, and the Iraqi Law, Article 21, which rules that the wife shall be entitled to the whole *specified* dower on consummation or death of either spouse.

The Shias concur with this ruling, with the reservation that if the husband dies before consummation without having specified a dower nor set any portion for her in the contract, neither dower nor a *mutat* (a present, see B.) shall be due to the wife.'[18]

Accepting these two grounds, the Hanafis add a third: the valid retirement between the two spouses which they deem as a consummation *de juro* if not *de facto*, relying on the authority of the Quranic verse, "How can ye take it (back) after one of you hath gone in unto the other and they have taken a strong pledge from you?" (4:21), interpreting "one going in unto the other" as valid retirement. They also quote a Tradition of the Prophet, "He who unveils his wife and looks to her shall be liable to pay her dower, whether there is intimacy or not."[19] A similar ruling attributed to Imam Ali is held by the Ismailis.[20]

This rule is adopted in Egypt where the Hanafi doctrine prevails, and in the Lebanon by the Sunnis. It is also held in the Jordanian Law, "A dower specified under a valid contract shall be payable in full on the death of either spouse or on divorce after valid retirement ..." (Art. 48).

The Shafiis and Malikis do not accept that valid retirement confirms the wife's right to the whole dower, invoking the authority of the Quranic verse: "If ye divorce them before ye have touched them and ye have appointed unto them a

---

[17] Al-Abiani, *Sharia Personal Status Provisions*, p. 81.
[18] Al-Hilli, *op. cit.* p. 21.
[19] Quoted by Abdullah, *op. cit.* p. 300.
[20] Qadi an-Numan, *op. cit.* Vol. 2, p. 179.

portion, then (pay the) half of that which ye appointed. ... " (2:237). However, the Malikis maintain that even without actual consummation, the whole dower shall be due to the wife if she moves into the matrimonial home to stay for a whole year.[21]

The Shias hold that valid retirement under a marriage contract shall not be a substitute for actual consummation, and shall not confirm the wife's right to the whole dower.[22]

On the other hand, the Hanbalis, whose doctrine under the Wahhabi version is strictly applied in the Kingdom of Saudi Arabia, concur with the three Hanafi grounds and add a fourth ground to confirm the entitlement of the wife to the whole dower; namely acts of undue familiarity (*al mulamasa al-fahisha*) by which is meant touching any part of a person of the opposite sex, even inadvertently, without there being any cloth or other substance between the parties of sufficient thickness to prevent warmth of body to be felt, or kissing or looking on his or her nakedness or lying together or embracing, provided:

(i)   that neither of the parties is below age when the desire first arises; and
(ii) that the act is done with desire on the part of at least one of the parties, even if that occurs in the presence of other people.[23]

Valid retirement (*al-Khilwat-us-Sahiha*) is used to describe the event of the husband and the wife, under a valid marriage contract, being together by themselves in a place where they are secure from observation without anything in decency, law or health to prevent their having sexual intercourse. On grounds of decency there must be no third person with the spouses, whether awake or asleep, in possession of the power of sight or blind, adult or a discerning child, except a little child without understanding. On grounds of law, neither spouse may be in a condition which prohibits intercourse, e.g. if either spouse is observing ordained fast, or performing the pilgrimage rite, or if the wife is during a menstrual cycle under the Quranic verse: "They ask thee concerning menstruation. Say: It is hurt and pollution (*adha*). So let women alone at such time and go not unto them till they are cleansed." (2:222) On grounds of health, neither party shall be too young or too ill to have sexual intercourse.

Apart from the confirmation of the whole dower, which is the opinion of the Hanafis and the Hanbalis, the valid retirement has the following effects in common with actual consummation according to the Sunnis:

(i)   establishment of parentage, which is an effect really of the valid contract *per se* and not of valid retirement nor even of actual consummation under certain conditions as explained in more detail in the chapter on parentage;
(ii) the necessity for the wife to observe *iddat* after separation;
(iii) the unlawful conjunction (see temporary prohibited degrees) and the prohibition to take a fifth wife during the *iddat*;
(iv) the establishment of the wife's right to maintenance, accommodation and clothing during the *iddat*.

[21] Abu Zahra, *op. cit.* p. 193.
[22] Al-Hilli, *op. cit.* p. 21.
[23] *Fatawa Alamgiri*, Vol. 1 (Cairo, 131OH), p. 13. Neil B.E. Baillie, *Digest of Muhammadan Law*, Vol. II (London, 1826), p. 24.

The last three effects relate to the observation of the *iddat* rather than valid retirement or actual consummation.

According to the Shias, the only effect of valid retirement is the establishment of the wife's right to maintenance and accommodation.[24]

The valid retirement differs from actual consummation in the following respects:

(i)   Actual consummation establishes a prohibited degree between the husband and any descendant of the wife. Here valid retirement does not create such a prohibited degree under the Quranic verse: "... your step-daughters under your guardianship, born of your wives to whom ye have gone in ...;" (4:2)
(ii) Coition with the wife revocably divorced during her *iddat* is deemed remarrying her, unlike valid retirement;
(iii) After consummation, divorce may be revocable or irrevocable, but after valid retirement, divorce can be only irrevocable even during the *iddat*.
(iv) Where a man has divorced his wife three times, it is lawful for him (except in Tunisia) to remarry her if there was actual consummation between her and her second husband from whom she is later lawfully separated through divorce or death. Valid retirement between her and her second husband shall not be enough to make it lawful for her after separation to remarry her first husband;
(v)   Inheritance: No mutual inheritance shall be established between two spouses who were separated after valid retirement, should either die during the *iddat*. By contrast, there shall be mutual inheritance between spouses if a revocable divorce took place after actual consummation and either spouse died during the *iddat*.

B. *Entitlement of the Wife to Half of the Dower and to the Mutat*

The wife shall be entitled to half of the specified dower if the marriage is dissolved before consummation by any act on the part of the husband, under the Quranic verse: "If ye divorce them before ye have touched them and ye have appointed unto them a portion, then pay the half of that which ye appointed" (2:237). On the basis of this ruling, jurists deduce the following four conditions for half the dower to be due to the wife:

(i)   that marriage is under a valid contract;
(ii) that the dower is validly specified in the contract;
(iii) that divorce occurs before consummation or valid retirement;
(iv) that divorce is due to an act on the part of the husband, other than his exercising the option of puberty or recovery from insanity, since in this case the contract is deemed null and void.

The Syrian Law decrees that on divorce before consummation or valid retirement, half of the dower should go to the wife if a valid contract included a validly specified dower (Art. 58). Concurring, (Art. 63/a), the Kuwaiti legislator adds that (b) the wife shall repay any excess she received of the half and (c) that if she made a gift to the husband of half or more of her dower, she shall repay nothing on divorce before consummation or valid retirement and shall repay

[24] Al-Hilli, *op. cit.*

the balance of the half, if her gift to him was less than that. If there was no valid specification of the dower, the wife shall be entitled not to the half dower, but to the *mutat* or present, under the Quranic ruling: "It is no sin for you if ye divorce women while yet ye have not touched them, nor appointed unto them a portion. Provide for them, the rich according to his means, and the straitened according to his means, according to custom". (2:236/7) It is thus left to custom to determine the amount of the *mutat*. Under Hanafi Law, it consists of three articles of dress or of their value provided that the value shall not be less than five dirhams, being half the minimum dower according to the Hanafis, or more than half of the dower of the equal. The Sunnis in general hold that the *mutat* is regulated by the circumstances of both husband and wife. The Shias stick to the Quranic text and consider the circumstances and condition of the husband only.[25] The Ismaili order the *mutat* without quantifying it.[26]

The *mutat* is expressly mentioned in the Jordanian Law (Art. 55) which specifies that the *mutat*, becoming due on divorce before the stipulation of dower and before consummation or valid retirement, shall be determined according to custom and the condition of the husband, provided that it shall not exceed half the dower of the equal.

The Syrian Law, followed by Kuwaiti Law (Art. 64), orders *mutat* for the wife (if there was no specified dower or if the stipulation thereof is irregular under a valid contract) on divorce before consummation or valid retirement (Art. 61/2). The Syrian legislator defines *mutat* as an article of dress to go out in worthy of the wife's equals, according to the condition of the husband, without exceeding the value of half of the dower of the equal (Art. 62).

The Moroccan Law stipulates that the wife shall be entitled to half of the dower if she is divorced before consummation by the husband of his own free will (Art. 22). The Jordanian legislator rules that if divorce occurred, under a valid marriage contract in which a dower was specified, before consummation or valid retirement, half of the specified dower shall be due (Art. 48). Iraqi Article 21 simply stipulates that the wife shall be entitled to half of the specified dower on divorce before consummation.

It must be stressed that the half due for the wife on separation before consummation (or valid retirement if applicable) is of the validly specified dower. Any addition thereto by the husband made after the contract shall not be halved, but shall be dropped altogether. However, if there is an inherent increase of the dower, involving, for example, an increase in the value of a garden or a mare, and if the increase occurs while the substance is still in the possession of the husband, such an increase shall be halved together with the specified dower on separation prior to consummation (or valid retirement if applicable). The same provision applies if the increase is connected with the dower, e.g. the building on a land given in dower or the rent of a house. If the increase occurs after the wife is in possession of the dower and *before the husband recovers his half by agreement or litigation*, the increase shall be the wife's, whether it is inherent in the dower or not, and whether it occurs before or after separation, unless it is added, like a building on a piece of land, in which case it belongs to the person who made it. If the increase occurs to the dower which the wife has actually

---

[25] *Ibid.*
[26] Qadi an-Numan, *op. cit.* Vol. 2, pp. 176–177.

received *after the husband recovers his half by agreement or litigation,* the increase shall be halved between them, unless it is added to the dower, in which case it shall belong to the person who made it.[27]

C. *The Loss by the Wife of the Whole Dower*

No dower, whether specified or proper (dower of the equal) shall be due to the wife if the marriage is dissolved before it is confirmed in either of the two following events:

(i) If the marriage is dissolved by the husband before consummation (or valid retirement if applicable) through exercising his option of puberty or recovery from imbecility or insanity, in which case he is lawfully entitled to apply for the marriage to be annulled. For example, a guardian, other than the father or grandfather, may exercise his powers of compulsory guardianship to contract a marriage for his ward. However, on the removal of grounds for guardianship, when the ward attains puberty or recovers from his insanity or imbecility, he may exercise his option and apply to the Court for annulment of his marriage. Should the judge order annulment, the husband shall be released of the whole dower, since the very contract becomes null and void, and since there would be no point in the husband exercising his lawful option if he is ordered to pay half the dower.[28]

(ii) If the marriage is dissolved before actual consummation (or valid retirement where applicable) by an act by the wife whether it is lawful or unlawful. Examples of lawful acts by the wife are her exercising her own option of puberty or recovery from imbecility or insanity where she has the lawful right to apply for the annulment of marriage, or if she were given the power to ask for a divorce, and she exercised it before consummation. Examples of unlawful acts are: apostasy, or, being a polytheist, her refusal to adopt Islam or any *kitabi* religion after the conversion of her husband to Islam, or committing with an older relative or a descendant of the husband an act that creates a prohibited degree through affinity.[29]

These grounds for the loss of the whole dower are adopted in the Jordanian Law (Art. 52). It also rules, according to the Sharia provisions, that no dower whatsoever shall be due

(a) if separation occurred at the request of the wife on grounds of a deformity or a defect on the part of the husband, or if her guardian applied for separation on grounds of inequality before consummation or valid retirement (Art. 49);

(b) if the contract is annulled before consummation or valid retirement, the husband shall recover any dower he may have paid (Art. 50);

(c) if the contract is annulled before consummation, at the request of the husband on grounds of a deformity or defect on the part of the wife, in which case the husband shall also recover any dower he may have paid (Art. 53).

The Moroccan Decree deprives the wife of the whole dower if the contract is

---

[27] Abdullah, *op. cit.* pp. 311, 312.
[28] *Ibid.* p. 316.
[29] *Loc. cit.*

annulled or rescinded by the husband on grounds of a defect of the wife, or by the wife on grounds of a defect of the husband, before consummation (Art. 22).

According to the Syrian Law, the wife shall lose the whole dower if separation occurs by an act of the wife before consummation or valid retirement (Art. 59).

Kuwaiti Article 65 rules that the wife shall lose all her right to any dower or *mutat* if the divorce is due to a cause emanating from her, before consummation or valid retirement.

The husband shall also be released of the whole dower if the wife makes a gift of remission of it to him, the dower being her exclusive property of which she can dispose in any way she likes.[30]

Under Yemeni Art. 36, half of the named *mahr* (dower) becomes due on divorce or dissolution by the husband if it takes place before consummation. If the dissolution is by the agreement of the two parties, or by the wife alone, then no part of the dower becomes due to the wife, and she has to return whatever she has received to which she is no longer entitled, or something similar to any gift she has received from him. Both schools of the Shia have the authority of a ruling by Imam Jaafar that a woman whose husband dies before consummation without having set a specific dower shall have no dower or *mutat*, but shall inherit from him and observe the *iddat*.[31]

7. Legal Disputes Over the Dower

The most widespread legal suits over the dower are related to disputes over the stipulation of the dower, the amount of the contract dower and the receipt of the dower. These disputes may occur during the spouses' life, during the existence of matrimony or after separation. They may arise between a surviving spouse and the heirs of the other, or between the heirs of each if they are both deceased.

A. Dispute over the Stipulations of the Dower

If the spouses differ on whether the dower in the contract was stipulated or not, with one party claiming that a certain amount was specified and the other denying it, the court shall apply the general juristic maxim to the effect that "Evidence is for him who affirms; the oath for him who denies". If evidence is available, the judge shall order the specified dower accordingly. In the absence of evidence, the denying party shall be ordered to make an oath, failing which the claim of the other party will be proved. If an oath is made, the judge shall dismiss stipulation and order the dower of the equal, provided that it shall not exceed the amount claimed by the wife if she is the party who affirmed the stipulation, and shall not be less than what is claimed by the husband if he is the affirming party.[32]

This provision is held by the Jordanian Law, Article 57. It is also followed in general by Article 69 of the Kuwaiti Law which rules, however, that if the wife fails to provide evidence, the statement of the husband under oath shall be held, unless he claims a dower that does not benefit her according to custom, in which

---

[30] *Ibid.*
[31] Qadi an-Numan, *op. cit.* Vol. 2, pp. 176–177 and Maghniya, *Fiqhul Imam*, Vol. 5, p. 279.
[32] *Ibid.* pp. 336, 337; Al-Hilli, *op. cit.* p. 28.

case, the judge shall order the dower of the equal, provided that it shall not be more than the amount claimed by the wife; this ruling to apply likewise in any dispute between a spouse and the heirs of the other, or between their respective heirs. A similar ruling occurs in Article 29/5 of the Sudanese Law.

It must be stressed that such a ruling applies only in the case where the wife is entitled to the whole dower, whether during the continuation of the marriage or after separation, for whatever reason after the whole dower is confirmed to the wife. If the dispute occurs where only half of the dower is due to the wife, the judge shall order half the specified dower, if proven, or the *mutat* if the stipulation is dismissed.[33]

B. *Dispute over the Amount of the Specified Dower*

If both spouses agree on the fact of the stipulation of dower but differ on the amount thereof, the party who claims the higher amount shall be required to submit evidence, in the absence of which the other party shall have to make an oath. Notwithstanding this general rule, if it is the wife who claims the higher amount but could not prove her case, the judge shall order the dower of the equal if the amount claimed by the husband is not fit for the equal of the wife according to custom, or if the amount claimed by the wife is less than the equal's dower. The same provision applies if the dispute is between the surviving spouse and the heirs of the deceased, or between the heirs of both deceased spouses.[34]

This opinion of the Hanafi Jurist Abu Youssof is adopted in its entirety in Egypt (Act No. 25/1929, Art. 19), in Syria (Art. 54/4), in Kuwait (Art. 69) and in Jordan (Art. 58). However, the Jordanian Article 59 rules that no suit in respect of a dispute between the spouses over the dower of the contract shall be heard if it differs from the recognized contract document, unless a written proof is available of their agreement at the time of marriage on a dower other than that stated in the document.

C. *Dispute over the Receipt of the Dower*

The wife is lawfully entitled to refuse her husband connubial intercourse or to submit to her husband's authority until the payment of the prompt dower agreed upon in the contract, or in accordance with the custom (Art. 21, Moroccan; Art. 13, Tunisian). In Syria, it must be paid to her in person if she possesses full legal capacity, unless she authorizes in the contract document an agent to receive it for her (Art. 60/1). In Jordan, the virgin, even if she is of full legal capacity, shall be deemed to have received the dower if it is paid to her guardian if he is her father, or agnate grandfather, unless she has prohibited the husband to pay it to her guardian (Art. 64).

By exercising this right, she shall not be deemed disobedient (*nashiza*) and, therefore, shall not lose her right to maintenance.

If the spouses dispute over the fact of payment of the whole or part of the prompt dower, with the husband alleging that he has paid the prompt dower to his wife and consequently she is disobedient if she refuses to submit to his

---

[33] Abdullah, *op. cit.* p. 338.
[34] *Ibid.* p. 339.

authority, and the wife denying it, she shall not be deemed disobedient. If the dispute occurs before consummation, the onus of the proof of payment shall be on the husband, since the dower, by the very fact of the valid marriage contract has become a debt on him from which he could only be discharged through actual payment. If he provides evidence to substantiate his claim, or if the wife refrains from making an oath if no evidence is available, the judge shall rule in his favour, otherwise his case shall be dismissed. The same rule applies if the dispute arises after consummation, unless the observed custom is that the wife would not submit herself to the husband until she receives her prompt dower, in which case the custom shall be sufficient proof of the payment. The same rules apply if the said dispute is between a surviving spouse and the heir of the deceased or between their respective heirs if they are both dead.[35]

There are three modern legal texts on this matter. The Moroccan Law rules, under Article 24, that in the event of the spouses disputing the payment of prompt dower, the claim of the wife shall prevail before consummation, while that of the husband shall apply after consummation. The Algerian Article 17 gives a similar ruling in the absence of any evidence, and applies it to the dispute over the fact of payment between the spouses or their heirs, provided that either claim be confirmed with an oath. The Kuwaiti Article 60 agrees with the Moroccan, adding the proviso: "in the absence of any contradicting evidence or custom".

The Jaafaris hold that the wife who denies receiving the dower shall be believed because the non-receipt is the original state of things (*asl*) until the contrary is proven, and the husband has to prove that he has paid it, regardless of consummation having occurred or not.[36]

---

[35] *Ibid.* pp. 341–342.
[36] Maghniya, *Fiqhul Imam*, Vol. 5, p. 294.

CHAPTER 5

Maintenance

1. Definition

Maintenance is the lawful right of the wife under a valid marriage contract on certain conditions. It is the right of the wife to be provided at the husband's expense, and at a scale suitable to his means, with food, clothing, housing, toilet necessities, medicine, doctors' and surgeons' fees, baths, and also the necessary servants where the wife is of a social position which does not permit her to dispense with such services, or when she is sick.

All the modern Arab Codes on personal status more or less repeat this general Sharia position with some slight modifications.

In Iraq, Jordan, Syria, Kuwait and Algeria, there is an identical provision that maintenance consists of food, clothing, housing and the amenities thereof, treatment fees according to custom, and servants for women whose equals have servants (Arts. 24/2, 66/a, 71/1, 75 and 78 respectively).

The Sudanese Article 65 rules that maintenance includes food, clothing, housing, medical treatment and all means of human subsistence according to decent custom. Omani Art. 44 is identical. Yemeni Art. 44 similarly makes it an obligation on the husband to provide his wife with accommodation, maintenance and clothing according to their status.

The Egyptian Law No. 100/1985 enumerates the components of matrimonial maintenance, by way of non-limitative illustration such as food, clothing, housing and medical expenses, adding "and any such other things as are dictated by the Sharia."

The Moroccan Decree simply states that it is the right of the wife to have lawful maintenance for food, clothing, medical treatment and housing (Art. 35/1).

The Lebanese Druze Personal Status Act No. 28/1948 rules under Article 28 that maintenance shall include food, clothing, housing, medical treatment and servants for the wife on the grounds of her social position, infirmity or sickness. This maintenance is an obligation that must be met by agreement or by court order.

The Jordanian Law (Article 78) rules that the husband shall be liable for the fees of the mid-wife and the physician summoned for a birth if necessary, and the medicine and the cost of birth according to custom and to his means, whether or not the state of matrimony exists.

Maintenance by her husband is the lawful right of the wife, irrespective of her means or her religion. This position is virtually unanimously held by the Muslim jurists and modern statutes. The only two exceptions are the Zahiris and the modern Tunisians. The Zahiri Andalusian jurist Ibn Hazm holds that maintenance shall be the duty of the affluent wife if the husband is destitute, since she is a presumptive heir herself under the Quranic ruling "The duty of feeding and clothing nursing mothers according to decent custom is upon the father of the child. No-one should be charged beyond his capacity. A mother should not be made to suffer because of her child, nor should he to whom the child is born because of his child. And on the father's heir is incumbent the like of that." (2:33) The modern Tunisian Personal Status Mijalla, which, while asserting that it is the husband's duty to provide for his wife and his children by her, according to his means, in all matters related to maintenance, rules that the wife shall contribute to the maintenance of the family if she has any means (Art. 23).

The entitlement of the wife to maintenance derives from the authority of the Quran, Prophet's Tradition and Consensus. The above mentioned Quranic verse enshrines such a right.

For the divorced woman, the Quran commands "Lodge them where ye dwell, according to your wealth, and harass them not so as to straiten life for them." (65:6)

As for Tradition, the Prophet preached in his last sermon "Show piety to women, you have taken them in the trust of God and have had them made lawful for you to enjoy by the word of God, and it is your duty to provide for them and clothe them according to decent custom."

The maintenance of the wife is deemed a debt on the husband from the date of withholding it once it is due. Only payment or discharge shall settle this debt (Arts. 79, Syrian; 24/1, Iraqi; 78, Kuwaiti; 1, Egyptian Act No. 25/1920). In Syria, it has priority even over the privileged dower debt (Art. 54/3. See Chapter 4 Section 1). Sudanese Article 70 rules that the wife shall not be ordered more than three years' maintenance in the event of a court claim, and such an order would be made subject to the husband's affluence. Omani Article 50 sets the maintenance at one year.

2. Entitlement to and Loss of Maintenance

Maintenance shall be due to the wife:

(a) under a valid marriage contract;
(b) if she places, or offers to place, herself in the husband's power so as to allow him free access to herself at all lawful times (the Arabic word is *Tamkeen*); and
(c) she obeys all his lawful commands for the duration of marriage.[1]

This Sharia provision has been enacted in the modern laws of Egypt, Jordan, Iraq, Kuwait, Syria, Sudan and Oman which make the wife's maintenance an

---

[1] Almost all the classical Sunni and Shia jurists add the condition that the wife, in order to be entitled to maintenance, shall not be too young to render conjugal rights to her husband. Only the Hanafi jurist Abu Youssof holds that maintenance shall be due to a child-wife if her husband retains her in the matrimonial house for company. The Zahiris rule that maintenance is the right of the wife by the very act of the marriage contract "even if she is in the cradle". However, this whole issue is now of no relevance since all modern Islamic laws of marriage prohibit child marriage. See Chap. 3.

obligation of the husband from the date of valid contract (Act No. 25/1920 Art. 1, and Arts. 67, 23, 74, and 72/1, 69 and 49, respectively) even if they were of different religions (Jordan, Kuwait and Syria), if she submits or offers to submit herself to him (Egypt), and even if she is staying at her family's home, unless the husband asks her to move with him and she refuses without a lawful excuse (same Jordanian, Iraqi and Syrian Arts.).

No maintenance, however, shall be due to the wife in the absence of any of the three conditions set out above.

A. The Non-Valid Contract

As explained in Chapter 3, a void, or an irregular marriage contract *before consummation*, is no contract at all and shall have no effect whatsoever. However, under an irregular marriage contract, *after consummation*, the wife shall not be entitled to maintenance, since the husband has no lawful right of access to her. They would be forbidden to live together as man and wife, and would be separated of their own free will or by a court order. If the marriage was, *prima facie*, regular, and the wife obtained a court order for maintenance before it transpired that the marriage was irregular (e.g. that the wife was a foster sister of the husband), he may claim back the money he spent on her maintenance. In the absence of such order, he has no such right to a refund.

The Jordanian Law expressly rules out any maintenance for the wife under an irregular contract, subsequent to consummation and before or after separation (Art. 42). The Iraqi Law confines any right of the wife under such circumstances to the lesser of the specified or proper (i.e. dower of the equal) dowers, or to the latter in the absence of any specification (Art. 22). Without really dissenting from this ruling, the Syrian Law grants the wife the right to matrimonial maintenance for as long as she remains unaware of the irregularity of her marriage (Art. 51/3).

B. The Lack of Access

Since it is the *tamkeen*, i.e. the availability of the wife for her husband, and not the marriage contract itself, that makes maintenance the lawful right of the wife, this right shall be lost if the husband is denied access to the wife, even when, in certain cases, this denial is due to a cause not proceeding from the wife, subject to certain conditions:

(1) Imprisonment and abduction

No maintenance is due to a wife who is in jail, even if she is innocent, provided that the cause of her imprisonment proceeded from her, and that she had a choice. This provision is adopted by the Iraqi Law which deprives of maintenance a wife jailed for a crime or a debt (Art. 25/2). The Sunni jurists generally agree that the jailed wife is not entitled to maintenance if her imprisonment is before consummation. The general opinion is that she would lose her maintenance even if she were jailed after moving to the matrimonial home, and even if she could not avoid being in jail. Only Abu Youssof dissents, granting her maintenance on the grounds of a lawful excuse.[2]

---

[2] Abu Zahra, *On Marriage*, p. 238.

The Shias restrict the loss of maintenance because of imprisonment, to the event of the wife being jailed for a debt which she can afford to pay. She would keep her maintenance right if she is jailed for a debt she owes to the husband and if she cannot avoid the sentence.[3]

The same rule applies for an abducted wife, with Abu Youssof again dissenting on the ground that she has no choice.[4]

(2) The working wife

The majority of Islamic jurists, both Sunnis and Shias, rule that there shall be no maintenance for the wife who goes out to work without permission of her husband. The same attitude is adopted expressly in the Jordanian Law, Article 68, and the Syrian, Article 73. It is also implied in the Iraqi Article 25 which deprives the wife of her right to maintenance if she goes out of the matrimonial home without permission or lawful excuse (para. 1). The Iraqi lawyer Naji includes in this category the case of a wife who has a job or a profession, is forbidden to work by the husband, but continues to do so.[5]

Following the opinion of more progressive Islamic jurists, notably Ibn-ul-Humam, The Egyptian Act No. 100/1985 adopts a more liberal approach, ruling that the wife shall not lose her right to maintenance if she goes out for a lawful job without her husband's permission, provided that her exercise of that conditional right (to work) is not abused or in conflict with the family's interests, and that she was not expressly forbidden by the husband to work. So it seems that while she does not need the husband's permission, she has to heed his prohibition.

In a similar view, Kuwaiti Article 89 does not consider it disobedience by the wife to go out for a lawful reason or lawful employment unless it is not in the family's interests.

The Ismailis maintain a ruling by Imam Ali that a woman who leaves the matrimonial home without her husband's permission shall lose her right to maintenance until she returns home.[6]

(3) The disobedient or rebellious wife (nashiza)

The wife working against her husband's wishes denotes disobedience. But a special juristic term, *nashiza*, is applied to the wife, defined in the Jordanian Act (Art. 69) and the Syrian Act (Art. 75) following the Sharia, as "the wife who leaves the matrimonial home without a lawful reason or denies her husband access to the home which she owns without first requesting him to accommodate her elsewhere." The Shias alone add another case of disobedience, *nushuz*, which is the woman denying her husband his conjugal rights while she is living with him.[7] The Shias also consider as *nashiza*, a wife who borrows money without an order by the judge or the husband.[8]

Among the lawful reasons for such disobedience, the Jordanian Law mentions

---

[3] Al-Hilli, *Jaafari Personal Status Provisions*, p. 44.
[4] Abu Zahra, *op. cit.*
[5] Muhsin Naji, *Commentary on the Personal Status Act* (Baghdad, 1962), p. 231.
[6] Qadi an-Numan, *op. cit.* Vol. 3, p. 204.
[7] Al-Hilli, *op. cit.* p. 45.
[8] *Ibid.* p. 44.

the wife leaving home because of her husband beating or maltreating her (Art. 69). Other such reasons are:

(i)   to have a co-wife living in the same house without the wife's consent (Arts. 67, Syrian; 26, Iraqi; 40, Jordanian);
(ii) to have the husband's kin living with the wife without her consent, except the husband's child below the age of discretion (Arts. 69, Syrian; 26, Iraqi).

The Jordanian Act also makes a further exception, that of the husband's incapacitated poor parents if he has no means to support them independently and they have no other place to live, provided that that will not interfere with the spouses' conjugal life (Art. 38);

In a similar ruling, Kuwaiti Article 85 adds to the husband's children below the age of discretion, his other children and his parents if need dictates that they should live with him, provided that they shall cause no injury to the wife.

(iii) the wife shall not obey any command by the husband that conflicts with the Sharia, and the judge shall order maintenance for her (Iraqi, 33);
(iv) if she has not received her prompt dower, or has not a decent home prepared for her (Syrian, 72/2; Iraqi, 23/2; and Jordanian, 67);

Kuwaiti Article 87 adds "or if he refused to give her maintenance and she could not enforce a maintenance court order against him because he apparently has no property";

(v)   the Shias consider as a lawful excuse the wife going to visit her sick father who needs her to stay with him, having nobody else to look after him, even if he is not a Muslim, and even if the husband denied permission.[9]

The *nashiza* shall lose her right to maintenance for as long as she remains disobedient (Arts. 74, Syrian; 69, Jordanian; 75, Sudanese; 54, Omani, 11, *bis* 2, added to Egyptian Act No. 25/1929 under Act No. 100/1985). According to Kuwaiti Article 88, no obedience order obtained by the husband against her shall be implemented using force, the only penalty of non-compliance thereto being the loss of her maintenance (see the Explanatory Note to the said Article).

The disobedient wife's lost right to maintenance shall be revived on the removal of the cause.

(4) Travelling

The wife is bound to travel with her husband to wherever he wishes, provided that she is safe and unless otherwise stipulated in the marriage contract (Arts. 37, Jordanian; 2/3, Iraqi; 78, Sudanese; 57, Omani), or if the judge rules she has a lawful excuse (Syrian Art. 70; Kuwaiti Art. 90). Otherwise she would lose her entitlement to maintenance (Jordanian Art. 37).

On the other hand, the wife's maintenance right shall be suspended if she travels, unaccompanied by her husband, for as long as she is away from him, whether she travels on her own or in the company of a kin in a prohibited degree. Abu Youssof makes an exception of the wife who travels for the first time to perform the religious duty of pilgrimage if she is accompanied by a kin in a prohibited degree, after the consummation of marriage, in which case she

---

[9] *Ibid.* p. 57.

is granted a "settlement" not a "travelling" maintenance.[10] Kuwaiti Article 91 enshrines this right of the wife. The Shias add to this the wife who travels for a desirable (*mandub*) or permissible (*mubah*) cause with the husband's permission.[11]

(5) Apostasy

The Egyptian legislator alone rules expressly that the wife shall lose her maintenance right if she apostasizes (Art. 1 Act No. 25/1920 amended under Art. 2 Act No. 100/1985). That the wife shall lose her maintenance right if she apostasizes can be inferred under the Sharia and other laws from the fact that apostasy renders the marriage contract void (see Chapter 3.B.(3)). Apostasy of the wife and its relevance to her right to maintenance is also dealt with by the Hanafis and Shias in the context of maintenance after divorce. The Hanafis rule that the irrevocably divorced wife shall not lose the right to maintenance (during *iddat*) except while she is in prison for apostasy. But the revocably divorced wife who apostasizes shall lose her right of maintenance, and shall not recover it on her subsequent return to Islam.[12]

Contrariwise, the Shias allow the divorced wife who apostasizes her right to maintenance if the divorce is revocable, but not if it is irrevocable. She also restores her right on reconversion.[13]

Tyabji suggests an explanation for this discrepancy between the Hanafis and the Shias. For the Hanafis, he takes the view that the reason is their disapproval of irrevocable divorces, some of which are even considered sinful, and therefore the husband is mulcted in maintenance in all circumstances after such irrevocable divorce. On the other hand, the Shias do not permit the disapproved kinds of divorce and a considerable part of the *iddat* expires before any pronouncement of divorce can become irrevocable under the Shia Law. This law considers divorces revocable and irrevocable on the same footing and a wife is more favoured during the period when the divorce is still revocable than after it has become irrevocable[14] (see Chapter 6).

(6) Loss of maintenance due to court procedure

Apart from the Sharia provisions in respect of the loss of the wife's right to maintenance, the Jordanian Law contains procedural provisions that would result in such a loss. Under Jordanian Law, Article 20, there shall be no maintenance for the period preceding agreement between the parties or application to the judge in respect of fixing an amount for maintenance. Under Article 17 of the Egyptian Act 25/1929, no *iddat* maintenance action shall be heard by the court for a previous period of more than a year from the date of the divorce. According to the Jordanian Act (Art. 80), if the divorcee was served with the document of divorce at least a month before the completion of her *iddat*, she shall lose her right to maintenance if she fails to claim it before the expiry of the *iddat*.

---

[10] Abu Zahra, *op. cit.* p. 240.
[11] Al-Hilli, *op. cit.* p. 44.
[12] Alamgir, *Al Fatawa Alangiriyya Almaarufa bil Fatawal Hindiyya*, Vol. 1, pp. 557/8.
[13] Al-Hilli, *op. cit.* pp. 83, 84.
[14] Tyabji, *Muhammadan Law* (Bombay, 1940), p. 323.

C. Assessment of Maintenance

The ultimate sources which made maintenance the right of the wife on her husband, namely the Quran and the Prophet's Traditions, did not discuss it in detail, but simply ruled that the husband shall spend according to his means: "Let him who hath abundance spend of his abundance, and he whose provision is restricted, let him spend of that which Allah hath given him. Allah asketh naught of any soul save that which He hath given it. Allah will vouchsafe, after hardship, ease." (65:7) It was left, therefore, to the jurists to assess the amount of maintenance which varies according to social environments, style of life and differences of persons, times and regions. The Hanafis rule that the matrimonial maintenance must be enough to satisfy the woman's needs, and therefore cannot be fixed *per se* and shall be assessed according to observed custom. The Shafiis dissent, ruling that maintenance is assessed under the Sharia, though they agree with the Hanafis that the condition of the husband must be taken into consideration whether he is affluent, impoverished or of average means. The Hanbalis assess the maintenance left unspecified in the Quran according to custom, considering again the conditions of the rich, the impoverished and the average.[15]

If the husband provides the wife with sufficient food, clothing and other basic needs and a decent home, there shall be no point in the wife requiring any maintenance from the court. This method of providing maintenance for the wife is called *tamkeen*, and is the normal way of living together as man and wife.

There is another method of maintenance for the wife which is the exceptional course of matrimonial life. Under this method called *tamleek*, (i.e. passing property) a certain amount shall be paid for the wife's maintenance whether by agreement or by court order. It can be either in kind such as food and clothing, or it may be an amount of money.

The judge, in assessment of the matrimonial maintenance, shall take into account the financial condition of the husband, regardless of the wife's condition, and the market prices. The judge's assessment may be revised upwards or downwards if this is requested by the interested spouse.

In assessing the house rent, the judge shall take into consideration the financial condition of the husband and the level of the rents. "Proper home" must fulfil four conditions:

(i)   to be fit for the husband's condition, and comparable to the home of his equals according to custom;
(ii) to be solely for the use of the spouses without any third party even of their spouses' kin except the husband's child who has not reached the age of discretion;
(iii) all domestic appliances must be provided in accordance with the husband's means;
(iv) the home must be in a decent neighbourhood among good neighbours where the person and property of the wife are securely safe.[16]

These are the general Sharia provisions adopted in the modern laws of Egypt (Act 25/1929, Art. 16), Syria (Art. 76), Kuwait (Art. 76) and Jordan (Art. 70).

---

[15] Explanatory Note to Egyptian Act No. 25/1929.
[16] Abdullah, *Personal Status*, pp. 368/375.

The Iraqi legislator alone rules that the wife's maintenance shall be assessed against the husband according to the condition of both spouses (Art. 27).

Maintenance may be increased or decreased in accordance with the change of the husband's condition and the market prices, Syrian Law (Art. 77) implies the right to ask for increase or decrease in the court order of the amount of maintenance. The Jordanian Law (Art. 71) follows the Syrian Law (Art. 77/2) in ruling that no application for such an increase or decrease shall be heard before the lapse of six months from the court order, save in exceptional emergencies, e.g. soaring prices. A similar ruling prevails in the Sudan (Art. 67:122). Kuwaiti Article 77 and Omani Article 46 make the time limit one year. The Iraqi and the Druze Codes (Arts. 28/1 and 29, respectively) allow such an amendment of the assessment of maintenance if there is any change in the condition of both spouses. Like the Jordanian and Syrian Acts, Iraqi Article 28/2 allows the consideration of increase or decrease of the ordered maintenance in the event of emergencies, without stipulating the time limit.

The judge shall order maintenance against the husband who fails to honour his obligation of maintenance as from the date of such failure (Arts. 78, Syrian; 30, Lebanon Druze Act; and 73, Jordanian).

The Algerian Article 78, provides that maintenance becomes due from the date of the commencement of court proceedings.

The Syrian Article paragraph 2 rules that no maintenance for more than four months prior to the legal action shall be ordered. The Jordanian Article empowers the judge to order the payment of maintenance in advance. The Jordanian, Iraqi and Lebanese Acts deal with the absent husband who leaves his wife without maintenance or moves to a destination far or near, or is considered missing (Arts. 76, 29 and 32, respectively). In this case, the judge shall assess the wife's maintenance as from the date of application to the court on the strength of the evidence submitted by the wife of the existent state of matrimony. She must also make an oath that the husband has left her no maintenance and that she is neither disobedient nor divorced, having counted her *iddat*.

The Iraqi Article adds that the judge may permit her if necessary to borrow on behalf of the husband. Sudanese Article 7(2) makes the decision that of the judge.

If the wife is awarded maintenance against the husband which cannot be collected from him, her maintenance shall be the obligation of any person whose duty it would have been to maintain her if she was not married, and he shall have the right to recover it from the husband (Arts. 80/1, Syrian; 75, Jordanian). If she borrowed maintenance from a stranger who is under no obligation to maintain her, the creditor has the choice to recover the loan from the husband or the wife (Arts. 80/2, Syrian; 33, Druze). The Jordanian and Kuwaiti laws remain silent on this point. The Iraqi Act adds that in the absence of any person willing to lend the money, with the wife incapable of earning a living, her maintenance shall be the duty of the State.

During the consideration of the court action, the judge may order a provisional maintenance of the wife against the husband. Such an order would be effective immediately (Arts. 82/2 and 2, Syrian; 31/1 Iraqi; 79a Kuwaiti; Art. 16, Egyptian Act No. 25/1920 and 71(1) Sudanese).

Algerian Article 80 enacts that the judge may order the payment of maintenance on the strength of evidence, for a period of one year prior to the commencement of court proceedings.

The accumulated sum of maintenance shall not be lost as a result of divorce or the death of either husband or wife.

Maintenance of the divorcee is an obligation on the husband and shall be ordered as from the date of counting the *iddat* (Arts. 83 & 84, Syrian; 80, Jordanian; and Art. 2, Egyptian Act No. 25/1920).

The maximum period of the maintenance during the *iddat* shall not exceed nine months in Syria, or one year in Jordan.

Jordanian Article 81 denies the divorced wife during her disobedience any maintenance during her *iddat*.

Iraqi Article 50 dissents, ordering maintenance during the *iddat* for the divorcee against her living husband even if she is disobedient, but rules out any maintenance during the *iddat* of death. The last ruling is upheld by Kuwaiti Article 164.

The obligation on the husband to provide maintenance for his wife lapses on any of the following occurrences: payment; discharge; the death of either spouse.

CHAPTER 6

Dissolution of Marriage

1. Introduction: Methods of Dissolution

Under the Sharia, marriage may be dissolved, during the life-time of the parties thereto:

(i) by the act of the husband in three forms:
   (a) repudiation (*talaq*),
   (b) injurious assimilation (*zihar*), or
   (c) vow of continence (*ilaa*)
(ii) by the spouses, either by mutual agreement (*khula* or *mubaraat*); or imprecation (*lian*)
(iii) by a judicial order of separation in a suit by the husband or the wife on various grounds: divorce (*tafriq*).

The most common procedure has been the *talaq*, which is the right of the husband. However, modern personal status legislators show an increasing tendency to curb such a power of the man to the extent that, under some legislation, no divorce shall be effective, or even allowed, outside the court.

Dissolution of marriage is dealt with in separate chapters of the modern Personal Status Laws of Syria, Tunisia, Morocco, Iraq, Jordan, Algeria, Sudan, Yemen, Oman and Kuwait. Although no comprehensive personal status compendium has been promulgated in Egypt, various legal provisions have been decreed on the subject of dissolution of marriage under Act No. 25/1920 (on judicial separation on grounds of defects) and Act No. 25/1929 (on conditions of validity of repudiation, further grounds for separation by court order, arbitration, the missing or jailed husband), both being amended by Act. No. 100/1985.

In the following sections, we shall deal with the various forms of dissolution of marriage in the order given above.

2. Dissolution by the Husband

A. Repudiation – Talaq

The definition of repudiation according to the Sharia is "the dissolution of a valid marriage contract forthwith or at a later date by the husband, his agent or his wife duly authorized by him to do so, using the word *talaq*, a derivative or a synonym thereof."

106

This definition is almost universally adopted by the modern Arab personal status codes: Arts. 87/2, Syria; 44, Morocco; 34, Iraq; 128, Sudan; 81, Oman, (which defines it as "the dissolution of a marriage contract in the Sharia set formula") and 87, Jordan, where a written document is required. There are, however, two exceptions where divorce can only be effected by the court, for the Druzes (of the Lebanon, Art. 37 and of Syria, Art. 307), and in Tunisia (Art. 30).

The definition quoted sums up all the conditions for repudiation to be valid, effective and binding. Analysing the definition in detail, these conditions can be treated under the headings of: the valid marriage contract, the husband who pronounces the *talaq*, and the formula used.

a. The Existence of a Valid Marriage Contract

Repudiation is an effect of a valid marriage contract whereby the duties and rights emanating from the marital status are terminated either forthwith, in the irrevocable divorce, or after the lapse of the *iddat* in the revocable divorce.

The termination of a non-valid marriage contract is not a repudiation proper but an annulment, whether separation between the two parties is effected by them on their own accord or by an order of the court, and whether it occurs before or after consummation.

The modern laws expressly adopt this provision by ruling that the object in the repudiation is the wife under a valid marriage contract or counting her *iddat* of a revocable divorce. No repudiation of any other woman shall be valid even if it is suspended (Arts. 86, Syria; 45, Morocco; 103, Kuwait; and 84, Jordan). Therefore, the woman shall not be liable to repudiation in the following cases:

(a) if she is married under an invalid contract, since repudiation is by definition a dissolution of a valid marriage;
(b) if she is in her *iddat* of an irrevocable repudiation;
(c) if she is in her *iddat* as a result of a court order for separation on the grounds of the option of puberty or option of recovery from insanity or mental derangement, or for the dower being less than that of the equal;
(d) if she has completed her *iddat*, even if it was of a revocable repudiation; and
(e) if she is a divorcée prior to consummation or valid retirement.

These provisions are unanimously accepted by the Sunnis and Shias.[1]

b. The Husband

Apart from the legal texts governing the divorce of the Druzes and the Tunisians, repudiation is the right of the husband on fulfilling certain requirements, which are majority, sanity, and acting on his own free will, not under coercion. He must be aware of his utterances, regardless of his being of legal capacity or placed under interdiction on grounds of prodigality or imbecility. In the absence of any of these conditions, no repudiation shall be valid. It follows that the repudiation shall be void if uttered in any of the following cases:

---

[1] *Cf.* Abdullah, *Personal Status*, pp. 423–426; Abu Zahra, *On Marriage*, pp. 289–291; Al-Hilli, *Jaafari Personal Status Provisions*, p. 59.

(i)   by the minor, even if he possesses discretion, and even if approved by his guardian, since it is the exclusive right of the husband;

(ii) by the insane or the mentally deranged;

(iii) by a person in a state of alcoholic intoxication;

This position of the Malikis, Shafiis and Hanbalis, as against the Hanafis, who allow repudiation by such persons, is adopted by the Egyptian legislator (Art. 1, Act 25/1929) and followed by the Laws of Syria (Art. 89/1), Morocco (Art. 49), Iraq (Art. 35/1), Jordan (Art. 88/a), Kuwait (Art. 102), Sudan (Art. 134a and b) and Oman (Art. 83a and b). The Shias concur;[2]

(iv) by a person under coercion (the same Articles);

The Shias concur[3] but the Hanafis allow such a divorce on the ground that the husband would have a choice;

(v)   a person in a state of rage to the extent of losing discretion (Arts. 89/1, Syria, 49, Morocco, 35/1, Iraq, 88/a, Jordan, 102, Kuwait). The Syrian and Jordanian legislators call a person under such a state "the stunned" "*al madhoosh*" who is defined as "a person who lost discretion because of rage or otherwise to the point of becoming unaware of his uttering" (Arts. 89/2 and 88/b, respectively). The same description occurs in Kuwaiti Article 102;

(vi) the fainting or sleeping person – Jordanian (Art. 88/a). A special case in this context is a person suffering from a terminal or mortal sickness (*marad al-maut*). Article 1595 of the Mijalla gives the following definition of such a sickness: "Mortal sickness is characterized by a strong likelihood of death. It renders the patient incapable of looking after his interest out-of-doors if he is a male or indoors if she is a female. The patient shall die within a year whether bed-ridden or not. ..." The Iraqi legislators consider a repudiation by such a person void if he dies of that illness, and his wife shall inherit from him. The same ruling prevails if he was in a state where death is most likely (Art. 35/2). The Egyptian legislator (Inheritance Act No. 77/1943 Art. 11) and the Syrian legislator (Art. 116) provide that the wife shall inherit from the husband who repudiates her irrevocably (against her consent) during his mortal sickness or in a state where he is most likely to die and then dies because of that sickness, or in such a state while the wife is still counting her *iddat* provided that her entitlement to inheritance shall persist from the time of the irrevocable divorce until his death. But they do not follow the Iraqi legislator in ruling out such a repudiation altogether as void.

The husband who fulfils all the necessary requirements may pronounce repudiation either by himself or through an agent duly authorized by him who shall act on his behalf within the terms of his power of attorney. The husband may also authorize the wife to effect her repudiation either in the marriage contract or thereafter. However, the husband cannot stipulate on his own accord the wife's right to effect her repudiation. In such a case the marriage contract shall be valid and that stipulation shall be void. But if it is the wife who stipulated that she be granted that power as a condition in the marriage contract, and the husband agrees, both the contract and the condition shall be valid and effective. The husband may authorize the wife to effect her repudiation at any time after the conclusion of the marriage contract in writing.

[2] Al-Hilli, *op. cit.* pp. 58, 59.

[3] *Ibid.*

c. The Formula

The Iraqi, Sudanese and Omani legislators refer to the legally appropriate formula to be used (Arts. 128, 81 and 34, respectively). This formula is left unspecified and therefore recourse must be had to the Sharia regulations. The formula used by the husband for the pronouncement of repudiation includes the medium of expression and the grammatical construction.

(1) The medium of expression

Repudiation by the husband can be through any medium denoting the termination of the marital relationship, by word of mouth, in writing, or by gesture for him who is incapable of either of them. This general Sharia provision is held in the Laws of Syria (Art. 87/1), Morocco (Art. 46), Jordan (Art. 86), Kuwait (Art. 104) and Sudan (Art. 129).

The word used may be explicit (*sarih*) or implicit (*kinaya*). An explicit pronouncement of repudiation shall employ the word *talaq* or a derivative thereof and shall take effect regardless of the intention (*niyya*), according to all the Sunni schools and the modern laws of Syria and Jordan (Arts. 93 and 95, respectively).

The Shia Ithna-Ashari not only require a specific form: "You are repudiated" or "this" pointing to his wife, or "so and so" "is repudiated", but also stipulate the intention.[4] In other words, it must be specifically related to the wife concerned. They also reject the use of any metaphor to effect repudiation, even if the intention is proven, and even if there is circumstantial evidence to corroborate the intention. Yemeni Article 58 also rejects metaphor.

On the other hand, the Sunni schools allow the use of metaphor for repudiation, provided that the intention can be established, a ruling followed in Egypt (Art. 4, Act 25/1929), the Sudan (Art. 129(b)), Syria (Art. 93), Jordan (Art. 95), and Kuwait (Art. 104).

There is an essential difference between the Shias and the Sunnis. The Shias, both Ismailis and Ithna-Asharis, hold that there can be no repudiation without the presence of two honest men (no women witnesses are accepted) as dictated by the Quran "... and take for witness two persons endowed with justice from among you and establish the evidence before God" (65:2) The Sunnis see no reason for requiring witnesses on the ground that repudiation is an established right of the husband, and hence needs no evidence.[5]

(2) Grammatical construction

The Sunnis allow the formula used in a divorce pronouncement by the husband to be either absolute, unconditional, with immediate effect (*munjaz*), or contingent (*muallaq*), subject to a condition, in the form of an oath, or relegated to some event in future.

The Shias differ again, recognizing only the absolute unconditional formula, although they allow the formal suspension, i.e. subject to a condition that actually exists, e.g. "You are repudiated if you are my wife".[6]

---

[4] *Ibid.* p. 60.
[5] Al Kashiful Ghataa, *op. cit.* p. 279; Qadi an-Numan *op. cit.* Vol. 2, p. 211.
[6] Al-Hilli, *op. cit.* pp. 65/66.

The absolute pronouncement of repudiation shall be valid and take effect forthwith, provided that the husband and the wife comply with the conditions mentioned above, in countries where the husband has still the right to repudiate his wife without recourse to the court.

As for the contingent formula of a repudiation pronouncement, the Sunni jurists, followed by the law-makers in Egypt, Syria, Morocco and Jordan, distinguish between three cases:

(i) A contingent pronouncement where the condition is meant to urge to do or abstain from doing something, as when a husband says to his wife, "If you leave home, you shall be divorced", or, "If I sell this article, my wife shall be divorced". This formula is construed as an oath. The classical jurists ruled that, as such, the husband shall have to choose, if the condition occurs, between a religious expiation (*kaffara*) or to effect repudiation.[7] The Andalusian jurist Ibn Hazm Al-Zahiri rules that this form shall be void without need to expiation. The modern laws maintain straightforwardly that this form of repudiation is null and void. Egyptian Article 2 of Act 25/1929 stipulates "No contingent repudiation shall occur if it is meant to urge the doing of or abstention from any act." The same article is repeated in Jordanian Article 89, Moroccan Article 52, Sudanese Article 130(a) and (b), Yemeni Articles 65/66, and Omani Articles 85/86. The Syrian Article 90 adds the repudiation meant as an oath or for emphasis. Moroccan Article 50 is more specific: "No repudiation shall occur using an oath." Jordanian Article 92 is more restrictive: "No repudiation shall occur using an oath such as 'Repudiation befall me' or 'My wife is prohibited to me' unless the repudiation formula implies that the wife is addressed or meant." Omani Article 56(a) concurs without the last reservation.

(ii) A contingent pronouncement where the intention is that repudiation shall occur if a certain thing happens, as when a husband says to his wife "If you commit adultery you shall be repudiated", or "If you release me of your deferred dower you shall be repudiated." The Sunni jurists, again with the exception of Ibn Hazm, rule that divorce shall duly occur if the condition happens. This ruling is maintained expressly in the Jordanian Law (Art. 96) and, by implication, in the Egyptian, Syrian and Moroccan Laws. Jordanian Article 96 reads, "It is valid to make repudiation subject to a condition and to defer it to the future. No refrain by the husband from suspended or deferred repudiation shall be admitted".

Both instances of contingent repudiations are dismissed in the Iraqi Article 36 which also rules out the third instance of non-absolute repudiation, following the Shia School.

(iii) A pronouncement deferred to the future is recognized as shown above in the Jordanian Article 96. The four major Sunni Schools agree that this is a valid repudiation, but differ on the time when it comes in force. For example, a husband says to his wife "You are repudiated in a year's time." The Hanafis and Malikis maintain that she shall be repudiated forthwith. The Shafiis and Hanbalis rule that divorce shall not occur until the end of the year. Ibn Hazm, and the Shias, consider it a void repudiation.[8] Kuwaiti Article 105 stipulates that repudiation should be unconditional (*munjaz*).

---

[7] Ibn Qayyim Al-Jouzia, *Alam-ul-Muwaqqeen*, Vol. 3, p. 71.
[8] Al Hilli, *op. cit.* p. 66.

d. *Modes of Repudiation*

A repudiation may be effected in two ways:

(i) *Sunnat*, in the sense of the right way, as well as a Tradition of the Prophet. It consists of one pronouncement uttered during a *tuhr*, that is a period of menstrual purity during which no sexual intercourse occurs. The *Sunnat* repudiation is again subdivided into *ahsan* (most approved) and *hasan* (good or approved):

    (a) The *talaq ahsan* consists of a single pronouncement made during a period of menstrual purity and followed by abstinence from sexual intercourse for the period of *iddat*;

    (b) The *talaq hasan* consists of three pronouncements made over three consecutive periods of menstrual purity during which no intercourse takes place. It becomes irrevocable on the third pronouncement.

(ii) *Bidat* (innovated or heretical) – any repudiation effected disregarding the above requirements. The four Sunni schools consider it valid, albeit a sin.

Only the *Sunnat* repudiation is valid under the Shia Law which stipulates that the wife at the time of divorce must not be in menstrual or puerperal courses if the marriage has been consummated and the husband and wife co-habited. Nevertheless, the repudiation shall be valid if it is pronounced during a menstrual period if the marriage has not been consummated or while the husband is absent, having left his wife in a period of menstrual purity during which there was no intercourse, for a length of time during which another period of menstrual purity has occurred.[9]

Yemeni Article 62 recognises both *Sunnat* and *Bidat* repudiations. Moroccan Article 47 reflects a similar tendency: "If repudiation is pronounced while the woman is during menstruation, the Judge shall force the husband to revoke repudiation."

Related to the timing of the divorce is the number of pronouncements of repudiation. The Shia have always maintained that three repudiation pronouncements at one sitting is counted as a single, first one, which is revocable, like the second, but the third is irrevocable, and makes the divorcee a prohibited degree to the first husband, who cannot re-marry her until she is duly married to and divorced from another. That was the rule in the reign of the Prophet and Abu Bakr and through the two years under Omar, who decreed that one declaration of repudiation associated with the number three should count as three pronouncements and render repudiation irrevocable.

The majority of Sunni jurists abided by this ruling which remained in force until modern legislators adopted the Shia position in the new Islamic Personal Status Statutes. It started with the Egyptian Law No. 25/1929 Article 3: "A repudiation in which a number is implied whether verbally or by a gesture shall be counted as one." The same provision has been adopted in Syria (92), Morocco (51), Iraq (37/2), Jordan (85), Kuwait (109), Algeria (51), Sudan (130/C), Yemen (64) and Oman (86/6). The Shia rule that the woman shall be eternally in a prohibited degree to the husband on the ninth pronouncement.[10]

---

[9] *Ibid.* p. 65.
[10] Al Kashiful Ghataa, *op. cit.* p. 280.

e. Revocable and Irrevocable Pronouncements of Repudiation

All forms of dissolution of marriage are either revocable – *raji*, or irrevocable – *bain*, in terms of their legal effects.

(1) The revocable repudiation

The revocable repudiation, which is usually the rule, does not dissolve marriage until the period of *iddat* is completed. At any time during this period, the husband has the option to revoke the pronouncement either expressly by word of mouth or implicitly by resuming marital relations, without the necessity of a new contract or a new dower, and without even the consent of the wife.

This provision is based on the Quranic ruling: "And their husbands have the better right to take them back in that period if they wish for reconciliation" coming a few lines after "Repudiated women shall wait concerning themselves for three monthly periods." (2:228)

This Quranic ruling is adopted in all Islamic countries even though it is not mentioned expressly except in the Jordanian Article 97, which adds that the husband's right to take back his wife during the *iddat* cannot be relinquished, a ruling adopted in Sudanese Article 139, and by the Shia. The Iraqi Article 38 requires the same proof for revocation of repudiation as for repudiation itself. On revocation, the Shia Ithna-Ashari and the Ismaili, unlike in the case of repudiation, do not require witnesses, nor even that the wife be informed of it, but consider it recommendable for the record.[11]

On the other hand, the marriage is dissolved forthwith on the utterance of an irrevocable pronouncement, apart from the Druzes, to whom every divorce is irrevocable for ever (Art. 38, Lebanese Act of 24/2/1948 and Syrian Art. 307/g). Usually every repudiation is deemed revocable except in certain cases listed by the Egyptian, Sudanese, Syrian and Kuwaiti legislators (Arts. 5, Egyptian Act No. 25/1929; 5, Sudanese Sharia Circular No. 41/1935; 94, Syrian and 110, Kuwaiti). These cases are:

(a) *A repudiation completing three divorces.* Under the Quaranic ruling "A divorce is only permissible twice: after that the parties should either hold together on equitable terms or separate with kindness." (2:229) The three repudiations must be separate, in three different sittings, divided by three *iddats* as explained in the Sunna repudiation. Three pronouncements of repudiation or one pronouncement combined with a number denoted verbally or by a gesture shall be counted as one (Arts. 3, Egyptian Act No. 25/1929; 3, Sudanese Sharia Circular No. 41/1935; 92, Syrian; 51, Moroccan; 37/2, Iraqi; 85, Jordanian; 109, Kuwaiti) (See above d.).

(b) *A repudiation prior to consumation.* The marriage is dissolved in this case immediately without any waiting period, under the Quranic verse: "O ye who believe! When ye marry believing women, and then repudiate them before ye have touched them, no period of *iddat* have ye to count in respect of them; so give them a present, and set them free according to decent custom." (33:49)

---

[11] Al-Hilli, *op. cit.* p. 69; Qadi an-Numan, *op. cit.* p. 241.

(2) *Types of irrevocable repudiation*

The irrevocable repudiation is again subdivided into minor – *bain bainoona sughra* and major – *bain bainoona kubra*. In the minor irrevocable repudiation, the husband may remarry his repudiated wife under a new contract, for a new dower and subject to her consent. Such is the case after the lapse of *iddat* of the first and second repudiation by the husband. In the major irrevocable repudiation, occurring after the third pronouncement by the husband, the wife becomes temporarily prohibited for the husband to remarry. He can only remarry her after she has been duly married to another, genuine consummation has taken place, her second marriage has been duly dissolved, and she has counted her *iddat*, or the second husband has died. This general Sharia rule is observed throughout the Islamic world, even codified in the Jordanian Article 100. Only Tunisian Article 19, prevents the husband for ever from remarrying the wife he has repudiated three times, following the Hanbalis who consider a marriage with a view to making the wife later lawful to her first husband void and religiously prohibited.

When the husband is allowed to remarry his wife whom he has previously repudiated and whose later marriage to another husband has since then been dissolved, the majority of jurists maintain that the former husband shall be entitled to three pronouncements anew. Indeed, Kuwaiti Article 108 rules that the former husband shall have such a right if his divorcée married another man and was later divorced from him.

On the repudiation becoming irrevocable, the wife shall be entitled to her deferred dower at once. Should either spouse die after an irrevocable repudiation, there shall be no inheritance by the surviving spouse on grounds of matrimony. The only exception is if the husband was on his deathbed and it could be proved that he was repudiating his wife with the malicious intention of depriving her of her inheritance rights. In this case, she would retain her inheritance rights, although he would not retain his, should she die before him.

To prove malicious intention, the following conditions must be fulfilled:

(i)   that the irrevocable repudiation occurs against her will;
(ii) that the husband died after an illness during which the repudiation occurred and before her *iddat* was completed;
(iii) that the irrevocably repudiated woman shall be eligible at the time of the repudiation to inherit; for example, that she was not then of another religion. If she was, and then converted to Islam after the repudiation, she shall not inherit from her Muslim husband.[12]

B. *Injurious Assimilation (Zihar) and Vow of Abstention (Ilaa)*

Zihar has been briefly referred to, *supra* Introduction (2), as a pre-Islamic formula in which the husband compares his wife to a relative within a prohibited degree, e.g. his mother. The Quran described this device, and rules as follows:

"God has indeed heard the statement of the woman who pleads with thee concerning her husband and carries her complaint to God: and God hears the arguments between both sides among you: for God hears and sees. If any men

---

[12] Abu Zahra, *op. cit.* pp. 316–320; Abdullah *op. cit.* p. 470; Al-Hilli, *op. cit.* pp. 68–70.

among you divorce their wives by *zihar* (calling them mothers), they cannot be their mothers: none can be their mothers except those who gave them birth, verily they use words iniquitous and false: but truly God is One that blots out (sins), and forgives. But those who divorce their wives by *zihar*, then wish to go back on the words they uttered, – (it is ordained that such a one) should free a slave before they touch each other: this are ye admonished to perform: and God is well-acquainted with (all) that ye do. And if any has not (the wherewithal), he should fast for two months consecutively before they touch each other. But if any is unable to do so, he should feed sixty indigent ones." (58: 1–4)

In *ilaa* the husband makes an oath of abstention from the wife for four months or more. This device is regulated in the Quran: "For those who take an oath of abstention from their wives, a waiting of four months is ordained." (2:336) The Hanafis maintain that such a divorce shall be irrevocable after the lapse of the four months. The Malikis, Shafiis, Hanbalis and the Shias make the separation subject to a pronouncement of divorce by the husband or to a suit by the wife. It is then deemed revocable, although Malik makes return to the married status contingent on consummation. The Moroccan and Kuwaiti Laws deal with this form of divorce (Arts. 58 and 123/124 respectively), giving the wife the right to apply to the judge who shall give the husband a delay of four months, after which a revocable divorce decree is issued.

More recently the Sudanese Personal Status Law of 1991 devotes a whole chapter to *zihar* and *ilaa* (and *lian*), the Yemeni Law of 1922 deals in two chapters with *zihar* and *ilaa*, while the Omani Law of 1997 treats *ilaa* and *zihar* in two Articles, 113 and 114.

The Sudanese Law, like the Yemeni, requires that the husband must enjoy the legal capacity necessary to pronounce repudiation, but then permits the wife to apply for divorce from the husband who fails to perform expiation to make her lawful again to him.

The Yemeni Law recognizes explicit and metaphoric *zihar* which is also either absolute or conditional. The wife becomes lawful again in the absolute *zihar* if the husband performs expiation, and in the conditional on the condition being fulfilled, or, if it is timed, on the time lapsing. The wife may apply for divorce and the judge shall give the husband a four month delay for expiation and then order divorce. Similar provisions apply for the oath of *ilaa*.

Under the Omani Law, the marriage is dissolved by the husband's *zihar* unless it is lifted by expiation within four months – exactly like the *ilaa* which is considered also as an oath.

Sudanese Article 193 allows the wife to apply for divorce because of the *ilaa* if the husband sticks to his oath for more than four months.

The Ismailis, on the authority of Imam Ali, hold that *zihar* shall be valid only when the wife is in the purity stage of her menstrual cycle without intercourse. If the husband takes an oath of *zihar* several times in one sitting, it will count as one, and requires one expiation. Otherwise several oaths shall require as many expiations. In a report of a Tradition of the Prophet, Imam Jaafar recites that a man confessed to the Prophet that he took an oath of *zihar* against his wife and asked what to do. The Prophet ordered him to perform expiation in the form of manumission of a slave, fasting two consecutive months, feeding sixty poor persons, all of which he could not afford. The Prophet then gave him a measure of wheat to feed sixty at which the man replied that he knew no-one in more need of food than he and his dependants. To which the Apostle of God replied "Go then and feed thyself and thy dependants."[13]

Al-Hilli does not mention *zihar* or *lian* in his manual on *Jaafari Personal Status Provisions*. Al Kashiful Ghataa, in his treatise entitled *The Origins of Shia* says of *zihar*, *ilaa* and *lian* "These are also grounds to make the wife unlawful to her husband in general, and under specific conditions dealt with in reference books of jurisprudence, but which are not dealt with here because of their rarity."[14]

3. Dissolution by the Spouses

A. By Mutual Agreement

Apart from the divorce effected by the husband, marriage may be dissolved by mutual consent by the wife giving the husband something for her freedom under the Quranic ruling, "And it is not lawful for you that ye take from women aught of that which ye have given them except in the case when both fear that they may not be able to keep within the limits imposed by God. And if ye fear that they may not be able to keep the limits of God, it is no sin for either of them if the woman ransom herself." (2:229)

This form is called *khula*, an Arabic word which means "To take off one's dress", relating to a metaphoric description of the spouses in the Quranic verse "They are raiment for you and ye are raiment for them". (2:187) As seen in the previous verse, it may be called "ransom". Some jurists use also the word *mubaraat* (mutual discharge). One of these words, or a derivative thereof, must be used in this context, otherwise it shall be deemed a divorce for a pecuniary consideration (*talaq ala mal*), as when a husband says to his wife, "You are divorced for such and such sum of money" and she accepts. Both forms have in common that the dissolution takes effect forthwith, the consideration becoming due from the wife provided that she has the legal capacity thereto. They differ in that the divorce for a pecuniary consideration does not deprive the wife of her rights under the marriage contract, e.g. deferred dower and maintenance.[15]

Khula is dealt with in separate chapters in the Laws of Syria (Arts. 95–104), Morocco (Arts. 61–65), Iraq (Art. 46), Jordan (Arts. 102–112), Kuwait (Arts. 111–119), Sudan (Arts. 142–150), Yemen (Arts. 72–74) and Oman (Arts. 94–97). Tunisian Article 31 allows divorce by the spouses' consent before the court, a provision required also by Iraqi Article 46/1. Under Shia Law, the *khula*, like divorce, must be effected in the presence of two male Muslim witnesses of approved probity, and it must not be conditional.[16] The Ismailis add that it must occur during a menstrual purity, during which there was no intercourse.[17] The Druzes combine the penultimate two provisions, allowing dissolution of marriage by mutual consent to be declared in the presence of two witnesses

---

[13] Qadi Numan, *op. cit.* pp. 222/3.
[14] Al Kashiful Ghataa, p. 287.
[15] Abu Zahra, *op. cit.* pp. 327–338; Abdullah, *op. cit.* pp. 486–506.
[16] Al-Hilli, *op. cit.* pp. 71–75.
[17] Qadi an-Numan, *op. cit.* Vol. 2, p. 219.

before the judge who shall issue a divorce decree (Lebanese Druze Personal Status Act/1948, Art. 42).

For the *khula* to be valid, the husband must possess legal capacity to pronounce divorce and the woman must be a lawful object thereof (Arts. 95/1, Syrian; 46/1, Iraqi; 102/a, Jordanian; 112, Kuwaiti; 144, Sudanese; 73, Yemeni and 95, Omani). A woman under the age of majority shall not be liable for the *khula* consideration without the consent of her guardian of property (Arts. 95/2, Syrian; 62, Moroccan; 106/b, Jordanian). The Moroccan and Kuwaiti legislators add as a condition for the husband's entitlement to the *khula*, consideration that the *khula* by the woman shall be of her own accord and free choice to leave the husband without coercion or harassment (Arts. 63 and 116 respectively).

The juristic qualification of *khula* differs in the case of the husband, when it is deemed an oath, from the case of the wife when it is considered to be compensation. Therefore, according to the Hanafis, the husband cannot withdraw from the *khula* and cannot retain the condition of option. On the other hand, the wife may withdraw her offer of *khula* before the husband gives his acceptance, or may leave the hearing before his consent is given, thus retaining the condition option, during which she may accept or reject the *khula* offer. This Hanafi rule is dropped in the modern laws of Syria (Art. 96), Jordan (Art. 103), and Kuwait (Art. 113), which grant both parties the right to withdraw the *khula* offer before it is accepted by the other party, following thereby the Hanbali and Zaidi jurists.

The consideration for the *khula* may be pecuniary, advanced or deferred, or may be the nursing, maintenance and custody of their child. This provision is codified in an identical text reading "Everything that is a lawful object of obligation is suitable as a consideration for *khula*" in the laws of Syria (Art. 97), Morocco (Art. 64), Jordan (Art. 104) and Kuwait (Art. 114). Following a general Sharia provision, the Jordanian legislator holds that if the consideration is unlawful, divorce shall be revocable, and the husband shall lose the consideration agreed upon (Art. 102/c). Sudanese Article 146 concurs.

The husband may receive from his wife in consideration for the *khula* an amount which is more or less than her dower (Iraqi Art. 46/3).

If the *khula* is for a pecuniary consideration other than the dower, it shall be payable and the two parties to the *khula* shall be discharged of all liabilities in respect of the dower and the wife maintenance (Arts. 98, Syrian; 105, Jordanian). The same provision shall apply if the two parties fail to specify any consideration at the time of *khula* (Arts. 99, Syrian; 106, Jordanian). But the Algerian legislator empowers the judge, in the case of such a failure, to order a consideration not exceeding the dower of the equal at the time of judgment (Art. 54).

If the two parties to the *khula* declare that there is no consideration, the case shall be one not of *khula*, but of a simple revocable divorce (Arts. 100, Syrian; 107, Jordanian; 97b, Omani).

The *iddat* maintenance shall not be dropped, nor shall the husband be discharged therefrom unless the *khula* contract contains expressly such a stipulation (Arts. 101, Syrian; 108, Jordanian).

If it is stipulated in the *khula* contract that the husband shall be spared the fees for the fosterage or custody of the child, or that the wife shall keep the child, free of charge, for a given period or shall provide maintenance for it, and later she marries and leaves the child or dies, the husband shall be entitled to claim the equivalent of the fosterage and custody fees and the maintenance of the child for the rest of the period. But if the child dies, the father shall have no right for such a claim for the period following its death (Arts. 102/1, Syrian, 109, Jordanian). The Sudanese concur.

The father shall be liable to the maintenance of the child if the mother is indigent at the time of *khula* or becomes so later; such a maintenance shall be a debt on the mother (Arts. 102/2, Syrian; 110, Jordanian).

A condition in the *khula* contract that the father shall keep the child for the period of custody shall be void while the contract remains valid, and the child's lawful custodian shall take it, and the father, if poor, shall be liable only for its maintenance, under the Jordanian Article 111 and also for its custody fees according to the Syrian Article 103 and Kuwaiti Article 1187.

No maintenance due to the child from the father may be set off against a debt to the father from the mother who has the custody of the child (Art. 104, Syrian). Moroccan Article 65 is even more sweeping "Nothing connected with the rights of children may be a consideration for *khula*, if the woman is destitute". Sudanese Article 145 concurs.

Of the modern statutes, only the Kuwaiti Personal Status Act, Art. 119, deals with a specific case: the *khula* by a wife who suffers from a fatal illness (*marad-ul-maut*) a case covered by the classical and Shia jurists whose provisions are applied by courts. They rule that *khula* in such a case shall be valid and the divorce shall be deemed irrevocable, as if the *khula* has taken place before her illness, and the consideration to be within one-third of her estate if the heirs do not consent to anymore, with the following reservations

(i)   In the event of the death of the wife while still in her *iddat*, the husband shall be entitled to the least valuable of three options: the *khula* consideration, his share of her estate or a third of her net estate, as if the *khula* consideration was a bequest.

(ii) In the event of the wife's death during her illness but after completion of her *iddat*, the husband shall be entitled to the lesser amount of the *khula* consideration, or a third of her net estate. He shall no longer be entitled to a share of her estate as the marriage tie has been broken in all respects.

(iii) In the event of the wife's death after her recovery from the illness during which the *khula* occurred, the husband shall be entitled to the *khula* consideration.

The effect of a valid *khula* is a divorce of minor irrevocability: i.e. the husband may remarry the ransomed wife, after her *iddat*, under a new marriage contract and dower.

If the *khula* includes no specified pecuniary consideration, repudiation provisions apply. If the consideration is specified without describing the deal as a *khula*, it will be also of minor irrevocability unless the consideration is void, when the dissolution becomes revocable, subject to there not being two earlier repudiations. The Ithna-Ashari allow the wife to withdraw the consideration when the husband may revoke repudiation provided she is still in her *iddat*.[18]

---

[18] Al Kashiful Ghataa, *op. cit.* p. 287.

B. Dissolution by Mutual Imprecation (Lian)

In the case of imprecation (*lian*), the husband affirms under oath that the wife has committed adultery and that the child born of her is not his, and she affirms under oath the contrary, according to the Quran:

> "And for those who launch a charge against their spouse, and have no witness but themselves, their solitary evidence is that they bear witness four times by God that they are solemnly telling the truth. And the fifth (oath) that they solemnly invoke the curse of God on themselves if they tell a lie. But it would avert the punishment from the wife, if she bears witness four times by God, that (her husband) is telling a lie; and the fifth (oath) is that she solemnly invokes the wrath of God on herself if (her accuser) is telling the truth." (24:6–8)

Classical jurists, both Sunni and Shia (Ithna-Ashari and Ismaili alike) agree that *lian* was the solution of a problem brought to the Prophet by a husband who complained that if he knew for sure that his wife was adulterous, or that her child was not his, he could not accuse her without bringing in four righteous male witnesses, or else would face the penalty of false accusation (*qadhf*). Nor could he stay with her with that certainty. The *lian* would spare him the necessity to bring in witnesses and saves him the *qadhf* penalty (eighty strokes of the whip). The wife would also avoid the penalty of adultery (stoning to death) if she refuted his accusation under oath.

Each spouse may ask the Imam or judge to perform *lian* before him. He would then order an irrevocable dissolution of marriage for life. An existing child or a child in the womb would not then be the husband's but that of the wife and her family within which it would have mutual inheritance rights.

Before *lian*, the husband can withdraw his accusation and pay the *qadhf* penalty, and the marriage continues, and any child will be his, and will inherit from him, although not vice-versa, but the woman remains prohibited to him for ever.

The modern Personal Status Laws of Sudan, Yemen and Oman deal with *lian*, the two former in some detail. The husband must be the first to make the oaths, followed by the wife (Sudanese Art. 200 (b), Yemeni 109). After the oath having been taken in that order, and in specific form, the judge orders their separation for ever, and the negation of the paternity (Yemeni Art. 110). If the imprecating man, during his lifetime, withdraws his denial of paternity, it shall be valid, the child will be his, and he will receive the *qadhf* penalty, but the prohibition against remarriage shall stand for ever. (Art. 112)

The Sudanese differ, ruling that the imprecating couple may remarry, under new contract and dower, if the husband admits he was lying and the *qadhf* punishment is inflicted upon him. (Art. 203)

The Omani Law simply rules that "Dissolution of marriage by way of *lian* is deemed recision." (Art. 118 (b)).

4. Dissolution of Marriage by the Court

In the case of *lian*, although applied for by both spouses, it is the court that decrees separation. In the present era, the court has an active role both in

Tunisia, and for the Druzes in Lebanon and Syria where divorce can only be effected before and by order of the judge. In some other countries, e.g. Iraq and Algeria, divorce even by the husband shall take effect from the time it is recorded with the court of jurisdiction of the locality if not before the judge.

Here I shall deal with the actual intervention by the court to effect dissolution of marriage. This is called "divorce proper" according to Black's *Law Dictionary* (5th ed., West Publishing Co., Paul Minn, 1979). In Arabic it is *tafriq* or *tatleeq* in the Sudanese Law, a subject of controversy among jurists. The Shia Ithna-Ashari allow the *tafriq* only in the event of the husband's impotence, provided that the wife shall apply to the court for divorce, and that she has not known about it at the time of marriage, and that she applies for divorce immediately she knows of her husband's impotence.[19] For the Lebanese Shias, divorce by the court does not apply.[20]

The Yemeni Law devotes a whole chapter (Arts. 43–57) to dissolution of marriage by the court which it calls recission (*faskh*) and considers it creating a separation of minor irrevocability – and should not be counted as a repudiation (Art. 56).

The Hanafis maintain that dissolution of marriage is the exclusive right of the husband, with the court having the right to intervene only in the event of a serious genital defect of the husband such as impotence or castration. The Hanafi jurist Muhammad adds insanity and leprosy. The other three major Sunni Imams, Malik, ash-Shafii and Ahmad ibn-Hanbal grant the wife the right to apply to the court for divorce on specific grounds, the judge in such a case being asked to act on behalf of the husband to redress an injury. This more liberal interpretation has been adopted in the Ottoman Family Rights Act, which is the law applicable to the Sunni Muslims of the Lebanon, followed by the laws of Syria, Morocco, Iraq, Jordan, Algeria, Kuwait, Sudan and Oman.

The Tunisian Mijalla, apart from investing the court with the exclusive power to effect divorce, rules that divorce shall be ordered:

(i)   at the request of either spouse on grounds under the said Mijalla;
(ii) by mutual consent of the two spouses;
(iii) at the request of the husband to obtain divorce or the wife applying for it (Arts. 30 and 31).

However, it adds that the judge shall not order divorce except after doing his utmost to resolve the grounds of dissent between the two spouses and finding it impossible to reconcile them.

As for the other said laws, there are five grounds for applying to the court for divorce:

(a) injury or discord;
(b) a defect on the part of the husband;
(c) failure to pay maintenance;
(d) absence of the husband without an acceptable excuse;
(e) the imprisonment of the husband.

I shall now deal with those grounds in the above order.

---

[19] Al-Hilli, *op. cit.* p. 76.
[20] B. Baylani, Lebanese Personal Status Acts (Cairo, 1971), p. 134.

A. Injury or Discord

The two Imams Malik and Ahmad Ibn-Hanbal maintain that the wife may ask the judge to order divorce if she claims that the husband has caused her such an injury as to make the continuation of the marital life between the likes of them impossible. They cite the following examples; beating, insulting or forcing her to an outrage. Imam Abu Hanifa and Imam ash-Shafii dissent, holding that injury is no sound ground for divorce as it can be remedied through reprimanding the husband, or the wife's refusal to obey him. According to the first opinion, the judge must be convinced of the validity of the wife's claim either on the strength of her evidence or the admission of the husband. If the injury is such as to make their continued life together unbearable and the judge cannot reconcile them, then he shall order an irrevocable divorce. If the wife cannot prove her case, or the husband makes no confession, the case shall be dismissed. If she repeats her complaint and requests a divorce and the court cannot establish the validity of her claims, the judge shall appoint two arbiters who are adult, of known propriety, well-acquainted with the spouses and capable of effecting a reconciliation. Preferably they shall be relatives of the spouses but otherwise they can be strangers. They shall investigate the causes of discord between the two spouses and attempt, as far as possible, to effect a reconciliation. Should they fail and the two spouses or the husband were to blame for the injury, or if the arbiters could not establish the facts, they shall decide on an irrevocable divorce. If the wife is to blame for the injury, they shall be separated through *khula*. Imams Abu Hanifa, Ahmad ibn-Hanbal and ash-Shafii make the arbiters' decision on divorce subject to being authorized thereto by the husband. Should the two arbiters fail to reach a consensus, the judge shall order them to make further investigations, and if they fail this time, he shall appoint two others, and their award shall be binding on him. This is all based on the Quranic verse: "And if ye fear a breach between them twain (the man and the wife), appoint an arbiter from his folk and an arbiter from her folk. If they desire amendment Allah will make them of one mind. ..." (4:35), and on another Quranic verse "A divorce is only permissible twice, and then (a woman) should either be retained in honour or released in kindness. ..." (2:29).

The jurists argue that should retaining in honour not be the case, then releasing in kindness shall prevail. The jurists also quote the authentic Tradition of the Prophet "There shall be no injury and no injury shall be remedied with another injury." The modern Islamic legislations have adopted these provisions (Egyptian Act No. 25/1929 as amended by Act No. 100/1985, Arts. 6, 7, 8, 9, 10 and 11; Syrian Arts. 112, 113, 114, 115; Tunisian Art. 32 as amended under Act No. 7/1981; Moroccan Art. 56; Iraqi Arts. 40, 41 and 42; Jordanian Art. 132 paras. a–i inclusive; Algerian Art. 53 paras. 6 and 7 and Art. 56; Kuwaiti Arts. 126 to 135; Sudanese Arts. 162–179 and Omani Arts. 101–108) with various additions as follows:

(a) Syria. Either spouse may apply to the court for divorce on the ground of injury by the other, and the judge shall effect an irrevocable divorce between them if he fails to reconcile them, having been convinced of the injury. If the injury is not proved, the judge shall adjourn the case for at least a month in the hope of a reconciliation being reached, failing which, with the applicant insisting

on the dissolution of marriage, the judge shall appoint arbiters in the above manner, who shall swear on oath to accomplish their brief in fairness and honesty.

The arbiters shall hold a meeting under the auspices of the judge to be attended by the spouses and those invited by the arbiters solely.

The failure of either spouse to attend such a meeting, having been notified thereof, shall not affect the award. If the injury, or most of it, is on the part of the husband, the arbiters, having failed to reconcile the spouses, shall award an irrevocable divorce. If they find the injury or most of it, on the part of the wife, or equally due to both spouses, they shall award a divorce and order the full dower or a commensurate part thereof to the injury. The arbiters may also award the divorce without establishing the injury on either party, releasing the husband of a part of the wife's right subject to her consent. Should the arbiters disagree, the judge shall replace them, or add to them an umpire with a casting vote. The judge may accept the arbiters' award or reject it, in which case he shall appoint for the last time two other arbiters. The Sudanese Law is similar.

The Omani Law concurs, ruling that the judge shall order divorce if (a) the wife applies for it on the ground of injury before consummation or valid retirement; (b) returns to the court the dower she has received and monies the husband has spent in respect of the marriage; (c) the husband still refuses to repudiate; and (d) no reconciliation has been attained (Art. 108).

(b) Tunisia. The new Article 31 as amended under Act. No. 7/1981 rules that the injured spouse shall be granted damages for any material or moral injury inflicted as a result of divorce at the request of either party. The woman shall receive damages for any material injury in the form of a monthly allowance, to run after the expiry of the *iddat*, to secure for her the same standards of living she was accustomed to during her marriage. Such an allowance shall be liable to revision upwards or downwards as circumstances change, and shall continue for the lifetime of the divorcee or until she remarries and her social status changes, or on acquiring such property as to enable her to do without such an allowance. It shall be a charge on the estate of the ex-husband on his death, to be settled through an agreement with the heirs or by court order for a lump sum to be determined with due consideration of her age at that date, unless she opts from the start for a lump sum in compensation for the material injury in a single payment.

Article 32 as amended under the same Act, provides that the court president, on failing to effect reconciliation between the two spouses, shall order all the necessary measures in respect of the matrimonial home, maintenance, custody of and access to the ward, unless the two parties agree expressly on leaving all or any such matters pending. His order shall be enforceable forthwith, and shall be liable for revision but not for appeal. The court shall rule in the first instance on divorce and all the matters related thereto, and determine the amount of the monthly allowance. Notwithstanding any appeal, the court orders in respect of custody, maintenance, monthly allowance, accommodation and access to the ward shall be enforceable forthwith.

(c) Iraq. Under Law No. 21/1978, amending some Articles of Law No. 188/1959, The Iraqi legislator, while granting both spouses leave to apply to the court for a divorce, distinguishes between the grounds of injury (Art. 40 – as amended) and of discord (Art. 41 – as amended).

Under injury, the Act lists the following grounds:

(i)   marital infidelity by either spouse;
(ii)   marriage contract being solemnized, without the Judge's permission, before either spouse completes 18 years of age;
(iii) marriage being concluded outside the court through coercion, and consummation having occurred;
(iv)   the husband taking another wife without the court's permission, without the wife having the right to set the criminal prosecution which shall be a public right.

Article 41 allows each spouse to apply to the court for a divorce in the event of any dispute between them, whether before or after consummation. The court shall then investigate the causes of discord, and, having found that it existed, shall appoint an arbiter related to the wife, and another related to the husband if possible, failing which the court shall order the spouses to elect two arbiters. If the spouses disagree, the court shall appoint the arbiters who shall try their utmost to reconcile them, failing which they shall report to the court on the responsibility for the injury. If they disagree, the court shall add an umpire with a casting vote. If the court is convinced of the continuation of dissension between the two spouses and fails to reconcile them, and the husband refuses to pronounce divorce, the court shall order a divorce. If divorce is ordered after consummation, the deferred dower shall be dropped if the injury is on the part of the wife, whether she is the applicant or the respondent, and she shall be ordered to repay an amount not exceeding half of the dower if she has received it in full. If both parties are responsible for injury, the deferred dower shall be divided in the proportion of their respective responsibility. If divorce is ordered before consummation and injury is proved on the part of the wife, she shall be ordered to repay the prompt dower she has received.

(d) Jordan. The Jordanian legislator (Art. 132), while allowing either spouse to apply to the court for divorce, distinguishes between the applicant being the wife or the husband. If it is the wife, and she can prove injury by the husband, the judge shall try his utmost to reconcile them, failing which he shall caution the husband to mend his ways, and shall adjourn the case for at least a month, at the end of which the judge shall refer the case to two arbiters (Art. 132/a).

If the husband is the applicant for divorce, and would prove dissension and discord, the judge shall adjourn the case for at least a month, at the end of which, without the husband withdrawing his application or reconciliation being reached, the judge shall refer the case to two arbiters (Art. 132/b) who shall record their findings in a report, and if they fail to effect reconciliation, and find against the wife, they shall award divorce for a consideration they set, provided it shall not be less than the dower.

If they find against the husband, they shall award an irrevocable divorce, reserving all the wife's rights as if it was the husband himself who effected the divorce (Art. 132/e).

If they find against both spouses, they shall award a divorce between them in the proportion of their respective injury. If they cannot apportion the injury, they shall fix the consideration at their discretion (Art. 132/f). If any consideration is awarded against the wife who is the applicant for divorce, she shall secure the payment thereof before the arbiters award divorce, unless the husband accepts the deferment of such consideration, and the judge shall order the divorce. If the husband is the applicant for divorce and the arbiters award a consideration against the wife, the judge shall uphold the award of both divorce and the consideration (Art. 132/g).

If the arbiters fail to reach agreement, the judge shall replace them, or add an umpire with a casting vote, and the majority award shall prevail. The judge shall rule according to the agreed findings of the arbiters' report if it conforms with the provisions of this Article 132/a–i inclusive.

(e) Algeria. The arbiters shall be kinsmen of the spouses, and shall submit a report of their findings within two months of their being appointed to reconcile between the spouses among whom there is a severe dissension without proving the injury.

It is considered an injury entitling the wife to apply to the court for divorce if the husband should abstain from connubial intercourse for more than four months (Art. 53/3) or commit a flagrant outrage (*ibid.* para. 7).

(f) Kuwait. If the two arbiters fail to reach an award, the court shall appoint a third, not being a kinsman of either spouse, with a casting vote and capable of repairing the rift (Art. 131/b). The three arbiters shall submit their unanimous or majority report to the court for decision. If they fail to agree or to report, the court shall proceed in the normal way (Art. 132/a and b). Injury shall be proven by the evidence of two men or a man and two women (Art. 133). Hearsay evidence, based on well-known facts about the life together of the two spouses, shall suffice to prove the occurrence, but not the absence, of injury (Art. 134). Evidence of the kin or a person connected with the person in whose favour the evidence is given shall be admitted, provided that witnesses possess the capacity thereto (Art. 135).

Yemeni Art. 54 provides that if the woman requests the court to order recision on the ground of discord, the judge shall investigate the cause. If it is proven, he shall appoint two arbiters from the respective two families to try reconciliation, or order the husband to repudiate. If the husband refuses, the judge shall himself order recision. The woman shall return the dower unless she gets her requested recision on proving that the husband is an alcoholic or a drug addict (Art. 55).

B. A Defect on the Part of the Husband

Divorce on the ground of a defect in either spouse is a subject of some controversy among Islamic jurists. To start with, there are two extreme positions. The Zahiris bar any divorce on account of a physical defect on the part of either the husband or the wife. According to Ibn Hazm "No marriage shall be nullified, once it is duly celebrated, by any leprosy, insanity, nor any other defect on the part of the wife, nor by impotence nor by a vaginal defect nor by any defect whatsoever."[21] On the other hand, the Hanbali jurist Ibn Qayyim maintains that every defect, whether on the part of the man or the wife, shall entitle the other spouse to petition for a divorce, since the contract was solemnized on the assumption of freedom from all defects, an implied condition based on custom, which ought to be fulfilled and was found to be lacking. He does not bother to enumerate

---

[21] Ibn Hazm, *Al-Muhalla*, Vol. 7, p. 109 (Cairo).

such defects, but gives the widest description of them as any shortcoming that causes aversion to the other spouse.[22]

Between these two extremes, there is a wide spectrum of juristic opinion. The Shias maintain that a wife who finds her husband impotent without having known it at the time of marriage is entitled to petition for divorce if she did not consent to the continuation of the marriage. She shall have the same right if impotence occurs after the contract and before consummation, but she shall lose that right if she does not apply for divorce and she knows about the defect. The judge shall investigate and if the husband declares that he has not consummated the marriage, the judge shall grant him a delay of a whole lunar year including Ramadan, the wife's menstrual cycles and any absences or illnesses of either spouse, to start from the date of petition, unless the husband was young, in which case the delay should count from the day he reaches puberty. At the end of the delay, if the woman still complains, the judge shall order a divorce. The wife may annul the marriage at the expiry of this delay without recourse to the judge. If she finds the husband mutilated, castrated, or insane, without having known that at the time of the marriage, and therefore asks for a divorce, it shall be granted forthwith. She also has the right to annul the marriage on her own. If the husband denies impotence he shall be believed on taking an oath; if he refrains and the wife takes an oath before the adjournment described, he shall be given a delay of a year. After the expiry of this delay, she shall have the choice at the same hearing. If she opts for divorce, it shall be granted. If she opts for the continuation, or leaves the hearing before making a choice, she shall lose that right.[23]

Imam Abu Hanifa and his disciples maintain that the judge has no power to order a divorce on the grounds of a defect on the part of the wife, as the husband possesses the right to repudiate her. They allow such a divorce to be ordered on the grounds of defects of the man. Abu Hanifa and Abu Youssof confine these defects to three genital ones: impotence, mutilation and castration, all being impediments of consummation and procreation, and constituting an injury to the wife. The judge, on the husband's refusal to repudiate, shall act on his behalf and order a divorce. A second disciple, Muhammad ibn ash-Shafii, adds the defects of insanity and leprosy. The three jurists set three conditions for such a divorce:

(i)   that the wife was not aware of the defect at the time of marriage;
(ii) that she petitions the court for a divorce and her case is proved;
(iii) that the judge shall order a divorce.

Mutilation shall entail a divorce forthwith. As for impotence and castration, the judge shall adjourn the case for a whole (lunar) year, not counting periods of the husband's being away, after which, in the absence of any improvement, the wife insisting on her application and the husband refusing to repudiate, the judge shall order an irrevocable divorce with the woman entitled to the whole dower if valid retirement had taken place.[24]

The three other Sunni Imams, Malik, ash-Shafii and Ahmad, allow a divorce

[22] Ibn Qayyim al-Jouzia, *Zad-ul-Maad*, Vol. 4 (Cairo, 1369H), pp. 30–31.
[23] Al-Hilli, *op. cit.* pp. 76–77.
[24] Al-Abiani, Sharia Personal Status Provisions, pp. 269–272; Abu Zahra, *op. cit.* pp. 354–359.

by the court on the grounds of such defects on the part of either spouse. But Malik maintains it shall be an irrevocable repudiation, arguing that if it is not by the husband, it is by a cause emanating from him, and the injury could only be remedied if this is an irrevocable repudiation. The Malikis also enlarge the scope of such defects, giving the most general description without listing them definitively. They consider silence by the wife to be an implicit acceptance which deprives her of the right to apply to the court. In the case of insanity, they rule that a divorce should be adjourned for a year.

Imam Ash-Shafii considers such a divorce a decree of annulment, since it is not effected by the husband personally and of his own free will. Imam Ahmad ibn-Hanbal concurs, but differs from ash-Shafii in that he does not consider the wife's silence an acceptance of the defect, unless she knew about it and consented to consummation.

The modern Arab legislations in general adopt the position that the wife is entitled to sue for divorce on the grounds of a defect on the part of the husband, and retain many of the previous provisions.

(a) Egypt. The Hanafi doctrine on divorce for a defect on the part of the husband that renders him incapable of consummating marriage was followed in Egypt until the promulgation of Act No. 25/1920 which implicitly retained this provision and added further such defects which it described without naming them. Chapter 3, Articles 9, 10 and 11 of the said Act gives the wife the right to apply to the court for a divorce, stipulating three conditions:

(i)   that the defect is of long standing and is incurable or only curable after a long time. If the husband can recover in a short time, the wife shall not be entitled to sue for a divorce;

(ii) that the continuation of marriage shall not be without an injury in view of such a defect such as insanity and leprosy, and that the injury shall affect her and her offspring. This condition shall be certified by medical experts;

(iii) that it is not proved that she consented having known of that defect. She shall not be entitled to sue for a divorce if the defect was existent at the time of the marriage, and she knew of it, and also, if, having not been aware of it at the time of the marriage, she did consent after acquiring that knowledge expressly or by implication. The same premise applies if the defect emerges later, and she consents to it. Such a divorce shall be irrevocable, at her request and by order of the court. Before the decree, there shall be no divorce, and all effects of marriage shall prevail.

(b) Syria. Divorce on grounds of the husband's defects is dealt with in Articles 105–108. There are two specific cases when the wife is entitled to sue for a divorce:

(i)   if the husband suffers from a defect that renders him incapable of consummating the marriage, provided that the wife is free from such a defect. With the exception of impotence, for which the right to apply for a divorce shall not lapse under any circumstances, the wife shall lose the right to petition for dissolution of the marriage by the court if she knew of the existence of the defect before the contract or if she consented to continue marriage thereafter;

(ii) if the husband becomes insane after the contract. The judge shall order a divorce forthwith if such a defect is incurable. If it is, the judge shall adjourn the case for a period not exceeding a year, at the end of which he shall order a divorce if no cure was found. Such a divorce shall be irrevocable.

(c) Morocco. The Moroccan legislator follows the Egyptian with some modifications. The wife may apply to the court for a divorce if she finds an incurable disease or one which it would take a long time to cure, during which time they cannot live together without great injury to her. Article 54/1 cites the examples of insanity, leprosy and tuberculosis. It is of no consequence that such a defect existed before marriage without her knowing about it or occurred after marriage, and she did not consent to stay with him. The judge shall adjourn the case for a year, at the end of which he shall order a divorce if no cure has occurred. This does not apply to incurable genital defects for which the judge shall order a divorce forthwith.

On the other hand, if the wife suffers from a defect such as insanity, leprosy, tuberculosis, or a genital disease which renders cohabitation impossible or unpleasurable, the husband, if he knew of such a defect before consummation, shall have the option to repudiate without incurring any liability, or to consummate marriage and pay the dower in full. If he knew it only after consummation, he may either retain her or repudiate her, and recover the balance of the least dower if it was the wife who misled him. If it was the guardian who misled him, then the guardian shall be liable for the monies paid by the husband. Recourse shall be made to medical experts to ascertain the defect. The divorce in this case is irrevocable.

(d) Iraq. Defects on the part of the husband are dealt with under paragraphs 4, 5 and 6 of Article 43, on the right of the wife to sue for a divorce by the court. She may apply to the judge if she finds her husband to be impotent or unable for any other defect to perform connubial intercourse due to organic or psychological causes, or if he becomes so defected after consummation, and a competent official medical committee certifies that such a defect is incurable. However, if the court finds that the cause is psychological, it shall adjourn divorce for a year, provided that the wife shall make herself available to her husband in the meantime. The wife shall also have the right to petition for dissolution if the husband is, or becomes, sterile after marriage without her having any surviving child by him. The same right shall prevail if she found after marriage that her husband was suffering from any such illness as to render living with him impossible for her without injury to herself. The examples cited are leprosy, tuberculosis, a venereal disease or insanity or the like, even if they occur later. However, should the court find, following a medical examination, that such a disease could be cured, it shall adjourn divorce until the actual cure; the wife meanwhile should avoid living with the husband. Nevertheless, the judge shall order an irrevocable (minor) divorce if there is no hope that the disease would be cured within a reasonable time and if the husband refuses to repudiate his wife.

(e) Jordan. Like the Syrian Law, the Jordanian legislator stipulates for the woman petitioning for a divorce on the grounds of the husband suffering from a condition she knows of rendering him incapable of consummation, such as mutilation, impotence or castration, that she herself should be free from any defect that makes connubial intercourse impossible. Except for impotence, she shall lose her right of option if she knew before the time of the marriage of such

a defect on the part of the husband or if she consented to live on with him having known of that defect after the contract (Arts. 113 and 114).

The law then distinguishes between incurable and curable diseases. The judge shall order a divorce forthwith if the disease is incurable. If it is curable, the husband shall be granted a delay of a year from the day she makes herself available to him, or from the time the husband recovers from another illness. This delay shall not include any periods, long or short, during which either spouse is suffering from an illness preventing intercourse, or any absence by the wife, but shall include her menstrual periods during which the husband is away. If the defect is not removed by the end of the delay and the husband refuses to repudiate marriage, the judge shall order a divorce if the wife presses her petition. If the husband claims at the beginning or end of the proceedings that he has consummated marriage, the wife shall be examined, and if found not to be a virgin, the husband shall be believed on taking an oath; if found a virgin, she shall be believed without an oath (Art. 115).

As for other diseases such as leprosy, tuberculosis or venereal disease, which would make the continuation of matrimonial life an injury to the wife, she may apply to the judge for a divorce whether the diseases occurred before or after consummation. The judge shall order a divorce forthwith if competent experts certify that there is no hope of recovery. If there is such a hope, the divorce proceeding shall be adjourned for a year at the end of which the judge shall order a divorce if there is no recovery, the husband refuses to repudiate and the wife insists on her petition. However, such handicaps as blindness or lameness of the husband shall be no valid ground for a divorce (Art. 116).

The husband, on his part, is entitled to apply for the annulment of the marriage contract if he finds his wife to be suffering from a genital impediment to connubial intercourse or a repugnant disease that makes life with her impossible without injury to himself, provided that he did not know of it prior to the marriage contract and has not accepted it expressly or by implication (Art. 117); and provided that such defects on the part of the wife have not occurred after consummation (Art. 118).

A genital defect on the part of either spouse shall be proved by a report of a medical practitioner or a midwife who shall be called to give evidence (Art. 119).

Insanity of the husband after the celebration of marriage shall entitle the wife to sue for a divorce, in which case the judge shall adjourn proceedings for a year at the end of which, if the husband has not recovered and the woman insists on her petition, the judge shall order a divorce (Art. 120).

The Jordanian Law is unique in (i) giving the wife the right to defer the court action or to leave it in suspense for a time after the institution thereof (Art. 121); (ii) in depriving both parties of the right to sue for a divorce if they renewed the marriage contract under the previous provision after a divorce decree was issued (Art. 122).

(f) Algeria. The Algerian Article 53/2 simply grants the wife the right to apply for a divorce on the grounds of defects that impede the achievement of the objective of marriage.

(g) Kuwait. The Kuwaiti legislator gives each spouse the right to ask for the marriage to be rescinded on finding with the other an injurious or disgusting defect, or such as to render enjoyment impossible, whether it occurred before or

after the contract, such right being waived if the defect was known before or expressly accepted after (Art. 139). But the wife shall not lose that right if the husband suffers from a defect which makes enjoyment impossible, e.g. impotence, inate or acquired, even if she expressly acquiesced (Art. 140). The court shall annul the marriage forthwith if the defect is incurable, otherwise it shall postpone trial for an appointed time at the end of which, if the defect is not cured and the applicant insists on rescission, the court shall issue a nullification decree (Art. 141).

Under the Sudanese Law, the wife may apply for divorce from her husband because he has a defect or a serious disease of which she was unaware before the contract, or which she knew and accepted after the contract. If it is curable within a year, the judge shall grant that delay before ordering divorce. (Art. 151) If the defect is impotence, whether before the contract, or after consummation, she shall retain her right to apply for divorce even after consenting to stay (Art. 154). The judge shall order divorce forthwith if it is medically proven that the impotence cannot be cured for more than a year. If it is curable within a year, a decision shall be deferred for a year (Art. 156).

The same provisions apply in general for all defects of either spouse under Omani Article 98, where there is no specific mention of impotence.

Similar rulings prevail under Yemeni Art. 47 with the option to apply for divorce retained and renewable only in respect of madness and all infectious and incurable diseases.

C. Failure to Pay Maintenance

The Islamic jurists differ on deeming failure by the husband to pay maintenance as a valid ground for the wife to apply to the court for a divorce. The Hanafis are categorical that such a divorce is not permissible whether the reason for the failure to pay maintenance is insolvency of the husband, or just refusal. They quote the Quranic verse: "Let him who hath abundance spend of his abundance, and he whose provision is measured, let him spend of that which Allah hath given him." (65:7) This, according to the Hanafis, covers the case of the husband who fails to maintain his wife because he is indigent. As for the husband who inflicts injustice on his wife by refusing to maintain her although he could afford it, the Hanafis rule that this injustice could be redressed without recourse to the divorce which is the most detestable to God of all permissible things, e.g. he could have his property sold, or could be put in jail until he resumes paying maintenance.[25]

The Shias, as previously mentioned, restrict the right of the wife to apply for divorce to impotence of the husband. Failure to maintain would only give the wife the right to apply to the court for an order against the husband.

The three Sunni Imams, Malik, Ahmad ash-Shafii and ibn-Hanbal, allow a divorce by the judge at the request of the wife on the husband failing to maintain her, and if he has no known property. They agree that the Quran decrees: "... either retaining in honour or releasing in kindness ..." (2:229) and abstention

---

[25] Abu Zabra, *op. cit.* pp. 347–354. Abu Zahra concurs with the Hanafi doctrine on the ground that there is no express provision at all in the Quran, the Tradition or the Prophet's Companions' consensus, to allow divorce because of failure to pay maintenance.

from paying maintenance does not conform to retention with honour. They also agree that failure to maintain is a grievous injury to the wife which should be remedied by the court under the authentic Prophet's Tradition: "There shall be no injury, and no injury shall be remedied by another." They also agree that if the judge has the power to order a divorce on the ground of a defect on the part of the husband, a divorce for failure to maintain should be *a fortiori* allowable.[26]

The modern law-makers adopt the position of the three Imams, Malik, ash-Shafii and Ahmad.

(a) Egypt. Act No. 25/1920, Article 4, reads as follows: "Should the husband abstain from maintenance of his wife, and has known property, a court order for maintenance shall be enforced on his property. If he has no known property, and refuses to declare whether he has means or is insolvent while insisting on abstaining from maintenance, the judge shall order a divorce forthwith. If he proves his insolvency, the judge shall grant him a delay not exceeding one month after which if he still fails to pay maintenance, a divorce decree shall be issued."

Under Article 5, a husband who is away for a short period shall have a court order for maintenance enforced on his property, if known. If not, the judge shall warn him, according to the normal procedure, fixing a time, at the end of which the judge shall order a divorce if the husband fails to send maintenance to the wife, or fails to return to support her. If the husband is away in a place where it is not easy to reach him, or is of unknown place of residence, and it is proved that he has no means from which the wife can get maintenance, the judge shall order a divorce forthwith. The same applies to the person who becomes insolvent and thus unable to pay maintenance.

Such a divorce shall be revocable, that is, the husband may resume matrimony if he proves his solvency and is prepared to pay maintenance for the *iddat.* Otherwise the resumption of marriage shall not be valid (Art. 6).

(b) Syria. Articles 110 and 111 deal with divorce for failure of maintenance. The wife may apply for a divorce if the husband living with her refrains from maintenance, has no known means, and fails to prove his insolvency. Should he prove his insolvency, or be away, the judge shall grant him a delay not exceeding three months on the expiry of which, if the husband persists in refusing to pay maintenance, the judge shall order a divorce. Such a divorce shall be revocable, with the husband having the right to resume matrimony during the *iddat* on condition that he proves his solvency and is willing to pay maintenance.

(c) Morocco. The Moroccan legislator follows closely the Syrian Law, while making it expressly clear that the divorce by the court shall be issued forthwith if the husband has no known property and refuses to declare whether he has means or is insolvent, while insisting on refusal to pay maintenance (Art. 53/1 and 2).

(d) Iraq. Paragraphs 7, 8 and 9 of Article 43 state that the wife may sue for divorce on the following grounds:

(i)   the abstention by the husband from paying maintenance without a lawful excuse after being given a notice to pay within sixty days;

---

[26] Abu Zahra, *loc. cit.*

(ii)   the impossibility of collecting maintenance from the husband on account of his being away or in jail for more than two years;
(iii) if the husband refrains from paying the accumulated maintenance ordered against him by the court, having been given notice by the enforcement officer to pay within sixty days. Such a divorce shall be irrevocable.

(e) Jordan. Under Article 127, if a husband refuses to pay maintenance to his wife who has obtained a court order to that effect, maintenance shall be taken from his property, if any. If he has no property, and has not stated whether he is of means or impoverished, or stated that he has means but insists on refusing to pay maintenance, the judge shall order a divorce forthwith. If he claims to be insolvent he shall have to prove it, otherwise a divorce shall be ordered forthwith. If he proves it, he shall be given a delay of not less than a month, and not more than three months, after which, if he has failed to pay maintenance, the judge shall order a divorce. Under Article 128, if the husband is away for a short period, and he has property from which maintenance may be taken, a maintenance order shall be given and executed on his property. If he has no property, the judge shall warn him and fix a time for him to pay. If the husband fails to send money for the maintenance of the wife, or has not come back himself to pay her maintenance, the judge shall order a divorce. If he is away and cannot be communicated with easily, or his whereabouts are unknown, and it is proved that he has no property from which the wife can get maintenance, the judge shall order a divorce without warning or fixing a time. The same provision applies to the person who cannot afford to pay maintenance.

Under Article 129, such a divorce shall be revocable if it occurs after consummation, and irrevocable if it is before consummation.

If the divorce is revocable, the husband may return to his wife during the *iddat*, if he can prove he has means through the payment of three months' maintenance out of the accumulated maintenance due to her from him, and showing his willingness to pay maintenance during the *iddat*, otherwise the resumption of matrimony shall not be valid.

(f) Kuwait. The Kuwaiti legislator is in general agreement with this provision, except that the judge shall issue an irrevocable divorce decree if the wife sues the husband more than twice for lack of maintenance and asks for a divorce on the grounds of injury (Art. 122).

(g) Algeria. Article 53, paragraph 1, grants the wife the right to sue for a divorce on account of the failure by the husband to pay maintenance after an order to that effect by the court, unless the woman knew of his insolvency at the time of the marriage.

(h) Sudan. Under Articles. 174–184, the wife may apply for divorce if her husband has no visible means, refuses to maintain her, and proves insolvent. The judge shall grant him a delay of one to two months to resume maintenance before ordering divorce. If the husband denies insolvency, the judge shall give him a delay to pay maintenance or repudiate before decreeing divorce forthwith.

If the husband is absent, but in a known place, without paying maintenance, the wife may apply for divorce, which the judge shall grant after warning the husband for a month, and the wife taking an oath that she is entitled to maintenance which she has been unable to get from her husband who has no known property. If the husband is away, and is of no known address, and the wife seeks divorce, the judge shall grant it after investigation, and the lapse of a month to enable his return. The wife must take the same oath as above. However, no divorce decree shall be granted if she has known of, and accepted, her husband's insolvency when they married.

Divorce because of insolvency or lack of maintenance is revocable if consummation has taken place, and the husband proves his ability and accepts his obligation to pay maintenance before the wife's *iddat* is over

(i) Yemen. Under Articles 50 and 51, the wife has the right to ask for recision if she cannot receive her lawful maintenance from an affluent husband, or from an insolvent husband who can, but declines to earn a living, and refuses to repudiate her.

(j) Oman. Article 109 rules that no divorce order shall be made against an insolvent husband if the wife knew of and accepted his insolvency before marriage, or if she has means of her own.

D. *Absence or Imprisonment of the Husband*

The absence of the husband or his imprisonment are valid grounds for the wife to apply for a divorce according to Imams Malik and Ahmad ibn-Hanbal, although they differ in detail. Both jurists agree that absence or imprisonment must cause actual, rather than anticipated injury to the wife, and would render her vulnerable to seduction. Absence or imprisonment must be for a long time, during which the wife suffers injury. Imam ibn-Hanbal sets that time at six months according to a tradition of Omar, the Second Patriarchal Caliph. Imam Malik is said to maintain the minimum of the duration of such an absence of one year or three years. Ibn-Hanbal stipulates that the absence should be without an acceptable cause. As for imprisonment, the wife, according to ibn-Hanbal, may apply to the court for a divorce after one year of the husband's imprisonment. All these periods are calculated according to the lunar year. Malik considers such a dissolution as an irrevocable divorce. Ibn-Hanbal considers it an annulment. While accepting the two Imams' position in principle, the modern Islamic legislators take an eclectic attitude.

(a) Egypt. Divorce by the court on account of the husband's absence or imprisonment is dealt with under Chapter 3, Articles 12, 13 and 14 of Act No. 25/1929. Under Article 12, if the husband is absent for a year or more without an acceptable excuse, his wife may ask the court for an irrevocable divorce should she suffer injury due to his absence, even though he has property from which she can get her maintenance.

Under Article 13, if it is possible to send messages to the absent husband, the judge shall fix a time for him with a warning that the wife would be granted a divorce by the court unless he returns to live with her, moves her to live with him, or divorces her. At the end of the delay, if the husband has not complied or submitted an acceptable excuse, the judge shall order an irrevocable divorce. Likewise, if no message could get to the absent husband, the judge shall grant the divorce without warning or setting a delay.

Under Article 14, the wife of the husband against whom a prison sentence of three years or more has been passed and become final may apply to the judge after one year of the husband's imprisonment for an irrevocable divorce on account of injury, even if the husband has property from which she could get maintenance.

The same provisions are ordered in Kuwaiti Articles 136, 137 and 138.

(b) Syria. Under Article 109, the wife whose husband has gone absent without an acceptable excuse, or who has received a prison sentence of more than three years, may apply to the court for divorce after one year of the absence or imprisonment, even if there is property of the husband from which she can get maintenance.

Such a divorce shall be revocable, with the released husband, on his return, having the right to get his wife back if she is still in her *iddat*.

(c) Morocco. Under Article 57, the wife may petition the court for an irrevocable divorce if the husband has been away at a known address for more than a year without an acceptable excuse, if she feels injured thereby, even if he has property from which she could get maintenance.

The provision of the Egyptian Article 13 is repeated in paragraph 2 of the same Moroccan Article.

(d) Iraq. Under Article 43, paragraph 1, the wife may apply for a divorce if the husband has received a prison sentence of three years or more, even if he has property from which she can get maintenance, or if the husband has deserted her for two years or more without lawful excuse, even if his address is known and he has property from which she can get maintenance.

(e) Jordan. Under Articles 128 and 130, the provisions of the Egyptian Articles 13 and 14 are adopted.

(f) Oman. Omani Article 111 is very similar to the Egyptian, except that if the absent husband has no known address, no divorce order shall be granted before at least one year from the date of absence. (Art. 111). As for imprisonment, Article 112 is the same as the Egyptian Law.

(g) Sudan. Similar provisions apply, except that the wife has to take an oath that she suffers injury and fears temptation from sin before she gets a divorce. (Art. 186/7/8) As for imprisonment, the sentence must be for a minimum of two years. (Art. 189).

(h) Yemen. Article 52 rules that the wife of the absent husband who is abroad, or of unknown address, may get her marriage rescinded after one year without maintenance and after two years of having received maintenance. For imprisonment, Egyptian ruling applies.

(i) Algeria. Under Article 53, paragraph 4, the wife may apply for a divorce if the husband has received a prison sentence of over a year for an offence that constitutes a disgrace to the family and renders the continuation of life together impossible. Under paragraph 5, she shall have the same right on his going absent for a year without an excuse or maintenance.

E. Other Grounds for Applying to the Court for Divorce

(a) The Syrian, Iraqi and Jordanian Acts (Articles 14/3, 6/4 and 9/1, respectively) grant the wife the right to apply to the court for a divorce if the husband fails to honour a stipulation agreed upon in the marriage contract. The Jordanian legislator adds that the wife may then claim all her matrimonial rights, Jordanian

Article 19/2 grants the same right to the husband who shall then be released of the wife's deferred dower, and the *iddat* maintenance.

(b) Under the Sunni Sharia, the nearest agnate guardian may apply to the court to nullify a marriage on the ground of non-equality between his minor ward and the husband. Dissolution of the marriage can be only by order of the judge, and until that order is issued, the state of matrimony shall hold and have full effect to the extent that should either spouse die during the court proceedings, the surviving spouse shall inherit. It shall constitute an annulment of the contract, so that the three pronouncements of repudiation to which the husband is entitled shall not decrease.

The Ottoman Family Law which governs the personal status of the Sunnis in the Lebanon adopts this provision in Articles 45 and 47, under which marriage can be dissolved by the court in the following instances:

(i)   if a major woman marries a husband who is not equal without the knowledge of her guardian;
(ii) if equality was stipulated in the contract and the husband was found not to be equal;
(iii) if the husband alleged being equal before the contract and was believed by the wife and her guardian and was proved to be not so after the marriage.

The right to apply for annulment is the guardian's exclusively in the first instance, and is equally shared by the wife and her guardian in the second and third instances.

These provisions are adopted in the Laws of Syria, Jordan and Kuwait: Articles 27, 29 and 32; 21 and 22; 34 and 38 respectively. Equality is to be considered at the time of the marriage only, and shall have no relevance if it ceases to exist thereafter (Art. 31, Syrian and 20, Jordanian). The right to apply for annulment on the grounds of non-equality shall cease on the wife becoming pregnant (Arts. 30, Syrian; 23, Jordanian). Kuwaiti Article 39 adds that this right shall also be lost on earlier consent or the expiry of one year after knowing of the marriage.

In Yemen, Article 48 considers equality in faith and morality with mutual consideration, and gives both spouses the right to request recision because of non-equality. Art. 53 rules that if a man has more than one wife and cannot afford their maintenance and accommodation, each of them may apply for recision of the marriage. The judge shall then give the husband the choice of keeping one and repudiating the others, and on his refusal to do so, shall order recision of those who request it.

5. Dissolution of Marriage by Operation of Law

Only a valid marriage can be dissolved, as both irregular and void marriage contracts need no dissolution, and the parties thereto shall separate of themselves, with the court only intervening to order them if they fail to do so.

Yet, a marriage contract that was valid to start with may become later invalidated to the extent that it is dissolved without any need for the husband to pronounce repudiation or for the court to order a divorce. This could happen in two ways:

A. Change of Religion

As previously explained in the Conditions of Marriage, no Muslim husband can take as a wife a non-*Kitabi* woman. Therefore, if after marriage a Muslim or a *Kitabi* woman becomes atheist or a non-*Kitabi*, the marriage shall be *ipso facto* dissolved; a ruling of Yemeni Article 49. However, the Kuwaiti legislators' Article 145/b, following a prevailing Maliki opinion and some Hanafi jurists, rule that the Muslim wife's apostasy shall not dissolve the marriage.

If a Muslim husband apostasizes, or if a non-Muslim husband refuses to adopt Islam after his wife has done so, the marriage shall be automatically dissolved. This ruling is held in Yemeni Article 49.

In more detail, the Kuwaiti Law, under the heading "Annulment on the Grounds of Religious Difference", (Art. 143) rules that:

(a) If the two non-Muslim spouses together convert to Islam, their marriage shall continue.
(b) If the husband only adopts Islam, if his wife is a *Kitabi*, marriage shall continue. If she is not, she shall be offered the opportunity to convert to Islam. If she accepts or becomes a *Kitabi*, they shall remain married – otherwise the marriage is nullified.
(c) If the wife only adopts Islam, the husband shall be invited to do the same; the marriage shall continue if he consents, and become nullified if he does not. If he lacks legal capacity, the marriage shall be dissolved forthwith if the wife has converted to Islam before consummation; if the marriage has been consummated, then the *iddat* has to be observed.

In all cases, the court shall not investigate the sincerity of the convert to Islam, nor shall it enquire into the motives of such a conversion (Art. 144).

As contradistinct from the wife, marriage shall be dissolved on the husband apostasizing. Nevertheless, if apostasy occurs after consummation and the husband reverts to Islam during the *iddat*, marriage shall be resumed as if there were no nullification (Art. 145/a).

B. The Creation of a Prohibited Degree

According to the Sunnis, if either spouse commits, with an ascendant or descendant of the other, an act that creates a prohibited degree through affinity, the marriage shall likewise be dissolved *ipso facto*.

These universal Sharia provisions apply by operation of the laws of marriage even though modern legislators, apart from the Kuwaitis and the Sudanese, keep silent on this issue, with the exception of the Egyptian Law (as explained under Apostasy, above) and Jordanian Law. The Sudanese rule that marriage shall be rescinded if an occurrence prevents its continuance under the Sharia (Art. 205). Jordanian Law decrees, under Article 51 that a dissolution of marriage, *inter alia*, through the husband refusing to convert to Islam if his wife does so, or his committing an act that creates a prohibited degree through affinity, shall be liable to pay half the specified dower before actual or assumed consummation. On the other hand, under Article 52 of the same law, the wife who apostasizes, or refuses to follow her husband if he converts to Islam when she is non-*Kitabi*, or commits with an ascendant or a descendant of the husband an act that creates a prohibited degree through affinity, shall lose all dower, and shall have to refund any dower she may have received. The Shias concur that apostasy of either spouse renders the marriage void forthwith without any recourse to the court.[27] However, unlike the Sunnis they rule that the wife's adultery or misbehaviour with her step-son does not annul the marriage if it occurs during it.[28]

6. Compensation of the Wife in the Case of Arbitrary Repudiation by the Husband

The husband, under the strictest Sharia provisions, has the right to repudiate, without the divorcée having any financial rights other than the whole dower if marriage was consummated, and the *iddat* maintenance. If such a repudiation occurred before consummation or valid retirement, the woman shall have no right to any dower if it was not validly specified, or was omitted altogether from the contract, and the only compensation for her in such a case is the *mutat*. The Quran left the amount of *mutat* to custom: "It is no sin for you if ye divorce women while yet ye have not touched them, nor appointed unto them a portion. Provide for them the rich according to his means and the straitened according to his means, a fair provision". (2:236)

The Hanafi jurists hold that the *mutat* is desirable for every divorcée after consummation, but that there is no mandatory or desirable *mutat*, prior to consummation, for a divorcée who is entitled to half the dower, nor for a widow.

The Ithna-Asharis hold, to the Quranic rule that the *mutat* shall depend on the husband's material condition, and can be paid in cash, clothing, or home furniture. No *mutat* is due (a) for a woman divorced before consummation; (b) for whom dower was validly specified; (c) for the widow. *Mutat* is desirable for the divorcee after consummation.[29] The Ismailis concur.[30]

This Quranic and Sharia ruling is adopted in Article 60 of the Moroccan Law: "Every husband shall have the obligation to provide *mutat* for his divorcée if divorce proceeded from him, according to his affluence and her means, except the woman for whom a dower was specified and was divorced prior to consummation."

However, the modern Islamic Personal Status Laws of Syria, Jordan and Egypt go much farther to safeguard the rights of the divorced wife.

All three Acts agree on the principles in general, namely that the wife shall be entitled, on repudiation by the husband after consummation of marriage, to the *mutat* compensation, but they differ on the amount thereof:

The Syrian Article 117 of the Decree No. 59/1953, as amended under Article 16 of Act No. 34/1975, reads as follows:

"If a man repudiates his wife and the judge finds that the husband's pronouncement of repudiation has been arbitrary without any reasonable cause, and that the wife would suffer misery and hardship therefrom, the judge may order for her against her ex-husband, in proportion with his means and his arbitrariness, a compensation not in excess of the amount of maintenance of her equals for three years, over and above the *iddat* maintenance.

---

[27] Al-Hilli, *op. cit.* p. 78.
[28] *Ibid.* p. 69.
[29] *Ibid.* p. 34.
[30] Qadi an-Numan, *op. cit.* Vol. 2, pp. 239–240.

The judge may order that such a compensation shall be paid in a lump sum or by monthly instalments as warranted by the circumstances."

In a similar vein, Article 134 of the Jordanian Provisional Law No. 61/1976 rules as follows:

"If the husband repudiates his wife in an arbitrary manner, e.g. without a reasonable cause, and she applies to the judge for compensation, the judge shall order for her against her ex-husband the compensation deemed by the judge to be fair, provided that it shall not be in excess of the equivalent of the maintenance due to her for a year. Such a compensation shall be paid either in a lump sum or by instalments as warranted by the circumstances, while taking into consideration the condition of the husband in respect to affluence or poverty. This shall not affect the other marital rights due to the repudiated wife, including the *iddat* maintenance."

The Egyptian legislator steers a middle course between the Syrian and Jordanian provisions in terms of the amount due. In another aspect, it is more generous towards the divorcée. Article 18 *bis* added to Act No. 25/1929 under Act No. 100/1985, rules:

"The wife with whom consummation occurred under a valid marriage contract, if she is repudiated by her husband without her consent nor for a cause proceeding from her, shall be entitled, over and above her *iddat* maintenance, to a *mutat* of no less than the maintenance of two years with due consideration given to the condition of the repudiating husband in terms of affluence or destitution, the circumstances of the repudiation and the duration of matrimony. The repudiating husband may be allowed to pay such a *mutat* by instalments."

The Tunisian legislators' position has been detailed in this Chapter under the Section headed Injury or Discord above (4a).

The Kuwaiti Law, under the heading of "Compensation for Repudiation", sums up the general provisions in this matter in Article 165, as follows:

"A. If a valid marriage is dissolved after consummation, the wife shall be entitled, over and above her *iddat* maintenance, to a *mutat* in an amount not in excess of a year's maintenance, according to the condition of the husband, which shall be paid to her in monthly instalments, on the completion of her *iddat*, unless the two parties agree otherwise in terms of the amount or method of payment.

B. The provisions of the previous paragraph shall not apply in the following events:
1. Divorce on the grounds of non-maintenance by the husband due to his insolvency.
2. Divorce on the grounds of injury if it proceeds from the wife.
3. Repudiation with the wife's consent.
4. Annulment of marriage at the behest of the wife.
5. Death of either spouse."

CHAPTER 7

The *Iddat*

1. Introduction: Definition and Objects

The word "*iddat*" is derived from the root "*adda*" meaning to count; in this case, it is the counting of days and months. By definition, the *iddat* is a waiting period, a period of abstinence, or a specified term during which the wife shall remain unmarried after the dissolution of marriage by divorce, death, or any other form of separation under certain conditions.

It constitutes for the woman a temporary prohibition to marry, to be lifted on the expiry of the term. Such a prohibition shall not apply to the man except if he is already married to four wives, including the divorcée in her *iddat*, and his aim is to avoid having more than four wives at one time, or to avoid unlawful conjunction (see Chap. 3 above) for the duration of the term.

There are three main objects of *iddat*:

(i)   to ascertain whether the wife is pregnant, and if so, the paternity of the child;
(ii) to provide the husband with an opportunity to return to his wife if the divorce is revocable;
(iii) to mourn the dead husband, in the case of the widow.

These provisions of the Sharia are generally adopted in the modern Codes for Personal Status. They are taken for granted in the Egyptian legislation, and mentioned explicitly in the laws of Syria, Tunisia, Morocco, Iraq, Jordan, Kuwait and Algeria. In the following sections we shall refer to the relevant articles, if any, of the general Sharia rules.

2. Conditions for Observing the *Iddat*

Under a valid marriage, the *iddat* shall be rigidly observed on divorce if consummation has actually occurred, or, according to the Sunnis, is deemed to have occurred, in conformity with the Quranic rulings: "Divorced women shall wait concerning themselves for three monthly periods." (2:228)

The Shias stipulate for the *iddat* to be observed that the marriage is actually consummated. Valid retirement without that requires no *iddat*.[1]

---

[1] Al-Hilli, *Jaafari Personal Status Provisions*, p. 79.

137

All Schools maintain that no *iddat* shall be observed on divorce if the marriage has not been consummated, according to the Quranic ruling: "O ye who believe! When ye marry believing women, and then divorce them before ye have touched them, no period of *iddat* have ye to count in respect of them." (33:49)

The *iddat* shall nevertheless be observed, under a valid marriage, on the death of the husband even if there was no consummation or valid retirement. This is the main difference between a valid and a defective marriage when no *iddat* shall be observed. This provision is adopted in Articles 126 (Syria) and 79 (Morocco), which both make valid retirement equivalent to actual consummation, and in Articles 47 (Iraq) and 155/b Kuwait.

Although the Shia temporary (*muta*) marriage is not liable to divorce, expiring at the end of the term or making a gift of the remainder thereof to the wife (see Chapter 3), the temporary (*muta*) wife shall observe an *iddat* of two complete menstrual cycles, if she has not reached menopause, or of forty-five days if she suffers from amenorrhoea, perhaps due to illness. If she is pregnant, she shall wait until her delivery or for forty-five days, whichever term is the longer.[2]

3. Duration of the *Iddat*

The *iddat* shall be calculated by menstrual cycles (cycles of menstrual purity for the Shias), by months or until the delivery of the baby. Counting shall commence from the time of divorce under a valid marriage, from last cohabitation under a defective contract or from the death of the husband.

Some modern Arab legislations endorse expressly these provisions, e.g. Syrian Article 125, Moroccan Article 78, Omani Article 119(b). Iraqi and Jordanian Articles 49 and 141 respectively add that the *iddat* shall start forthwith, even if the woman is not aware of the occurrence. Sudanese Article 207(1) concurs. Yemeni Article 80 rules the start from the date of the woman becoming aware of dissolution, not of its occurrence.

The Kuwaiti Article 156 succinctly sums up as follows:
"The *iddat* shall start:

(a) Under a valid contract, from the date of the repudiation or the husband's death.
(b) Under a defective contract, from the date of separation or the man's death.
(c) Under consummation with semblance of the right thereto, from the date of the last cohabitation.
(d) Under a court decree of divorce from the date it becomes final."

A. Iddat *Calculated by Menstruation*

In the case of a woman subject to menstruation, whose valid marriage has been dissolved after actual or presumed consummation for a reason other than the death of her husband, and who was not pregnant at the time of dissolution, the *iddat* shall extend for three complete menses, on the expiration of which the prohibition to remarry shall be lifted. This provision is based on the Quranic

---

[2] Tayabji, *Muhammadan Law*, pp. 121–122.

ruling: "Divorced women shall wait concerning themselves for three monthly courses." (2:228)

Schools differ on the interpretation of the prescribed three menses. Of the Sunnis, the Hanafis maintain that it means three menses between which two periods of menstrual purity intervene; the Shafiis and Malikis count three periods of menstrual purity. The latter is also the opinion of the Shias, who stipulate that divorce can only be pronounced when the wife is not menstruating or puerperal. The *iddat* for the Shias is terminated at the onset of the third menstruation. Nevertheless, according to the Sunni schools, if a wife is divorced while menstruating, that menstrual period shall not be counted for the purposes of the *iddat*.

The ambiguity of the term "monthly courses" (in Arabic, *quru*) in the Quranic text persists in Articles 48/1 (Iraqi), 135 (Jordanian) and 58 (Algerian). The Moroccan, Syrian, Sudanese and Omani Codes are more specific, counting three periods of purity (Art. 73) and three of menstruation (Art. 121/1) and three complete menstrual cycles (210d and 121c) respectively. Yemeni Article 82a specifies three menstrual cycles apart from that in which she was divorced. The Jordanian Article adds that the woman's claim to have completed her *iddat* before three months shall not be accepted, and Article 136 goes on to rule that if the woman did not see blood at all or only once or twice during the said period, it shall have to be ascertained if she has reached menopause, in which case she shall observe an *iddat* of three months, otherwise she should complete a lunar year. The same provision is adopted in the Syrian Article 121/3, further dating the *iddat* from divorce or annulment. The Tunisian legislator does not calculate *iddat* by menstruation at all, but by months (Art. 35). The Kuwaiti legislator (Art. 57) combines both, ruling (c-1) that the *iddat* of the non-pregnant, otherwise than at the death of the husband, shall be three complete menstruations in a term not shorter than sixty days for those who menstruate.

B. Iddat *Calculated by Months*

The *iddat* shall be counted by months in two cases:

(i) For the woman who is not subject to menstruation, either because she has not reached puberty, or has reached menopause, under the Quranic ruling: "Such of your women as have passed the age of monthly courses, for them the prescribed period, if ye have any doubts, is three months for those who have no course. ..." (65:4)

To these two classes of women, the Shias add those who suffer from amenorrhoea because of a congenital defect, or from fostering (suckling a child) or some illness.[3]

Three lunar months shall be counted if divorce occurs at the start of the month calculated according to the Islamic calendar even if any month is less than thirty days, otherwise ninety days shall be counted.

These provisions are adopted in full in Kuwaiti Article 157.

Syrian Article 121/3 rules an *iddat* of three months for the woman in menopause, excluding the pre-adolescent girl who is not lawfully capable of marriage under the Syrian law. The same provision is adopted under Algerian Article 58.

---

[3] Al-Hilli, *op. cit.* pp. 79–80.

Moroccan Article 73 counts three months for the woman in menopause, and the one who does not menstruate. Omani Article 121 concurs, adding that if the latter did see blood before the end of the three months, she shall count again for three menstrual cycles, and specifies a three month period for one who does not know her cycle, and one year for one who has stopped menstruation before menopause. The same provision applies under Yemeni Art. 82. The same *iddat* is stipulated for the woman who reached puberty and did not menstruate at all, under Iraqi Article 48/2. The Jordanian Article 137 follows the Syrian provision while further qualifying the women as having married under a valid contract, and were separated from their husbands after valid retirement, whether by divorce or annulment if they have reached menopause. The Tunisian Article 35 simply decrees that the divorced woman who is not pregnant shall count three complete months.

(ii) For the widow, under a valid marriage, if she is not pregnant. In this case, the *iddat* shall be four lunar months and ten days as prescribed in the Quran. This shall be counted as one hundred and thirty days from the death of her husband.

This provision is adopted without any modification under Articles 123, 35, 74, 48/3, 143, 59, 109(1), 81 and 120a of the Personal Status Codes of Syria, Tunisia, Morocco, Iraq, Jordan, Algeria, Sudan, Yemen and Oman, respectively.

Kuwaiti Article 158 follows suit (para. a), adding two interesting rulings (b and c):

"(b) In the event of an irrevocable separation under repudiation or dissolution, if the man dies during the *iddat*, the woman shall complete her *iddat* and shall not move to the *iddat* of the death of the husband, without prejudice to the provisions of case (5), paragraph (c) of the preceding article.

 (c) The woman with whom cohabitation occurred with semblance of the right thereto, under a defective contract or without any contract, if the man dies shall observe an *iddat* of separation, not of death."

Case (5), paragraph (c) of Article 157 referred to, provides that the woman shall observe the longer term of the *iddat* of repudiation or of death of the husband if she has been repudiated by the husband to trick her out of inheriting from him, should he die before she completes her *iddat*.

Yemeni Article 83 rules that the *khula* woman shall count one menstruation if she menstruates, or else three months.

C. Conversion from One Form of Calculating the Iddat to Another

The above-mentioned periods of *iddat* must not be combined, but it is possible to convert from one form of counting to another as follows:

(i) Conversion from *iddat* calculated by months to *iddat* calculated by menstruation: The woman whose *iddat* is calculated by months following the dissolution of marriage for a reason other than the death of her husband, and who menstruates before the expiration of the *iddat* calculated by months, shall start a fresh *iddat* of three complete menses. However, she shall not be required to do this if menstruation occurs after the expiry of the first *iddat*.

(ii) Conversion from *iddat* calculated by menstruation to *iddat* calculated by months: The *iddat* shall be counted afresh for three months if it started by counting menses, and these either become irregular, or are interrupted or terminated by the advent of menopause, provided that this change occurs before the expiry of the original three menses.

(iii) Conversion from the divorce to the death *iddat*: A woman who is revocably divorced and whose husband dies during her *iddat* shall interrupt the divorce *iddat* and start afresh, counting the death *iddat* of four months and ten days. This ruling does not apply to an irrevocably divorced woman, except that if his death occurred during his death illness whilst counting her *iddat*, and if it can be proved that he fraudulently intended to deprive her of her inheritance, the irrevocably divorced woman shall observe the longer death *iddat*, although this will include the period already counted for the divorce *iddat*.

The conversion from the divorce to the death *iddat* as stipulated above is codified under Articles 127, 77, 48/4, 143, 157/c-5, 212, 82/d and 123 of the Laws of Syria, Morocco, Iraq, Jordan, Kuwait, Sudan, Yemen and Oman respectively. The Tunisian and Algerian Laws keep silent on this point. The Syrian Article 127, paragraph 2, adds that if the husband dies during an *iddat* of an irrevocable divorce, the woman shall observe the longer term of the death or the divorce *iddat*.

D. *Termination of* Iddat *on the Delivery of a Baby*

In the case of a woman who is pregnant at the time of dissolution of marriage, the *iddat* shall be observed until the delivery of the baby (or babies, in the case of multiple birth), under the general Quranic ruling: "And if they carry (life in their wombs), then spend (your substance) on them until they deliver their burden. ..." (65:6)

The Sunnis observe this rule rigidly, regardless of the grounds for separation, whether under a valid, defective or even void marriage contract, or on the death of the husband, however short the period may be. The Shias maintain the same opinion generally, but differ in ruling that the pregnant widow shall observe the longer period of *iddat* until the delivery, of four months and ten days.[4]

All the modern Arab Personal Status Laws agree that the *iddat* of the divorced woman who is pregnant shall be terminated on delivery of her child (Arts. 124, 35, 72, 48/3, 140, 60, 157/b, 209/2, 81 and 121/b of the Laws of Syria, Tunisia, Morocco, Iraq, Jordan, Algeria, Kuwait, Sudan, Yemen and Oman respectively). However, a maximum term for pregnancy is set at one year (Arts. 35, Tunisian; 76, Moroccan and 160, Kuwaiti), or ten months (Art. 60, Algerian) calculated from the date of divorce or death of the husband.

Miscarriage shall terminate the *iddat*, provided that some organs of the embryo are identifiable (Arts. 124, Syrian; 140, Jordanian and 157/b, Kuwaiti).

Sunnis and Shias alike rule that an identifiable foetus must be taken from the mother in order to be absolutely sure that the delivery is complete.

---

[4] *Ibid.* pp. 80–81.

4. Rights and Obligations of the Spouses During *Iddat*

The *iddat*, being a transitional period between actual separation and final termination of marriage under a revocable pronouncement of repudiation, creates, while it lasts, certain obligations and rights for both spouses. These include a temporary legal bar to marriage, the mutual entitlement to inheritance, maintenance and residence of the wife.

A. The Marriage Bar

During the *iddat* of a revocable divorce, the husband may resume the conjugal relationship with the wife without her consent. The wife is prohibited from marrying another man, and the husband is prohibited from marrying a fifth wife, or marrying a relative of the wife which would be in a prohibited degree to her had she been a man. A marriage contracted during the *iddat* shall be defective, under Sunni law, but shall be void under Shia law.

B. Parentage

A child born during the *iddat* shall be the husband's.

C. Mutual Rights of Inheritance

Under a revocable divorce, on the death of either spouse during the *iddat*, the surviving spouse shall inherit. Under an irrevocable divorce, the surviving partner shall only inherit if it is established that the partner who died during the *iddat* as a result of a death-illness, intended fraudulently, by causing dissolution, to deprive the spouse from inheritance.

D. Maintenance

The right to maintenance of the woman during her *iddat* may be established, controversial, or may be lost altogether as detailed in the following paragraphs.

(i)   Maintenance shall be the inalienable right of the woman during her *iddat* in the following two cases:
   (a) if the dissolution is under a valid marriage by way of a divorce pronounced by the husband or ordered by the judge for reasons proceeding from the husband; or
   (b) if separation was by way of annulment by the husband or by the wife, but through no fault of hers, e.g. if, on recovery from insanity, she exercises her option to terminate marriage which has been consummated.[5] The Shias dissent, ruling that the wife shall lose her maintenance during the *iddat* of divorce due to using her option on reaching majority.[6]

Maintenance of the wife during her *iddat* shall also be imperative on the husband in cases of separation through a vow of continence (*ila*), imprecation

---

[5] Abu Zahra, *On Marriage*, p. 384.
[6] Al-Hilli, *op. cit.* p. 83.

(*lian*), refusal by the husband to profess Islam after his wife's conversion thereto, or his apostasy.[7]

(ii) While maintenance is unanimously held to be the right of a woman during her *iddat* of a revocable divorce, there is controversy over the right to maintenance during the *iddat* of an irrevocable divorce. However, it is unanimously agreed that in this case the woman shall be entitled to maintenance if she is pregnant, under the Quranic ruling: "And if they carry (life in their wombs), then spend (your substance) on them until they deliver their burden. ..." (65:6)

Schools differ on the entitlement to maintenance during the *iddat* of an irrevocable divorce if the woman is not pregnant. The Shias[8] and the Sunni Shafiis rule that there shall be no maintenance in this case apart from lodging, under the Quranic imperative: "Let the women live (in *iddat*), in the same style as ye live, according to your means." (65:6) The Hanafis, whose opinion is upheld by the modern Islamic states' legislation in this respect, rule that maintenance shall be due, relying on the generality of the Quranic provision: "Let the man of means spend according to his means. ..." (65:7) applying it to all divorced women whether revocably or irrevocably repudiated, without restriction. This generally is retained in Article 162.

(iii) The woman in her *iddat* shall not be entitled to any maintenance in three cases:

(a) if the *iddat* is subsequent to consummation under a void marriage contract, or to co-habitation under a semblance of legality;

(b) in the *iddat* of death, since maintenance is an obligation which shall not pass from the deceased husband to the heir;

(c) if the marriage was dissolved for some cause of a criminal nature originating from the woman, such as the wife's apostasy or her misbehaviour so as to establish a supervening prohibition. The Shia differ, making maintenance due for a wife in this case, since misbehaviour does not render the marriage void if it occurred during but not before marriage.[9]

E. Residence

According to all schools, the *iddat* must be observed by a revocably divorced woman at the matrimonial home, under the Quranic ruling: "And turn them not out of their houses, nor shall they (themselves) leave, except in case they are guilty of some open lewdness." (65:1) This is both the woman's right and duty. Remaining in the husband's home is considered a continuation of the right of the husband to be obeyed, a right he retains until the completion of the *iddat*.

The Sunnis extend that duty to remain in the husband's residence to include the duration of the *iddat* following separation under a valid contract for whatever reason, including death and irrevocable divorce. The Shias restrict that duty to the duration of *iddat* of a revocable marriage and preferably the *iddat* of death.[10]

The Sunnis rule that should the woman leave the matrimonial home during

---

[7] Al-Ghandour, *Divorce.*

[8] Al-Hilli, *loc. cit.*

[9] Al-Hilli, *loc. cit.*

[10] *Ibid. op. cit.* p. 82.

her *iddat* without an acceptable excuse, she shall forfeit her right to maintenance until she returns. Among the acceptable excuses allowed by both the Sunnis and the Shias for the woman leaving the matrimonial home during the *iddat*, is fear of the house collapsing, its location in a remote area, fear for the safety of her person or property there, or forceful ejection by the landlord. A woman in her *iddat* of revocable divorce may then move to another home chosen by her husband, while a woman in the *iddat* of death may go wherever she chooses.[11]

Algerian Article 61 adopts the Quranic ruling above, and reads as follows: "Neither the divorced wife nor the widowed shall leave the matrimonial home during her *iddat* of divorce or death of the husband except in case she is guilty of some open lewdness. ..."

Jordanian Article 146 is more detailed:

"The woman observing an *iddat* of a revocable divorce or of death shall stay during her *iddat* at the home in which the spouses have lived together before separation. If she has been divorced or her husband has died while she was staying elsewhere, she shall return forthwith to her matrimonial home. The woman observing her *iddat* of divorce shall not leave her home except for a necessity; the woman in her *iddat* of the death of the husband shall only go out on some essential business, and shall not sleep in a place other than her home. If the spouses have to move elsewhere, the woman in an *iddat* of divorce shall move to wherever the husband chooses. If the woman in an *iddat* of the death of the husband is obliged to move, it shall be to the nearest location to her home."

Kuwaiti Article 161 confirms this ruling in respect of a woman revocably divorced, moving, if necessity dictates, only to a home appointed by the judge, and deems her *nashiza* if she left home without justification.

---

[11] *Ibid.*

CHAPTER 8

Parentage

1. Introduction: The Children's Rights

The child's first right is to establish parentage, a right both of the child and the father. This right may commence *in utero*, for example the baby may inherit from its father so long as the father's death occurred not more than two hundred and seventy days before the baby's birth. The child's first right is followed by the right of upbringing – the right to maintenance by the father, and fosterage and custody by the mother, if these are assigned to her. After passing the age of custody, the minor shall have the right to care and guardianship by its agnates. If it has possession of property, it shall need administration and guardianship of its property, a need shared by those who lack legal capabilities.

In this chapter, I shall deal with the right of parentage. The following chapters will deal with the other rights of fosterage, custody, maintenance and guardianship, in that order.

2. General Provisions of Parentage

Parentage of a child to its parents may be established through marriage, acknowledgment or evidence. One of the most important rights emanating from marriage is the establishment of parentage, i.e. maternity and paternity of the offspring of the spouses.

This legal relationship between parent and child gives rise to rights and obligations such as mutual rights of inheritance, guardianship and maintenance. It shall be the duty of the parent to ensure that such needs are satisfied with the interests of the child deemed paramount to any other consideration.

Parentage confers upon the child the status of legitimacy. Parentage is only established in the natural father and mother of a child. Adoption is not recognized in the Sharia, under the Quranic ruling: "... nor hath He made those whom ye claim (to be your sons) your sons. This is but a saying of your mouths. But God sayeth the truth and He showeth the way. Proclaim their real parentage. That will be more equitable in the sight of God. And if ye know not their fathers then (they are) your brethren in the faith and your clients." (33:4/5)

This principle is expressly codified in the Algerian Article 46, "Adoption shall be prohibited under the Sharia and the Law", and in Kuwaiti Article 167 and Yemeni Article 135 "No parentage shall be established through adoption even

145

of a child of unknown parentage", and is unanimously adopted in Islamic States, with the exception of Tunisia, where Act No. 27/1958 allows adoption under certain conditions and according to certain procedures which will be presented later in this chapter. Moroccan Article 83/3 rules adoption in the literal sense null and void, while adoption for the purpose of rewarding or bequeathing, i.e. to accord a person the status of one's child, shall not establish parentage, and shall be deemed as a will.

Maternity is established only in the natural mother of a child, and it cannot be disclaimed whether birth occurred under a valid or invalid contract, or without any contract whatsoever. This Sharia provision is expressed in the Moroccan Article 83/2 "Illegitimate filiation is utterly void for the father, and shall have no effect whatsoever, but for the mother it shall be the same as the legitimate, because it is her child," and in Yemeni Article 122 "Filiation of the child to its mother is established once birth is established even without her acknowledgment and without any condition or restriction."

No paternity can be established for the illegitimate offspring. Apart from acknowledgment and evidence (see below) paternity can only be established for the offspring of wedlock, whether under a valid contract, an irregular contract, or under a semblance of the right to marital intercourse. Such cases are subject to the minimum and maximum terms of pregnancy.

The minimum term of pregnancy is unanimously reckoned to be six lunar months, under two Quranic verses: "And We have commended unto man kindness to his parents: in pain did his mother bear him, and in pain did she give him birth, and the bearing of him and the weaning of him is thirty months." (46:15) "And We have commended upon man concerning his parents: His mother beareth him in weakness upon weakness, and his weaning is in two years ..." (31:14)

By subtracting from thirty the twenty-four months for weaning, the pregnancy term was said to be six months. A child born in less than six months from the time of the marriage is deemed by all the four Sunni Schools to be illegitimate. The Ithna-Asharis, while concurring in principle, allow a child born under a valid marriage contract less than six months after consummation, to be acknowledged by its father if he declares that it was not an offspring of unlawful intercourse, and if he is not known to be telling a lie.[1] Some Sunni scholars agree.[2]

The maximum term of pregnancy used to be a matter of controversy among jurists, ranging from two to five years, but in practice it has been laid down as one lunar year. To the Shia Ithna-Ashari, the maximum term for pregnancy is nine lunar months, with the same reservation mentioned above for a child born within less than the minimum term for a child born more than nine months after consummation under a valid contract.[3]

The minimum term of six months for pregnancy is approved by all modern Arab Personal Status Laws which are almost unanimous on a maximum term of one year, with the exception of Algeria, where this term is reduced to ten months (Arts. 42 and 43). Under the Lebanese Druze Personal Status Act of 24/2/1948, Article 137, the minimum term for pregnancy is one hundred and

---

[1] Al-Hilli, *Jaafari Personal Status Provisions*, p. 85.
[2] Abu Zahra, *On Marriage*, p. 388.
[3] Al-Hilli, *op. cit.* p. 85.

eighty days, and the maximum is three hundred days. However, the Syrian Article 128 specifies a solar year, while the Jordanian Article 185 stresses that the year is a lunar one. Kuwaiti Article 166 defines the minimum and maximum term of pregnancy as six lunar months and three hundred and sixty-five days respectively. Moroccan Article 84 makes the two terms subject to the provisions of Article 76 which deals with cases of suspicion which should be referred by the court to medical experts to decide thereon. Iraqi Article 51 simply refers to the minimum term for pregnancy with the implication that the Sharia rule in this context shall prevail (Art. 1, paras. 2–3).

Apart from these general rules, provisions of paternity differ under a valid marriage from those under an irregular marriage, or consummation with a semblance of the right to marital intercourse.

3. Paternity Under a Valid Marriage Contract

Jurists are unanimous that the valid marriage contract is the ground for establishing the parentage of the father of a child born during its continuation. The Sunnis calculated the pregnancy term from the time of the contract, not of consummation. Some among them, namely the Hanafis, consider the contract in itself a sufficient ground for establishing parenthood by the husband regardless of consummation. The Hanbalis, Malikis and Shafiis require the possibility of consummation, i.e. the husband having reached puberty and having access to his wife.[4]

The Shias stipulate that the marriage must be consummated, and count the pregnancy term from the time of consummation rather than of contract.[5]

The Syrian, Moroccan, Kuwaiti and Iraqi codes rule that the pregnancy term shall start from the date of the marriage contract and that the parentage of the child shall be established if meeting between the spouses has been possible (Arts. 120/1a and b, 85, 169/a, and 51, respectively). The Syrian Article cites the two examples of the husband being in jail or away as proof of the impossibility of such meeting.

On the other hand, the Jordanian Article 148 rules that the six months (minimum term for pregnancy) shall be counted from the date of consummation or valid retirement.

Once a child is born under a valid marriage contract within the specified limits of the pregnancy term, and consummation having been possible, its parentage is established, and the husband can only deny his fatherhood through one of two devices:

(i) denial at the time of birth or during preparations for it if the husband is present, or at the time of his learning of it if he is absent;

(ii) the imprecation (*lian*) (see Chap. 6): *Lian* should be made before a judge who shall order the separation of the spouses. This separation is technically an annulment, not a divorce proper, and shall be irrevocable. The husband shall disclaim paternity of the child born to his wife provided that he has

---

[4] Abu Zahra, *op. cit.* p. 386.
[5] Al-Hilli, *op. cit.* p. 85.

not previously acknowledged his paternity, or acquiesced in its being attributed to him, and his marriage was valid. There shall be no rights of inheritance between the two, or maintenance for the child, although prohibited degrees of relationship between the man and the child shall be created.

The Sunnis hold that the child may not give evidence against the husband,[6] but the Shias rule that the child may.[7]

Notwithstanding the above provisions, the Shia Ithna-Ashari maintain that the denial of paternity shall not be effective if the husband or wife dies after the renunciation of the child before the *lian*, or during it before they complete it.[8]

Those Sharia provisions are expressly asserted in the modern Codes of Syria and Kuwait. Syrian Article 129/3, reads, "If these two conditions (see above) are met the parentage of the child shall not be denied except through imprecation."

The whole of section 2 of Chapter 4, Book III, "Birth and Legal Effects Thereof", is devoted to the Denial of Parentage, which is the heading with the sub-title (*Lian*). It consists of Articles 176 to 180 inclusive. It repeats the general provisions for *lian*, specifying that a man may deny the parentage of a child within seven days of the birth, or the awareness thereof, provided that he has not acknowledged parentage whether expressly or by implication in cases when the parentage of the child is established in the wedlock, under a valid marriage existing or dissolved, or through consummation under a defective contract or with semblance of the right thereto. The *lian* suit procedure must be taken within fifteen days as from the time of birth or knowledge thereof. Once *lian* is effected between a man and woman, the judge shall declare the non-parentage of the child to the man who shall not be liable to any maintenance of the child, nor shall there be any mutual inheritance between them, and the child shall belong to its mother. If the man confesses to the effect that he was lying when he accused his wife and denied parentage of the child, that parentage shall be established even after the court's declaration of non-existence.

Although those general provisions on the denial of parentage are not asserted in other countries' Codes, they are observed by the highest courts of Arab States, i.e. the Cassation Courts. It must also be stressed that the denial of parentage of a child can only be made through a final conclusive court decision. Moroccan Article 90 sums up the rule as follows: "Only a decision of the judge shall rule out a child's parentage or a wife's pregnancy by a certain man."

On the other hand, if the husband denies parentage of a child, no parentage suit shall be heard if it is proved

(a) that the wife has not met the husband from the time of the contract;
(b) that the child was born more than a year from the husband's absence;
(c) that a divorcée or a widow gives birth to a child after more than a year from the time of divorce or death of the husband (Arts. 15, Egyptian Act No. 25/1929; 147, Jordanian).

The Syrian legislator distinguishes between two cases of parentage under a valid marriage depending on whether the child is born during the continuation of marriage, in which case the above provisions prevail, or is born after separation

---

[6] Abdullah, *Personal Status*, p. 577.
[7] Al-Hilli, *op. cit.* p. 87.
[8] *Loc. cit.*

or the death of the husband. Article 130 rules that if the divorcée or the widow has not declared that she has completed her *iddat*, the parentage of her child shall be proved if born within a year from the date of divorce or death. It shall not be proved if it is born after that, unless it is acknowledged by the husband or the heirs. Article 131 rules that a divorcée or a widow who declares having completed her *iddat* shall have a child's parentage proved if born within less than one hundred and eighty days from the time of declaration, or less than a year from the time of divorce or death.

4. Paternity Under an Irregular Contract or With a Semblance of the Right, or After Separation

A. Under an Irregular Contract

According to all schools, the pregnancy term shall be counted from the time of consummation, not of contract, for an irregular contract. A child born to a woman between six months at least and nine months at most after that time, shall be attributed to the husband under an irregular contract, before or after separation, and shall not be denied through *lian* which can only be made under a valid contract. No paternity shall be established if the child is born within six months of cohabitation, regardless of the date of contract.[9]

This provision is adopted in Articles 132 (Syrian, the term is 180 days), 86/1 (Moroccan), 172/a (Kuwaiti), and 148 (Jordanian, which makes valid retirement equivalent to consummation). If the child is born after separation, its parentage shall not be established unless the birth occurs within a year from separation (Arts. 132/2, Syrian; 86, Moroccan; 148, Jordanian, and 172/b, Kuwaiti), which makes the term three hundred and sixty-five days.

B. Consummation with a Semblance of the Right to have Lawful Sexual Intercourse

In the absence of any marriage contract, whether valid or irregular, i.e. in the case of consummation with a semblance of the right thereto (e.g. if the woman is thought by the husband to be his lawful wife, or not to be in a prohibited degree, without knowing that the contrary is the case), the child born within the above limits shall be attributed to the man on the strength of his acknowledgment, provided that he shall not declare it is an issue of adultery.[10]

This Sharia provision is observed throughout the Islamic countries and is mentioned expressly by the Syrian and Moroccan Laws which rule that: "The woman who is without a husband if she has had sexual intercourse with a semblance of the right thereto, if she gives birth to a child between the two limits of the pregnancy term, shall have its parentage to her partner established," (Arts. 133/2 and 87, respectively). Algerian Article 40 also acknowledges the offspring of cohabitation with a semblance of the right thereto. It is dealt with in the same Kuwaiti Article dealing with parentage under an irregular marriage contract (172/a and b).

---

[9] Abdullah, *op. cit.* pp. 579–580.
[10] *Ibid.* p. 581; Al-Hilli, *op. cit.* p. 88.

C. After Separation

A child born after separation, whether through revocable or irrevocable divorce, annulment or death, shall be attributed to the husband if the interval between separation and birth is one lunar year or less.[11] According to the Shias, no paternity shall be established for a child born after nine months from the death of the husband even if it is acknowledged by the heirs. Nevertheless, under Shia Law, a husband may acknowledge a child born to his divorced wife after more than a year of separation, provided that he is not known to be lying.[12]

5. Settlement of Disputes Between Spouses over the Fact of Birth and the Identity of The Child

A. During the Continuation of a Valid Marriage

Any dispute between the husband and wife over the fact of birth or the identity of the newborn child shall be settled by the evidence of the midwife or the physician, according to the Hanafis, of two women, according to the Malikis, of four women according to the Shafiis, and of four women, two men, or a man and two women, according to the Shias. Jurists are unanimous that the witnesses must be known to be honest.[13]

B. After Separation

A dispute over the fact of birth between a woman in her *iddat* of revocable or irrevocable divorce and her husband, or between a woman in her *iddat* of death and the heirs, shall be settled, according to the Shias, by the same evidence as above, namely four women, or two men, or one man and two women, even if the husband or the heirs have acknowledged the fact of pregnancy.[14] The Sunnis require the evidence of two men or a man and two women to settle a dispute over the fact of birth, but rule that the evidence of the midwife shall suffice to establish birth if pregnancy has been acknowledged by the husband or the heirs, or if it was observed.[15]

6. Paternity Through Acknowledgement

Apart from marriage, whether valid, irregular or with a semblance of a right to marital intercourse, parentage can also be established through acknowledgement which could be by the father, by the mother, or by the child itself.

---

[11] Abdullah, *op. cit.* pp. 582–583.
[12] Al-Hilli, *op. cit.* p. 88.
[13] Abdullah, *op. cit.* pp. 583–586; Al-Hilli, *op. cit.* p. 90.
[14] Al-Hilli, *loc. cit.*
[15] Abdullah, *loc. cit.*

A. By the Father

A man may either expressly or implicitly acknowledge a child as lawfully his, upon which the paternity of that child shall be established in the man, provided the following conditions are met:

(i)   that the child so acknowledged is not known to be the child of another man;
(ii) that the ages of the parties are such that they could be father and child;
(iii) that the acknowledgement is made in such a way that the father is indicating that the child is legitimate, and not the offspring of unlawful intercourse (*zina*);
(iv) that the child, if of discretion, confirms or acquiesces in the acknowledgement; such confirmation shall not be required if the child has not reached the age of discretion.[16] Kuwaiti Article 173(a) adopts all these provisions. The Shias do not require such confirmation by the child, even when it is of discretion.[17]

B. By the Mother

A woman may declare her maternity of a child and her acknowledgement shall be valid on meeting the above requirements, if she was not married nor in her *iddat* at the time of the birth. This ruling is adopted in as many words in Kuwaiti Article 174/a. If the mother is married, or in her *iddat* of marriage, her acknowledgement shall not establish the paternity of the husband without his confirmation.[18]

Under the Shias, the mother of a child may claim, after the death of a man, that she was his wife, and that the child is his. Her claim shall be sustained if approved by the heirs, and shall be dismissed if they deny that she was a wife of the deceased, or if she was not Muslim at the time of his death.[19]

C. By the Child

A child may also acknowledge the parentage of a father or a mother. This acknowledgement shall be subject to the same conditions enumerated above, namely that the child is of unknown parentage, that it is not the issue of unlawful intercourse, that the age difference admits of such a relationship, and that the acknowledgement is confirmed by the parent. This ruling is the subject of Kuwaiti Articles 173/b and 174/b.

The other modern Arab Personal Status Codes adopt the above rules in general, with some variations in detail:

(a) Syria. Article 134/1 establishes the parentage of a child to a father who makes a declaration to that effect, even if during a fatal illness, provided that the child is of unknown parentage and the age gap warrants such a kinship. Under the same Article, paragraph 2, a married woman or one in her *iddat* may make a declaration of her child being her husband's or ex-husband's without

---

[16]*Ibid.* p. 588.
[17]Al-Hilli, *loc. cit.*
[18]Abdullah, *op. cit.* p. 587.
[19]Al-Hilli, *op. cit.* pp. 90–91.

the parentage being established, unless the husband confirms it, or she provides evidence thereto. Under Article 135, the acknowledgement of a person of no known parentage of a father or a mother, shall have such a parentage established if it is confirmed by the person acknowledged, provided that the age gap between them warrants such a relationship.

(b) Tunisia. Parentage may be established through the wedlock, the acknowledgement by the father, or through the evidence of two or more trustworthy people (Art. 68). If disputed, parentage shall not be established for a child born to a wife who definitely has not met her husband, or who gave birth a year after the husband's absence or death or the date of divorce (Art. 69). No acknowledgement shall be accepted if the contrary thereto is conclusively proved. An acknowledgement by a person of unknown parentage of a father or mother shall be established if it is confirmed by the person acknowledged, whose age admits such a kinship, and who shall then have all the rights and duties of parents *vis-à-vis* the children. The paternity of a child born to the wife within six months or more from the date of a valid or irregular contract shall be established in the husband (Art. 71). Such a child's paternity, if disputed by the husband, shall only be denied by order of the judge (Art. 75), who shall then order the permanent separation of the two spouses as well (Art. 76).

(c) Morocco. Only the father has the right to acknowledge a child of unknown parentage. Such an acknowledgement shall be established, even when made during a death-illness, provided that the deponent is a male of sound mind, and not belied "by sheer reason or custom" (Art. 92). Acknowledgement shall be proved beyond any doubt by an official certificate or in the deponent's own handwriting (Art. 95).

(d) Iraq. Parenthood acknowledgement, even during the death-illness, shall establish the parentage of the person acknowledged who is of unknown parentage, if the like may be born to the like. Except that if the deponent is a woman, the parentage of the child to her husband shall only be established if it is confirmed by him, or if evidence is produced (Art. 52/1 and 2). The acknowledgement by a person of unknown parentage of any paternity or maternity shall be established if it is confirmed by the person acknowledged to whose like the like can be born (Art. 53).

(e) Jordan. The same above provisions apply, albeit worded differently. Under Article 149 the deponent's acknowledgement of parentage even during a death-illness, shall establish that parentage to a person of unknown parentage provided the age gap warrants such a relationship, and with confirmation of the person acknowledged if the child has reached puberty. The acknowledgement of a person of unknown parentage of a father or mother shall establish parentage if confirmed by the person acknowledged and warranted by the age gap.

(f) Algeria. Parentage is established through valid marriage, acknowledgement, evidence, and cohabitation with a semblance of a conjugal right thereto (Art. 40). Paternity of the child shall be established to the father, under a lawful marriage contract with the possibility of the spouses meeting, unless lawfully denied (Art. 41). Parentage shall be established by acknowledgement of the filiation, paternity or maternity, even if made during a death-illness, if it stands to reason or custom (Art. 44).

Apart from acknowledgement and wedlock, all degrees of kinship, e.g. of a father, mother, child or brother, etc., may be established through evidence by two men, or one man and two women according to the Sunnis, but only by two men according to the Shias. This general Sharia rule is codified under Articles 68 (Tunisia), 89 (Morocco) and 40 (Algeria). All that is required of the witnesses is that they be trustworthy.

Apart from filiation, maternity and paternity, acknowledgement of any other kinship shall not affect any person other than the deponent unless it is confirmed by the person affected (Arts. 136, Syria; 93, Morocco; 54, Iraq; 45, Algeria; 103, Sudan).

7. Adoption

Acknowledgement by a parent of a child of unknown parentage as his or hers naturally, differs from adoption, which is the taking a child of known or unknown parentage, but known for sure not to be his or her own child. Adoption was widespread among the Arabs before Islam, and remained valid during the early days of Islam until it was prohibited under the Quranic edict "... Nor hath He made those whom ye claim to be your sons your sons. This is a saying of your mouth. ... Proclaim their real parentage. That will be more equitable in the sight of God. And if ye know not their fathers, then (proclaim them) your brethren in faith and your clients." (33:4/5)

Adoption has since then been unacknowledgeable throughout the countries which apply the Sharia Personal Status Provisions in spite of the fact that it has been expressly prohibited only in four instances:

(i)   under the Moroccan Article 83, paragraph 3, "Adoption as understood customarily is void and shall produce no legal effect. Adoption for the purpose of rewarding or bequeathing, known as according a person the status of one's child, shall not establish a parentage, and shall be subject to the provisions of the will";
(ii) under Article 46 of the Algerian Act No. 84/1984, "Adoption shall be forbidden, under the Sharia and the law";
(iii) under Article 167 of the Kuwaiti Personal Status Laws "No parentage shall be established through adoption even if the adoptee is of unknown parentage".
(iv) Article 135 of the Yemeni Personal Status Law contains an identical prohibition.

However, there is only one exception to this virtual unanimity – Tunisia. On 4/3/1958, Act No. 27 in respect of Public Guardianship Taking into Care and Adoption, was promulgated in an obvious attempt to find a remedy for the growing numbers of foundlings and children of refugees, according to the Explanatory Note issued by the Ministry of Justice. The Act tried to steer a middle course between the social and the Sharia exigencies. On the one hand, it granted the right to adopt to every adult, whether male or female, on complying with the conditions of being married, possessing civil rights, being of sound character, mind and body, and capable of looking after the adoptee. Other conditions are attached concerning the adoptee and third parties. The difference in age between the adopting parent and the adoptee shall be a minimum of fifteen years, except when the adoptee is a child of the adopter's spouse; the adoptee need not be Tunisian (Art. 10). In all cases, the consent of the adopter's spouse must be obtained (Art. 11). The adoptee itself must be a minor, whether male or female (Art. 12). The District Court shall issue the adoption order after ascertaining compliance with the requirements and confirmation of all those concerned and present, including the natural parents or the representative of the relevant administrative authority, the adopter and spouse; the adoption order shall then be final (Art. 13). The child shall bear the name of the adoptive parent, and shall enjoy all rights and liabilities of real children, of maintenance, custody and inheritance (Arts. 14 and 15).

On the other hand, honouring the Sharia rule, all the prohibited degrees for marriage purposes shall remain observable by the child if his relatives are known (Art. 15).

8. Legal Effects of Parentage

The establishment of a child's parentage creates forthwith certain rights and duties, the most important of which are fosterage, custody, maintenance and guardianship, which shall be dealt with in the following chapters.

I shall here deal with those rights connected with mutual inheritance which will not be dealt with in the chapter on inheritance.

A direct acknowledgement of parentage as explained above shall establish forthwith the reciprocal rights of inheritance between the parties concerned, subject to the provisions stated.

An indirect declaration of parentage which affects a third party shall be binding only on the person who makes it, and shall require that further evidence as to the kinship of the beneficiary be provided by the maker of the declaration. For instance, if an orphan acknowledges a man of unknown parentage to be his brother, his acknowledgement shall be effective only on him, and not on the other heirs if they dispute the claim. The acknowledged brother shall receive half the deponent's share, according to the Sunnis,[20] or the balance between that share and what the deponent deserves under his acknowledgement according to the Shias. By way of illustration, a man dies leaving two sons: A, who acknowledges the brotherhood of C, and B, who disputes this kinship. B shall receive half the estate, A shall get one third and C shall inherit one sixth. Obviously, if A is the only heir, he shall get a half, and C shall get the other half.[21]

If the deponent dies leaving no heir, his estate shall devolve on the acknowledged person if

(i)   the person is of unknown parentage;
(ii) the person is not proven to have a different parentage;
(iii) the deponent has not withdrawn acknowledgement;
(iv) there is no impediment to inheritance (Art. 41, Egyptian Inheritance Act No. 77/1943).

---

[20] Abdullah, *op. cit.* p. 589.
[21] Al-Hilli, *op. cit.* p. 91.

9. The Foundling

A foundling is a newborn baby, abandoned by its parents on grounds of poverty or shame, and so unable to fend for itself. Care of a foundling is a religious duty if there is any risk that the baby might otherwise die. Once found and taken into care, a foundling must never again be abandoned. The baby's finder has sole right to its guardianship unless he is unfit or is non-Muslim and a Muslim disputes that right, in which case, the Muslim shall be the guardian; if they are of the same religion, the judge should decide who shall be the guardian.[22]

A foundling is considered under Sunni law to be a Muslim if found in a Muslim locality, or a Christian or a Jew if found by such a person in his own locality.[23] Under Shia law, a foundling shall be deemed a Muslim regardless of the religion of its finder, or the place where the baby is found.[24]

If there should be any money on the foundling, it shall belong to the foundling. Its guardian shall use the money for its upbringing on authorization by the court. If the guardian spends his own money on the foundling, he shall be entitled to recover his expenses either from public funds, or from the foundling when it comes of age and can afford it. The guardian has the right to educate the foundling, or to provide for its learning a trade.

If any man claims paternity of the foundling, such a claim shall be valid subject to the previously mentioned conditions of acknowledgement, but the foundling shall remain a Muslim regardless of the religion of the putative parent.[25]

Under Shia law, a married woman may claim a foundling as her child. The claim shall be accepted if supported by her husband who shall then be acknowledged as the father, or if the woman proves giving birth to it. If she is unmarried, cannot prove the birth, or is not supported by her husband, the custody of the foundling shall be given solely to her.[26]

If a baby who is proved to be a foundling has no money, remains unclaimed and its guardian refuses to provide for it, its maintenance shall be a charge on public funds to provide for its needs in respect of food and clothing.[27]

Only the Tunisian Law includes provisions on the foundlings, adopting many of the above rulings. Anyone who pledges to provide maintenance for a foundling and obtains permission of the judge thereto, shall be under the obligation of maintenance until the foundling is capable of earning a living, unless it has means of its own (Art. 77). The finder shall have the custody of the foundling unless its father appears, claims it, and the judge grants him custody (Art. 78). Whatever property is found on the foundling shall remain its own (Art. 79). If the foundling dies leaving no heir, its earnings shall revert to the treasury, but the finder may claim back from the State his expenditure by way of maintenance of the foundling within the limits of its earnings (Art. 80).

---

[22] Abu Zahra, op. cit. p. 400.
[23] *Ibid.*
[24] Al-Hilli, *op. cit.* p. 92.
[25] Abu Zahra, *loc. cit.*
[26] Al-Hilli, *op. cit.* p. 94.
[27] Abu Zahra, *loc. cit.*; Al-Hilli, *loc. cit.*

CHAPTER 9

Child's Rights during Infancy: Fosterage and Custody

1. Fosterage

Parentage is a right for the child and the father. Once established, it is followed
by the child's right to be brought up, a right which imposes a duty on the father,
namely maintenance, and another on the mother, namely fosterage and custody
until the end of infancy.

Fosterage has already been discussed in the context of giving rise to a prohibited degree for marriage purposes. As a right of the child, it creates an obligation
on both parents and raises the question of wages.

A. Fosterage as a Duty of the Mother

During the first stage of its life, the infant needs feeding through suckling. It is
the mother's duty, in the first instance, to feed her baby, under the Quranic
ruling "The mothers shall suckle their offspring for two whole years for those
who wish to complete the suckling." (2:233) Although the verse is in the indicative
mood, all Muslim jurists agree that it is imperative, setting a religious duty on
the mother to feed the baby, whether she is married to its father or divorced
and has completed her *iddat*.

However, they differ on whether she should be ordered by the court to suckle
the infant. The Hanafis maintain that the mother may be compelled by the
father to nurse her infant child if no suitable nurse other than the mother is
available, if neither the father nor the infant has any property, or if the infant
refuses any other breast but the mother's.[1]

This Hanafi position is adopted under the Jordanian Article 150, and is very
similar to the Shia's, with the sole addition that the mother may be exempted if
a third woman agrees to hire, at her expense, a wet nurse for the infant.[2]

The Malikis hold that the mother shall be under the legal and religious
obligation to feed her baby free if she is married to its father or revocably
divorced from him, unless it is not the custom of her class to suckle its babies.
They make an exception in the latter case if the baby refuses any other breast,
when she is then entitled to a wage like a divorced mother.[3]

---

[1] Al-Abiani, *A Brief Commentary on Personal Status Sharia Provisions*, p. 318.
[2] Al-Hilli, *Jaafari Personal Status Provisions*, p. 95.
[3] Badran, *Children's Rights*, pp. 50–51.

156

The Hanbalis maintain that it is the duty of the father alone to provide for the feeding of the baby.[4]

Some Zahiris rule that the mother shall be compelled to suckle her baby whether she or her husband like it or not, unless she is divorced, has no milk, or her milk is not wholesome for the baby.[5]

Iraqi Article 55 makes it the duty of the mother to suckle her baby unless pathological conditions prevent her from so doing.

Kuwaiti Article 186, ruling that the mother shall be obliged to suckle her baby if it cannot be fed on anything except her milk, steers a compromise between the protection of the baby from disease or death and the respect of the mother's will.

The Yemeni Law, Arts. 136 and 137, provides that it is the duty of the mother to suckle her baby if it is impossible for another woman to suckle it, and shall have priority to suckle her child unless she demands higher wages than normal for her class and that of the child. If the child is suckled by another woman, then the suckling will take place at the home of the mother unless she has lost her right to custody. The woman who suckles a child other than her own is entitled to maintenance and attire fitting her class from the provider according to his class, for a term not longer than two years from the birth of the child. Such wages shall be a debt which shall not lapse except by payment or discharge.

B. The Father's Duty in Respect of Fosterage

If the mother does not have to suckle the baby and refuses to do so, or if she is dead and no woman volunteered to feed it, the father shall hire a wet nurse for the baby. The nurse will not have to stay at the home of the custodian (*hadina*) in order to suckle the baby unless expressly stipulated in the contract.[6]

In the absence of any agreement on a specific arrangement for suckling, e.g. that the baby be taken to the nurse's home for feeding and brought back to the custodian's, the baby shall be suckled at the mother's or other custodian's home, since the two rights of fosterage and custody are distinct, and the mother's refusal to feed the baby does not deprive her of the right of custody.[7]

This generally held Sunni position is not followed by the Shia Jaafaris, who maintain that if the mother refuses to suckle her baby when she is not under any obligation to do so, she shall lose her right to custody, and the father shall hire a wet nurse who shall not have to feed the infant at the mother's home.[8]

If the hire duration expires before the baby can do without suckling, the wet nurse shall be compelled to extend the period until weaning if the baby refuses any other breast.[9]

In all cases it is the father who shall be liable for the wages for feeding the baby whether they are to the mother or to the wet nurse, unless the infant itself has property. If the father is destitute, unable to earn a livelihood or dead, the wages for suckling the baby shall be payable by the person whose duty it is to

---

[4] *Ibid.*
[5] *Ibid.* p. 52.
[6] Abdullah, *Sharia Personal Status Provisions*, p. 595.
[7] *Ibid.*
[8] Al-Hilli, *op. cit.* p. 95.
[9] *Ibid.* p. 96. .

provide maintenance for the baby (Arts. 152/1, Syrian, adding "whether it is natural or artificial feeding"; 112, Moroccan; 56, Iraqi).

C. Wages for Fostering

Only the Shia Ithna-Asharis rule that the mother is entitled to receive payment for nursing her own infant during the continuation of marriage, during or after the *iddat* of a revocable or irrevocable divorce – and the husband may hire her for fostering.[10]

The Sunni Schools and the modern laws (Arts. 152/2, Syrian; 113, Moroccan; 152, Jordanian; and 189/a, Kuwaiti) rule, on the contrary, that no wages for fostering shall be paid to the wife during the continuation of marriage or in the *iddat* of a revocable divorce.

However, such wages shall be payable after the expiry of the *iddat* under the Quranic ruling on the divorced woman "... and if they give suck for you give them their due payment". (65:6) The mother shall then receive the wages for the equal, which shall be commensurate with the condition of the person whose duty it is to pay (Art. 153, Jordanian).

Since suckling the infant is not only the mother's duty but also her right, she shall have priority thereto unless a wet nurse is available who offers to nurse the baby free of charge or for less wages than the mother, under the Quranic verse "No mother shall be treated unfairly on account of her child, nor father on account of his child" (*Sura* Baqara, II, verse 233), the father being held responsible for the cost of nursing. This ruling is unanimously held, with the Shias adding that the mother shall then lose her right to custody, but could retain her right to access,[11] while the Sunnis again distinguish between the two rights. Articles 153 (Syrian) and 114 (Moroccan) stress that suckling even free of charge by a wet nurse shall take place at the mother's home, if the mother asks for wages and the father is destitute.

According to the Sunnis and Shias alike, pursuant to the Quranic ruling: "The mothers shall suckle their offspring for two whole years for those who wish to complete the suckling", (2:233) the fosterage wages shall be payable for a maximum of two years (Art. 153, Jordanian, and 188/b, Kuwaiti).

Nursing wages shall be a valid debt on the father under the Sharia to be settled only through payment or discharge (Kuwaiti Art. 187), and shall be a charge on the estate in the event of the death of the father.

2. Custody

Custody is an established right for the baby from the time of its birth. It is one form of guardianship of the child which the jurists divide into three categories:

(i) guardianship of the infant (*hadina* or *hidana* in Arabic) during the early years of life, when the infant needs women to look after it;

(ii) guardianship of education (*wilayat al-Tarbiyya*) believed under the Sharia to be the duty of men rather than women;

---

[10] *Ibid.*
[11] Al-Hilli, *op. cit.* p. 96.

(iii) guardianship of property (*al wilayatu alal maal*) if the child has any property, a task again for men rather than for women.

This section will deal with the first form of guardianship, leaving the two other forms to later chapters.

Custody under the Sharia is defined as the caring for the infant during the period when it cannot do without the women in a prohibited degree who have the lawful right to bring it up. (A person in a prohibited degree to another person – be it a child – of the opposite sex – means that it is illegal for those persons to contract marriage. For further details see under Chapter 3, Section 7, "Marriage Impediments"). There are similar definitions enshrined in three modern North African Laws: "... the caring for the child at its home and looking after its upbringing" (Art. 54, Tunisian); "... the protection of the child as far as possible from any potential cause of injury thereto and the provision for its upbringing and safeguarding of its interests" (Art. 97, Moroccan); "... the catering for a child, its upbringing and education in the religious faith of its father, and provision for its protection, health and righteousness" (Art. 62, Algerian).

The Yemeni Law, Art. 138, gives the most comprehensive definition: "*Hadana* is carefully looking after the infant who cannot look after itself, bringing it up and protecting it from what would destroy or injure it, without prejudice to the rights of the guardian. It is a right of the infant which cannot be waived. The guardian's entitlement shall be lost through certain impediments, but regained when they are removed."

A. The Persons Entitled to Custody

All Schools, Sunni and Shia alike, hold that the mother, whether she is separated or living with her husband, has the first claim to the custody of her infant, but she cannot be compelled to undertake it due to her inability to do so, unless there is no-one else to undertake it.

If she is dead or disqualified (see next section), Schools differ widely on the person to whom the custody of the child should pass. These differences are reflected in the modern and Personal Status Legislations.

(1) The Hanafis

The second claim to the custody of the child, if the mother is not available or eligible, goes to the following persons in the given order:

(a) the maternal grandmother, how-high-soever;
(b) the paternal grandmother, how-high-soever;
(c) the full, uterine and consanguine sister, in that order;
(d) the maternal aunts, in the same order;
(e) the paternal aunts, in the same order.[12]

The general rule is that since the mother has prior right, the relations on her side are given preference over those on the father's side, and among the latter the order is from the full to the uterine to the consanguine relations. (A full

---

[12]Badran, *op. cit.* pp. 64–65.

brother is, for example, a brother born of the same two parents; a uterine brother is only from the mother's side, and a consanguine brother is from the father's side.) If there is no woman either from the maternal or paternal side, then the right of upbringing goes to the agnates in the same order of priority as the inheritance, beginning with

(a) the father;
(b) paternal grandfather, how-high-soever;
(c) full brother;
(d) consanguine brother (N.B. a uterine brother is not an agnate);
(e) sons of the full brother;
(f) sons of the consanguine brother;
(g) their descendants how-low-soever;
(h) paternal uncle;
(i) paternal uncle's son, provided always that no agnate male shall be entrusted with the custody of a female minor whom he is not prohibited to marry.[13]

The above order is held by the Lebanese Druze Personal Act 1948 Article 57, the Syrian Act No. 59/1953 as amended by Act No. 34/1975 Article 139, the Sudanese Law Article 10, and the Yemeni Articles 141–142. The Jordanian Provisional Act No. 61/1976, Article 154 follows closely, "The real mother has prior right to the custody of her child, and to bring it up for the duration of marriage and after separation, such right passing from the mother to the woman next to her in the order set by Imam Abu Hanifa." This is the order cited above, except that, unique in that respect, the Jordanian Law seems to confine the right of the custody of the infant solely to women.

(2) The Malikis

Failing the mother, custody shall go to her mother, how-high-soever, then the full uterine maternal aunt, then the mother's maternal aunt, and then her paternal aunt, then the father's mother, then his mother's mother, then his father's mother; the nearer excludes the further, and those related through the mother shall have precedence over those through the father. Failing these, custody should go to the father, then the sister, then the father's sister, then the father's paternal aunt, then maternal aunt, then the daughter of the full brother, then uterine brother, then consanguine brother, then the daughter of the sister in the same order. Failing these, custody shall go to the guardian, male or female, then the brother, then his son (failing a maternal grandfather), then the paternal uncle, then his son, the nearer preferred to the further.

This order is followed in Morocco and in Kuwait. Article 99 of the Moroccan Personal Status Decree reads:

"Custody is a duty of the parents as long as they live together in matrimony; on the dissolution of marriage, the mother shall have the first claim to the custody of her child, then her mother, then her mother's mother, then the mother's full sister, then her uterine sister, then her consanguine sister, then the father's mother, then the father's maternal or paternal grandmother

---

[13] *Ibid.* pp. 66–67.

how-high-soever, then the sister, then the paternal aunt, then the father's paternal aunt, then the father's maternal aunt, then the sister's daughter, then the brother, then the paternal grandfather, then the brother's son, then the paternal uncle, then his son. In all cases, the full relation shall have precedence over the uterine, who is followed by the consanguine.

Article 100 reads:

"The guardian shall take precedence over all other agnates for the male ward and the female ward while she is a minor, and in the event of her majority if he is in a marriage prohibited degree to her, or if he is married and trustworthy." "This order shall be observed if the first is eligible or available then to the next."

Article 189 of the Kuwaiti Law No. 51/1984 repeats the Maliki order of eligibility for custody, and adds, in paragraph c, that in the event of equal claims for eligible custodianship, the judge shall select the best among them for the ward.

(3) The Shafiis
The eligible custodians may be a group of men and women, solely females or solely males.
  In the first case, the mother shall have priority over the father, followed by the mother's mother, how-high-soever, provided she is a presumptive heiress, failing which the father, then his mother, then her mother how-high-soever, provided she is a presumtive heiress – failing which the nearest female kin, then the nearest male kin.
  In the second case, i.e. of only female relatives, priority goes to the mother, then her mother, then the father's mother, then the sister, then the maternal aunt, then the daughter of the sister, then of the brother, then the paternal aunt, then the daughters of the maternal aunt, the paternal aunt, the paternal uncle and the maternal uncle, in that order.
  In the third case, when only male kin are available, priority goes to the father, then the grandfather, then the brother-german, then the consanguine brother, then the uterine brother, then the son of the brother-german or consanguine brother, then the full then the consanguine paternal uncle, then his son, who "not being a prohibited degree, shall appoint a trustworthy person, e.g. his own daughter, to take care of the female minor".[14]

(4) The Hanbalis
Priority goes to the mother, then her mother, then her mother's mother, and so on, then the father, then his mother, how-high-soever, then the grandfather, then his mother, then the sister, the maternal then the paternal aunt, then the father's maternal then paternal aunt; in all these categories the order going from the germane to the uterine to the consanguine, the same order being followed with nieces and cousins.[15]

---

[14] Al-Jazeeri, *Jurisprudence According to the Four Doctrines*, Vol. IV, pp. 595–596.
[15] *Ibid.*

(5) The Ithna-Asharis

The Shia Ithna-Asharis grant the mother the prior right to custody of the male infant until it is weaned at two, and of the girl until she is seven; the right passes then, if the mother is dead or disqualified, to the father, failing which to the father's father, then to grandparents, consanguine sisters, then to the nephews and nieces in the same order, then to the maternal aunts and uncles, then the paternal aunts and uncles, then to the children of paternal and maternal uncles, then to the mother's maternal aunt, the father's maternal aunt, and so on. In the event of a tie, a lot shall decide. If no kin of a prohibited degree for marriage is available or eligible, the infant shall be looked after by a non-prohibited agnate such as the daughters of paternal or maternal uncles or aunts, failing which the judge shall appoint an honest, trustworthy woman.[16]

(6) Other, more eclectic, modern Arab legislations

(a) Tunisia. Tunisian Article 57 rules that custody of the children is the right of their parents as long as the marital condition stands. Article 64 rules that any person entitled to the custody of the children may relinquish his right thereto, whereupon the judge shall appoint a different guardian. In the event of the termination of marriage due to death, the custody shall be given to the surviving parent. If the marriage is dissolved while the spouses are alive, custody shall be granted to either of them or to a third person. The judge shall take into account the welfare of the ward in making any decision (Art. 67).

(b) Algeria. Algerian Article 64 gives the mother the priority, followed by her mother, then the maternal aunt, then the father, then the father's mother, then the next nearest of kin, provided that the ward's interest shall be observed in all cases.

(c) Iraq. The Iraqi Act No. 188/1959 as amended under Act No. 21/1978 moves nearer to the Shia position. The persons entitled to the custody of the infant are described under Articles 57, the relevant parts of which read as follows:

> "(1) The mother has prior right to the custody and upbringing of the infant, both for the duration of marriage and after separation, unless the ward suffers injury thereby. ... (7) In the event of the mother becoming disqualified or of her death, custody shall pass to the father, unless the infant's interest dictates otherwise, in which case custody shall pass to whomever the court shall choose, with the best interest of the child being the paramount consideration. ... (8) If neither parent is eligible for custody, the court shall entrust the custody of the child to a trustworthy person, female or male, and may likewise order the child to be brought up in a state-run nursery if available. (9) In the event of the father's death or disqualification, the child shall remain with its mother for as long as she remains qualified, with any of its female or male kin having the right to challenge her right thereto until it reaches the age of majority."

---

[16] Al-Hilli, *op. cit.* p. 100.

B. *Eligibility for Guardianship*

The right to the custody of the infant is subject to certain conditions, some of which are common to females and males, others are for females and a third group for males.

(1) *Common conditions for custody*

According to Sharia, both women and men have to comply with the following conditions to be eligible for custody.

(a) Majority, sanity and freedom. The minor, the insane and the imbecile, and the slave, need to be looked after by another; *a fortiori*, they cannot look after an infant.[17]

These conditions, save for freedom, are adopted in the modern legislations (Arts. 137, Syrian; 55, Lebanese Druze Act; 58, Tunisia; 98, Morocco; 57(2), Iraq; 155, Jordan; 190/a, Kuwait; 122(a)(b), Sudan.

(b) Ability to bring up the ward, look after its interests and protect it both physically and morally. Kuwaiti Article 190/a incorporates this phrase to the letter. Therefore, no person shall be entrusted to the custody of a child if he or she is incapacitated due to a handicap, old age, disease, occupation, or moral corruption. Moroccan Article 98/5 and Tunisian Article 58 both specify the condition of freedom from any infectious disease. The Sudanese legislative circular of 16/2/1927 adds that even living with a patient suffering from an infectious disease shall debar a person from being entrusted with the custody of a child. Syrian Article 139(2) rules that a female shall not lose the right to custody of her children because of her work, provided that she secures their care in an acceptable way, a ruling generally held by the Egyptian courts.[18] However, the ability of the working person to care for the infant shall be left to the discretion of the court. Sudanese Law also adds honesty and freedom from infectious diseases (112c).

(2) *Conditions for the female custodian (hadina)*

In addition to those common conditions, a female custodian (*hadina*) shall also fulfil the following requirements:

(a) Marriage restrictions. Although the Tradition implies that the mother, and, *a fortiori*, any other female custodian, would lose the right to custody of the child once she married, it is not always interpreted so sweepingly. The Hanafis and Malikis deprive the woman of the right to custody should she marry a stranger (a person outside the child's paternal or maternal family) or a relation of the child who would not, in other circumstances, be prohibited from marriage to the child, such as a cousin. However, should she marry a relation of the child who would be prohibited from marriage to it in any circumstances, such as the child's uncle, then the custodian would not lose her right to custody, and loving care for the infant would then be assumed, even if the wife's attention to the child may compromise part of her services to her husband.[19]

---

[17] Badran, *op. cit.* p. 68.
[18] *Ibid.* p. 69.
[19] Abdullah, *op. cit.* p. 604.

This ruling is held in Articles 137 (Syrian), 156 (Jordanian) and 113(a) Sudanese. Kuwaiti Article 191/a concurs, adding the condition "if the marriage is consummated". Iraqi Article 57(2) stipulates that the woman shall not be married to a stranger. Moroccan Article 105 deprives a woman of the right to custody on marrying a stranger not in a prohibited degree to, or a guardian of the ward, unless she herself is a guardian or a foster mother of the baby, and provided that the baby does not reject her breast. However, in Article 106, the next person in line for the custody of the child shall lose that right on keeping silent for a year after knowing of consummation of such a prohibited marriage by the woman with custody. A similar ruling is stipulated in Tunisian Article 58: a female shall be entitled to the custody of the infant provided that she has no husband with whom marriage has been consummated unless the husband is in a prohibited degree to or guardian of the infant, ... or the next in line to the right of custody shall remain silent for a year after knowing of consummation of marriage without claiming that right, ... or the woman is a wet nurse, or both a mother and a guardian of the ward. However, the same Articles give the court discretion to allow the woman to keep the child, even if she is married, if its welfare so requires. Again, Article 191/b of the Kuwaiti law deprives the next in line for custody of that right on keeping silent for a year without any excuse, after learning of the consummation of marriage and adds that ignorance of this provision is no excuse.

On the other hand, the Jaafaris maintain that any marriage with a man, even in a marriage-prohibited degree to the infant, shall deprive the woman of the right to custody if the infant's father is alive and eligible, such right passing then to the father. In the absence of a father, the mother shall retain that right after her marriage, taking precedence over the grandfather.[20]

Should that impediment to custody be removed on the dissolution of marriage, the woman shall recover her right to custody according to the Jaafaris, Hanafis, Shafiis, and Hanbalis, and Articles 141 (Syrian), 110 (Moroccan), 158 (Jordanian), 193 (Kuwaiti) and 121 (Sudanese), all of which apply to all cases of temporarily losing that right. The Malikis rule out any such recovery.

(b) Relationship to ward. The woman shall be a relation in a prohibited degree to the ward. A stranger, even in a prohibited degree on fosterage grounds, shall not be eligible.

(c) Residence. She shall not live with the ward in a home where it is not liked. This provision is expressly stated in the Jordanian Article 155.

(d) Religion. Only the Jaafaris and Shafiis require that no non-Muslim woman is qualified for the custody of a Muslim child born to a Muslim father, although a *kitabi* shall have the custody of a *kitabi* infant.[21] The Hanafis, followed by the Jordanian legislator (Art. 155), consider apostasy a sufficient reason to deny a woman her right to custody.

Generally speaking, other Sunni jurists and legislators do not insist on the identity of religion between the female and her ward, provided that it shall be brought up in the faith of its father (Algerian Art. 62). However, the Sunnis rule that if there are reasonable grounds to think that the *hadina* would influence

---

[20] Al-Hilli, *op. cit.* p. 99.
[21] *Ibid.*

the infant's religious beliefs, e.g. her teaching it the articles of her faith, performing her religious rites in front of it, accompanying it to her church, making it eat pork or drink wine, the ward shall be taken away from her. The Zahiri, Ibn Hazm maintains that identity of religion is not a condition during fosterage, but it becomes necessary thereafter.[22]

The Kuwaiti Article 192 of the Personal Status Law reads as follows:

"The non-Muslim *hadina* of a Muslim child shall be entitled to its custody until it starts to understand about religion, or until it is feared that it may become familiar with a faith other than Islam, even if it does not understand about religion." "In all cases, such a child shall not remain with such a *hadina* after it has reached five years of age.

Articles 59 (Tunisian) and 108 (Moroccan) deal in almost identical terms with the case of a female eligible for the custody of a child and professing a faith other than the father's. Again, she loses her right to custody on the ward completing its fifth year of age, unless she is the mother and there is no fear of her bringing it up according to a religion different from the father's.

A similar ruling is given in Sudanese Art. 114 which provides (1) that the ward shall follow the better religion of the two parents, and (2) that if the *hadina's* faith is not that of the Muslim father of the ward, she shall lose the right to custody on the ward reaching five years of age, or when it is feared she might exploit her *hadana* to bring up the child in a faith different from that of its father.

(e) The disobedient wife. Article 145 of the Syrian Personal Act rules that if the wife becomes disobedient and the children are over five years of age, the judge may, at his discretion, grant their custody to either spouse provided that due care shall be taken of the children's interests on reasonable grounds.

(3) Conditions for the male custodian (hadin)

In addition to the general conditions of eligibility, the male custodian (*hadin*) shall comply with the following two requirements:

(i) To be a relative within a prohibited degree to the female ward. Therefore, a cousin shall not be eligible for the custody of his female cousin.

This general rule is held under Tunisian Article 58 and Kuwaiti Article 190/b in which both add the condition that such a relative shall have living with him a woman capable of looking after the child. Article 99(2) of the Moroccan Personal Decree grants the guardian, without any qualification, the right to custody of a female minor.

(ii) To profess the same religion as the ward, if the *hadin* is a male agnate. The reason is that his right to custody is based on his right to inheritance, a condition of which is the identity of religion. If the non-Muslim infant has two full brothers, a Muslim and a non-Muslim, its custody shall pass to the non-Muslim.

---

[22] Ibn Hazm, *Al Muhalla*, Vol. 10, p. 323.

However, a non-agnate relative is not required to be of the same faith as the ward, since the right to custody here is based on a kinship within a prohibited degree, not on the right to inheritance. This case has no room in the Shia Law which requires identity of religion whether the custodian is a *hadin* or *hadina*.[23]

The Sudanese Article 113(b) concurs with the Shia Law and adds that the male *hadin* has a woman with him fit to look after the infant.

C. Wages for Custody

The *hadina* may be the mother or not. The mother, according to the Hanafis, shall not be entitled to custody wages during the continuation of marriage or the *iddat* of a revocable divorce, since in both cases she receives matrimonial or *iddat* maintenance. But the mother who receives no such maintenance, e.g. if she is in an *iddat* of the death of the husband, or has been divorced on a discharge or has completed her *iddat*, shall be entitled to custody wages. She shall have that right also if she has ceased to receive her *iddat* maintenance on the expiry of one year after her being divorced.[24]

This Hanafi ruling is held in the modern Arab Personal Status Laws, Articles 104 (Moroccan), 57(3) (Iraqi) and 160 (Jordanian). Syrian Article 143 rules that the mother shall not be entitled to custody wages for the duration of matrimony or during the *iddat* of divorce, without qualifying it as revocable. The same ruling is adopted under Kuwaiti Article 199/a, which extends it to the duration of a *mutat* ordered by the court for the *hadina* against the ward's father. Paragraph 199b provides that the *hadina* must receive wages until the boy reaches seven and the girl nine years of age.

The *hadina* who is not the mother shall receive wages for custody unless she offers it free. This is accepted by all schools and adopted in Sudanese Article 124. The Shafiis and Hanbalis rule that even the mother may ask for wages for custody. The Jaafaris maintain that such wages are not imperative. But the mother is not compelled to give custody free, but may ask for wages. The father then shall have the choice between paying her such wages or taking the infant away from her. If custody is not incumbent on the father, and no person volunteered for it free of charge, the mother may be granted the wages she demands unless she asks for more than the wages of the equal.[25]

Wages for custody shall be payable from the time of agreement or court order, or from the time the mother undertakes it without any need for agreement or court order.

The infant shall be liable for the custody wages if it has property, under the Sunni and Shia Laws. If it has no property, such wages shall be due from and according to the means of the person who is liable for the maintenance of the infant (Arts. 143, Syrian; and 159, Jordanian). Moroccan Article 103 adds that such wages are distinct from maintenance and suckling wages. Tunisian Article 65 specifies the wages for custody as confined to the cost of serving the ward, preparing meals, and laundry, according to custom. Algerian Article 72 orders that the father shall provide or rent a home for the infant who has no property with which to provide maintenance and dwelling for itself.

---

[23] Al-Hilli, *op. cit.* p. 99.
[24] Al-Abiani, *op. cit.* p. 336.
[25] Al-Hilli, *op. cit.* p. 100.

Under the Sunni law, if the female entitled to the custody of the child refuses to take it without wages, and a woman offers to accept custody free of charge, the volunteer, if she is a relative in a prohibited degree and the infant has property, shall have precedence over the female entitled to custody, whether the father has property or not, as this would save any cost incurred by the infant and provide loving care for it.[26]

The volunteer shall also be preferred to the mother if in a prohibited degree and neither the infant nor its father has property, pursuant to the Quranic verse "A mother should not be made to suffer because of her child nor a father on account of his child". (2:233) The father in this case would suffer hardship to pay the mother wages.

It is evident, therefore, that a stranger who volunteers for fosterage is preferable to a mother who demands wages if the stranger is offering free suckling or asks for wages lower than those asked for by the mother, whether or not the infant or the father has property.

Under the Jaafari Law, however, if the infant's mother refuses to look after it free of charge, and a volunteer fit for custody, even if she is a stranger, can be found, or if the father is able to provide custody, even with the help of others such as a servant or his own wife, the mother shall be given the choice between free custody or handing the infant over to the volunteer or to the father, without prejudice to her own right to access.[27]

D. *Place for Custody*

(1) *When the mother is the hadina*

The infant shall stay normally with its mother at the matrimonial home during the continuation of marriage. The mother then shall not, without the husband's permission, move to a different place, with or without the infant, until it can do without her and custody is terminated.[28] This provision is held under the Syrian Article 148/1.

If the mother is divorced, she shall keep the infant with her at the place where she spends her *iddat*, which place she cannot leave or be made to leave, under the Quranic verse, "Expel them not from their houses nor let them go forth unless they commit open immorality." (65:1). Since staying on in the matrimonial home is a duty to honour both the right of the husband and the right of the Sharia, she shall not leave it with her child, even with the husband's permission.[29]

Having completed her *iddat*, she may move with the child to a city near enough to her previous home to allow the father to travel to see his child and return to spend the night in his own home.[30] Tunisian and Moroccan Articles 61 and 107 rule that the *hadina* shall lose her right to custody if she moves to or settles in a different town where it would be difficult for the father or guardian to look after the interests of the child.

She can move to a remote town on two conditions: that it is her town of origin, and the place where she married the father. Otherwise she shall have to

---

[26] Abdullah, *op. cit.* pp. 620–621.
[27] Al-Hilli, *op. cit.* p. 101.
[28] Abdullah, *op. cit.* pp. 611–615.
[29] *Ibid.*
[30] *Ibid.*

obtain the father's consent. This provision adopted in Sudanese Article 119(1) and (2) is also held under Syrian Article 148 (2), (3) and (4), which allows both the mother and her mother to move after the completion of the *iddat*, without the guardian's permission, to her home town where her marriage was solemnized, and to travel directly with the child within the territory to the town where she lives or works for a public authority, provided a relative in a prohibited degree to her lives there. Jordanian Article 164 makes the travelling of the guardian or the *hadina* with the minor to a town within the Kingdom subject to its not unfairly influencing the attitude the child has in favour of the other party, otherwise the child shall be taken away by the other party: Article 166 allows the *hadina* to leave the Kingdom with the ward, only with the consent of the guardian and after ascertaining that its interests are secured. Kuwaiti Article 195/a prevents a *hadina* from travelling to another state to stay there without permission of the guardian, and 195b forbids the guardian, whether he is the father or not, from travelling with the ward for a stay away from its home without permission of its *hadina*.

The Sunnis and Shias allow the mother to travel with the child even to a place remote from the father's residence during her *hidanat* (period of female custody) provided no injury to either parent ensues, since custody is at the time exclusively hers and not shared with the father.[31]

(2) If the hadina is not the mother

The *hadina* who is not the mother shall remain in the town where the father lives. She cannot travel with the infant anywhere without the father's or the guardian's permission. This provision, held expressly under the Lebanese Druze Personal Act, Article 66, and the Syrian Article 149, is observed both by the Sunnis and the Shias, who confine the right to give such permission only to the father.

Under Algerian Article 69, a custodian who wishes to reside abroad shall refer to the judge to confirm or cancel custody, taking the ward's interest into consideration.

It transpires from the above rules that in the *hidanat* a balance should be struck between the ward's interests and the rights of both parents, combining the *hidanat* of the mother or female relative with the supervision and guardian-ship of the father.

In the same vein, no father may travel with the infant without permission of its mother during her custodianship.[32] This Hanafi provision is expressly held under Sudanese Article 120, Syrian Article 150 and Tunisian Article 62 which adds "unless the ward's interests require otherwise". The Shia Jaafaris concur, adding that if the father takes the child away from the mother who has lost her right to custody because of marriage, he may travel with it until the mother recovers the said right.[33] This provision is also held under Article 65 of the Lebanese Druze Personal Act.

---

[31] Al-Hilli, *op. cit.* p. 102.
[32] Al-Abiani, *op. cit.* p. 339.
[33] Al-Hilli, *op. cit.* p. 102.

The Malikis, Shafiis and Hanbalis rule that the father has the right to travel with the ward in both cases.[34]

E. Access

Under the Sharia, no *hadina*, mother or not, may prevent the father from seeing his child in her custody. However she shall not be compelled to send it to his home, but shall be ordered to bring the child to a place where the father can see it.[35]

Nor can the father, to whom the child has been handed, bar the mother who has lost her right or has terminated its custody, from seeing it but, again, he shall not be compelled to send it to her residence, but shall be ordered to bring it to a place where she can meet it.[36]

The classic juristic texts do not define the frequency of such access for each parent. But by analogy with the wife's right to see her own parents, each parent of the child shall see it once a week.

Like the mother, the female relatives, such as the maternal aunt or the sister, have the right of access to the child, but less frequently, usually once a month.[37]

The Shia Ithna-Asharis maintain that the mother shall retain her right to access to the child even if she does not suckle it[38] or loses her right to its custody.[39] The right of access is secured for both parents under the following articles:

Art. 148 (5) Syrian:

"Each parent shall have the right to see children entrusted to the custody of the other periodically at the place where the ward lives, and if this is disputed, the judge shall order such right to be secured and the method to put it into effect forthwith without any need for a ruling by the Court of the First Instance. Any person who objects to access or the method thereof shall refer to the court. Any non-compliance with the judge's order shall render the offender liable to the sanctions of Article 482 of the Penal Code."[40]

Art. 66 Tunisian:

"If the child is under the care of one parent, the other parent shall not be prevented from visiting and supervising it. The said other parent shall incur the expenses of the child travelling to visit her or him if she or he asks for such a visit."

Art. 111 Moroccan:

---

[34] Badran, *op. cit.* p. 82.
[35] *Ibid.* p. 85.
[36] *Ibid.*
[37] *Ibid.* p. 86.
[38] Al-Hilli, *op. cit.* p. 96.
[39] *Ibid.* p. 101.
[40] Article 482 of the Syrian Penal Code reads as follows: "The father, mother, or any other person who does not comply with a judge's order, by refusing or delaying to bring in a minor under 18 years of age, shall be liable to imprisonment for three months to two years and a fine of S.£100.00."

"If the child is in the custody of one parent, the other shall not be prevented from seeing it and following its conditions. If the other parent asks for the child to be taken to visit him or her, this request shall be granted for once a week at least unless the judge rules otherwise in the interests of the child."

Under Article 20 of the Egyptian Act No. 25/1920 as amended by Act No. 100/1985, both parents, and, in their absence, grandparents have the right of access to the minor. If it is difficult to reach an amicable arrangement, the judge shall arrange for access, provided that it shall be at such a place as to spare the child any psychological stress.

The access order shall not be executed forcibly, but should the person entrusted with the custody of the minor refuse to carry out the order without a reasonable excuse, he (she) shall first be warned by the judge, and, on repeating the offence, the judge may issue an enforceable order passing custody provisionally to the next in line for the right thereto, for a period set by the court.

Article 196 of the Kuwaiti Personal Status Law rules as follows:

(a) The right of access is confined exclusively to the parents and grandparents.
(b) The *hadina* shall not stop any such person from seeing the ward.
(c) In the event of such prevention, and on one party refusing to go to see the child at the other's place, the court shall order a regular time, and a suitable place of access to the child, where the rest of its kin may see it.

Sudanese Art. 123 rules as follows: "In the event that:

(a) the ward is in the custody of one parent, the other shall have the right of access to, and the company of the child, and the judge's order for access shall be directly enforced;
(b) one of the ward's parents is absent or dead, the relatives of the ward in a prohibited degree shall have the right of access to the child in the manner decided by the judge;
(c) the ward is not in the custody of either parent, then the judge shall designate those of its relatives in a prohibited degree who shall have the right of access."

F. Duration of Custody

As previously stated, the Jaafaris rule that the mother's custody of the child shall continue for the duration of suckling for the male child, and for the female child till the age of seven, although some jurists make the duration of custody seven years for the boy and nine for the girl.[41] The latter view is held under Article 64 of the Lebanese Druze Personal Act.

However, these terms are made by the Jaafaris subject to no injury being suffered by the child as a result of being taken away from the mother. The father shall be compelled to take the child into his care if the mother refuses to keep it with her or it is detrimental to the child if it remains with her.[42]

The four Sunni Schools differ on the ages when the female custody of the children should come to an end.

The Hanbalis do not distinguish between the boy and the girl. They hold that

---

[41] Al-Hilli, *op. cit.* p. 101.
[42] *Ibid.*

the duration of female custody for both of them shall run from birth till the seventh year of age, at which time the child shall be given the choice between either parent, and its choice shall be respected.[43]

The Shafiis do not distinguish to start with, between the boy and the girl during the female custody period, to which they set no definite term. It shall continue until the infant reaches discretion and is assumed capable of making a choice between the two parents, which choice shall be observed. On reaching this stage, things change between the boys and the girls. If the boy chooses his mother, he shall stay with her for the night and spend the day-time with his father, who shall then undertake his education. The girl who opts to stay with her mother shall live with her day and night. Lots shall be drawn between the parents if the child opts for both. If the child remains silent on the matter, it shall stay on with its mother.[44]

The Malikis rule that female custody for the boy shall continue from birth till he reaches puberty, and for the female until she gets married.[45] This ruling is enshrined in Article 102 of the Moroccan Personal Decree, and Article 109 thereof, while granting the father and other guardians of the ward the right to look after its education and guidance, rules that the ward shall spend the night with its *hadina*, and nowhere else, unless the judge orders otherwise in the interests of the ward. The same provision is repeated in the Tunisian Article 60. Kuwaiti Article 194, following the same trend, rules that female custody for the boy ends on his reaching puberty, and for the female, on her marriage and its consummation.

According to the Hanafis, female custody for both boys and girls alike starts from birth. It comes to an end on the boy reaching an age where he can achieve a degree of independence, becoming able to feed, clothe and cleanse himself. This age is set by some at seven, by others at nine years of age. However, the prevailing Hanafi opinion is that custody for the boy ends at seven years, whether or not the *hadina* is the mother.[46]

According to Muhammad ibn Al Hassan, whether the *hadina* is the mother or grandmother or any other female, the custody for the girl ends with her reaching puberty, an age set by the Hanafis at eleven or nine years, which is the prevailing opinion. Other Hanafi jurists hold that the girl may stay in the custody of her mother or grandmother until the age of womanhood; but only until the age of puberty if the *hadina* is another female.[47]

The relevant Articles in the modern Arab Personal Laws are set out below in chronological order of their promulgation:

Syria
   Art. 146: "Custody shall come to an end for the boy on completing nine and for the girl on completing eleven years of age."

Tunisia
   Art. 67: "The ward shall live with the *hadina* until the age of seven years

---

[43] Badran, *op. cit.* p. 87.
[44] *Ibid.*
[45] *Ibid.*
[46] Qadi Khan, *Al Fatawa Khaniyya*, Vol. I, pp. 423–424.
[47] *Ibid.*

for the boy and nine for the girl, after which age the ward shall be handed over to its father if he so requests, unless the judge shall rule it fittest to keep the ward with the *hadina*."

Iraq

Art. 57: "... (4) The father may supervise the conditions of living and education of the minor until it reaches the age of ten. The court may extend the custody of the minor until it completes fifteen years, if the interests of the minor so require on the strength of evidence submitted by specialised medical and grass-root committees, provided that the minor shall spend the nights with its *hadina*. (5) On the ward completing fifteen years of age, it shall have the right to live with either parent it chooses, or with a relative, until it reaches eighteen years of age, if the court finds such a choice sensible ... (9) If the minor's father dies or loses his eligibility, the minor shall remain with his mother, if she still remains eligible, without any female or male relatives thereof having the right to dispute her custody until it reaches the age of majority."

Jordan

Art. 161: "Custody entrusted to a female other than the mother shall end on the boy completing nine and the girl eleven years of age."

Art. 162: "Custody by the mother who devotes herself entirely to the care and education of her children shall run until they reach puberty."

Egypt

Art. 20 of Act No. 25/1929 as amended by Act No. 100/1985: "The female's right to custody of the child shall come to an end on the boy reaching the age of seven and the girl reaching the age of nine years.

Algeria

Art. 65: "Custody for the boy shall end on his reaching ten years and for the girl on reaching marriage age. The judge may extend custody for the boy until he is sixteen years old if the *hadina* is a mother and has not remarried. Provided always that decision on the termination of custody shall be subject to the ward's interests."

Yemen

Art. 148 rules that when the ward, whether male or female, can do without others, and becomes independent, then, if its father and mother differ in opinion as to the ward's interests, it can chose between them. If the guardianship is awarded to a person other than the father or mother, the judge shall choose the person he deems the best in the interests of the minor, after first consulting that minor.

With the termination of female custody, a new phase begins: the guardianship of the person of the minor, which is its right and a duty of the guardian and cannot be renounced, subject to certain conditions which will be discussed in detail in a later chapter.

CHAPTER 10

Maintenance for Descendants, Ascendants and Collaterals

1. General

The general Sharia and legal rule is that, with the exception of the wife, whose maintenance is the duty of the husband regardless of her or his means, maintenance of every person shall be out of his own property (Art. 154, Syria; 58, Iraqi; and 167, Jordanian). Even the minor shall only be entitled to maintenance by its father if it has no property (Egyptian Art. 18 *bis*, secondly, Act No. 25/1929 as amended by Act No. 100/1985).

I have already discussed in Chapter 5, maintenance as a lawful right of the wife under a valid contract, during the continuation and after the dissolution of marriage. In this chapter, we are going to deal with maintenance as the right of children, the fourth such right due to established parentage, and of other poor relations who are classified into two categories of kinship:

(a) Lineal kinship (Al Qaraba al-Amoudia) between ascendants and descendants, whether immediate, between the child and its parents, or intermediate, i.e. grandparents and grandchildren. Such kin are always within the prohibited degrees of marriage.

(b) Collateral kinship (Qarabat-ul-Hawashi), which may be within the prohibited degrees, like siblings and their descendants, uncles and aunts, or not within the prohibited degrees, like cousins.

Maintenance includes basically food, raiment and lodging. Tunisian Article 50, Moroccan Article 127 and Yemeni Article 159 add education and whatever is considered necessary according to custom. Jordanian Article 170 includes medical treatment fees. It shall be assessed according to the means of the maintainer (Art. 52, Tunisian), after achieving self-sufficiency (Art. 128, Moroccan), and taking into account the cost of living (Art. 79, Algerian).

Maintenance of descendants and ascendants, unlike that of collaterals, shall be due without a court order. It shall run, for collaterals, from the date of legal action (Arts. 161, Syrian; 130, Moroccan, only for parents; 63, Iraqi; 175, Jordanian; and 80, Algerian). The Algerian Article allows the judge to order maintenance with retrospective effect not exceeding a year. For the children, the same Syrian Article 161 empowers the judge to order maintenance against the father as from four months at most prior to the legal action.

173

2. Relatives Eligible for Maintenance

Islamic jurists and modern Arab Personal Status Laws are unanimous that maintenance is a right of the minors who have no property, on their father, and a right for the poor parents on their children who have means to provide it. However, they differ on the extent of this lineal kinship which establishes the right of maintenance. They differ even more on the entitlement to maintenance in respect of other, collateral relatives.

(a) The Malikis confine maintenance exclusively to immediate parents and children, quoting the Quranic verses "But if they (parents) strive with thee to make thee ascribe unto Me as partner that of which thou hast no knowledge, then obey them not. Consort with them kindly." (31:15) "Mothers shall suckle their children for two whole years for those who wish to complete the suckling. The duty of feeding and clothing nursing mothers in a seemly manner is upon the father of the child. No-one should be charged beyond his capacity." (2:233) and "... and kindness to parents." (17:23) The Malikis argue that these Quranic texts must be taken at their face value to mean just the father, mother and child. They also cite the Prophet's Tradition, "Thou and thy property are thy father's", extending it to the mother by analogy.[1]

This Maliki doctrine is adopted by the Moroccan Law, Article 128, although it makes it a duty upon the prosperous to provide subsistence for the needy (Art. 132). Moreover, Article 131 rules that whoever makes a covenant to maintain another person, whether a minor or a major for a specific period, shall be bound by his covenant, the judge determining according to custom the unspecified period.

(b) The Shafiis follow the Malikis in ruling the entitlement to maintenance solely of children and parents, quoting the same authorities. But they extend the denotation to include all the lineal kin, grandchildren how-low-soever and grandparents how-high-soever, on the grounds that they share the same inheritance provisions. They argue that two Quranic verses on inheritance apply equally to children and grandchildren "God chargeth you concerning your children: to the male the equivalent of the portion of two females ..." and to parents and grandparents "... and to his parents a sixth of the inheritance if he has a child." (4:11)

This Shafii doctrine[2] is adopted in Tunisia and Algeria. Under the Tunisian Article 43, "Those entitled to maintenance on grounds of kinship are of two categories: the parents and the father's parents how-high-soever and the lineal children, how-low-soever." Algerian Article 77 reads as follows, "The maintenance of the ascendants shall be incumbent on the descendants and *vice versa*, according to means, needs and the degree of kinship in inheritance." Kuwaiti Article 200 reads "There shall be no maintenance to any relatives apart from ascendants how-high-soever and descendants how-low-soever."

(c) The Hanbalis, adopting the enlarged Shafii denotation of ascendants and descendants, add to those entitled to maintenance, and those on whom it is

---

[1] Abu Zahra, *Personal Status*, p. 414.
[2] Ash-Shafii, *AL UMM*, Vol. 5, p. 89.

incumbent, the presumptive heirs. These are the relations who would inherit from the person to whom or from whom maintenance is claimed if he were immediately to die, whether or not they are within a prohibited degree. They derive their position from the Quranic ruling "... And on the heir is incumbent the like of that" (2:23) following provisions on maintenance and from the general juristic rule, "Disadvantage is an obligation accompanying enjoyment." Since the entitlement to maintenance according to the Hanbalis is derived from the right to inheritance rather than to the kinship within a prohibited degree, they make it conditional on adherence to the same faith, which is an essential condition for inheritance.[3]

The modern laws of Syria, Iraq and Jordan follow this Hanbali doctrine, except that they do not stipulate the common faith in respect of ascendants or descendants, following the Hanafis instead.

(d) The Hanafis derive the right to maintenance for relations other than ascendants how-low-soever and descendants how-high-soever from a prohibited degree of kinship, rather than from the right to inheritance as the Hanbalis do. They base their position on the Quranic verse "kindness unto parents and unto near kindred". (4:36) They interpret "near kindred" as those within a prohibited degree being the strongest blood kinship. They also quote a reading by Abdullah ibn Masud of the above cited verse of the Quran, "... and on the heir, *who is a cognate within a prohibited degree*, is incumbent the like of that" to which they accord status of a Tradition, it having been heard from the Prophet. Therefore, no son of a paternal uncle shall be eligible for maintenance although his right to inheritance is prior to that of a maternal uncle who can claim maintenance.[4]

This Hanafi interpretation is observed by the Egyptian courts, in the absence of any codified text on this subject.

Ibn Hazm Al-Zahiri holds that maintenance by the relatives shall be due for ascendants, descendants, brothers, sisters and wives in the first place, being all equal in terms of entitlement, followed by the cognates within a prohibited degree, and those from whom the would-be maintainer would inherit, if in need and without means of livelihood.[5]

The Shia Ithna-Asharis grant the right to maintenance to descendants, ascendants, and poor cognates who are presumptive heirs whether or not they are within a prohibited degree, provided that they adhere to a common faith, except for the wife, ascendants and descendants.[6] This ruling is held under Article 80 of the Lebanese Druze Personal Act.

Yemeni Law rules no maintenance for relatives who are not of the same religion except for the ascendants, and the maintenance for relatives shall be assessed immediately the need arises (Art. 157).

3. Maintenance of Descendants

Islamic jurists are unanimous that a child who has no property of its own is entitled to receive maintenance, in the first instance from its father, under two

---

[3] Ibn ul Qayyim, *Zad ul Maad*, Vol. 3, p. 164.
[4] Badran, *Children's Rights*, pp. 104–105.
[5] Ibn Hazm, *Al-Muhalla*, Vol. II.
[6] Al-Hilli, *Jaafari Personal Status Provisions*, p. 108.

authorities: the Quran "The duty of their feeding and clothing according to seemly custom is upon the father of the child" (2:233), and the Tradition of the Prophet who told a woman complaining to him of the parsimony of her husband, "Take of his property what suffices for you and your child according to fair custom."

However, this right is subject to two conditions:

A. that the child is in need, i.e. indigent and unable to earn a living; and
B. that the father has the means to provide maintenance from capital or income.

These two conditions shall be dealt with more fully in the following paragraphs.

A. The Child in Need

Inability to earn a living can be a matter of age, and physical or mental condition.

According to Sunni and Shia Sharia, a boy with no property of his own shall lose his right to maintenance by his father on reaching the age at which he can earn a living, even before puberty, but shall retain that right if he cannot work due to an illness or handicap.

However, according to the Sunnis, the maintenance of a student shall continue after that stage, provided that the course of studies he pursues is religiously acceptable.

The son who has reached majority shall also be entitled to maintenance by his father if the son is incapable of earning a living because of a chronic disease, a mental or a physical handicap and has no private means, or, according to both Sunni and Shia jurists, is of such a social status as to render it impossible to be employed to do a menial job.[7]

As for the daughter who has no property, the condition of her being in need is fulfilled by the very fact of her sex, even though she may have the ability to earn her own living, e.g. through sewing at home, which she cannot be obliged to do. The duty to maintain her shall pass to her husband once she marries.[8] However, if she later ceases to be maintained, for example, on divorce or because of disobedience to her husband, her father shall be bound, once more, to maintain her.[9]

Here are the relevant Articles of the modern Arab Personal Status Law on this subject in chronological order:

Arts 67 and 68 Lebanese Druze Personal Act – 67:

"Maintenance in its three categories shall be incumbent upon the father for his poor minor child, whether male or female, until the male reaches the age for earning a living and is capable thereof, and until the female marries": 68: "It is the duty of the father to provide maintenance for his poor adult son who is incapable of earning a living due to an incapacitating handicap and for his poor adult daughter unless she marries."

Art. 155 (Syria):

1. "If the child has no property, its maintenance shall be the duty of its

---

[7] Abu Zahra, *On Marriage*, p. 415.
[8] Abdullah, *Sharia Personal Status Provisions*, p. 630; Al-Hilli, *op. cit.* pp. 102–103.
[9] Al-Abiani, *Commentary*, p. 349 Al-Hilli, *op. cit.* p. 104.

father unless he is indigent, incapable of providing maintenance or earning a living due to a physical or mental handicap.

2. The children's maintenance shall continue until the female marries and until the boy reaches the age at which his like earn a living."

Art. 46 (Tunisia):

"It is the duty of the father, how-high-soever, to provide maintenance for his minor children and those who are incapable of earning a living, how-low-soever. Maintenance of the female shall run until it becomes a duty on her husband, and for the male until he reaches sixteen years of age and becomes capable of earning a living."

Art. 126 (Morocco):

"1. It is the duty of the father to provide maintenance for his minor children and those who are incapable of earning a living.
2. Maintenance for the female shall continue until it becomes a duty of her husband, and for the male until he reaches puberty and becomes of sound mind and capable of earning a living.
3. Unless he is a student following a course of studies, in which case his maintenance shall continue until he completes his course or reaches the age of twenty-one."

Art. 59 (Iraq):

"1. If the child has no property, its maintenance shall be incumbent upon its father unless he is indigent, incapable of providing maintenance or earning a living.
2. Children's maintenance shall continue until the female marries and the boy reaches the age at which his like earn a living, unless he is a student.
3. The adult son who is incapable of earning a living shall be deemed similar to the minor."

Art. 168 (Jordan):

"(a) If the child has no property, its maintenance shall be incumbent solely upon the father unless he is indigent and incapable of earning a living because of a physical or mental handicap.
(b) Children's maintenance shall continue until the female who is not self-sufficient through her work or earnings marries, and until the boy reaches the age at which his like can earn a living unless he is a student."

Art. 169:

"The father who has means and has to maintain his children shall also have to provide the costs for their education throughout their learning stages until the child obtains its first university degree, provided that the child shall be successful and be possessed of the capability to learn, due consideration being taken in all cases of the financial condition of the father and provided that maintenance shall be within sufficiency limits."

Art. 18 *bis*, (Egyptian Act No. 25/1929 as amended by Act 100/1985):

"If the minor has no property, its maintenance shall be incumbent on its father. The children's maintenance by the father shall continue until the girl marries or earns what is sufficient for her maintenance and until the son completes fifteen years of age and is capable of earning a suitable income. If he reaches that age while he is incapable of earning due to a physical or mental handicap, or because of his pursuing a course of learning that is fit for his like and for his aptitude, or because of such an earning not being available, his maintenance by his father shall continue. The father is under the obligation to provide his children with decent accommodation according to his means, and at a level that befits their like. The maintenance of the children by the father shall be due from the date he refuses to provide for them."

Art. 202 (Kuwait):

"The father who has means, how-high-soever, shall provide maintenance for his indigent child incapable of earning a living, how-low-soever, until it can do without it."

Art. 75 (Algeria):

"The maintenance of the child shall be a duty incumbent on the father, unless it has means. For the males it shall run until the age of majority and for the females until they marry. Maintenance shall go on if the child is incapable because of a mental or physical defect, or is a student and shall lapse once it becomes possible to earn a living."

Arts. 158–160 (Yemen):

"Maintenance of the minor or insolvent child, or of the insane, shall be incumbent on its father, how-high-soever, who has means, or is capable of earning; if not, then the affluent mother or other relatives in the order of inheritance. If the child has means, its maintenance will be incumbent upon its own means.

Maintenance of a major insolvent son who is unable to earn or is in full time study up to the completion of secondary school education, is incumbent on his affluent parents until he reaches the age of twenty.

An affluent father shall provide for the marriage of his insolvent son to one wife if needed."

A special case in this context is the daughter-in-law: According to both Sunni and Shia jurists, the father is under no obligation to provide maintenance for the wife of his impoverished son unless he guarantees it. However, he may be ordered to maintain her, and all expenses he incurs shall be a debt to be repaid by his son when his condition improves.

This provision is enshrined in Article 74 of the Lebanese Druze Personal Act and Article 157 of the Syrian Personal Law.

B. Capability of the Father to Provide Maintenance

This is the second condition for the children to be entitled to maintenance by the father. As previously stated, the father who is possessed of sufficient means or is capable of earning a living shall be solely liable for the maintenance of his needy children.

If the father is impoverished, but can earn a living, he shall be ordered to do so, under pain of imprisonment if he refuses. If he cannot earn enough for himself and his children, or if no livelihood is available, the obligation of the children's maintenance shall pass to the person next to the father. Here Shias and Sunnis part ways.

The Shias hold that this liability shall be upon the father's father, failing which, upon the latter's father and so on how-high-soever, then to the children's mother, then to her father and mother and so on. All maintenance so paid cannot be claimed back from the father when his financial conditions improve.[10]

According to the Sunnis, this obligation passes to the mother if she has means, otherwise to the father's father whose duty it is to provide maintenance to his son, and likewise to his grandchildren. In both cases, the maintenance so paid shall be a debt repayable by the father when he can afford it.[11]

But if the father is incapable of earning a living due to a chronic illness, paralysis or a handicap, he shall be released from the obligation to maintain his children as if he were dead. The children's maintenance shall then be incumbent upon the nearest relatives without being a repayable debt.[12] The Shias rule that the order of maintaining relatives shall be the same as in the case of the impoverished father.[13]

The Sunnis set a different order for the obligation to maintain the children whose father is dead. Relatives are either ascendants, how-high-soever, or collateral. They also may or may not be presumptive heirs. There are three possible contingencies: (i) that all the relatives are ancestors; (ii) that some are ascendants and others are collateral; (iii) that they are all collateral.

(i) In the first contingency, four cases are possible: (a) that some are and some are not presumptive heirs, but they are all equal in nearness. Here it is upon the presumptive heir that maintenance shall be incumbent, e.g. the father's father rather than the mother's father; (b) the same case but not equal in nearness: here maintenance shall be incumbent upon the nearest regardless of the right to inheritance, e.g. upon the mother rather than her father, and upon the mother's father, who does not inherit rather than the father's father who does: (c) and (d) that they are all presumptive heirs but vary in the degree of nearness: here maintenance for the children shall be shared in proportion to the presumptive inheritance, e.g. a mother's mother and a father's mother shall bear maintenance equally as they are equal in nearness and in inheritance share; a mother shall contribute one third and a father's father two thirds of the maintenance according to their shares, although they are different in nearness to the child.

(ii) In the second contingency, two cases are possible: (a) that some are presumptive heirs and others are not; here maintenance shall be incumbent upon the ascendants regardless of the right to inheritance, e.g. a father's father shall be liable for maintenance rather than a full brother, and a mother's father, who does not inherit rather than a full brother who does; (b) that both ascendants and collateral relatives are presumptive heirs; here they

[10] Al-Hilli, *op. cit.* p. 103.
[11] Al-Albiani, *op. cit.* p. 344.
[12] *Ibid.*
[13] Al-Hilli, *loc. cit.*

shall be liable for the maintenance of the child according to their inheritance shares, e.g. a mother shall be liable for one third and a full brother for two thirds.

(iii) In the third contingency, all the collaterals shall contribute to the maintenance in the proportion of their inheritance shares.[14]

Here are the relevant clauses in the modern legislations:

The Lebanese Druze Personal Act

"69. The maintenance of the child shall be the duty of the father exclusively, unless he is insolvent and unable to earn a living, in which case he shall be deemed like the dead and the obligation shall pass on to the person upon whom the maintenance of the child is incumbent in the event of the non-existence of the father.

"70. The obligation of the maintenance of the child in the event of the father being insolvent shall pass to the mother before any other relative. If both parents are insolvent and have children who are entitled to maintenance, it shall be ordered against the nearest relative if he has means and he shall be compelled to render it. Maintenance paid by a relative shall be a debt repayable by the father once his condition improves, whether the maintainer is a mother, a grandfather or any other.

"71. If the minor's father is deceased and it has ascendants who have means, if some of them are (presumptive) heirs and others are not, but are all equal in nearness, the (presumptive) heir shall be committed to the maintenance of the minor; if they vary in nearness, the nearest shall be ordered to provide maintenance; if all the ascendants are (presumptive) heirs, they shall share the obligation to maintain the minor in the proportion of their inheritance rights.

"72. If some of the relatives of the poor child whose father is dead are ascendants and others are collateral, and if one category are (presumptive) heirs and the others are not, the ascendant rather than the collateral shall be ordered to pay maintenance whether or not he is a (presumptive) heir; but if both ascendants and collaterals are (presumptive) heirs, maintenance shall be ordered against them in the proportion of their inheritance rights."

Syria Art. 156:

"(1) If the father is unable to provide maintenance and is not incapable of earning a living, the maintenance of the child shall be ordered against the person upon whom it is incumbent in the event of the non-existence of the father.

(2) Such a maintenance shall be a debt for the maintainer on the father to be repaid by him when his condition improves."

Tunisia Art. 47:

"In the event of the father's indigency, the mother's obligation shall precede that of the grandfather to maintain her children."

---

[14] Al-Abiani, *op. cit.* pp. 345–347.

Morocco Art. 129:

"If the father is incapable of providing maintenance for his children and the mother has means, their maintenance shall be incumbent upon her."

Iraq Art. 60:

"(1) If the father is unable to provide maintenance, the maintenance of the child shall be ordered against the person upon whom it is incumbent in the event of the non-existence of the father.

(2) Such a maintenance shall be a debt for the maintainer to be repaid by the father if his condition improves."

Jordan Art. 170:

"(2) If the father is indigent and unable to provide physician's fees, (medical) treatment or the cost of education, and the mother has means and can afford all that, she shall be compelled to pay such expenses which shall be a debt she can claim back from the father at better times. The same applies if the husband is away and no maintenance can be received from him.

(3) If both father and mother are indigent, the person upon whom maintenance is incumbent if the father were not existent shall be liable for the maintenance for (medical) treatment or education, to be repaid by the father to the maintainer at better times."

Art. 171:

"If the father is indigent, capable of earning a living and his earnings just suffice for his needs, or if he cannot find a job, the obligation to maintain the child shall pass to the person upon whom maintenance would be incumbent if the father were not existent, such maintenance being a debt for the maintainer on the father, to be repaid in better times.

Algeria Art. 76:

"In the event of the father being incapable (of providing maintenance) the children's maintenance shall be incumbent upon the mother if she has means to provide it."

Kuwait Art. 202:

"The father who has means, how-high-soever, shall provide maintenance for his destitute child who is incapable of earning a living, how-low-soever, until it can do without it."

Art. 203:

"(a) If the father is insolvent and the mother has means, the maintenance of her child shall be incumbent upon her, and shall be a debt on the father repayable if his circumstances improve; the same applies if the husband is absent and no maintenance can be exacted from him.

(b) If both father and mother are indigent, the maintenance shall be incumbent on the one whose duty it would be to provide maintenance had it not been for the parents, and shall be a debt on the father to be claimed back from him when his circumstances improve."

4. Maintenance of Ascendants

Sunni and Shia jurists are unanimous that it shall be a duty on the child who has means, whether minor or major, male or female to provide maintenance for its poor parents, grandfathers or grandmothers, whether they are Muslim or *kitabi* and whether they are capable or incapable of earning a living, this being its duty unshared by anybody else.

If the father suffers from a handicap or is afflicted by a severe illness that makes him in need of a wife to look after him or to a servant to help him, maintenance of such a wife or a servant shall be incumbent on the child who has means. However, the child shall be responsible for the maintenance of only one step-mother if there are more than one.[15]

This is also the ruling of Yemeni Article 162 which adds that the rich son shall provide a wife for his poor father, and that if the father is old or sick and needs a wife to care for him or a servant to help him, the maintenance of the wife or the servant shall be borne by the rich son.

The maintenance of a needy woman married to a person other than the child's father shall be incumbent upon her husband not upon the child, who shall nevertheless be ordered, if it has means, to maintain her, such a maintenance being deemed a debt against her husband who is indigent or absent, to be repaid on the improvement of his condition or on his return.[16]

A poor son shall not be liable for the maintenance of his poor father unless the son is earning and the father is handicapped and cannot earn a living. In the latter case, the father shall share the son's livelihood as a matter of religious piety. The needy mother shall be deemed like the handicapped father, even if she suffers no handicap. The poor son who supports a family shall make his needy parents join them and thus support the whole lot without being obliged to support his parents separately.[17]

The above provisions are adopted, almost verbatim, in Articles 75, 76 and 77 of the Lebanese Druze Personal Law 1948. Here are the relevant Articles from the other modern legislations:

Syria Art 158:

> "It is the duty of the child who has means, whether male or female, a minor or a major, to provide maintenance for its poor parents, even if they are able to earn a living, unless the father shows himself as insisting on a preference for unemployment over any job that is worthy of his like, out of sluggishness or obstinacy."

Tunisia Art 44:

> "It is the duty of the child or children who have means to provide maintenance for the poor father and mother and paternal grandfathers and grandmothers."

---

[15] *Ibid.* p. 352; Al-Hilli, *op. cit.* p. 106.
[16] Al-Hilli, *loc. cit.;* Al-Abiani, *op. cit.* p. 353.
[17] Al-Abiani, *op. cit.* pp. 353–354; Al-Hilli, *op. cit.* pp. 106–107.

Art. 45:

"If there are many children, the obligation of maintenance (of the parents) shall be shared in the proportion of their means, not according to their number nor to their inheritance rights."

Morocco Art. 125:

"Maintenance of parents by the children, if they are more than one, shall be shared according to the children's means, not their inheritance rights."

Art. 128:

"No man shall be liable to provide maintenance for his parents and children until he has secured sufficient maintenance for himself."

Iraq Art. 61:

"It is the duty of a child who has means, whether a minor or a major, to provide maintenance for his two poor parents even if they are able to earn a living, unless the father shows his insistence to opt for unemployment."

Jordan Art. 172:

"(a) It is the duty of the child who has means, be it a male or a female, a minor or a major, to provide maintenance for his two poor parents, even if they are able to earn a living;

(b) If the son is poor but can earn a living, he shall be compelled to provide maintenance for his two poor parents."

Algeria Art. 77:

"The maintenance of the ascendants shall be incumbent on the descendants and *vice versa* according to means, need and degree of kinship in inheritance."

Kuwait Art. 201:

"The child who has means, be it male or female, shall have incumbent on it the maintenance of its poor parents, grandfathers and grandmothers, even if they profess a different faith or can earn a living. If there are many children, they shall contribute in proportion to their means."

Yemeni Art. 161;

The maintenance of the poor father, how-high-soever, and mother, how-high-soever, even if they are cable of earning, shall be incumbent-on-the rich child, how-low-soever, male or female, major or minor, and shall be borne by the rich children of the same generation in the order of inheritance. The maintenance of the mother, then the father shall have priority over that of other relatives.

5. Maintenance of Other Relatives

In Section 2 above, we discussed the various opinions of the Sharia Schools on the relatives, other than ascendants and descendants, that are eligible for maintenance by their relatives. In Section 4 we discussed the maintenance obligation of collateral relatives for children whose father is incapacitated or dead.

Before quoting the relevant provisions in modern Arab Personal Status Laws it must be pointed out again that the Laws of Tunisia and Algeria, adopting the Shafii Doctrine, enlarge the mutual rights of maintenance to encompass ascendants and descendants how-high or how-low-soever. The Moroccan Law, following the Maliki school, limits such mutual rights to the immediate parents and children. However, it rules under Article 131 that: "Whoever undertakes to provide maintenance for another person, who may be a minor or an adult, for a limited period, shall have to honour his commitment. If the period is not limited, the judge shall rely on custom to define it." In a similar vein, Tunisian Article 49 reads as follows: "Whoever undertakes to provide maintenance for another person whether a major or a minor for a limited period shall be bound by his commitment. If the period is not limited *per se* his word for it shall be accepted."

Moroccan Article 132 also rules "The sustenance of the needy is a duty upon him who has excess."

The Articles dealing with the maintenance of collateral relations in other Arab modern Personal Status Laws are now quoted:

The Lebanese Druze Personal Act

Art. 80:

"The maintenance of every poor cognate in a prohibited degree shall be the duty of every presumptive heir among his relations who have means even if they are minor, in the proportion of their inheritance rights from him."

Syria Art. 159:

"The maintenance of every indigent relative who is unable to earn a living because of a physical or mental handicap shall be the duty of the presumptive heirs among his relatives who have means according to their respective inheritance shares."

Art. 160:

"No maintenance shall be due in the event of difference of religion except for ascendants and descendants."

Art. 161:

"The maintenance for relatives shall be ordered from the date of the court action. The judge may order maintenance for the children against their father to cover a period prior to the legal action provided that it shall not exceed four months."

Iraq Art. 62:

"The maintenance of every indigent relative who is unable to earn a living shall be the duty of the presumptive heirs among his relatives who have means according to their respective inheritance shares."

Art. 63:

"The maintenance for relatives shall be ordered by the court from the date of the court application."

Jordan Art. 173:

"The maintenance of the indigent minors and of every indigent adult who is unable to earn a living because of a physical or mental handicap shall be the duty of the presumptive heirs among their relatives who have means according to their inheritance shares. If the presumptive heir is indigent, maintenance duty shall pass to the next in the order of inheritance to be repaid by the first presumptive heir when he has means."

Art. 174:

"In the event of a dispute over the state of having or not having means, the evidence of means shall prevail except in the case of purported contingent destitution, when the evidence of the purporting person shall prevail."

Art. 175: same as Iraqi Art. 63.

It is obvious from the above that according to Shia and modern legislations there are the following differences between the maintenance for the wife, the lineal and the collateral relatives:

(i) Only the wife is entitled to maintenance by the husband, regardless of her means or his financial conditions. Every other kin, whether lineal or collateral, shall not have the right to maintenance unless he (or she) is needy and the maintainer has means and earns more than his immediate needs.

(ii) Adherence to a common faith is not a condition of eligibility for maintenance in the case of the wife, ascendants or descendants, but is an essential condition for the collaterals' right to maintenance, as it is based on possible inheritance which cannot occur between persons of different religions.

(iii) The wife shall be entitled to maintenance by her husband from the date of the valid marriage subject to the conditions set out above in the relevent chapter. For ascendants and descendants it may start with retrospective effect before the date of a court application. For collaterals it begins from the date of the legal action.

CHAPTER 11

Guardianship

1. Definition

Djurdjani in his *Tarifat* gives the following definition of Guardianship (*wilaya* or *walaya*): "The carrying through of a decision affecting a third person whether the latter wishes or not."[1]

Guardianship may be of persons or property. The guardian of a person may or may not be the same as the guardian of property. It is mainly a duty incumbent on a person on the grounds of kinship, by testament or by court order towards another person of imperfect or no legal capacity. There are three grounds under the Sharia for being placed under guardianship: minority, insanity, and, within limits, the state of being female.

A special form, namely marriage guardianship, has been dealt with in Chapter 3, 3.C. The earliest form of guardianship of the person, custody of the child, forms the subject matter of Chapter 9, 2.B. This present chapter deals in more detail with the remaining provisions of guardianship of the person and the whole subject of guardianship of property.

Apart from the classical references of Islamic jurisprudence, guardianship of the person and of property is treated in the Personal Status Acts of the Lebanese Druzes, Syria, Tunisia, Morocco, Algeria, Sudan and Oman. The Kuwaiti Personal Status Law devotes a chapter (Articles 208 to 212 inclusive) to the Guardianship of the Person, connecting it with the child custody. Guardianship of the Property is left out, and therefore the authoritative Maliki opinion shall prevail (Art. 343). The Jordanian Personal Status Law does not mention guardianship of property, and deals with guardianship of the person only in the context of the custody of the child. Therefore recourse must be had to the authoritative Hanafi opinion on this subject pursuant to the general Article 183 of the said Act. In Egypt, Decree No. 118/1952 assesses the cases for the dismissal of the guardian of the person, while Decree No. 119/1952 deals fully with the guardianship of property. Articles quoted in the following paragraphs refer to the said Acts.

---

[1] Djurdjani, *Tarifat*, p. 275.

2. Categories of Guardians

Guardians fall into three main categories according to the grounds of their guardianship and their relationship to the ward:

A. *The Natural Guardian (al waley)*

Under the Moroccan Law (Art. 148), and the Lebanese Druze Law (Art. 81), the father is the natural guardian of the child. Tunisian Article 154, as amended under Act No. 7/1981 rules that the minor's natural guardian is the father, or mother in the event of the father's death or loss of legal capacity. A testamentary guardian appointed by the father does not take over unless the mother has died or lost her legal capacity. On the death or loss of legal capacity of both parents, without the minor having any testamentary guardian, the judge shall appoint a guardian. Under Article 155, amended likewise, those guardians shall not lose their guardianship without court order on legal grounds. Shia doctrine rules that the natural guardian is the father and the grandfather jointly and severally.[2] Under the Sharia, and Article 1 of the Egyptian Act No. 119/1952, the guardian is the father, then the valid grandfather. Sudanese and Omani Laws, Arts. 234 and 159 respectively, are identical, ruling that guardianship of the person is vested in the father, then the agnate in his own right in the order of inheritance. In all these cases, the natural guardian is of the person and the property of the minor. The Syrian Article 170 distinguishes between the two: under paragraph 1, the father, then the agnate valid grandfather, shall have the obligation of the guardianship of both the person and the property of the minor; under paragraph 2, other relatives in the order of inheritance shall have guardianship of the minor's person, but not its property. Kuwaiti Article 211 simply requires of the *waley* to be trustworthy and capable to look after the minor's interests, and professing the same faith (paragraph a); on losing any such requirement he shall lose his guardianship (paragraph b). This last ruling is repeated in both Sudanese and Omani Laws (237 and 163). The Sudanese conditions require that the guardian is Muslim, has reached majority, is of sound mind, honest and capable of discharging the duties of guardianship (236). Omani Art. 161 is almost identical, but Art. 162 rules that no non-Muslim shall be the guardian of a Muslim.

The *waley* shall be removed if he is deemed missing, or is jailed on being convicted of a criminal offence for more than a year (Art. 21, Egyptian Act 119/1952). The Syrian Article 174 adds as further grounds for the removal of the *waley* the attachment of his property, and makes disqualification because of imprisonment subject to the condition that as such it would be detrimental to the minor's interests. Under Article 175, the court shall appoint a special guardian should any conflict arise between the interests of the minor and the guardian. Kuwaiti Article 209, along similar lines, is more elaborate: (a) guardianship of the person shall go to the father, then the agnate grandfather, then to an agnate by himself in the order of inheritance provided he is in a prohibited degree; (b) the court shall choose the fittest if there are various eligible candidates for

---

[2] Al-Hilli, *Jaafari Personal Status Provisions*, pp. 109–111.

guardianship; (c) in the absence of any eligible candidate, the court shall appoint a suitable guardian.

B. The Testamentary Guardian (al wasey al-mukhtar)

The father may appoint in a testament, a guardian to look after his children, including those born after his death, (and he may also revoke such an appointment). This is the ruling of Sudanese Article 234a and Omani Article 170a, which adds that he may also appoint a guardian to look after the minor children of his son placed under interdiction after his death. Immediately on the father's death, such guardianship shall be submitted to the court for confirmation (Art. 151 of Moroccan Law). Article 28 of the Egyptian Act 119/1952 requires in addition that the appointment shall be confirmed in a formal deed or in an informal document with the authentication of the father's or *al wasey al-mukhtar's* signature, or written in the father's handwriting and signed by him.

Articles 178 (Syrian), 27 (Egyptian) and 153 (Moroccan) set out the qualifications for a *wasey* who must be of good character *(adl)*, fit to carry out his task, of full legal capacity and of the same religion as the minor. The same Egyptian and Syrian Articles and the Moroccan Article 154 exclude expressly as unfit to be a *wasey* the following categories:

(i)   any person convicted of an immoral or dishonest offence;
(ii) any person declared bankrupt by the court until he is rehabilitated;
(iii) any person (or, in Syria and Egypt, any person or any ascendant, descendant, or spouse of that person) who is involved in either a legal dispute with the minor or indeed any family conflict which may endanger the minor's interests. The Egyptian and Syrian Articles add any person whom the father before his death, on the strength of a written document, barred from being appointed as a *wasey*.

Under Sudanese and Omani Laws (Art. 244 and 172) the testamentary guardian must be of full legal capacity, trustworthy, capable of discharging guardianship duties, and have never been convicted of theft, betrayal of trust, trickery, forgery or any offence against decency or honour, nor been declared bankrupt in a legal dispute against the minor, or in animosity with it. The Omani Law further requires him to be Muslim if the minor is Muslim.

C. The Curator (al-qayyim, or in Northern African Law, al muqaddam)

The curator is a guardian appointed by the court for the minor, born or conceived, who has no *wasey* (Moroccan Arts. 148 and 152) or for the insane, the idiot, the imbecile or the prodigal (Syrian Art. 163). The same qualifications for the *wasey* shall apply to the curator.

Article 68 of the Egyptian Act 119/1952 sets the order to be followed for the eligibility of the curator as the adult son, failing which the father, failing which the grandfather, failing which, another person appointed by the court.

Both the Syrian Law, Articles 163/2 and 3, and 202–206 inclusive, and the Egyptian Act, Articles 74 to 79 inclusive, add another category of guardianship, namely the Judicial Agent (*al wakeel al qadaiee*), to be appointed by the court to look after the property of a person who has gone missing without anyone knowing whether he is alive or dead.

In the following sections, we shall deal with guardianship of the person, legal capacity and interdiction, guardianship of property, and the provisions in respect of the missing person, in that order.

3. Guardianship of the Person

Guardianship of the person of the infant has been dealt with in the Section on "Custody" (Chapter 9.2). The father, failing which the agnate grandfather, takes over from the mother or other *hadina* when the child reaches a certain age. In fact, their guardianship can be exercised even during the female's *hadana*. It is defined under Article 170/3 of the Syrian Act No. 59/1953 as amended by Act No. 34/1975 to include "the authority to discipline, to provide medical care, to educate, to direct to a craft for a living, to give consent to marriage and all other matters related to the care of the person of the minor." Paragraph 4 of the same Article deems the failure by the guardian to see to the completion of the minor's education till the end of the compulsory stage as a sufficient reason for depriving him of the guardianship, just as the *hadina* who objects to or shows negligence in her guardianship may be so deprived. The tasks of the guardian of the person, under Kuwaiti Article 210, include looking after the interests of the ward and seeing to his protection, education and suitable preparation for life's duties, without prejudice to the provisions of *hadana*.

The guardianship of the person of the minor ends on the boy reaching puberty unless he is insane, when it will continue by the same guardian even if he is not the guardian of property or the maintainer.

The guardianship of the person of the girl is either in respect of marriage, which has been dealt with in Chapter 3, 3.C. or in respect of care and protection. This latter guardianship comes to an end on the girl reaching the age at which she can fend for herself and is no longer in need of anybody to protect her from dangers that threaten her dignity and honour, or reaches a station in her life of education or career at which she can safeguard her interests without recourse to her guardian for help. Such a guardianship is also deemed to terminate on marriage, with the husband providing the care and protection under the marriage relationship, rather than by way of guardianship of the person.[3]

However, guardianship of the person shall be resumed on the occurrence of any mental defect that renders the person in question of defective or no legal capacity.

4. Legal Capacity (*al-ahliyyat*)

The ultimate ground for guardianship of whatever form, is the state of inadequacy of the ward, being of partial or nil legal capacity, to care for its persons or manage its property. Only full legal capacity can qualify a person to act independently of any guardian.

The Sharia recognizes two types of legal capacity: capacity of obligation (*ahliyyatul wujub*) which is the capacity to acquire rights and duties, and the

---

[3] Abu Zahra, *Guardianship of the Person*, pp. 46–67.

capacity of execution (*ahhliyyatul adaa*), i.e. the capacity to contract, dispose and validly fulfil one's obligations.[4]

The capacity of obligation is established for every human being from the time of being an embryo, before actual birth, to the time of death and after, until the estate is divided and debts are repaid.[5] It covers, therefore, a longer span than the legal personality which, according to Arab modern codes of civil law, commences from the time a child is born alive and ends at death (Arts. 29/1, Egyptian; 31/1, Syrian; 34/1, Iraqi; 29/1, Libyan; 25, Algerian; and 30/1, Jordanian). However, the same Articles under paragraph 2, rule that the Law [of Personal Status] determines the right of a child *en ventre de sa mere*, i.e. part of the capacity of obligation.

It is the capacity of execution that constitutes the full legal capacity to enjoy civil rights and it is the inalienable right for every person who attains majority, being in possession of mental faculties and not under any legal disabilities (Arts. of the Civil Codes 44/1, Egyptian; 46/1, Syrian; 46/1, Iraqi; 44/1, Libyan; 40, Algerian; 43/1, Jordanian).

Although they all agree on the age of majority being an essential requirement to acquire legal capacity, they differ on that age. In Lebanon, Syria, Iraq, Jordan, Sudan and Oman, it is eighteen complete solar years; in Algeria, nineteen years; in Tunisia, twenty years (Arts. 153 of Personal Status Mijalla); in Egypt, Libya, Kuwait and Morocco (Art. 137 of the Personal Status Decree) "twenty-one years completed in accordance with the Gregorian calendar."

The Sharia jurists did not set any specific age of majority, although they set an age for puberty ranging from fifteen years for the boy and the girl according to the bulk of jurists, seventeen years maximum according to Malik, to seventeen for the girl and eighteen for the boy according to Abu Hanifa.[6] The Shias date puberty from the appearance of the signs, otherwise at the age of fifteen years for the boy and nine for the girl, again distinguishing between puberty and majority.[7]

The opposite of full legal capacity is nil legal capacity, which is the case of the person devoid of discretion owing to youth, feeble mindedness or insanity (Civil Code, Arts. 45/1, Egyptian; 47/1, Syrian; 96 and 108, Iraqi; 45/1, Libyan; 42, Algerian; 44/1, Jordanian; Personal Code, Arts. 156 and 163, Tunisian; 134, Moroccan; 217, Sudanese and 141d, Omani). Again, Arab legislators vary on the age of discretion, making it from seven (Egypt, Syria, Iraq, Libya, Kuwait, Jordan, Sudan and Oman), under twelve (Morocco), under thirteen (Tunisia) to under sixteen (Algeria) all in Gregorian calendar years. The age of discretion under the Sharia and the law is seven years.

A half-way house between the nil and full legal capacity is partial legal capacity. This is the status of the person who has reached the age of discretion but has not attained majority, as well as a person who has attained his majority but is a wastrel or an imbecile.

Persons of nil or partial legal capacity are governed, as the case may be, by the rules of the natural or legal guardianship or curatorship subject to the

---

[4] Abu Zahra, *Theory of Contract*, p. 272.
[5] *Ibid.* p. 273.
[6] *Ibid.* pp. 283–284.
[7] Al-Hilli, *op. cit.* pp. 124–125.

conditions and in accordance with the rules laid down by the Law (Civil Code, Arts. 47, Egypt; 49, Syria; 46/2, Iraq; 46, Jordan; 44, Algeria; Personal Status Code of Morocco, Art. 136, Sudan 221 and Oman 144). These provisions follow the Hanafi doctrine.[8]

Such persons shall have their dispositions in the matter of their property restricted in the following manner:

(i) A person who is devoid of legal capacity, i.e. a minor devoid of discretion and the insane shall have all his legal dispositions deemed void (Civil Code, Arts. 110, Egypt; 111, Syria; 96, Iraq; 110, Libya; 117, Jordan; 87, Kuwait; Personal Status Code, Arts. 156 and 163, Tunisia; 139 and 146, Morocco; 82 and 85, Algeria).

(ii) A person of partial legal capacity, i.e. a minor possessing discretion, an imbecile or a wastrel, shall have his dispositions of property deemed valid if they are wholly to his advantage and void when wholly to his disadvantage.

His dispositions of property which may be, at the same time, profitable and detrimental, may be annulled if this is in his interests or ratified by the guardian of his property (Civil Code Arts. 111, Egypt; 112, Syria; 97, Iraq; 111, Libya; 118, Jordan; 99, Kuwait).

It follows that the person of partial legal capacity may accept gifts, being wholly advantageous, but cannot make donations, being wholly detrimental. As for other dispositions such as sale, purchase, bartering, letting, etc., which may be partly advantageous and partly detrimental to such a person, they shall be left to the guardian or curator at his discretion.

5. Interdiction (*Hajr*)

Interdiction denotes both the status and act of imposing legal restrictions on the capacity to dispose of property in such a way as to render the acts of the person placed under interdiction legally null and void. Its object is the verbal utterances of the interdicted person who shall therefore be liable for his unlawful deeds and responsible for making good, out of his own property, any damage he causes.

The persons that are liable to interdiction are those described in the previous Section (4) as possessing nil or only partial legal capacity. However, in addition thereto, Shia and some Sunni jurists urge the authorities to pronounce interdiction against the irresponsible *Mufti* who teaches the public reprehensible tricks, the ignorant physician who is a danger to his patients, and the bankrupt transport contractor who receives his payment in advance and deprives people of the performance of their *hajj* or the like.[9]

The Sharia, followed by modern personal laws, distinguishes between several types of mental defectiveness: insanity, mental derangement, prodigality and imbecility.

The insane (*majnoon*) is afflicted with a mental illness which renders him incapable of sound judgment or rational behaviour, usually accompanied by a

---

[8] Abu Zahra, *Theory of Contract*, pp. 300–301.
[9] Al-Hilli, *op. cit.* p. 123; Al-Zailaie, *Tabyeen*, Vol. 5, p. 193.

state of confusion and excitement. Insanity may be intrinsic when a person reaches puberty in the state of being insane, or transient if insanity occurs after puberty. It may be permanent or temporary; under Islamic jurisprudence, insanity in general shall render the person afflicted interdicted without requiring a court ruling to that effect, and all his acts shall be without effect, even if authorized by the guardian. On restoration of sanity, the interdiction shall be removed without necessitating a court ruling, and all his acts shall be valid and effective.[10]

The mentally deranged (*maatooh*) by definition is a person suffering from a mental handicap which makes him mix sane and insane utterances.[11] Such a person may be either in possession or devoid of discretion, and his acts shall be treated in the same way as those of the minor possessing or lacking discretion respectively.

It must be stressed that the above Sharia provision is followed by the Civil Code of Iraq (Art. 94), Jordan (Art. 127/1), and Kuwait (Art. 85), whereby the minor, the insane and the mentally deranged may all be placed under interdiction without requiring a court decision. Nevertheless, under the Civil Codes of Egypt (Art. 113), Libya (Art. 113), Syria (Art. 114), and Tunisia (Personal Code Art. 161), Morocco (Personal Code Art. 145), the courts shall pronounce or lift interdictions on all persons suffering from insanity, mental derangement or imbecility and on prodigals in accordance with the rules and procedures prescribed by the law.

Under the latter Civil Codes, an act entered into by a person suffering from insanity or mental derangement after the registration of the sentence of interdiction is null. Before such a registration, such an act is null only if the state of insanity or derangement was a matter of common notoriety at the time the contract was entered into or if the other party had knowledge thereof (Arts. 114, Egyptian; 115, Syrian; 114, Libyan). Tunisian Personal Status Article 163 rules that the acts of the insane are unconditionally null, while the acts of the feeble-minded are voidable before interdiction if his feeblemindedness was known before the act. According to Moroccan Personal Status Article 146, the acts of both the insane and the prodigal are null if they are entered into during the state of insanity or prodigality.

The prodigal (*safeeh*), such as the spendthrift, is a person who is unnecessarily wasteful or lavish, and lacks sound judgment while being of sound mind (Personal Status Art. 164, Tunisian; and 144, Moroccan). The Hanafis refuse to place the prodigal under interdiction which they consider de-humanizing, but the majority of jurists rule that he should be placed under interdiction in order to protect him and his interests. If the act or contract is liable to rescission, it can either be binding, in which case it can only be rescinded by mutual agreement, or non-binding, being subject to an option, in which case the prodigal may rescind it unilaterally.[12]

The imbecile (*dhul ghafla*) is a person who can easily be defrauded in property transactions due to his naiveté. The provisions in respect of the prodigal's acts

---

[10] Abdullah, *Sharia Personal Status Provision*, pp. 660–661.
[11] Djurdjani, *op. cit.*
[12] Abdullah, *op. cit.* pp. 666–667.

shall apply in this case.[13] The Moroccan and Tunisian Personal Status Laws use the same word (*safeeh*) to denote both the prodigal and imbecile (Arts. 144 and 164, respectively).

The prodigal and the imbecile, under the Sharia, can only be placed under interdiction by an order of the court which shall also lift it. A legal disposition by them after the registration of the order shall be tantamount to that of a minor possessing discretion: before registration it shall only be void or voidable if unfair advantage has been taken of them or if there has been fraudulent collusion (Civil Code, Arts. 115, Egyptian; 116, Syrian; 109, Iraqi; 115, Libyan; 129, Jordan; 85, 99 and 101, Kuwait).

More explicitly, the Tunisian Personal Status, Art. 165 maintains that all acts entered into by the prodigal before the sentence of interdiction are valid, effective and irrevocable; after the sentence, their validity shall be subject to the ratification thereof by the guardian. Article 166 adds that the prodigal's declarations on financial matters shall be void.

However, the constitution of a *waqf*, or the execution of a will by a person placed under interdiction for prodigality or imbecility is valid if the interdicted person has been duly authorized by the court. Acts of management carried out by a person under interdiction for prodigality or imbecility, who has been authorized to take possession of his property, are valid within the limits provided by the law (Civil Code, Arts. 116, Egypt; 117, Syria; 116, Libya; 130, Jordan; 102/104, Kuwait). The law referred to is the series of Sharia provisions in respect of guardianship by the *waley*, *wasey* and *qayyim* (curator), codified, with some modification, in Book Four (Legal Capacity and Agentship) of the Syrian Personal Status Act, and in the Egyptian Decree No. 119/1952 on Guardianship of Property and in the Kuwaiti Civil Code Articles 85 to 109 inclusive.

6. Guardianship of Property

In addition to those persons interdicted due to their nil or partial legal capacity, guardianship of property is imposed upon the absent and missing persons whose exercise of their full legal capacities is virtually impossible. The powers of the guardians of property vary with their categories under the provisions of the Sharia and the law.

A. The Natural Guardians

The father's powers to administer the property of his child depend on his character. If he is known to be reliable, of sound business judgment, or even if nothing is known of him to his disadvantage, he shall have full capacity to dispose of his ward's property as if it was his own, save making a gift for no consideration as this constitutes a disposition that is wholly to the disadvantage of the ward.

A father who is not a spendthrift nor unreliable but is not endowed with sound business judgment shall have his disposition of the ward's property restricted subject to the condition of it being to the ward's advantage.

---

[13] *Ibid.* p. 673.

But a father who is known to be unreliable, a spendthrift and of poor business judgment shall exercise no guardianship of his ward's property. Indeed, he shall be himself subject to guardianship of his own property.

A general Sharia and Civil Code provision rules that no-one may contract with himself, in the name of the person he represents, either for his own benefit or that of a third party without the authority of his principal who, nevertheless, may ratify the contract. The Hanafis make an exception from this general provision for the father who may buy the minor's property for himself or sell his property to the minor, it being taken for granted that the reliable wise father shall have his ward's best interests at heart.

The valid (or agnate) grandfather is the equal to the father in all dispositions of the ward's property, according to the Shias and Muhammad ash-Shaibani. Abu Hanifa and Abu Youssof confine the grandfather's powers over the property of the minor to those of the testamentary guardian.

These are the general Sharia rules on the natural guardian of the property of the minor. There are a number of modifications thereto in the modern Arab Laws.

The Tunisian and the Moroccan Personal Laws, Articles 155 and 149, respectively, make the natural guardianship of the minor's property the legal duty of the father solely. Algerian Article 87 makes it the legal duty of the father and on his death, of the mother. Moroccan Article 150 adds that the judge shall prevent the destitute father from taking possession of his child's property and to safeguard it shall appoint a supervisor to watch over the acts of the father.

Algerian Article 88 rules that the natural guardian shall carefully dispose of the minor's property and shall be liable therefor in accordance with the requirements of the public law. He shall have to obtain the court's authorization for:

(i)   the sale, division, mortgage or a compromise arrangement of the real property;
(ii)   the sale of movables of a particular interest;
(iii) the investment of the minor's property by way of giving or receiving loans, or buying a company's shares;
(iv)   the letting of the minor's property for more than three years or for more than one year after the minor reaches the age of majority.

Syrian Article 172 makes guardianship of the minor's property the sole right and duty of the father and the agnate grandfather, from whom it shall not be withdrawn unless their dishonesty or poor management is proven. Neither of them may make a gift of any of the minor's property or usufructs, nor sell or mortgage its real property, without permission of the judge who must be convinced of the sound grounds therefor.

Article 110 (1) of the Kuwaiti Civil Code gives guardianship of the property of the minor to its father, then the testamentary guardian chosen by the father, then the paternal grandfather, then to the guardian appointed by the court with due observance of the provisions of Article 112. Under paragraph (2), the father and his father are forbidden to withdraw from guardianship without an acceptable excuse. Under Article 112 (1), a Kuwaiti minor whose guardianship of the property is not established in his father, testamentary guardian or grandfather, shall have that guardianship undertaken by the Administration of Minors' Interests, according to the law, unless the Government appoints another guardian (2). The court may, from time to time and at the request of any interested party, appoint another guardian instead of the Administration of Minors' Interests, if the minor benefits therefrom.

Articles 103 and 124 of the Iraqi and Jordanian Civil Codes respectively allow as valid, a disposition by the father or agnate grandfather of the minor's property if it is of the same value or only slightly less. If, however, they are known to be of poor management sense, the judge may restrict or cancel the guardianship.

The Egyptian Act No. 119/1952 introduces further restrictions and amendments to the Sharia provisions on guardianship of the property:

To start with, it drops the distinctions between the spendthrift, reliable and unreliable father, requiring only of the natural guardian (who is the father then the valid grandfather in the absence of a testamentary guardian, see Art. 1) that he should possess legal capacity to administer his own property (Art. 2). It excludes from the guardianship any gift made to the minor if stipulated by the donor (Art. 3). The natural guardian cannot, without the court's permission and in order to discharge a humanitarian or family duty, make a gift of any of the minor's property (Art. 5), dispose of the minor's immovables to his advantage or to that of his wife or their kin to the fourth degree (Art. 6), dispose of the immovables, goodwill or security of a value in excess of £E300 (Art. 7), give or receive loans on the minor's behalf, carry on with a business transferred to the minor (Art. 10), or accept a gift or a legacy to the minor encumbered with certain obligations (Art. 12). He cannot without permission and the supervision of the court, dispose of any inheritance to the minor if the propositus has so specified (Art. 8). He cannot mortgage the minor's immovables as a security for a debt on him (Art. 6). Nevertheless, these restrictions do not apply to any property given to the minor by way of gift, whether express or implicit, by the father (Art. 13). Following the Hanafi rule, the father may enter into a contract on the minor's behalf to his or to a third party's advantage, unless otherwise provided by the law (Art. 14).

The Egyptian legislator adopts Muhammad ash-Shaibani's opinion treating the valid grandfather in the same way as the father, save for the provision that the grandfather cannot, without the court's permission, dispose of the minor's property, conclude an arrangement with the creditors thereon, or forego or reduce security (Art. 15). Again, while the father is only liable for a gross mistake, the grandfather shall be liable in the same way as the testamentary guardian (Art. 24).

The *waley* shall compile a list of all the minor's property, failing which the court may rule that the said property is jeopardized (Art. 16), in which case the court may dismiss or reduce the powers of the *waley* (Art. 20).

The *waley* may receive maintenance for himself from the property of the minor if it is due on the latter and may give maintenance in the same way to those who are entitled thereto (Art. 17).

B. *The Testamentary Guardian and the Curator*

Generally speaking the testamentary guardian (*wasey*) and the curator (*qayyim*) enjoy fewer powers than the *waley*.

Under the Sharia and the modern laws of Syria (Art. 176) and Algeria (Art. 92) the father or the grandfather may appoint a testamentary guardian. This right is confined to the father solely under the Laws of Morocco (Art. 149). Egyptian

Art. 28 gives that right to the father or a donor who bars the father from disposing of the gift.

Over and above the restrictions imposed on the father in respect of the property of his ward, the testamentary guardian and the curator cannot, without the court's permission, undertake the following: any act that involves a transfer or creates a real right; invest; liquidate or borrow the minor's property; let a real property of the minor for more than three years or for a period extending to a year after the minor reaches the age of majority; give maintenance to whom it is due from the minor's property without a conclusive court decision; meet obligations incumbent upon the estate or the minor without a final court decision; institute court actions unless there is a risk of an injury to or a loss of a right of the minor; withdraw court actions or waste the right to appeal against court decisions; or, spend money in respect of the marriage or education of the minor (Arts. 39, Egypt; 182, Syria; 158, Morocco).

The tasks to be performed by the *wasey* or the *qayyim* include depositing with the treasury or a bank appointed by the court, in the name of the minor, all the monies received and all valuable possessions such as securities and jewellery, from which nothing can be withdrawn without the court's permission. He shall submit an annual account duly documented of all dealings on behalf of the minor.

Jurists differ on the entitlement of such a guardian to fees, under the Quranic verse "Who so is rich, let him abstain generously; and who so is poor, let him take thereof according to decent custom" (*Sura* An-Nisa, IV, verse 6). Egyptian Article 46 rules that such guardianship shall be for no consideration unless the court, at the request of the guardian, orders fees for him or grants him some remuneration for a specific task. Syrian Article 187 follows suit adding that no fees may be ordered for a period prior to the application. Moroccan Article 157 (3) allows fees according to decent custom if the guardian applies therefor. Kuwaiti Article 144 (Civil Code) follows suit.

Guardianship both of the person and of property comes to an end on the ward reaching the age of majority unless the court orders the continuation thereof thereafter if the ward is insane or feeble-minded (Arts. 18, 47, Egyptian; 189/b, Syrian).

For the guardian, it ends on his resignation, loss of legal capacity, being dismissed or going missing (Arts. 47, Egyptian; 189/a–h inclusive, Syrian; 164, Moroccan; 82, Iraqi).

Guardianship of the property of a missing or absent person is invested in a general Agent left by such a person to be confirmed by the court, or in a legal deputy appointed by the court (Arts. 74 and 75, Egyptian; 204, Syrian). In both cases, the agent shall exercise the same power as a *wasey*. The missing person is one about whose life or death there is uncertainty, or who is known to be alive without knowing his whereabouts (Art. 202, Syrian). An absent person is one who has been away from home for over a year (Art. 203, Syrian). "Missing" shall end on the return of the missing person, or his death in fact or *de juro* on reaching eighty years (according to Art. 205, Syrian). Absence, under Egyptian Article 76 comes to an end on the cause thereof being removed, on the death of the absentee or on a judgment being issued by the competent Personal Status Court declaring him dead.

Similar provisions apply under Sudanese and Omani Personal Status Laws, Articles 252 to 266 and 179 to 197 respectively.

CHAPTER 12

Inheritance

1. Historical Background and Legal Sources

Succession to the estate of the deceased "propositus" is governed by compulsory rules laid down in the Quran. These rules constitute the doctrine of *Faraiid*, that is, the Prescribed Portions, described by the Prophet as a major part of the discipline of law.[1] The power to make a legacy is limited to one third of the estate, the remaining two thirds to be distributed among heirs according to the rules of *Faraiid*.

Although the whole set of rules may seem to fit in admirably, no principle appears to the system and the rules have to be memorized without any guide or clue unless they are approached historically and related to their formation in their pre-Islamic customs. For instance, the first, and, in some respect, the most important, group of heirs, the sharers (*As-hab-ul-Furud*) includes, among others, the spouses, parents and uterine siblings, but the son is conspicuously excluded therefrom. This can only be understood against the background of the customary law of succession in the pre-Islamic society, the main characteristics of which could be summed up as follows:

(i) Females and cognates were excluded from inheritance. In certain cases women even constituted part of the estate. A stepson or brother took possession of a dead man's widow or widows along with his goods and chattels.[2] The Quran forbade this custom: "O ye who believe! It is not lawful for you forcibly to inherit women." (4:19)

   Similarly, male minors who were unable to carry arms were deprived of any share in the estate.

(ii) The nearest adult male agnate or agnates succeeded to the entire estate of the deceased. Male agnates who were equally distant to the propositus shared together the estate *per capita*.[3]

(iii) Descendants were preferred to ascendants, who in turn were preferred to collaterals.

(iv) The adopted son, even if his real father was known, had the same right to the estate as the real sons if he was able to carry arms.

(v) Mutual inheritance between two men was recognized through a contract of alliance. The famous formula was for one of them to say to the other: "My blood is your blood, my destruction is your destruction, you inherit me and

---

[1] Al-Bardisi, *Islamic Law of Inheritance and Wills*, p. 13.
[2] Al-Ghandour, *Inheritance under Islam and the Law*, p. 3.
[3] *Loc. cit.*

I inherit you, you pursue my blood feud and I pursue yours."[4]

The Islamic Law of Inheritance has not entirely abolished the customary pre-Islamic law, but rather introduced radical changes to it. The doctrine of shares then becomes understandable once it is realized that the sharers consist of those who are not entitled to succeed under the customary law, in the circumstances in which they are granted the right to take their respective shares.

These innovations were not promulgated at once but in stages and in answer to specific questions.

To start with, fraternization between the Muhajireen (migrants from Mecca) and the Ansar (the citizens of Medina) entitled each to inherit from the other. This provision was abrogated after the conquest of Mecca under the two Quranic verses: "And those who accept faith subsequently and left their homes and strove along with you, they are of you; but kindred by blood have prior rights against each other in the ordinance of God." (8:75) and "Blood relations among each other have closer ties in the ordinance of God than believers and Muhajireen." (33:6) Earlier, bonds of brotherhood were temporarily approved to establish the right of inheritance, under the Quranic ruling: "And unto each we have appointed heirs of that which parents and near kindred leave; and as for those with whom your right hands have made a covenant, give them their due." (12:33)

Later, inheritance through adoption was abrogated, as an inevitable consequence of the Quranic abolition of the whole institution of adoption.

The right of inheritance for the kindred was first established through the will; "It is prescribed for you, when one of you approacheth death, if he leave wealth, that he will bequeath unto parents and near relatives according to decent custom. This is due from fear of God. And who so changeth the bequest after hearing it, the sin thereof is only upon those who change it." (2:180–181) This ruling was the first parting from the customary law which denied women and children the right to inherit, as parents include both father and mother, and near relatives comprise both children and adults.

The stage was now set for the final phase of legislation on inheritance, in the famous verses of *Sura* Nisaa. The principle covering females and males is laid down in verse 7: "Unto the men belongeth a share of that which parents and near kindred leave and unto the women a share of that which parents and near kindred leave, whether it be little or much – a legal determinate share." Three verses later, the detailed distribution of the shares:

"Allah chargeth you concerning your children: to the male the equivalent of the portion of two females, and if there be women more than two, then theirs is two-thirds of the inheritance, and if there be one then the half. And to his parents a sixth share of the inheritance to each if he left children; and if he left no children and his parents are his heirs, then to his mother appertaineth the third; and if he have brethren, then to his mother appertaineth the sixth, after any legacy he may have bequeathed, or debt. Your parents or your children: Ye know not which of them is nearer unto you in usefulness. It is an injunction from Allah. Lo! Allah is All-Knowing, All-Wise.

---

[4] Madkoor, *Succession under the Islamic Jurisprudence,* p. 16.

And unto you belongeth a half of that which your wives leave, if they have no child; but if they have a child then unto you the fourth of that which they leave, after any legacy they may have bequeathed, or debt. And unto them belongeth the fourth of that which ye leave if ye have no child, but if ye have a child then the eighth of that which ye leave after any legacy ye may have bequeathed, or debt. And if a man or a woman leave neither parent nor child, and he have a brother or a sister then to each of them twain the sixth, and if they be more than two, then they shall be sharers in the third, after any legacy that may have been bequeathed or debt not injuring. A commandment from Allah. Allah is All-Knowing, Most Forbearing." (4:11–12)

At the end of the same *Sura*, there is a provision on the collaterals:

"They ask thee for a pronouncement. Say: God hath pronounced for you concerning those who leave no descendants or ascendants. If a man die childless and he have a sister, hers is half the heritage, and he would have inherited from her had she died childless. And if there be two sisters, then theirs are two-thirds of the heritage, and if they be brethren, men and women, unto the male is the equivalent of the share of two females." (4:176)

Tyabji explains the different Sunni and Shia interpretations of the Quranic enunciations on inheritance in the following manner: although the existence of a few common principles underlying the Quranic amendments to the pre-Islamic customary law is recognized by all, there has been much divergence of opinion as to what those principles were and what was implied in them. Taking the Hanafis to represent the Sunnis, and the Ithna-Ashari the Shia, he sums up the main differences between the two sects as follows:

"I. The Hanafis allow the frame-work or principles of the pre-Islamic customs to stand: they develop or alter those rules in the specific manner mentioned in the Quran, and by the Prophet.

II. The Shias deduce certain principles, which they hold to under-lie the amendments expressed in the Quran, and fuse the principles so deduced with the principles underlying the pre-existing customary law, and thus raise up a completely altered set of principles and rules derived from them."[5]

The Shia interpretation of the law does away entirely with the priority of the agnates over the cognates and makes the estate devolve (subject to the rights of the husband or wife) upon the nearest blood relations, who divide it amongst themselves *per stirpes*, allotting to females half the share allotted to males in each grade.[6] Far more important to explain, the difference between the two Schools is the basic methodological divergence with the Sunni allowing Traditions recited by the Prophet's Companions accepting their *Ijmaa* and using analogy, and the Shia accepting only Traditions transmitted by their Imams, whose *Ijmaa* is the only concensus they adopt.

---

[5] F.B. Tyabji, *op. cit.* pp. 825–826.
[6] *Ibid.* p. 829.

The Quranic enunciations quoted in the previous section is the main authority recognised by them all, and is complemented by Tradition and *Ijmaa* as understood by the Sunni and Shia. Some modern Arab states have promulgated laws of inheritance based on the established Sharia rules without sticking to any one particular doctrine. They are as follows in chronological order:

Egypt. The Hanafi doctrine remained the inheritance law of the land until 1943 when Act No. 77/1943 was promulgated. This is mostly derived from the Hanafi School with some amendments from other Schools, the most important of which are the return, under certain conditions, to the surviving spouse of the residue of the estate, the non-exclusion by the grandfather of brothers and sisters from inheritance, the order of priority among heirs and the sharing in the estate of the full brothers and sisters with the uterine.

Syria. The Syrian Legislative Decree No. 59/1953 on Personal Status includes Book 6 on Inheritance, comprising eight chapters and forty-two articles (260–301 inclusive) and is based on the Egyptian Law with some amendments.

Tunisia. The Personal Status Mijalla of 1956 contains Book 9 on Inheritance, comprising eight chapters and sixty-eight articles (85–152 inclusive), based mainly on the Maliki doctrine.

Morocco. Personal Status Decree No. 1-58-112 contains Book 6 on Succession, comprising nine chapters and seventy-three articles (225–297 inclusive) based on the Maliki doctrine.

Iraq. Until 1959, succession was governed by the respective Sunni and Jaafari Sharia Laws. An attempt was made to unify the succession provisions in the Personal Status Act No. 188/1959 which dealt with the will and inheritance under the same Chapter 8. Article 74 rules that the heirs and their shares would be subject to the provisions of Articles 1187–1199 of the Civil Code, in respect of the succession to the rights of disposition of State land. These provisions were derived from the Ottoman Laws and incorporate many of the Sharia rules on inheritance, but differed on two main themes:

(i) the grandchildren were given the right to inherit the share of their dead father in their paternal grandfather's estate to the exclusion of the great uncles, which is a Shia ruling;

(ii) males and females were given equal shares.

However, this Article was abrogated under Article 3 of Act No. 11/1963 which further added a whole new Chapter, 9, dealing exclusively with inheritance. Article 90 restores the Sharia provisions in respect of the distribution of shares as applied prior to the promulgation of Act No.188/1959.

Jordan. The Personal Status (Provisional) Act No. 6 1/1976 includes two detailed Articles (180 and 181) on the sharing of full and uterine siblings, and on return. For all other issues on inheritance, the general Article 183 refers to the authoritative Hanafi opinion.

Algeria. The Family Act No. 84/1984 devotes a whole Book, III, to Inheritance, comprising ten chapters and fifty-eight articles (126–183 inclusive).

Kuwait. Act No. 51/1984 in the Matter of Personal Status, devotes a whole part, III, comprising seven books and fifty-four articles (288–341 inclusive) to inheritance, adopting an eclectic approach.

Sudan. Law No. 42/1991 on Personal Status for Muslims, devotes Book Five to Inheritance, Articles 344 to 397.

Yemen. Law No. 20/1992 on Personal Status, deals with Inheritance in Book Six, Arts. 299 to 347.

Oman. Personal Status Law issued by Decree No. 32/97 devotes Book Five to Inheritance, Articles 232 to 279.

2. Components of the Estate

The jurists of all Muslim Schools are unanimous that the inheritable estate comprises:

(i)   real and movable property, whether in the deceased's actual possession or not, e.g. in the hands of a leaseholder or a usurper;
(ii) monies due to the deceased but left uncollected by him at the time of death, e.g. debts owing, revenues from pious foundations (*waqf*), blood-money, etc.;
(iii) rights *in rem*, not being monies *per se*, but apt to be assessed in or related to monies such as water rights, rights of way and rights of mortgage;
(iv) certain rights of rescission, i.e. in the case of a defect, the right of the buyer to cancel the sale contract (*khiyaru-l-ayb*), and the right of the buyer to choose from among several objects (*khiyarush-shart*).

There is no distinction in the Islamic Law of Inheritance between movable and immovable property in their being inheritable, except that under the Shia Law a childless widow shall not take any share in her deceased husband's land, but shall receive her share in the value of the trees and buildings standing on the land.[7] There is, however, controversy over the inheritability of a usufruct (*manfaa*) as contradistinct from the thing or substance (*ayn*), *res in commercio* (*mal*).

The Hanafis rule that a usufruct, not being a tangible, assessable substance, cannot be inherited, but the general consensus of the jurists other than the Hanafis is that usufruct is inheritable.[8] The Egyptian Civil Code on ownership rules that this object is a right as contradistinct from the thing, which is the subject of rights. Therefore the inheritance is established of usufruct, lease, patent rights, etc., all of which fulfil the essential elements of property, namely utility, assessability, and acquirability. Some purely personal rights are considered by the Hanafis not to be

---

[7] *Ibid.* p. 149.
[8] Abdul Latif, *op. cit.* pp. 32–33.

inheritable, but in some Islamic countries, such as Egypt and Tunisia, such rights are inheritable. One example is the right of acceptance of a will. Should the legatee die after the testator, but before accepting the legacy, then the right of acceptance passes to his heirs. A further example is the right of pre-emption (*Shufaa*), i.e. the right of the nearest neighbour in preference to all other persons to acquire by compulsory purchase, in certain cases, immovable property.

3. Charges on the Estate

The Hanbalis, some Hanafis and the Shias maintain that the estate of the deceased should be applied successively in payment of:

(i)   the funeral costs, including the death-bed charges and the burial expenses according to decent custom;[9]
(ii)   the debts of the deceased, payable from the gross estate;
(iii) valid and effective legacies within one-third of the remainder;
(iv)   the shares of the heirs from what is left. If there are no heirs, the net estate shall devolve on the Treasury.

This order is followed in Egypt (Art. 4), Syria (Art. 262/1), Iraq (Art. 87), Algeria (Art. 180), Iran (Art. 869), Kuwait (Art. 291), Sudan (Art. 345), Yemen (Art. 302), Oman (Art. 233) and Jordan (Art. 1093 of the Civil Code).[10]

On the other hand, the Malikis, Shafiis, Zahiris and the authoritative Hanafi opinion put the payment of the deceased's debts before the funeral and internment expenses. This opinion is observed in both Tunisia and Morocco, where Articles 87 and 218 respectively apply, being the Hanafi distinction between debts secured by a charge on the estate, and uncontested debts on the deceased, which are payable after the funeral costs.

A. Debts Equal to or Exceeding Assets of the Estate

In this case the assets are distributed among the creditors in proportion to their claims. Consequently, the creditors have the right to nullify any transactions such as sales, purchases or gifts, which were concluded by the deceased during his death-illness[11] if such transactions affect the value of the debts.

The executor and/or guardian appointed by the deceased before his death, or by the judge, should the deceased fail to nominate an executor or guardian, shall dispose of the estate to repay the debts and deal with the creditors.

---

[9] The Egyptian legislator in fact goes beyond the Hanbalis and extends the funeral costs chargeable on the estate of the deceased even to those whose maintenance was incumbent on him, if they had died shortly before him (Art. 4 of the Inheritance Act).

[10] Under the legacy laws of Egypt, Syria, Morocco, Tunisia, Iraq, Jordan, Kuwait and Oman, the mandatory will takes precedence over the voluntary will. See Chap. 13 on Wills.

[11] Death-illness (*marad-ul-maut*) is one which it is highly probable will end in death. Art. 1595 of the Mijalla which codifies the Hanafi jurisprudence gives the following definition: "Death-illness is one where there is preponderance of apprehension of death, and which renders the patient incapable of attending to ordinary avocations, out-of-doors for the male and in-doors for the female. The patient would die in this state of affairs within a year. Should the illness linger on for a year, unchanged, the patient shall be deemed like a healthy person unless his condition gets worse and death follows before the lapse of one year, in which case the condition from the time of worsening to death shall be deemed a death-illness.".

The executor and/or guardian shall discharge the debts of the estate with funds derived from claims recovered, cash in hand, proceeds of the sale of movables, and, if the funds so obtained are insufficient, with the proceeds of the sale of immovable property of the estate (Civil Code, Arts. 893, Egypt; 854, Syria; 1104, Jordan).

B. *Assets of Estate Exceeding Debts*

If the estate exceeds the value of the debts, the executor nominated by the deceased shall also act as a guardian and as an agent of such heirs as are minors or absent. He shall repay the debts in cash if available from the assets, or else shall sell any such part of the estate as is sufficient to repay the debts, even if there are majors among the heirs. He shall not sell any real property apart from what is absolutely necessary to repay the debts on the estate.

Should the deceased have failed to appoint an executor, the judge shall appoint an executor to administer the estate for the benefit of the minors and pay the debts, This need will not arise should all the heirs be adults, in which case they themselves will settle with the creditors.

C. *When there are no Debts*

In this case the heirs shall be fully entitled to deal with the estate. An executor appointed by the deceased shall have more restricted powers with regard to a major than with regard to a minor. He shall collect the debts due to the estate, proceed to the partition of the inheritance, sell the movables for the absent major heirs to avoid the loss or destruction thereof, and execute the will if there is one. No judge in this case shall have the power to appoint an additional executor. Should any dispute arise between partners, they shall have recourse to the court to settle the dispute.

D. *Order of Payment of Debts*

The first debts due for payment are charges on the property or the purchase price of anything bought and unpaid for before death. These are followed by debts incurred while the deceased was suffering from the death-illness. Last come the debt arising from an acknowledgement made during the death-illness which is not considered a legacy and therefore is not restricted to one third of the estate. Valid legacies are deducted from the remaining assets within this limit.

The remainder shall be distributed among the heirs. It should be pointed out that the heirs have no right on the estate until all debts have been paid. But heirs can, if they so wish, pay all the debts due on the estate and thereby acquire the whole estate for themselves. In such a case, neither the creditors nor the judge can refuse to allow such a procedure. After the payment of debts, and legacies which may not exceed one third of the net estate, the heirs for their part may nullify any transactions as may affect their prescribed shares. Such transactions are usually unilaterally disadvantageous; e.g. a donation or a sale for less than the value; as they are regarded as a legacy if they are made during the death-illness and therefore are subject to nullification or approval by the heirs should they exceed the prescribed one third.

4. Grounds for Inheritance

Under classical Sharia, there are three grounds for inheritance: marriage, consanguinity and clientage. Clientage of both manumission (*Wala-ul-Itq*), (i.e. the personal relationship between the patron and the client or the slave freed by him, both being called *mawla*), and clientage of oath of brotherhood (*Wala-ul-Muwalat*) no longer exist, and therefore will be omitted. Yemeni Article 303 refers to it in order to dismiss it.

The modern Personal Laws of Syria (Art. 263-1), Tunisia (Arts. 89, 90), Morocco (Art. 225), Iraq (Art. 86-b), Algeria (Art. 126), Sudan (Art. 348) and Oman (Art. 236) confine grounds for inheritance to consanguinity and valid marriage.

Marriage under a valid contract is a ground for inheritance between spouses. The right of the wife to inherit cannot be frustrated by irrevocable divorce during the death-illness of the husband if he dies during the *iddat*. Conversely, the husband inherits if the wife has caused the dissolution of the marriage during her death-illness, and dies during the *iddat*. This rule is enshrined in the Algerian Personal Status Act which orders mutual inheritance between spouses even if there was no consummation of marriage (Art. 130), no inheritance under a void marriage contract (Art. 131), and inheritance by the survivor should either spouse die before the divorce decree is issued or death occur during the *iddat* of divorce (Art. 132).

Consanguinity is the blood relationship between the deceased and the heirs, including descendants, ascendants, siblings, uncles and aunts, etc. Their shares, priorities and entitlement vary between the Sunnis and Shia, and depend on their closeness to the deceased and whether they are of the patriarchal or matriarchal lineage.

5. Conditions of and Impediments to Inheritance

For the succession to the estate to take effect, two conditions should be fulfilled:

(i) Death of the succeeded propositus, whether in fact or by court decision in the case of the missing person of whom it is not known for sure whether he is alive or dead. The judge may base his decision on circumstantial, not necessarily conclusive, evidence. Islamic law does not recognize any interest expectant on the death of another; and until that death occurs, which gives birth to the right as heir of the person entitled thereto under the rules of succession, he possesses no right at all (Arts. 1, Egyptian; 260/1, Syrian; 85, Tunisian; 86-c/1, Iraqi; 127, Algerian; 288, Kuwaiti; 349(a), Sudanese; 300, Yemeni and 237, Omani).

(ii) The certainty that an heir has survived the deceased. (Arts. 2, Egyptian; 260/2, Syrian; 85, Tunisian; 220, Moroccan; 86-c/2, Iraqi; 128, Algerian; and 289a, Kuwaiti). It follows:

(a) A missing person shall not inherit forthwith. But his share shall be set aside for him to collect if he is found to be alive. If he is deemed dead under a court ruling, that share shall be redistributed among the other heirs. The inheritance of the missing person will be dealt with in more detail in a separate section of this chapter.

(b) If a man dies, leaving a pregnant wife, the life of the child in her womb is not established at the time of the death of the propositus, and therefore it shall not inherit immediately. But in view of the probability of its being born alive later, a provisional share for it shall be reserved until it is born and its exact share is known. If it is still-born, there shall be no inheritance. The inheritance of the unborn child is the subject of a separate section of this chapter.

(c) If two or more persons who are competent to inherit from each other die without it being known for certain which has died first, they shall not inherit from each other. For the purpose of this provision, it is irrelevant whether they died simultaneously or at different times, in the same accident or not. Their respective estates shall be divided among their heirs who survive them at the time of the death of the propositus. This general Sharia provision is adopted in Article 3 (Egypt), 261 (Syria), 86 (Tunisia), 224 (Morocco), 129 (Algeria), 290 (Kuwait), 352 (Sudan), 301 (Yemen) and 240 (Oman).

Apart from the two conditions set out above, i.e. the actual or presumed death of the propositus and the sure survival of the heir, a third condition is the non-existence of any impediment to inheritance. The three conditions are summed up in the two Algerian Articles 127 and 128.

There are three main grounds for exclusion from succession: homicide; difference of religion; difference of domicile.

A. Homicide

Anyone who has caused the death of the deceased shall be excluded from succession, be he a murderer or an accomplice, or should he, by perjury, cause a death sentence to be passed and executed. (Complicity in murder shall include those pointing out the victim and those keeping watch during the murder.)

For homicide to be an impediment to inheritance, four conditions should be fulfilled:

(i) That it is deliberate. Therefore, homicide committed in retaliation or as a punishment laid down by the Quran (*hadd*) shall not exclude the murderer from inheritance.

(ii) That the murderer is criminally responsible. Therefore a minor under fifteen, an insane person, an imbecile or a person in a state of trance due, for example, to drugs, shall not be barred.

(iii) That the homicide is not an act of legitimate defence of life or property.

(iv) That there is no justification for homicide, e.g. in the case of a husband surprising his wife and her lover in the act of adultery and killing both or either of them.

While accidental homicide shall not bar the killer from inheritance, it shall, under Shia Law, exclude him from any share in the blood-money (i.e. an indemnity which may be claimed for the death) (*diya*), but not from the rest of the estate.[12] The same provision applies in the case of the minor and the insane.

---

[12] Al-Hilli, *op. cit.* p. 145.

The same view is adopted by the Algerian Law Article 137. These provisions are held under Articles 5 (Egypt), 264-a (referring to 223) (Syria), 88 (Tunisia), 229 (Morocco), 292 (Kuwait), 350 (Sudan), 304 (Yemen) and 238 (Oman), Algerian Article 135/1 and 2, with paragraph 3 adding the person who has had prior knowledge of the murder or the planning thereof without reporting it to the competent authorities. Article 136 goes on to rule that any such person debarred from inheritance shall not exclude any other heir.

B. Difference of Religion

Among Muslims: under Sunni Law, there shall be no inheritance by a non-Muslim of a Muslim and *vice versa* (Arts. 6, Egypt; 264, Syria; 228, Morocco; 293/a and b, Kuwait; 351, Sudan; 305, Yemen and 239, Oman). Kuwaiti Article 294 rules that: (a) the apostate shall not inherit from anyone; (b) his property before and after apostasy shall devolve on his Muslim heirs on his death, otherwise on the Public Treasury; (c) an apostate who adopts the nationality of a non-Muslim State shall be deemed dead and the estate goes to Muslim heirs; (d) if he returns to Islam after adopting a non-Muslim State as his domicile, he shall recover the balance held by his heirs or the Treasury. Algerian Article 138 rules that *lian* and apostasy debar from inheritance. Under Shia Law, a Muslim may inherit from a non-Muslim, or an apostate.[13] The Ismailis concur.[14]

Among non-Muslims: non-Muslims may inherit from one another even if they differ in religion (Kuwait, 293/b).

C. Difference of Domicile

Under the Sharia, difference of domicile does not bar inheritance among Muslims or among subjects of Muslim States, even if they are non-Muslims. But it shall bar inheritance between non-Muslims if one of them is subject to the laws of a non-Muslim State. Therefore, if a Christian dies in Egypt and has heirs living in England or in America, they shall not inherit from him because of the difference of domicile. However, the Egyptian Law of Inheritance, Article 6, restricts this impediment to one condition, namely that the law of the non-Muslim State bars foreigners from inheritance; otherwise, this impediment shall not apply. Therefore, if, for example, a member of the Jewish faith dies in Egypt, and his heirs are subjects of a foreign State which does not bar foreigners from inheritance, they will inherit from their Egyptian kin. The same provision is held in Article 264-c of the Syrian Personal Status Act, Yemeni Article 305, and Article 293/d of the Kuwaiti law.

So far the Sunnis and Shias, both Ithna-Ashari and Ismaili, follow fundamentally the same rules, except for some slight differences which have been pointed out. They part ways when it comes to the distribution of the estate among heirs. They differ so much over those who should inherit and, once they are specified, over what portions are due to each, that it will be best to consider the Sunnis, the Ithna-Ashari and the Ismaili separately in the remaining sections.

---

[13] *Ibid.*
[14] Qadi an-Numan, *op. cit.* Vol. 2, p. 320.

6. The Sunni Law of Inheritance

A. Introduction and General

There are three classes of heirs: sharers, residuaries, and distant kindred.

(i) Sharers are those who are entitled to a fixed share (*Fard*) of the inheritance.
(ii) Residuaries are those who take no fixed share but succeed to the residue after the claims of the sharers are satisfied. If there are no sharers, the residuaries will succeed to the whole estate.
(iii) Distant kindred are those relations by blood who are neither sharers nor residuaries. If there are no sharers nor residuaries, the estate will be divided among such of the distant kindred as are entitled to succeed thereto.[15]

There are certain cases in which heirs are excluded, or have their shares reduced due to the existence of other heirs who themselves take no share, because they are excluded by nearer heirs. The following example may demonstrate the point at issue. A man dies leaving behind him his father, mother and two sisters. In this case the father will exclude the two sisters. The two sisters, though themselves excluded, will reduce the share of the mother from one-third to one-sixth, and the rest, being five-sixths, will go to the father as a residuary. The same will be the result if there are two brothers, or one brother and one sister, instead of two sisters.

Total exclusion debars a person absolutely from succeeding to the estate. It arises, for example, when the deceased leaves its father's mother, its mother's maternal grandmother, and its father. In such a case, the father's mother, being the nearer true grandmother, would completely exclude the mother's maternal grandmother, and the father's mother herself is excluded by the father. Thus the father will take the whole as residuary.

As to the doctrine of proportionate abatement (*aul*), if, on assigning their shares to the sharers, it is discovered that the total of shares exceeds the unity, the share of each sharer is to be proportionately reduced by diminishing the fractional shares to a common denominator, and increasing the denominator in order to make it equal to the sum of the numerators.

Return (*rudd*) is the converse of proportionate abatement. In the case of return, the total of the shares is less than the unity. In the *rudd* case, the shares undergo what may be called a rateable increase, while in the *aul*, it is a rateable decrease.

The doctrine of return applies if there is a residue left after satisfying the claims of sharers. In the absence of a residuary, the residue reverts to the sharers, apart from the spouses, in proportion to their shares.

B. Sharers

Sharers are those heirs who are entitled to a fixed share of the inheritance, and whose specific shares should be given in the first instance after payment of funeral charges, debts and legacies, before distributing the inheritance among

---

[15] The Egyptian Law (Arts. 39, 40), following the Sharia, includes the manumitter, in the absence of distant kindred, followed by his agnates. Since this is only of academic interest, in view of the abolition of slavery, it has been left out altogether. The Tunisian Law drops the distant kindred, making the Treasury the heir of a deceased who leaves no sharers or residuaries (Art. 144).

the second class of heirs, i.e. residuaries. The sharers are twelve in number: husband, wife, father, mother, true grandfather how-high-soever,[16] true grandmother how-high-soever,[17] daughter, son's daughter how-low-soever, full sister, consanguine sister, uterine brother and uterine sister.

The sharers constitute the first and the most important group of heirs. Conspicuous by their absence from this group are the sons. The reason, as explained above, is that sharers consist entirely of those who were not entitled to succeed under pre-Islamic customary law, which excluded females and cognates, gave the nearest male agnates the entire estate of the deceased, and preferred descendants to ascendants, and the latter to collaterals.

We shall now deal with each of the twelve sharers who are entitled to a fixed share.

(i) The husband shall inherit half of his wife's estate when there is no child or child of a son how-low-soever, and a quarter if there is.

(ii) The wife inherits a quarter of her husband's estate when there is no child or child of a son how-low-soever, and one-eighth if there is. Two or more wives collectively inherit a quarter or one-eighth, which shall be divided equally among them.

The husband and wife cannot be utterly excluded from succession to the estate of their spouse, although their share may be reduced as above. However, no spouse shall have a return if there is a residue, unless there is no residuary or distant kindred.[18] The Hanafis and Hanbalis rule out any return to the spouse.[19] However, for the inheritance by either spouse to take effect, two conditions must be fulfilled:

(a) That the marriage contract is valid because there shall be no reciprocal inheritance under an irregular marriage contract.
(b) That the marriage stands *de facto* or is deemed so to stand on the death of a spouse, while the wife is still in her *iddat* of a revocable repudiation. Under Hanafi and Maliki (but not Shafii) Law, the wife is entitled to inherit if the irrevocable repudiation is made during the husband's death-illness, and the wife has not expressly or implicitly consented to the repudiation (*talaq*). This rule is adopted in the Egyptian, Syrian and Kuwaiti Laws of Personal Status.

Similarly, if the marriage is dissolved by an act proceeding from the wife during her death-illness, and then she dies during the *iddat*, the husband is entitled to inherit.

(iii) The father shall inherit, as a sharer, one-sixth when there is a child of the deceased or child of a son how-low-soever. When there is no child or child of a son how-low-soever, the father inherits as a residuary. He inherits both as a sharer and a residuary when there are only daughters or son's daughters how-low-soever.

(iv) The mother shall inherit one-sixth (a) when there is a child of the deceased

---

[16] A male ancestor between whom and the deceased no female intervenes.
[17] A female ancestor between whom and the deceased no false grandfather intervenes. "False grandfather" means a male ancestor, between whom and the deceased a female intervenes.
[18] Arts. 30, Egyptian; 288/2, Syrian; 167, Algerian; 318, Kuwaiti.
[19] Abu Zahra, *On Estates and Inheritance*, pp. 202–203.

or child of a son how-low-soever; or (b) when there are two or more brothers or sisters of the deceased, or even one brother and one sister, whether full, consanguine or uterine. She shall inherit one-third when no child or child of a son how-low-soever exists, and no more than one brother or sister (if any); but if there is also a spouse and the father of the deceased, then she shall inherit only one-third of what remains after deducting the share of the spouse.

(v) The true grandfather shall be excluded by the father and a nearer true grandfather. If there are no full or consanguine brothers or sisters, he shall inherit one-sixth as a sharer with a son or a son's son how-low-soever. He shall receive one-sixth as a sharer and again as a co-residuary with the daughter and a daughter of a son how-low-soever. He shall inherit solely as a residuary if there is no other heir.

When the deceased leaves full or consanguine brothers or sister, the Imam Abu Hanifa, following the opinion of some eminent Companions of the Prophet, including Abu Bakr, the first Patriarchal Caliph, rules that the true grandfather excludes the siblings. All the other three Imams (Malik, as-Shafii and ibn Hanbal) and the two Hanafi Companions (Abu Yousoof and Abu Shaibani), following the opinion of Imam Ali ibn-Abi-Talib, maintain that the siblings are not excluded, but again differ on the share of the true grandfather with the presence of siblings.

The Imam Malik, whose doctrine is followed in Tunisia, Morocco, Algeria and Kuwait, rules that the grandfather shall take the more advantageous to him of one-third of the estate, or as a co-residuary with the siblings if there is no sharer; if there is, then the better part of his entitlement as a co-residuary, one-sixth, or one-third of the residue. In the famous Akdari case, the total of his and the sister's shares are divided between them in the proportion of two to one. This provision of Tunisian Article 146 is further illustrated in the Moroccan and Algerian Articles 258 and 175 respectively: A woman dies leaving a husband, a mother, a full or consanguine sister and a true grandfather. The shares of the grandfather and the sister shall be added together, and then divided with the male taking twice as much as the female. With proportionate rebatement, the whole estate shall be divided by twenty-seven, the husband receiving nine, the mother six, the sister four and the grandfather eight parts.

Under the Egyptian Law (Art. 22), the true grandfather shall receive the more advantageous to him of the share of a brother as a co-residuary, or as a sharer (one-sixth) if there are brothers and sisters. If there are sisters who inherit as sharers, he shall get the more advantageous to him as a sharer (one-sixth) or as a co-residuary. This provision is also adopted under Syrian Article 279.

(vi) The true grandmother whether maternal or paternal is excluded by the mother according to all Islamic jurists, followed by all the modern legislators. They are almost unanimous, except the Hanbalis, that the paternal grandmother is excluded by the father or the grandfather through whom she is related to the deceased, a provision enshrined in Articles 25 (Egyptian), 283/1,2 (Syrian), 141 (Tunisian), 255 (Moroccan), 161 (Algerian), and 313/c (Kuwaiti). A nearer true grandmother shall exclude a further one. In the absence of any such exclusion the true grandmother shall inherit one-sixth, and two of the same degree shall share the one-sixth.

(vii) The daughter of the deceased shall inherit half if there is no son. If there are two or more daughters and no son, they shall together inherit two-thirds of the estate. If there is a son (or sons), the daughter (or daughters) become a co-residuary – taking half a son's share, after deduction of the portion of other sharers.

(viii) The son's daughter, how-low-soever, is excluded by a male descendant nearer to the deceased and by two daughters or daughters of a son nearer to the deceased unless she is made co-residuary with a son's son of the same or lower degree of nearness if she cannot inherit otherwise, in which case she shall get half of the share of a male. With one daughter or son's daughter nearer to the deceased, she gets one-sixth, to be shared if there are two or more in the same degree. If there is no daughter or son's daughter nearer to the deceased, one son's daughter shall receive one-half of the estate, two or more shall receive two-thirds.

(ix) The full sister of the deceased is excluded from inheritance by a child, a child of a son how-low-soever, and the father. In the absence of a male residuary, one full sister shall get one-half, two or more shall share two-thirds. With the full brother she takes as a residuary, the brother taking a double portion. In default of a full brother and other residuaries, the full sister shall take, and two or more shall share, the residue after the shares taken by a daughter or daughters or a son's daughter or daughters how-low-soever.

(x) The consanguine sister shall be excluded from inheritance by the father, the son, the son's son how-low-soever, the full brother and the full sister if co-residuary with daughters, whether with or without a consanguine brother. She shall also be excluded by two full sisters unless there is a consanguine brother with whom she becomes a residuary. She gets, on her own, one half, with another like sister or more, they all share two-thirds. She shall take or share with like sister/s one-sixth if there is a full sister and no consanguine brother. With a consanguine brother or brothers with whom she becomes a residuary, they shall share the residue left of the estate after the other sharers receive their dues, with the brother taking twice as much as the sister.

(xi) The uterine brother is excluded by any descending heir whether as a sharer or residuary, and any male ascendant entitled to inherit. If not so excluded, he gets one-sixth on his own, and shares one-third with brother/s or sister/s.

(xii) The uterine sister follows as for the uterine brother above.

Table 1 describes the sharers, their normal shares, the conditions under which these are inherited, and their variations.

C. Residuaries

The residuaries shall inherit the residue of the estate after the sharers take their allotted shares or shall inherit the whole estate if there are no sharers after payment of funeral expenses, debts and legacies. There are three groups of such relatives in the following order:

(1) The residuaries in their own right (asaba bil nafs)

These are all the male relatives between whom and the deceased no female intervenes. There are four categories of such relatives in the following order of priority:

Table 1. TABLE OF SHARERS – Sunni Law

Sharers	Normal share of: One	Normal share of: Two or more divided equally	Conditions for inheritance of normal share	Share as varied by special circumstances
Father	1/6		When there is a son or son of a son h.l.s.	The father inherits as a sharer and a residuary with a female descending heir and as a residuary in the absence of any descendant.
True Grandfather	1/6		When there is a son or son of a son h.l.s. and no father or nearer true grandfather.	With no father, the same as for father above. With full or consanguine brothers or sisters (a) according to Malik, the more advantageous of 1/3 or a brother's share in the absence of sharers, with a sharer the more advantageous of a brother's share, 1/6 or 1/3 of the residue, taking twice a full sister's share out of their shares total (b) Egyptian Law – the more advantageous of a brother's share of 1/6 or as a residuary with sisters inheriting as sharers.
Husband	1/4		As for father above.	1/2 when there is no child or child of a son h.l.s.
Wife (or Wives)	1/8	1/8	As for father above.	1/4 when there is no child or child of a son h.l.s.
Mother	1/6		As for father above, OR when there are two or more brothers or sisters, or one brother and one sister, whether full, consanguine or uterine.	1/3 when no child or child of a son h.l.s. and no more than one brother or sister (if any). When there is also a wife or husband as well as the father, only 1/3 of remainder after deducting the husband's or wife's share.
True Grandmother	1/6	1/6	When no mother and no nearer true grandmother either paternal or maternal.	Paternal true grandmother is entirely excluded by the father and a grandfather through whom she is related to the deceased.

Heir			Condition	Notes
Daughter	½	⅔	When there is no son.	She becomes a residuary with a son, taking half his share.
Son's Daughter h.l.s.	½	⅔	When there is no son, daughter, higher son's son, higher son's daughter or equal son's son.	No share at all with a higher son's son. No share with two daughters or two higher son's daughters, unless she becomes a residuary with an equal or inferior son's son when she gets half his share. ⅔ on her own share with like son's daughter, when there is one daughter or higher son's daughter if there is no male co-residuary.
Uterine Brother or Sister	⅙	⅓	When no child, child of a son h.l.s., father or true grandfather.	A male receives the same share as a female.
Full Sister	½	⅔	When no son, son of a son h.l.s., father or full brother.	No share at all with a male descendant h.l.s., or a father. Only the Hanafis make a true grandfather exclude her as well. She becomes a residuary with a full brother taking half the share of a male, sharing one third with uterine siblings, and a residuary by a female descendant, e.g. daughter or son's daughter h.l.s. if there is no full brother.
Consanguine Sister	½	⅔	When no son, son of a son h.l.s., father, full brother or sister or consanguine brother.	No share at all with the father, an inheriting male descendant h.l.s., a full brother or a full sister becoming residuary with daughters. No share when there are two full sisters unless there is a consanguine brother with whom she becomes a residuary and takes ½ his share. ⅙ as a sharer on her own or sharing it with like sister/s when there is one full sister and no consanguine brother. As a residuary with an inheriting female descendant.

(i)   The son and the son's son how-low-soever.
(ii) The male ascendants of the deceased, that is, the father and the true grandfather, how-high-soever.
(iii) The descendants of the father of the deceased, that is, full or consanguine brothers and their sons, how-low-soever.
(iv) The descendants of true grandfathers, how-high-soever, e.g. the deceased's full or consanguine paternal uncles and grand-uncles and their sons and grandsons. Only the Malikis, among the Sunnis, differ on the priority of the true grandfather over the full or consanguine brothers, making them of the same right to succession to the estate, after the father and before the male descendants of the said brother. The Hanafis rule that the true grandfather excludes the full or consanguine brothers from inheritance in the same way as he unanimously excludes the uterine, a ruling adopted in Omani Article 251(2) and Yemeni Article 316(2). But most modern Arab legislators, following the Malikis, treat him as equal to the agnate brothers, provided his share shall not be less than one-sixth.[20]

The above order of priority is followed in that each category shall exclude any other below. Within the same category, the nearest, i.e. with fewer links to the deceased, excludes the more distant. If they are equal in the category and nearness, the stronger relative, i.e. related to the deceased through both father and mother, e.g. a full brother, shall take precedence over the consanguine. If they are equal in all these aspects, they shall receive equal shares.

(2)   The residuaries through another (asaba bil ghayr)

These are all female sharers who need a residuary in his own right to share with. There are four such female sharers: the daughter with the son; the son's daughter, how-low-soever, with an equal or lower son's son; the full sister with the full brother; and the consanguine sister with the consanguine brother, whether of the same or different mother. They shall share the residue after the sharers, with the male receiving twice the portion of a female. In the previous section on the sharers, those females usually receive one half if on her own, and share two-thirds if many.

(3)   The residuaries with another (asaba maa al ghayr)

There are only two females in this class, the full and the consanguine sisters, who are both sharers, but, in the absence of a male agnate, they become residuaries with the daughter/s or the son's daughter/s how-low-soever or even one daughter and one or more son's daughters. A residuary with another differs from a residuary through another in that she does not share with her co-residuary, but inherits the residue left after the sharers take their share.

Notes on the distribution among sharers and residuaries. There are five heirs (referred to as "Primary Heirs") that are always entitled to a share of the inheritance and are never excluded entirely, although their share could be reduced. They are the child (son or daughter), father, mother, husband and wife.

---

[20] Arts. 22, Egyptian; 279, Syrian; 158, Algerian; 297–309, Kuwaiti; 379(c), Sudanese.

The child of a son, how-low-soever, true grandfather, how-high-soever, and true grandmother, how-high-soever are considered as substitutes of the primary heirs who exclude them if they exist.

Near male relatives can be excluded in some cases. For example, if a woman leaves a husband (share, one-half), the mother (share, one-sixth) and a uterine brother (share, one-third), the inheritance is exhausted, and nothing is left over for full brothers.

D. Distant Kindred

Distant kindred are those relations by blood of the deceased who are neither sharers nor residuaries. They consist of males or females related to the deceased through one or more female links. They are called in Arabic *dhawu-l-arham* or *ulu-l-arham* (relatives by virtue of the womb), and are entitled to inherit only on failure of any heir who belongs to the class either of the sharers (except a spouse) or residuaries. Distant kindred are divided into four classes in the following order of priority:

(1) Descendants of the deceased through a female link

(i) Daughters's children how-low-soever;
(ii) Children of son's daughters how-low-soever.

When there is only one, he/she shall inherit the whole estate in the absence of sharers and residuaries, and shall inherit the residue when there is a surviving spouse after his/her share is deducted. If there is more than one in this category of different degrees of kinship, the closest shall exclude the others.

If they are equal in degree of kinship, a child of a sharer shall exclude the others.

If they are equal in degree without any being the child of the sharer, or if all are children of a sharer, they shall inherit collectively (Arts. 32, Egyptian; 291, Syrian; 168, Algerian; 321, Kuwaiti; 393, Sudanese; 326, Yemeni and 263, Omani).

Nevertheless, their exclusion from inheritance is subject to the provisions of the modern Arab laws on the mandatory will, as explained in the next chapter on wills. Algerian Articles 169/172 inclusive enact the same provision as a rule, on inheritance, where the grandchildren take the place of their ascendant as an heir.

(2) Ascendants of the deceased through a female link

These are the false grandfather or false grandmother, how-high-soever. The closest to the deceased shall exclude the others. If they are equal in degree, the ascendant of a sharer shall exclude the others.

If they are equal in degree and ascendants of sharers, or none of them is an ascendant of a sharer, the father's cognates shall inherit two-thirds and the mother's one-third, with the male within each group taking a double portion to the female. This ruling is held under Articles 33 (Egypt), 292 (Syria), and 322 (Kuwait), 294 (Sudan) and 265 (Oman).

(3) Descendants of the deceased's parents who are neither sharers nor residuaries

(i)   Male or female children of full, consanguine or uterine sisters;
(ii) Daughters or son's daughters of full, consanguine or uterine brothers, how-low-soever;
(iii) Sons of uterine brothers and their children how-low-soever.

The closest in kinship, even a female, shall exclude the others. If they are equal in degree, the descendant of a residuary shall exclude that of a distant kindred, otherwise they shall be treated as if they were residuaries among themselves, the descendant of the two parents excluding a consanguine descendant who shall exclude a uterine one. If they are equal in both aspects, they shall equally share (Arts. 34, Egyptian; 293, Syria; 323, Kuwait; 396, Sudan and 364, Oman).

(4) Descendants of the deceased's immediate grandparents (true or false)

These are in brief all paternal aunts (*ammat*), all maternal aunts and uncles (*khalat wa akhwal*) and uterine paternal uncles (*aamam li umm*) – in the following detail:

(i)   Uterine paternal uncles of the deceased and full or half maternal uncles or aunts.
(ii) The children of (i) above, how-low-soever, and daughters or son's daughters of full or consanguine paternal uncles, how-low-soever, and the children of said females, how-low-soever.
(iii) The deceased's father's uterine paternal uncles, full or half paternal aunts, full or half maternal aunts or uncles; the deceased's mother full or half paternal or maternal aunts or uncles.
(iv) The children of (iii) above how-low-soever, the daughters and son's daughters of the deceased's father's full or consanguine paternal uncles how-low-soever and the children of said daughters how-low-soever.
(v)   The deceased's father's paternal aunts or uncles, and their full or half maternal aunts or uncles, and the deceased's mother's mother's or father's mother's full or half paternal or maternal aunts or uncles.
(vi) The children of (v) above how-low-soever and the daughters and son's daughters of the deceased's father's father's full or consanguine paternal uncles how-low-soever and the children of said females how-low-soever.[21]

For class (i) above, if the group consists solely of paternal relations or maternal relations, those related to the deceased through both parents shall exclude the consanguine who shall have priority over the uterine. If they are equal, they shall share. If the class combines both paternal and maternal relations, those of the father's side shall receive two-thirds and on the mother's side one-third, with distribution running on the above lines. These provisions shall also apply to classes (iii) and (v) above.

For class (ii) above, the nearer kin shall exclude the more distant regardless of the side. On being equal in distance and of the same side, the stronger kinship shall have priority if they are children of a residuary or a cognate, and the

---

[21] Al-Bardisi, *op. cit.* p. 76.

paternal side shall exclude the maternal, with the distribution running in the afore-mentioned fashion.

These provisions shall also apply to classes (iv) and (vi) above (Arts. 35 and 36, Egyptian; 295 and 296, Syrian; 324 and 325, Kuwaiti).

For all distant kindred, the male shall receive the share of two females (Arts. 297, Syrian; 327, Kuwaiti and 271, Omani).

E. Miscellaneous

(1) The acknowledged person

If the deceased has acknowledged as a kin a person of unknown parentage, the acknowledged person shall be entitled to the deceased's estate, provided that its parentage to a third person is not established, that the deceased has not revoked his acknowledgement, that there is no impediment for the acknowledged person to inherit, and that he/she is alive at the time of the actual death of the deponent (Arts. 41, Egyptian; 298, Syrian; 328, Kuwaiti; 276, Omani).

(2) The unborn child

The Sunni jurists are unanimous that an unborn child who is a prospective heir shall inherit if it already exists as an embryo, at the time of the death of the propositus, and if it is later born alive. Its existence as an embryo then can be inferred from the time span between the death of the propositus and its actual birth, namely within the maximum and minimum duration of pregnancy.

The jurists agree that an unborn child of the propositus who has died while the marriage was standing shall inherit if it is born within the minimum limit of pregnancy, i.e. within six months according to the majority of jurists, and nine months according to the Hanbalis, after the death of the father. If the death occurred while the wife was counting her *iddat* of an irrevocable marriage, the child shall inherit if born within the maximum duration of pregnancy, over which they differ, from two years according to the Hanafis and one lunar year (354 days) according to the Maliki jurist Muhammad ibn-ul-Hakam.[22]

The Egyptian legislator (Art. 43) rules that if a man dies leaving his wife or divorcée during her *iddat*, her unborn baby shall inherit from him if born alive within 365 (i.e. a solar year) days at most from the date of death or separation. The Tunisian and Kuwaiti legislators (Arts. 150 and 330 respectively) follow suit. The Algerian legislator (Art. 43) holds that the child's parentage shall be established if it is born within ten months from the date of separation or death. Syrian Article 300 reads as follows: "If a man dies leaving his wife or divorcee during her *iddat*, her unborn child shall not inherit from him unless it is born alive with proven parentage to him in the manner shown under this law", namely if it is born less than 180 days after the declaration of the termination of the *iddat* and less than one year after separation or death (Art. 131).

If the propositus is not the father of the unborn child, e.g. if he is a brother or grandfather, the unborn child shall not inherit from him unless:

(i) if it is born alive within 365 days at most after the death or separation whilst its mother is counting her *iddat* of death or separation, and the propositus died during the *iddat*; or

---

[22] Abdul Latif, *op. cit.* p. 151.

(ii) if it is born alive within 270 days at most from the date of the death of the propositus and the marriage was standing at the time of death (Arts. 43, Egyptian; 150, Tunisian and 330, Kuwaiti). This way, the existence of the embryo at the time of the propositus' death is certain.

On complying with these conditions, the unborn child shall have set aside for it from the deceased's estate the larger share of a male or female (Art. 42, Egyptian; 299, Syrian; 329, Kuwaiti; 274, Omani). Concurring to this provision the Tunisian (Art. 147) and Algerian (Art. 173) legislators add that if it excludes entirely all other prospective heirs, no shares shall be given and the whole estate shall stay undivided until the child is born. After the birth, the share set aside shall be adjusted upwards or downwards (Arts. 44, Egyptian; 301, Syrian; and 321, Kuwaiti).

(3) The hermaphrodite or person of non-determined sex

Such **a** person shall take whichever portion is less, whether that of the male or female (Arts. 46, Egyptian and 334, Kuwaiti).

(4) The illegitimate child

The illegitimate child or child whose paternity was solemnly contested (*lian*) shall not inherit from the wife's husband, but is eligible to inherit from, and be inherited from, the mother and her kindred (Arts. 47, Egyptian; 303, Syrian; and 152, Tunisian). Kuwaiti Article 335 concurs, adding that the time span under Article 330 shall be observed, i.e. to be born alive within 365 days maximum from the date of death or separation.

(5) The missing person

If a person dies, and among his heirs is a missing person, the estate shall be divided on the basis that that missing person is present until it is known for sure whether he is alive or dead. If he is discovered to be alive, he shall take his share of the inheritance. If it is duly proved that he died after the deceased, his share shall go to his heirs. If his death is duly confirmed before that of the propositus, the missing person shall not be entitled to any share. If he is found to be alive after his death has been declared by a court, he shall receive his share that has been given to the other heirs (Arts. 45, Egyptian; 302, Syrian; 151, Tunisian; and 115, Algerian). Under Articles 332 and 333 of the Kuwaiti law, the missing person appearing after his being declared dead by the court shall take back what is left of his original share with the other heirs.

7. The Shia Law of Inheritance

A. Introduction and General

The main difference between the Sunni and Shia Laws of Inheritance is that the Sunni distinguish between the agnates, the *asaba*, i.e. the persons related to the deceased without the intervention of female links, and the cognates, *dhawui-al-arham*, related to the deceased through one or more female links, while the Shias do not acknowledge such a distinction.

The difference emanates from a Tradition attributed by Tawoos, a narrator of *Hadeeth,* to the Prophet "Give *faraids* (prescribed shares) to those entitled thereto, and the residue shall go to the male agnate who deserves it most." The Sunnis believe it but the Shia reject it, denying its attribution to the Prophet and do not trust Tawoos.

Those to whom the Quran assigned a prescribed share are known as 'the sharers' *'As-haabul Furud'*. There are nine Shia sharers (instead of the Sunni twelve). Three are male: the father, the uterine brother and the husband should his wife die first. Six are female: the wife should her husband die first, the daughter, the full sister, the consanguine sister the uterine sister and the mother. Those missing from this list but included in the Sunni list are the grandfather, the grandmother and the son's daughter, all of whom inherit by kinship.

Those who inherit by kinship receive the residue after the sharers receive their prescribed portions. Of these residuaries, the male's share is twice that of the female. They are divided, according to their closeness to the deceased, into three classes, the higher of each class excluding the lower, but all those in the same class are equal within the male/female divide.

The first class: The parents and the children, male and female, how-low-soever.

The second class: The grandfathers and grandmother how-high-soever, and the brothers and sisters who in turn are replaced by their children, male or female, should they have predeceased their own parent.

The third class: The maternal and paternal uncles and aunts, with their children whether male or female, replacing them in the event of their earlier death.

Again no member of the second class or third class can inherit at all under kinship, in the event of the existence of any member of the class above them.

Spouses and mothers are always sharers, and sons are always residuaries, but always inherit as members of the first class.

The Iranian Law sums up this classification in Articles 893–98 inclusive which read as follows:

"Article 893 – An heir may be either a sharer, both a sharer and a residuary, or a residuary.

Article 894 – The sharers are those heirs who have a prescribed portion in the estate, such a portion being called a share.

Article 895 – Shares are one-half, one-quarter, one-eighth, two-thirds, one-third and one-sixth of the estate.

Article 896 – The sharers are the mother and the surviving spouse.

Article 897 – The heirs who are both sharers and residuaries are the father, the daughter or daughters, the full or consanguine sister or sisters, and the uterine sisters and brothers.

Article 898 – All heirs who are not specified in the previous two articles are residuaries."[23]

The following sections deal with the provisions on the entitlement of heirs in more detail.

---

[23] Quoted by Abu Zahra, *Inheritance According to the Jaafaris,* pp. 82–83. We owe a great deal to this valuable reference in the section on the Shia Law of inheritance. All references to Abu Zahra in the notes below are made to this book.

B. *The Spouses*

It must be noted that in all classes, the sharer, if any, shall have priority, and that residuaries come after the sharers. Since the spouses are always sharers, and therefore shall have priority over other sharers, and since they are the only sharers who are not necessarily blood relations, and notwithstanding the above order, I shall begin with them, following the Iranian Law, although the Shia jurists begin otherwise.[24]

Both the Sunnis and the Shias give the widower half the estate of the deceased wife if she has left no child, and a quarter if she has; the widow shall receive one-quarter or one-eighth respectively. Both schools rely on the authority of the Quranic verse:

"And unto you belongeth a half of that which your wives leave, if they have no child; but if they have a child then unto you the fourth of that which they leave, after any legacy they may have bequeathed or debt. And unto them belongeth the fourth of that which ye leave if ye have no child, but if ye have a child then the eighth of that which ye leave, after any legacy ye may have bequeathed or debt." (4:12)

However, the two sects differ on the meaning of the child which reduces the share of the widower and widow from a half to a fourth, and from a quarter to an eighth respectively.

The Sunnis maintain that such a child is any descendant whose relation to the deceased can be traced without the intervention of female links, e.g. a son's son or daughter. Under that definition a daughter's son is no descendant of the deceased and therefore shall not reduce the share of the surviving spouse.

The Shias consider that every descendant of the deceased, whether related through male or female links, is a child which shall reduce the share of the surviving spouse. Therefore, with a daughter's son or daughter, the widow shall receive one-eighth and the widower one-quarter of the net estate. The Shias quote the authority of a Tradition ascribed to the two Imams, Jaafar as-Sadiq and Muhammad al Baqir to that effect. They also use the term "posterity" (*dhurriyya*) to denote all descendants however they are related to the deceased.[25]

If there was no posterity in this general sense of the term, and there were no other sharers or blood relations, the widower shall receive the residue by way of "return" (*radd*). The widow, according to the most authoritative Ithna-Ashari opinion, is not entitled to any such return.[26] The Iranian Law adopts this ruling in Article 905 which reads as follows:

"Every sharer shall receive his portion of the estate. The remnant shall devolve upon the blood relations. If there are no blood relations of the same class as the sharers to participate with them in the residue of the estate, such residue shall be added to the shares of the sharers as an additional right of inheritance except for the surviving spouse. Nevertheless the husband who is the sole heir to his deceased wife shall receive the

[24] Abu Zahra, *op. cit.* p. 84.
[25] Abu Zahra, *op. cit.* p. 85.
[26] Al-Hilli, *op. cit.* p. 144.

residual part of the estate as an additional portion"[27] (that is, by way of return).

Like the Sunnis, the spouses can mutually inherit if the marriage stands *de facto* or is deemed to stand on the death of a spouse while the wife is still in her *iddat* of a revocable repudiation whether or not there was consummation. This does not apply, however, in the event of marriage during a death-illness where the Shias differ from the Sunnis and distinguish between the husband and wife: the wife shall not inherit from a husband who married her during his death-illness and died before consummation which renders the marriage void.[28] Contrariwise, the husband shall inherit from a wife who married during her death-illness and died before consummation as her death then does not render the marriage void.[29]

Another difference between the husband and wife in terms of inheritance is that the husband shall inherit the half or the quarter of all the estate left by the wife without distinction between real and movable property. As for the wife, the most authoritative Imami opinion is that a widow with a child by the deceased shall receive her share of both real and movable assets of the estate, but a childless widow shall receive nothing from the land left by the deceased and shall only take her share of the value of machinery, buildings and trees.[30] A different Imami opinion does not distinguish between widows who have a child by the deceased and those who do not. This opinion rules that a widow shall not inherit any real property but only the value of the buildings and the household effects. It is this latter ruling that the Iranian Law has adopted in Articles 946, 947 and 948 as follows:

"Article 946 – The Sharia share of the husband in the estate of his wife shall be calculated in all the property left by her. However, the wife's Sharia share in her husband's estate shall be taken from his following assets only:

(i)   All his movable possessions of whatever kind.
(ii) Buildings and household effects.

Article 947 – The wife shall take her share of the value of the buildings and household effects but shall take no part of the substance of said buildings and household effects. The value thereof shall be assessed on the basis that such buildings and household effects shall remain on the land without the owner of the land being entitled to any consideration therefor.

Article 948 – In the case described in the previous Article, if the heirs refuse to pay the value of the buildings and household effects, the surviving wife may demand her share in substance."[31]

C. Blood Relation Heirs of the First Class

These include the immediate parents and the descendants. They are considered by the Shia to be of the first class: any member whereof surviving shall exclude

---

[27] Quoted by Abu Zahra, *op. cit.* p. 86.
[28] *Ibid.* p. 88. It is noteworthy that the Malikis, of all Sunni schools, concur with the Shias in this ruling.
[29] *Ibid.* p. 89.
[30] Al-Hilli, *op. cit.* p. 149.
[31] Quoted by Abu Zahra, *op. cit.* p. 90.

all other relatives, be they brothers, sisters, uncles or aunts. The reason is that the shares of children and parents are defined in the same Quranic text with the omission of all others:

"God chargeth you concerning your children, to the male the equivalent of the portion of two females, and if there be women more than two, then theirs is two-thirds of the inheritance and if there be only one then the half. And to his parents a sixth of the inheritance, if he left children. If he left no children and his parents are his heirs, then to his mother appertaineth the third, and if he have brethren, then to his mother apperaineth the sixth, after any legacy he may have bequeathed, or debt. Your parents or your children: You know not which of them is nearest unto you in benefit. It is an injunction from God. Lo! God is All-Knowing, All-Wise." (4:11)

Moreover, according to the Shia, the inheritance by brothers and sisters is subject to the non-existence of ascendants and descendants, under the Quranic verse:

"And if a man or a woman has a distant heir, having left neither ascendants nor descendants (*kalalat*), and has a brother or a sister, then to each of them twain the sixth, and if they be more than two, then they shall be sharers in the third." (4:12)

The inheritance by brothers or sisters is also described in the Quran as *kalalat*:

"They ask thee for a pronouncement say: God hath pronounced for you concerning those who leave no ascendants or descendants as heirs (*kalalat*). If a man die childless and he has a sister, hers is half the heritage that he would have inherited from her had she died childless. And if there be two sisters then theirs are two-thirds of the heritage. And if they be brethren, men and women, unto the male is the equivalent of the share of two females." (4:176)

Unlike the Sunnis, children are interpreted by the Shia, strictly following the Quranic texts without reference to any exegesis, to include all descendants of the deceased, through male or female links, while parents are restricted to the immediate father and mother.

(1) The shares of mother and father

The mother on her own, without a spouse or a member of the first class or a group of brothers or sisters, shall receive the whole estate: one-third as a sharer and the residue by way of return. If she inherits with a husband, he shall take his share of one-half. A wife shall take a quarter, and the mother in both cases shall receive what is left: one-third as a sharer and the residue by way of return.

Likewise if the father is on his own as an heir, he shall inherit the whole estate. With a spouse he shall receive the rest after the spouse's share.

With both parents surviving, the mother shall get one-third and the father the residue. Both with one spouse, the mother shall receive one-third of the whole estate, the spouse his or her share and the father what is left thereafter.

With a number of brothers and/or sisters, the mother's share is reduced to one-sixth on five conditions:

(i)   The number should be two brothers, or four sisters or one brother and two sisters. Less than that, the mother's share shall not be reduced.
(ii) Siblings should be on both sides or on the side of the father. Uterine siblings shall not reduce the mother's share, since she is the link through which they are related to the deceased.
(iii) The father must be alive, in which case the father shall receive what is left over after the siblings take their share and the mother her sixth.
(iv) They must not be debarred from inheritance through any impediment as a debarred person shall not exclude or reduce the share of any other heir.
(v)   They must actually exist. A sibling unborn at the time of the death of the deceased shall not be counted in the quorum and shall not reduce the mother's share to one-sixth.

The Shia School does not accept this condition which has also been dropped from Article 892 of the Iranian Law which reads as follows:

"If the propositus has left a number of brothers and/or sisters, the mother's share shall be reduced to one-sixth of the estate on the following conditions: 1. That the propositus leaves two brothers, or one brother and two sisters or four sisters. 2. That their father is alive. 3. That they are not debarred from inheritance. 4. That they are full or consanguine brothers and/or sisters."[32]

(2) The parents with one female descendant as heir

A parent with a female descendant shall take her/his share of one-sixth and the descendant her share of a half, the residue being further divided between them in the proportion of their share, with the parent getting a quarter and the daughter three-quarters of the residue. For example, with the deceased leaving a wife, a mother and a daughter, the wife shall receive one-eighth, the mother one-sixth and the daughter one-half, the residue being then distributed between the mother (one-quarter) and the daughter (three-quarters).

If the deceased has left a father, a mother and a female descendant, without brothers to reduce the share of the mother, each parent shall receive one-sixth, and the female descendant her share (one-half). The residue shall be shared between them, one-fifth to each parent and three fifths to the daughter.

If there are brothers, they shall reduce the mother's share to one-sixth and exclude her from return, although they themselves inherit nothing. Therefore, in the previous case, but adding brothers, the mother shall get only one-sixth, the father one-sixth and the daughter one-half. The residue shall be shared between the father (one-quarter) and the daughter (three-quarters). Only Mueen-ud-Deen Al Misri dissents, ruling two-fifths of the residue to the father and three-fifths to the daughter, on the ground that the father should get the mother's one-fifth of the residue which she has lost due to the existence of the brothers.[33]

Article 908 of the Iranian Law deals with this case as follows:

[32] Quoted by Abu Zahra, *op. cit.* p. 108.
[33] *Ibid.* p. 109.

"If the propositus has left a mother and/or a father and an only daughter, each of the surviving parents shall take one-sixth, the daughter a half and the residue shall devolve by way of return to all heirs in the proportions of their Sharia shares. However, if the mother is partially excluded, she shall take no part of the return."[34]

(3) The parents with more than one female descendant

With two or more daughters, each parent shall take one-sixth, and the daughters shall take two-thirds. If it is only one parent with the daughters, he/she shall receive one-sixth, the daughters two-thirds and the residue shall be divided in the proportions of one-fifth for the parent and four-fifths to be shared by the daughters.

With a surviving spouse, both parents and more than one daughter, the spouse shall take his/her share, each parent one-sixth, and the residue, being less than two-thirds, shall be shared by the daughters. Here we find a distinct difference from the Sunnis, as the Shias do not allow *aul* (proportional increase). If the sum total of the fractions of shares exceeds unity, the deficit is borne solely by the females whose share is reduced if there is a male.

This case is covered by Article 909 of the Iranian Law:

"With one or both parents surviving with more than one daughter, all the daughters shall equally share two-thirds of the estate and each surviving parent shall take one-sixth of the estate, the residue, if any, to be distributed among all heirs in the proportion of their Sharia share. However, if the mother is partly excluded, she shall have no part of the return."[35]

(4) The parents with children as heirs

If there is a male among the children surviving the deceased, inheriting with one or both parents, the parents shall take their share, and the residue shall be divided among the children, the male receiving the share of two females under the Quranic verse: "God chargeth you concerning your children: to the male the equivalent of the portion of two females." (4:11) Therefore there is no return in this case. The children, male and female, shall take whatever is left after the sharers receive their portions. If a man leaves his wife, a father and mother, son and daughter; the wife shall take one-eighth, the father one-sixth, the mother one-sixth and the rest shall be divided between the son (two-thirds) and the daughter (one-third). Here, the Imamis concur with the Sunnis, both applying a clear Quranic ruling.

(5) The children's shares

An only child of the deceased shall take the whole estate if on its own: a son through kinship, and a daughter as a sharer (one-half) and by way of return (one-half). On the same grounds, an only child with a spouse of the deceased, shall take the whole residue after deducting the spouse's share. More than one child, males and females, shall share the whole estate if there is no sharer, and

---

[34] *Ibid.*
[35] *Ibid.* p. 110.

the residue if there is a sharer, the male taking twice the portion of the female. If they are all males or females they shall equally share such a residue. These rules are adopted under Iranian Article 907 which reads as follows:

> "If the propositus has left a child or several children, without leaving a father or a mother, the estate shall be divided in the following manner:
> 1. If there is only one child, male or female, it shall succeed to the whole estate.
> 2. If there are a number of children, all being males or females, they shall share the whole estate equally.
> 3. If there are both males and females, the male shall receive twice as much as the female."[36]

The eldest son, provided that he is not a prodigal nor an adherent to an unorthodox doctrine (that is other than Imami) shall get his dead father's Quran, sword, seal and robes as a prior charge before even the legatees. This is not a matter of inheritance, but an act of favouritism dictated by the legislator in return for the said son performing on behalf of his dead father what the latter missed in respect of the rites of prayers and fasting.[37]

(6) The grandchildren's shares

Every grandchild shall be excluded by a direct child of the deceased, under the general Shia rule that within the same class of blood relations, the nearest excludes the more remote. A daughter's daughter shall be excluded by a daughter or a son, a son's son shall not inherit if there is a son or a daughter, and so forth. But grandchildren may inherit with the parents, being of different categories (descendants and ascendants) albeit of the same class. This ruling is enshrined in Article 901 of the Iranian Law: "If the propositus leave any child, even an only child, the grandchildren shall not inherit anything."[38]

The entitlement of grandchildren to the estate is governed by three basic rules:

(i)   The higher descendant shall exclude the lower on whatever side, e.g. the daughter's son shall exclude the son's son's son.

(ii) A descendant shall inherit the share of its ascendants, whether male or female. Suppose a deceased left a son's daughter and a daughter's son; they shall get respectively the shares of the son and the daughter had they been alive. This is known as the principle of representation which is rejected by the Sunnis.[39]

(iii) If a dead child of the deceased has left several children, they shall share their parent's portion, had he been alive, with the male taking twice as much as the female. As an example, the deceased left a son and a daughter of his daughter, and a son and a daughter of his son. The daughter's son shall take two-thirds, and her daughter one-third of their mother's share, had she been alive. The son's daughter shall take one-third and his son two-thirds of their father's share.

---

[36] Abu Zahra, *op. cit.* p. 112.
[37] *Ibid.* p. 113.
[38] *Ibid.* p. 114.
[39] Except in the special case of the mandatory will in modern Arab laws, cf. Chap. 13.

Iranian Articles 911 and 912 sum up these provisions as follows:

"Article 911 – if the propositus has left no children, their children's children shall take their place under the right of representation, and shall as such be considered heirs of the first class and shall share the estate with the surviving parent or parents of the deceased. As for distribution among grandchildren it shall apply by stirps, that is to say, the heirs of each descendant shall inherit the share of their ascendant whom they represent and who forms their link with the propositus. For example, the share to be inherited by the children of the propositus' son shall be twice that devolved upon the propositus' daughter.

Article 912 – The descendants of the deceased, how-low-soever, shall inherit in accordance with the previous article."[40]

The children's children shall inherit in the same manner as their ascendants, vis-à-vis other sharers. A daughter's children shall share in the return in the same way as their mother would have done. The son's children shall take, on the ground of blood relationship, the residue after the parents' and the spouse's shares. A spouse inheriting with grandchildren shall take only his/her share and nothing by way of return, exactly as if their parents had been alive.

Parents do not exclude children's descendants and shall inherit with them as if those descendants' ascendants were alive.

Representation applies only to descendants, not to parents or grandparents.

D. Blood Relation Heirs of the Second Class

Brothers and sisters and their descendants share with the grandparents the same second class of blood relationship, because both categories relate to the deceased via a parent. To make a grandfather or a grandmother equal to a brother or a sister respectively is a rule maintained also by the bulk of Sunni jurists. However, Sunnis and Imamis (Shias) differ in three important issues:

(i)   While the Sunnis accord a grandparent the status of a sibling, they stipulate a minimum for his share, one-sixth or one-third according to different jurists. The Shias do not rule any such minimum.

(ii) The grandfather considered by the Sunnis as an equal to the brother is a "true grandfather", i.e. an ascendant between whom and the deceased no female link intervenes. The Imamis place any grandfather in the same status for inheritance as siblings, and their descendants, whether there was or not a female link intervening between him and the deceased. Likewise, they consider a grandmother as an equal for inheritance purposes to a sister, regardless of the way she is linked to the deceased.

(iii) The true grandfather, under the Sunni doctrine, excludes the children of brothers and sisters. Contrariwise, he does not exclude them according to the Shias. Grandparents shall share with the descendants of brothers and sisters, be they full, consanguine or uterine.

The members of the second class shall only inherit if there is no member

---

[40] Abu Zahra, *op. cit.* p. 115.

whatsoever of the first class of blood relations, i.e. immediate parents and descendants, how-low-soever.

There are three possible eventualities for the inheritance by the second class: no grandparents and only brothers or sisters or their children; grandparents on their own; and grandparents sharing with brothers or sisters or their children.

(1) No grandparents, but only brothers and/or sisters

The brothers and sisters shall inherit with the surviving spouse, if any, taking his/her prescribed share, the uterine sister or brother her/his share, the residue devolving on the full or consanguine brothers and sisters.

The uterine brothers and sisters are not excluded by the full brothers and sisters, but shall take their share with them. Contrariwise, consanguine brothers or sisters are utterly excluded by full siblings, whether the latter inherit as sharers or residuaries. Here the Imamis differ from the Sunnis who rule that the consanguine brothers and sisters shall inherit with a full sister who shall only exclude the consanguine if she is a residuary with the daughter.

Uterine sisters shall share equally with uterine brothers in absolute conformity with the Sunnis ruling under the Quranic verse: "... but if more than two, they share in a third." (4:12) But a male shall receive twice as much as a female if there are full or consanguine sisters with full or consanguine brothers, again in conformity with the Sunnis, under the Quranic verse: "If there are brothers and sisters the male shall have twice the share of the female." (4:176)

Uterine brothers and sisters shall not take part of any return if there are full brothers or sisters who shall share the return.

Full brothers or sisters of the deceased shall take the whole estate, the male taking twice as much as the female if there is no sharer. If there is a sharer, e.g. a spouse or uterine brothers or sisters, the full siblings shall get the residue.

If the deceased left only consanguine brothers and sisters, they shall receive the shares that would have been for full brothers and sisters: one sister shall receive one-half, two or more shall receive two-thirds and the brothers shall equally share the residue.

The Iranian Law Articles 918–922 and 927 cover the inheritance of brothers and sisters as follows:

918. If the propositus left full brothers or sisters they shall utterly exclude the consanguine but not the uterine brothers and sisters.
919. If the propositus left only full or consanguine brothers or only full or consanguine sisters they equally share the estate.
920. If the heirs are full brothers and sisters or consanguine brothers and sisters, the male shall receive twice the share of a female.
921. If the heirs are the deceased's uterine brothers and/or sisters they shall equally share the estate.
922. If the estate is shared by full brothers and sisters with uterine or consanguine brothers and sisters, the devolution shall be in the following manner:

If there is only one uterine brother or sister, he/she shall receive one-sixth of the estate and the residue shall devolve on full brothers and sisters. If there is no uterine brother or sister, the sixth shall be taken by the consanguine brothers and/or sisters under the rules set above. If there are several uterine brothers and/or sisters, they shall share one-third equally between them, with the full brothers and/or sisters receiving the residue which shall be divided according to the rules set above.

927. In all cases treated in this section, the surviving spouse shall first of all receive his/her Sharia share, being half the estate for the widower and a quarter for the widow. The prescribed share shall also go to the relations of the deceased on the mother's side, be they ascendants or brothers and sisters. If the sum total of shares exceeds the estate due to the survival of a spouse of the deceased, the shares of the full brothers or consanguine brothers and/or sisters or of ascendants shall be reduced accordingly."[41]

(2) Nephews and nieces

If the deceased left no brothers or sisters, the estate shall devolve on their children, if any. No child of a brother or sister shall receive any part of the estate with any brother or sister surviving. If the deceased left a uterine brother and a son of a full brother, the latter will receive nothing of the estate which shall be entirely taken by the uterine brother, in accordance with the fundamental Imamis' rule that the proximity overrides any other consideration within the same class of blood relations. Applying the same rule, the nearest in degree of kinship among the children of brothers and sisters shall exclude the more remote. The son of a uterine sister shall succeed to the whole estate excluding the grandson of a full brother and so on.

Again, applying the principle of representation, distribution of shares among the members of the same class with the same degree of proximity to the deceased proceeds by stirps, not per capital. The children of several brothers or sisters of the deceased shall take, between them, the share their father or mother would have taken had he/she survived the deceased, e.g. the deceased left a son of a uterine brother, a son of a full sister and a son of a consanguine brother. The first shall take one-sixth, the second shall take one-half as a sharer, and by way of return, the two portions being those of the uterine brother and the full sister. Like his father, the son of a consanguine brother shall be excluded by the full sister or her son who represents her in this case.

The children of a full brother or sister shall share their father's/mother's prescribed portion with the male taking twice the portion of a female. Those of a uterine brother or sister shall share equally their father's/mother's share, according to the rules outlined above.

The distribution of the estate among the nephew and nieces is canonized in Article 925 of the Iranian law as follows:

"In all cases treated in the previous Articles, if the deceased left no brothers or sisters, the children of brothers and sisters shall succeed to the estate by the right of representation and shall share with the surviving ascendants of the deceased, the distribution being by stirps, i.e. the heirs of each collateral

---

[41] Abu Zahra, *op. cit.* pp. 122–123.

shall succeed to their ascendant's share through whom they are related to the deceased and shall take the prescribed portion to which the said ascendant would have been entitled had he/she survived the deceased. Therefore, the children of the full uterine or consanguine brother or sister shall take the portion of the full, uterine or consanguine brother or sister. In dividing the estate among the members of the same class, the male shall take twice the share of a female if the heirs are children of full or consanguine brothers or sisters. But if they are children of uterine brothers or sisters, they shall share their ascendant's share equally."[42]

(3) Grandparents on their own

Grandparents how-high-soever are considered in the same degree of kinship to the deceased as brothers and sisters and their descendants how-low-soever, having the same links with one deceased, namely a parent of whatever sex.

A grandfather or a grandmother on his/her own shall succeed to the whole estate after the surviving spouse receives his/her share.

The nearest grandparent to the deceased, whether maternal or paternal, male or female, shall exclude a more distant grandparent. A maternal grandfather shall exclude a paternal great-grandmother and shall succeed to the whole estate and so on.

If more than one grandparent survives the deceased and they are equally near, there are three possibilities:

(i)   That they both be on the father's side, for example the father's father and mother. Here the grandfather shall receive two-thirds and the grandmother one-third, the male taking twice the share of a female as in the case of full or consanguine brothers and sisters.

(ii)   That they both be on the mother's side, e.g. the deceased's maternal grandfather and grandmother. The link is the mother and therefore each grandparent shall receive one-half of the estate, as in the case of uterine brothers and sisters.

(iii) That they be on the mother's and the father's side, e.g. the deceased's maternal and paternal grandparents. In this case, the maternal grandparents shall take one-third and the paternal shall take the residue. The maternal grandmother shall share the third equally with the maternal grandfather. Of the residue, the paternal grandfather shall take two-thirds and the maternal grandmother one-third.

If grandparents are heirs with a spouse, a sole grandparent shall take the residue after the spouse's share. If more than one in the same degree, the maternal grandparents shall share the residue equally and a paternal grandfather shall take two-thirds of the residue leaving one-third for the paternal grandmother.

If paternal and maternal grandparents succeed to the estate with a surviving spouse, the maternal grandparents shall equally share one-third of the whole estate, the spouse shall get his/her prescribed share and the residue shall go to the paternal grandparents, with the male taking twice the share of the female, as in the case of surviving father and mother of the deceased. The mother would

---

[42] *Ibid.* pp. 125–126.

have taken one-third of the whole estate, the spouse his/her share and the father the residue.

These provisions are adopted in the Iranian Article 923 which reads as follows:

"If the sole heirs of the deceased are grandfathers or grandmothers, the estate shall be divided among them in the following manner:

If it is solely the grandparent, whether on the mother's or father's side of the deceased, she/he shall succeed to the whole estate. If there are several grandparents, the estate shall be distributed among them on the basis that the male shall receive twice the share of the female on the paternal side, while the maternal grandparents shall receive equal shares.

If the paternal grandparent inherits with the maternal grandparent, one-third of the estate shall be equally shared among the maternal grandparents and the remaining two-thirds shall devolve on the paternal ascendants, with the male receiving twice the share of a female."[43]

(4) Grandparents with brothers and/or sisters

Grandparents do not exclude brothers or sisters nor even their descendants. They shall inherit together, the grandfather as a brother and the grandmother as a sister sharing the estate with brothers and sisters or their children.

Maternal grandparents shall share with uterine brothers and/or sisters or their descendants, taking one-third of the estate to be shared equally between male and female, e.g. the deceased's mother's father and mother shall equally share one-third with the uterine brothers and/or sisters. They shall succeed to the whole estate as sharers, and by return if there are no paternal grandparents or full or consanguine brothers/sisters. If there are paternal grandparents, they shall share with full and/or consanguine brothers/sisters with the male taking the portion of two females.

Again, according to the principle of proximity, the nearest grandparent to the deceased shall exclude the more distant, and share with brothers/sisters. The mother's mother of the deceased shall exclude the mother of the father's father. Likewise, the nearest nephews and nieces of the deceased shall exclude the more remote, and share with grandparents.

A few examples illustrate these general rules:

(i) A deceased left a father's mother, a uterine brother, a uterine sister, a full brother, a full sister, a consanguine brother and a consanguine sister. The uterine brother and sister shall equally share one-third. The consanguine brother and sister shall be excluded by the full brother and sister. From the residue, the father's mother shall receive the same as the full sister who shall get half of the full brother's share.

(ii) A deceased left a mother's mother, a father's mother and a uterine brother. The brother shares the third equally with the mother's mother, while the father's mother, replacing a full sister, shall succeed to the whole residue as a sharer and by return.

(iii) A deceased is survived by a father's father, a full brother's son, a full sister's

---

[43] *Ibid.*

daughter, a uterine brother's son and a uterine sister's daughter. The relations on the mother's side shall share equally one-third, i.e. the uterine siblings' children shall get the share of their respective parent. The residue shall devolve on the grandfather, the full sister's daughter (representing her mother) and the full brother's son (representing his father), with the male taking twice the share of the female.

Article 924 of the Iranian Law rules as follows on the inheritance of grandparents with brothers and sisters.

"If the ascendants of the deceased inherit with the uterine brothers/sisters, two-thirds of the estate shall go to the deceased's relations on the father's side, with the male getting twice the share of the female and the remaining one-third to the relations on the mother's side, to be shared equally between them.

However, if the deceased leaves only a uterine brother or sister the share that devolves to either of them shall not exceed one-sixth."[44]

Although the immediate parents, being of the first class, exclude the grandparents who belong to the second class of relations, the Imamis strongly recommend that the father or mother who receives more than one-sixth should give the excess, up to one-sixth, to his or her surviving ascendant. However, they restrict this voluntary recommended grant to the immediate grandparent and not any further.[45]

E. Blood Relation Heirs of the Third Class

This class includes the descendants of grandparents both maternal and paternal. They come after the grandparents and brothers and sisters because they relate to the deceased through the grandmother or grandfather and are therefore more remote. For the same principle of proximity, the descendants of the first grandparent have priority over, and exclude, those of the second grandparent, and so forth. The son of an uncle excludes the brother of a grandparent. In general, the cousins, how-low-soever, have priority over the descendants of the second grandparent.

The whole estate shall devolve on any such relative if he/she is the only surviving heir. With a surviving spouse, he/she shall take the residue after deducting the spouse's share.

To the general rule of proximity, there is one major exception: the son of a full brother to the father shall have precedence over and exclude the consanguine brother of the father. This exception, on the authority of a Tradition of the Imam Ali-ibn-Ali Talib, is confirmed in this case. A maternal uncle or a spouse shall exclude such a cousin.[46]

When equal in the degree of proximity to the deceased, those relations on the

---

[44] *Ibid.* p. 131.
[45] *Ibid.* p. 132.
[46] Al-Hilli, *op. cit.* p. 155. This provision enables the Shias to assert the priority of Ali's claim to the Imamat over Al-Abbas, who was a consanguine uncle to the Prophet, while Ali's father, Abu Talib, was a full brother of Abdullah, the Prophet's father.

mother's side shall succeed to one-sixth of the estate if only one and shall equally share one-third if several, as if they were uterine brothers and/or sisters. Those relations on the father's side shall share the residue, with the male taking twice the share of a female. This distribution shall follow the share of a spouse, if any.

The relations on the side of both mother and father shall exclude those solely on the father's side, but not on the mother's side.

Iranian Articles 928–938 inclusive deal with the inheritance of uncles and aunts and their descendants in the following manner:

"928 – If the deceased left no relatives of the second class, the estate shall devolve on heirs of the third class.

929 – A sole relation of the third class shall succeed to the whole estate. Among several such relations, the distribution of the estate shall proceed according to the following provisions:

930 – If the deceased left full or consanguine paternal aunts/uncles or maternal full or consanguine aunts/uncles, the maternal and paternal aunts/uncles who are the consanguine sisters/brothers of the deceased's mother/father shall be excluded by their full siblings, but shall replace them if there are not any.

931 – If the deceased left only paternal aunts/uncles, they shall equally share the estate if they are uterine brothers/sisters of the deceased's father. If they are full or consanguine brothers/sisters of the deceased's father, they shall share the estate with the male taking twice the portion of a female.

932 – If the deceased left paternal aunts/uncles who are uterine sisters/brothers of the deceased's father, together with paternal aunts/uncles who are full or consanguine sisters/brothers of the deceased's father, the aunt or uncle who are the uterine sister/brother of the deceased's father shall take one-sixth if on his/her own and one-third to share equally if more. The residue shall devolve on the deceased's aunts and uncles who are full or consanguine sisters/brothers of the deceased's father with the male taking twice the share of the female.

933 – If the deceased left solely maternal aunts/uncles, they shall share the estate equally, whether they are the deceased's mother's full, uterine or consanguine sisters/brothers.

934 – If the deceased left maternal full or consanguine aunts and uncles together with uterine maternal aunts and uncles, one-sixth of the estate shall go to the uterine maternal aunt or uncle if alone; if they are several, they shall equally share one-third. The residue of the estate shall go to the aunts and uncles who are full or consanguine sisters and brothers of the deceased's mother to be shared equally between them.

935 – If the deceased left one or more paternal uncles and aunts with one or more maternal uncles and aunts, one-third of the estate shall go to the maternal uncles and aunts, and two-thirds to the paternal uncles and aunts.

Maternal uncles and aunts shall share equally. However, if there is among them a uterine brother or sister of the deceased's mother, he/she shall take one-sixth of the total share of maternal uncles and aunts. If there are several maternal uncles and aunts who are uterine brothers/sisters of the deceased's mother, they shall share equally one-third of the said total share. As for the two-thirds which go to the paternal uncles and aunts, it shall be divided on the basis that the male shall take twice the portion of a female. However, if there is among the paternal uncles and aunts of the deceased a uterine brother/sister of the deceased's father, he/she shall get one-sixth of the total share of paternal uncles and aunts; if there are several, they shall equally share one-third of the said total. The remaining five-sixths or two-thirds of the rest for the paternal uncles and aunts shall be divided, as the case may be, between full paternal uncles and aunts, or those who are consanguine brothers/sisters of the deceased's father, according to the rule that the male shall take twice the portion of a female.

936 – Paternal and maternal uncles and aunts shall exclude paternal and maternal cousins. However, if the deceased left a paternal cousin who is the son of a full brother of the deceased's father, and a paternal uncle who is a consanguine brother of the deceased's father, the full paternal cousin shall exclude the consanguine paternal uncle.

937 – If the deceased left with the full paternal cousin a maternal uncle or aunt or several paternal uncles and aunts, the full paternal cousin shall be excluded from inheritance, even if the paternal uncles and aunts are consanguine brothers/sisters of the deceased's father.

938 – In all cases provided for in this section, there shall be first taken from the estate the share of the surviving spouse, which is half the estate for the widower and a quarter for the widow, then the share of blood relations on the deceased's mother side. The residue shall be divided among the relations on the father's side."[47]

9. The Ismaili Law of Inheritance

The only known authority on Ismaili jurisprudence is '*Daaim ul Islam*' by Qadi an-Numan at-Tameemi, Chief Justice under the Fatimid Empire in Egypt, who devotes Part 15 of the second volume to the Ismaili Law of Inheritance, under the title '*Kitabul Faraid*', the Book of Prescribed Shares. It deals with the subject in nine chapters: children's inheritance; parents' inheritance with children and siblings; spouses on their own or with others; siblings and grandparents; *Dhawul Arhaam* (Cognates) *Asabaat* (Agnates) and other kin; definition of *Sihaam* (shares) and rejection of *Aul* (proportional abatement); impediments to inheritance; interpretation of some ambiguous rulings; with a summary and some illustrations. The provisions are based on Quranic verse, Prophet's Tradition and rulings by the Imams. Qadi an-Numan refers several times to a *Saheefatu Faraaid* (Sheet of Prescribed Shares), claimed to have been dictated by the Prophet and written in the handwriting of (the first) Imam Ali.

Ismaili rules on inheritance are based on the same principles of the Ithna-Ashari interpretation of the holy texts, mainly (a) that the word for children in the Quranic texts, '*walad*', covers both sons and daughters, an interpretation accepted sometime by the Sunnis themselves; and (b) the paramount importance

---

[47] Abu Zahra, *op. cit.* pp. 137–140.

attached to the Quranic ruling "But kindred by blood have prior rights against each other in the Book of God" a ruling asserted in two verses: 8:75 and 33:6.

Qadi an-Numan attacks the (Sunni) opponents who deny that the daughter's children are heirs to their grandfather, but claim that they are the descendants of their fathers. He accuses the opponents of maliciously intending to deny the Prophet's daughter, Fatima, her legitimate rights to inherit from her father. He claims that they are thereby defying Quranic and *Sunna* rulings. The Quran describes Jesus as a descendant of Ibrahim through a daughter, Mary, not a son (6: 85). As for the *Sunna*, Qadi an-Numan quotes reports that the Prophet used to call al-Hassan and al-Hussayn, his grandsons by Fatima, his two sons and children, and when he saw each of them for the first time, he had said, "Show me my son." The Qadi suspects that behind the Sunni position, the ultimate motive is to deny the Imams their divine rights to rule and guide.

The Ismaili inheritance law follows closely the Ithna-Ashari. The heir can be a sharer '*dhu fard*' if such heir has a prescribed portion under the Quran, or can inherit under kinship according to its degree of closeness to the deceased. Any privilege that may be enjoyed under the Sunni law is denied to the '*asaba*' (Agnates).

The shares are the same as under the Ithna-Ashari Law. There are six shares: two thirds, one half, one third, one quarter, one sixth and one eighth. The sharers fall into six categories: children, father, mother, father's side, mother's side and the spouses. They correspond to the Ithna-Ashari's nine sharers. The three remaining sharers of the Sunni Law, the two grandparents and the son's daughter are dropped from the Ismaili list as they are from the Ithna-Ashari and for the same reason – they inherit under kinship.

Like the Ithna-Ashari, the heirs under kinship fall into three classes, the higher class excluding the lower, and members of the same class have the same right to inherit if they are of the same degree of closeness to the deceased, otherwise the closer always excludes the remote. The classification runs as follows:

The first class: The parents and children, male and female, how-low-soever.

The second class: The grandfathers and grandmothers how-high-soever, and the brothers and sisters, who in turn are replaced by their children, how-low-soever, male or female, should they have predeceased their own parent.

The third class: The maternal and paternal uncles and aunts, with the children, how-low-soever whether male or female, replacing them in the event of their earlier death.

The first charge on the estate is the funeral expenses, followed by repayment of debt, then bequest, then distribution of the residue.

The sharers are first to receive their prescribed shares, followed by the heirs under kinship, with strict observance of priority of class. If the shares and entitlements are equal to the estate, there is no problem. If the entitlements exceed the assets, then the Sunni '*aul*' (proportional abatement) comes into force. The Ismailis, like the Ithna-Asharis, reject '*aul*' and stick to the six shares defined above, without fifths, sevenths or ninths. They hold that "Sharers shall not suffer reduction, no '*aul*'" on the authority of a report by the sixth Imam Jaafar, reciting from his fathers up to the Apostle of God in the 'Sheet of Shares' Qadi an-Numan cites from reports by the Imams Ali, al-Baqir and Jaafar as-Sadiq that they worked out, without any reduction, shares which had been abated. Relying on the Book of God, they gave priority to what was granted priority under the holy text and deferred what was deferred, and kept all shares already reduced at their minimum value. An example: A woman was survived by her husband, uterine brothers and consanguine sister. Imam al-Baqir (the fifth imam) ruled that the widower should receive one half of the estate (3 shares), the uterine brothers 2 shares, and the residue of one share to the consanguine sister. This is similar to the Ithna-Ashari ruling that no abatement shall be suffered by a spouse, the mother or the father, but shall be confined to the daughters and sisters because a share does not go from a maximum to a minimum.

If the assets exceed the entitlements, then we have the '*radd*', (the return). The excess goes back to the heirs *pro rata*, but only to those entitled. Here we come to the only difference with the Ithna-Ashari, who allow the return to the widower if there is no other heir; i.e. he receives one half as a sharer and the balance by return, i.e. the whole estate. A widow shall receive just her share of quarter of the estate, and nothing more at all. This provision is enshrined in the Irani Law, as shown previously. The Ismailis differ, maintaining that the surviving spouse shall not receive anything above the respective absolute maximum, of one half for a husband and one quarter for a wife, even if there is no other heir! The general rule is that only heirs under kinship are entitled to return.

Apart from this difference, the Ismailis apply the same rules as the Ithna-Ashari in respect of distribution of portions and eligibility of heirs to inherit.

CHAPTER 13

Wills

1. Legal Interpretation

The topic of the will is dealt with in the Egyptian Act No. 71/1946, and in separate chapters of the Personal Status Acts of the Lebanese Druzes, Syria, Tunisia, Morocco, Iraq, Algeria and Kuwait. It is referred to in the context of priority of charges on a deceased's estate, coming after the confirmed debts and before inheritance. The only reference thereto in the Jordanian Personal Status Act concerns the Mandatory Will (Art. 182). Where there are no specific legal texts on wills in the Arab States, recourse is made to the teachings of a specific school of Islamic jurisprudence, e.g. the Hanafi in Jordan (Art. 183).

2. Definition and General Provisions

Islamic jurists give various definitions of the will, the most common of which is "A transfer of ownership for no consideration to take effect after death".[1] Others define it as "A gift made by a person to another of a substance, a debt or a usufruct, in such a way that the beneficiary shall take possession of the gift after the death of the testator."[2] The first definition is adopted in the Lebanese Druze Article 145 and Algerian Article 184, and by the Shias.[3] Moroccan Article 173 reads: "The Will is an act by which the author thereof creates on the third of his property a right which becomes exigible on his death."

The Egyptian Article 1, followed by the Syrian Article 207, Kuwaiti Article 213, Sudanese Article 286 and Omani Article 198, define the will as "A disposition of the estate to take effect after death", with the Iraqi Article 64 adding, "implying transfer of ownership for no consideration." Tunisian Article 171 adds further "whether the property bequeathed is a substance or a usufruct." According to the Explanatory Memorandum to the Egyptian Article, this definition is the most comprehensive, as it includes a discharge of a debt, or a right linked to property, like the deferment of a debt falling due. By "estate" is meant everything left by the deceased to devolve on heirs, including property, usufruct or any other right related to property.

---

[1] Al-Abiani, *A Short Commentary*, pp. 440–441.
[2] Sabiq, *Sunna Jurisprudence*, Vol. 3, p. 414.
[3] Al-Hilli, *Jaafari Provisions on Personal Status*, p. 132.

According to some Arab legislators, a will can be made by word of mouth, in writing or by an intelligible gesture for a mute or an illiterate. To this Hanafi opinion, the Egyptian and Kuwaiti legislators add the Maliki opinion that certification is a condition for the validity of contracts for no consideration, requiring a written document for any suit to confirm a will if it is disputed; the Kuwaiti allowing, if needs be, the evidence of two right witnesses to prove a verbal will (Arts. 2, Egyptian; 208, Syrian; 214, Kuwaiti; 292, Sudanese and 204, Omani).[4]

It is a condition for the validity of a will that it shall not contravene the Sharia (Syrian Art. 209, according to Islam or the religion of the non-Muslim testator; Egyptian Art. 3). An example is a bequest for a mistress.[5] Moroccan Article 174 requires for the validity of a will that it shall not contain any contradictory, ambiguous or illegal stipulations. Kuwaiti Article 215 stipulates for the validity of a will that it shall not be for a sin, or the motive thereof shall not contravene the intentions of the legislators; non-Muslim testators can make a valid will unless it is prohibited under the Islamic Sharia.

A will may be subject to a valid condition, i.e. a condition to the welfare of the testator, the beneficiary or others, not contravening the Sharia (Arts. 4, Egyptian; 201/1, 2, 3, Syrian). An invalid condition shall be void without invalidating the will (Arts. 210/4E, Syrian; 172, Tunisian; 291, Sudanese and 199(b), Omani). Kuwaiti Article 216, paragraphs a/b/d, concurs, while ruling (paragraph c) that a will suspended on a non-valid condition shall be void.

3. The Testator

The testator must possess the legal capacity to make a disposition for no consideration (Arts. 5, Egyptian; 211/1, Syrian; 293, Sudanese and 205, Omani). The Iraqi legislator adds (Art. 67): "and be the owner of what he bequests". The Algerian Article 186 spells it out more clearly, requiring the testator to be of sound mind, not under nineteen years of age (i.e. the Algerian age of majority). The Shias explain it more fully: the testator must be "free, adult, of sound mind and acting of his own free-will".[6]

Nevertheless, the Syrian Law (Article 211/2) makes the will by a person put under interdiction on grounds of prodigality or naïvité, valid, subject to a court order. Egyptian Article 5 adds to the same ruling a person who has reached eighteen calendar years of age, i.e. three years under the Egyptian age of majority. This ruling, adopted also by Kuwaiti Article 217, follows the Shafii opinion, but is more restricting than that of the Hanafis, Malikis and Hanbalis, who allow a will by a prodigal, and is adopted under Tunisian Article 178 provided that such a will is passed by the court.[7] The Shias allow a will by a boy of ten and a prodigal under interdiction if it is for charity.[8] Exceptionally the Hanafis allow a bequest for his funeral expenses by a boy possessing discretion.[9]

---

[4] Hanafi, *The Wills Act*, pp. 2–3.
[5] *Ibid.* p. 6.
[6] Al-Hilli, *op. cit.* p. 132.
[7] Abu Zahra, *On the Wills Act*, pp. 65–66.
[8] Al-Hilli, *op. cit.* p. 132.
[9] Al-Abiani, *op. cit.* p. 442.

As for insanity, the Hanafis rule that a will shall be void if the testator becomes continuously insane until death, setting for such madness a duration of a year (Muhammad) or a month (Abu Youssof). The Malikis and Hanbalis dissent.

The Egyptian (Art. 14) and Syrian (Art. 220/a) legislators steer a middle course, ruling that the will shall be void if the testator became continuously insane until death. The Iraqi legislator (Art. 72/2) rules that the will shall become void on the testator losing his legal capacity until his death.

According to the Sunni and Shia jurists, no will by a testator whose estate is exhausted with debts shall be effective unless the creditors allow it, debts having priority over any will.[10]

This provision is adopted in Articles 38 (Egyptian) and 238/3 (Syrian).

Kuwaiti Article 217/d makes an apostate's will valid on return to Islam.

4. The Beneficiary

The beneficiary of a will may be an individual or individuals, a more or less defined group of persons, or an organization, or the proceeds of a bequest may be used for some purpose. In the event of many beneficiaries, under the Hanafis the whole bequest shall be taken by the surviving beneficiaries if one or more die before the testator, unless each beneficiary was allotted a definite part of the bequest, with each having such a part of the bequest as he would have taken if all the beneficiaries had survived the testator.[11] For the Shias, a bequest to a person who predeceased the testator shall pass to his/her heirs.[12]

According to the Sharia, the beneficiary must be identifiable, in existence at the time of the making of the will, and not a belligerent nor murderer or accomplice to the murder of the testator; and not an heir.

Identification of the beneficiary may be by recognized name, such as "A, the son of B" or a named mosque or institute; by demonstration, such as "this woman" or "the embryo in this woman's womb" or by description, such as "the poor of my village". No will shall be valid if the beneficiary is unidentifiable or not clearly identified. A will shall be unanimously deemed void if it is made to "a person" without identification. A will made to "either of these two men" is held by Abu Hanifa to be void because it is not clear which of them is meant.[13] Egyptian and Syrian Laws require the beneficiary to be known (Arts. 6/1, 212/a, and 218 respectively). Sudanese and Omani Laws, 295/b and 208/b respectively concur.

The beneficiary must be existent at the time of the making of the will. This is imperative if the beneficiary is identified by name or demonstration. If the beneficiary is identified by description such as "the children of A", the majority of Sunni jurists, except the Malikis, stipulate that while the beneficiary may not have existed at the time of the making of the will, it must exist at the time of the testator's death; consequently, children born more than six months after the death shall not be entitled to any part of the bequest.[14] The Malikis, followed

---

[10] Abu Zahra, *op. cit.* p. 67; Al-Hilli, *loc. cit.*
[11] Badran, *Inheritance, Wills and Gift*, p. 133.
[12] Al-Hilli, *op. cit.* p. 136.
[13] Madkoor, *Inheritance and Wills*, p. 330.
[14] Al-Abiani, *op. cit.* pp. 448–449.

by Moroccan Article 178, allow the entitlement of the embryo born after the testator's death.[15] The Shias allow up to nine months, provided that it is possible through the symptoms of pregnancy, to presume its existence at the time of the making of the will.[16] The Egyptian Law (Art. 6/2) adopts the Maliki opinion, as does the Algerian Article 187. Iraqi Article 68/1 follows the Hanafi position, as does the Sudanese Law (Art. 295) and the Omani Law (Art. 208). Tunisian Article 184 stipulates that the embryo must exist at the time of making the will, and that it is born alive.

Under Shia Law, it is irrelevant whether the pregnant woman is married or in her *iddat* of divorce or death.[17] The Hanafis distinguish between two cases: where the testator acknowledges and where he fails to acknowledge the existence of the embryo beneficiary at the time of making the will. In the first case, the will shall be valid if the child is born within two years of the making of the will, whether the mother is married or in her *iddat* of divorce or death. In the second case, there is a further distinction between two contingencies: if the mother-to-be is actually or deemed to be married, e.g. in her *iddat* of a revocable divorce, when the will shall be valid only if the child is born less than six months after the making of the will, but if she is in her *iddat* of an irrevocable divorce or of death, the will shall be valid if the child is born within two years.[18] This Hanafi doctrine was adopted in Egypt until the promulgation of the Will Act 71/1946 which made the minimum and maximum terms of pregnancy for the purposes of the will nine months (270 days) and one solar year (365 days) respectively, while maintaining the basic Hanafi provisions (Art. 35).

In the event of multiple births, the babies born alive shall share the bequest equally. Algerian Law, Article 187, Egyptian Will Law, Article 36, and Syrian, Article 237 all concur.

Apart from individuals, the beneficiary may be a juristic person or a charitable object, in which case it is not required to be in existence at the time the bequest is made. The same ruling is defined in the following modern legislation, Syrian Article 213/1/2, and Egyptian Will Law, Articles 52, 53, 57.

It is a condition for the will to remain valid at the time of the death of a testator that the beneficiary shall not be a belligerent, according to the Sunnis, Hanafis and the Shia Ithna-Ashari.[19] Difference of religion on its own does not invalidate a will, unlike inheritance. Nevertheless, the modern Egyptian, Syrian, Tunisian and Kuwaiti Will Acts stipulate only the principle of reciprocity in so far as a national of a foreign country is concerned (Egyptian Will Law, Art. 9 and Syrian Art. 215/1/2; Tunisian Arts. 174, 175 and Kuwaiti Art. 221).

The Hanafis rule that no will is valid for a beneficiary who causes the death of the testator, whether the will is made before or after the act causing death. The Shafiis and some Hanbalis and Malikis consider the will a form of gift and therefore do not deem homicide of whatever kind to render a will void. The authoritative Maliki opinion and some Hanbalis hold that a will shall become void if the beneficiary murdered the testator after the making of the will. But if the cause of death preceded the making of the will, it shall be valid in deference

---

[15] Hanafi, *op. cit.* p. 11.
[16] Al-Hilli, p. 133.
[17] *Ibid.*
[18] Al-Abiani, *loc. cit.*
[19] Madkoor, *op. cit.* p. 335.

to the wish of the testator who decided to benefit his murderer whom he knows.[20] This ruling is adopted in Moroccan Article 179.

Under the Iraqi Law, Article 68/2, a murderer of the testator shall be disqualified as a beneficiary. The Algerian Article 188 disqualifies a beneficiary who murders the testator with intent. Egyptian and Syrian Articles 17 and 223 respectively set as a ground for the disentitlement to mandatory or voluntary will, the murder of the testator with intent, whether the murderer is a principal agent, an accomplice or a perjurer whose false evidence resulted in a death sentence against the testator being passed and executed, if the killing was for no just cause or reasonable excuse, and the murderer was of sound mind and not under fifteen years of age. The Egyptian Article adds that using excess force in self-defence is a reasonable excuse. Kuwaiti Article 227 concurs in full.

A great controversy surrounds the last requirement of a beneficiary, namely that the beneficiary should not be an heir. At one extreme, the Zahiris and some Malikis, Shafiis and Hanbalis rule that a will to an heir is utterly void, on the authority of a Tradition of the Prophet to that effect. They deem it as an act of injustice against the other heirs even though they may allow it, in which case it shall not be a bequest but a gift.[21] This ruling is repeated twice (Arts. 176 and 179/d "the beneficiary shall not be a presumptive heir at the time of the death of the testator") by the Moroccan legislator. The Ismailis on the authority of *Ijmaa* of three Imams, Ali, Abu Jaafar and Abu Abdullah, declare it unlawful and a defiance of God's Book.[22] At the other extreme, the Shia Ithna-Asharis and Zaidis accept as valid a will to an heir within one-third of the net estate without requiring the consent of the other heirs.[23] A middle course is steered by the Hanafis, the Hanbalis, the Shafiis and the majority of Malikis, who hold that a will to an heir is valid subject to the consent of the other heirs by adding to the Tradition of the Prophet "except if allowed by the heirs".[24]

Article 37 of the Egyptian Will Act equates an heir with a non-heir as a valid beneficiary of a will without requiring the consent of the heirs, following the Ithna-Ashari opinion. The Syrian Article 238/2 and Tunisian Article 179 makes such a will to an heir subject to such an approval. Article 70 (Iraqi) simply rules that the bequest shall be within one-third of the estate, and any excess shall be subject to the heirs allowing it, without specifying that the beneficiary must be an heir. Algerian Article 189, following the Hanafis, rules that no will is valid for an heir unless approved by the heirs after the death of the testator.

5. The Bequest

A bequest may be real or movable property, monies, rights *in rem*, all of which are inheritable, or it may be a usufruct (whether for life or for a definite period), or anything that is capable of being transferred. The bequest need not be in existence at the time of making the will, but must exist at the time of the testator's death. It must be capable of being inherited or transferred, owned by

---

[20] *Ibid.* p. 338.
[21] *Ibid.* pp. 341–342.
[22] Qadi an-Numan, *op. cit.* Vol. 2, p. 296.
[23] Al-Hilli, *op. cit.* p. 133.
[24] Madkoor, *op. cit.* p. 343.

the testator and in existence at the time of his death; and it is limited to within one-third of the estate.

Like the inheritable estate, a bequest must be capable of being assessed, acquired and used, such as property, both movable and immovable, rights and usufructs, apart from personal non-pecuniary rights and uses. No testator can create by will an estate repugnant to law. Things that are outside the ambit of trade and cannot be the object of property and the sale of which is void, e.g. animals not ritually slaughtered (*mayta*), blood and pigs, cannot be valid subjects of a Muslim's will. The same applies to things in which there is no ownership (*mal mubah*), such as air and water, rivers and public roads.[25]

This leads to the second condition of a bequest, that it shall be in existence and owned by the testator. This condition applies to property as contradistinct from usufruct. A will shall be void if the bequest, being a defined property *per se* or part of a defined whole, is not existing *at the time when the will is made*, since no person has the right to dispose of property he does not own. Such a will shall remain void even if the testator subsequently becomes the owner of the subject of the bequest, unless a new will is then made. Nevertheless, if the subject of the bequest is part of the whole property or class of property, e.g. a quarter of one-third of the estate or of books or animals, the will shall be valid provided that such property exists *at the time of the death of the testator*. A bequest need not be in the actual possession of the testator at the time of his death, but may be in the hands of a third party, e.g. a trust with a lien or a debt with a debtor, or even in the possession of a usurper.[26]

That the bequest shall not exceed one-third of the estate is a condition for a valid will to take effect. A Muslim who leaves heirs cannot dispose by will of more than one-third of what remains of his estate after payment of funeral expenses and debts. The remaining two-thirds of the estate is distributed according to the Inheritance Law among his heirs. A bequest in a will in excess of the legal one-third may be validated by the consent of the heirs, expressly or by implication, after the death of the testator, although the Shias allow such a consent to be given before the death of the testator, in which case the heirs cannot withdraw it after his death.[27] Where some and not all of the heirs consent to the bequest, it shall be payable to the beneficiary from the shares of the consenting heirs alone.[28]

Some Shia and Abadi jurists,[29] followed by Druzes (Lebanese Art. 148 and Syrian Art. 307/h) allow a bequest of the whole or any part of the estate to an heir or non-heir.

The dispositions regarding the bequests are summed up in the Egyptian Article 10 as follows: "The bequest is stipulated to be (1) an object that can be inherited or may be an object for a contract during the life of the testator: (2) a valuable asset in the possession of the testator if it is a property: (3) owned by the testator, if it was definite *per se*, at the time of the will." The whole Article is adopted in Kuwaiti Article 222 with the addition of "with due observance of paragraph (a) of Article 216" which allows a will to take effect in the future, and to make it

---

[25] *Ibid.* pp. 368–369.
[26] *Ibid.* pp. 370–372.
[27] Al-Hilli, *op. cit.* p. 133.
[28] Madkoor, *op. cit.* p. 374.
[29] *Loc. cit.*

subject to a valid condition. The valid condition of the Egyptian Article is repeated under paragraph (b) of the Syrian Article 216 of which paragraph (a) rules that the ownership of the bequest must be transferable on the death of the testator, and a valuable asset according to his religious law. Iraqi Article 69 simply requires the transferability of the ownership of the bequest after the death of the testator. Algerian Article 190 allows the testator to make a bequest of the property which he owns or is going to own before his death, be it a substance or a usufruct. Moroccan Article 188 simply rules that the bequest must be capable of being taken possession of.

6. The Mandatory Will

According to the Explanatory Note to the Egyptian Will Act No. 71/1946, this is a disposition created as a remedy to a growing source of complaint, namely the position of the grandchildren whose parents die during the lifetime of their father or mother, or die, or are deemed to die with them, e.g. as a result of a sinking ship, building collapse, or fire. Such grandchildren rarely inherit on the death of their grandparent, as they are often excluded from inheritance, even though their dead parents might have contributed to the growth of the grandparent's wealth. Indeed, on the death of their father, they might have been supported and maintained by their grandfather who would have left them part of his property but died too soon for that, or was prevented from so doing through some temporary events.

On these grounds, Article 76 rules that if the deceased has left no will for the descendants of a child of his who died before, or is deemed to have died with him, bequeathing to such grandchildren the share of the estate that would have devolved on the child had he been alive, there shall be a mandatory will in the amount of such share within the limits of one-third of the estate, provided that the said descendant is not an heir, and that the deceased has not given thereto, for no consideration, by another disposition, the amount due thereto. If the gift is less than the said amount, the will shall be for the balance. Such a will shall be to the benefit of the first class of the descendants of the lineal daughters or sons, how-low-soever, with every ascendant excluding the descendant of the respective child but not any other's descendant. The share of every ascendant shall be divided among the descendants thereof according to the rules of inheritance as if the ancestor(s) through whom they are related to the deceased had died after him. Under Article 77, if the beneficiary who is qualified to benefit of a mandatory will has been left in a will by the deceased, a bequest in excess of what is due thereto, the excess shall be deemed a voluntary will. If the deceased left a will for only some of those qualified for a mandatory will, the rest shall be entitled to their due. Under Article 78, the mandatory will shall take precedence over all voluntary wills.

In the Explanatory Note, the legislator derives the doctrine of the mandatory will for the non-heirs among relatives, from a multitude of followers, jurists, and the authorities of jurisprudence and tradition, among whom are Saieed ibn ul Musayyab, Al Hassan al-Bisri, Tawoos, Imam Ahmad ibn-Hanbal, Dawood Al-Tibri and Ibn Hazm. The ultimate authority is the Quranic ruling: "It is prescribed for you, when one of you approacheth death, if he leaves wealth, that he bequeath unto parents and near relatives in kindness. This is a duty for all those who ward off evil."[30]

While Abu Zahra praises this doctrine as asserting a just and equitable principle,[31] some other Egyptian jurists criticize it. Sheikh Sanhouri objects that it is based on the premise that the orphaned grandchildren are entitled to compensation for the lost share of their dead parent. But that parent would not have been entitled to any share if it differed in religion from the propositus, and therefore there would be no room for compensation, an opinion shared by his disciple Professor Madkoor.[32]

However, the whole doctrine of the mandatory will, with all the provisions related to in the Egyptian Law, has been adopted by the Syrian and Omani legislators (Art. 257, 1a–c and 2, and 229/230 respectively) and the Jordanian legislator under Art. 182, which is the only text therein dealing with the will. The Iraqi legislator added the doctrine of mandatory will under Article 74, paragraphs 1 and 2 of Law No. 188/1959 as amended by Law No. 72/1979. The Tunisian legislator added the whole doctrine under the heading of "Mandatory Will" in Articles 191 and 192, as per Law No. 77/1959 dated 19 June 1959. There is no mention of the mandatory will in the Algerian Law No. 84-11/1984 under that name, but identical provisions are enacted under the heading *"Tanzeel"*, i.e. according a grandchild the status of a child for the purposes of inheritance (Book Three: On Inheritance, Chapter Seven, *"Tanzeel"*. Arts. 169–172, inclusive). The same expression with similar provisions is used in Article 83, paragraph 3 of the Moroccan Law. Again it constitutes the object of a whole chapter (VII) of the fifth Book (on Wills), Articles 212 to 215 inclusive, but *tanzeel* here could apply to any person, not necessarily a grandchild, whom the testator wishes to be treated as an heir of his but who is in fact a beneficiary of a will. In the sixth Book (on Succession) the Moroccan legislator devotes a whole chapter (VII), Articles 266 to 269 inclusive to the mandatory will, incorporating all provisions of the Egyptian doctrine.

The Kuwaiti legislator introduced the mandatory will under Law No. 5/1971. It is referred to in the Personal Status Law No. 51/1984 under Art. 291 which sets the mandatory will third in priority of charges on the estate, following funeral expenses and debts of the deceased and preceding voluntary wills and distribution of heirs' shares. The Kuwaiti Law differs from the Egyptian in that it does not give the orphaned beneficiary the amount of the whole share of its predeceased parent, but the proportion that child would have got of the share of the parent.

---

[30] Sura Baqara II, verse 180.
[31] Abu Zahra, *op. cit.* p. 198.
[32] Madkoor, *op. cit.* pp. 449–450.

CHAPTER 14

Waqf

1. Definition

The term *waqf* (*habs*) literally means to prevent, restrain. In legal terms it means "to protect a thing, to prevent it from becoming the property of a third person (*tamlik*)".[1]

According to Islamic jurists, *waqf* is the permanent dedication by a Muslim of any property, in such a way that the appropriator's right is extinguished, for charity or for religious objects or purposes, or for the founder of the *waqf* during his lifetime and after his death, for his descendants, and on their extinction, to a purpose defined by the founder.[2] It follows that there are two categories of *waqf* – a charity *waqf* and a "family endowment".

According to Abu Hanifa: 'It signifies the appropriation of any particular thing in such a way that the appropriator's right in it shall continue, and the advantage of it shall go to some charitable objects; or it is the detention of a specific thing in the ownership of the *waqif* or appropriator, and the devoting or appropriating of its profits or usufruct in charity, or the poor, or other good objects. ...'[3]

According to the two disciples of Abu Hanifa, whose opinion is accepted by the Hanafi school: "*Waqf* signifies the appropriation of a particular article in such a manner as subjects it to the rules of divine property, whence the appropriator's right in it is extinguished, and it becomes the property of God by the advantage of it resulting to His creatures."[4] Shia textbook "*Sharaiul Islam*" considers *waqf* as a contract, the fruit or effect of which is to tie up the original and to leave its usufruct free.

Algerian Law Article 213 states that "*Waqf* is the detention of property. ..."

Islamic jurists hold the view that *waqf* is an imperfect form of ownership in which ownership and utility are never combined at the same time by the same person.[5] The *waqif* is considered a juristic person to be represented by the administrator thereof (*al mutawali*) who is merely a manager of the *waqf*. Under the Sharia, when *waqf* is created, all rights of property pass out of the *waqif* and

---

[1] Sarakhsi, *Mabsut*, XII, p. 27.
[2] Yakan, *Waqf*, p. 7.
[3] Neil B. E. Baillie, *Digest of Mohammadan Law Part I* (1st edn 1826), pp. 459 (557).
[4] *Minhaj* Book, p. 232.
[5] Abu Zahra, *On Waqf*, p. 89.

rest in God Almighty. The founder of a *waqf* may constitute himself the first *mutawali* (administrator). A *mutawali* may be a female, or even a non-Muslim. Equally, a body of persons in the form of a committee may be entrusted with the administration of the *waqf*, but no minor or a person of unsound mind can be appointed a *mutawali*. Muslim Law does not recognize any right of inheritance to the office of *mutawali*. If the founder and his executor are both dead, and there is no provision in the *waqfiya* document for the succession to the office, the *mutawali* at the time may, on his own death-bed, appoint a successor.[6]

According to the Sunni Law, the essentials of a valid *waqf* are:

(i)   a permanent dedication of property;
(ii) the dedicator (*waqif*) should be a person professing the Muslim faith, of sound mind, and of age[7], and must have full right of disposal over his property;
(iii) the dedication should be for a purpose recognized by Islamic Law as religious, pious or charitable.

The essentials of a valid *waqf* under the Shia Law are as follows:

(a) it must be perpetual;
(b) it must be absolute and unconditional;
(c) possession must be given of the item dedicated;
(d) it must be taken out from the dedicator. That is, he should not retain any interest.

Under Shia Law, a *waqf* is not completed unless either possession of the *waqf* property is delivered to the first beneficiaries, or they are authorized to administer the *waqf* property, or where the *waqf* created is for the benefit of a body of persons, a *mutawali* is appointed, and possession is delivered to him.[8]

A dedication by way of *waqf* may be either oral or in writing.

2. The Object of the *Waqf*

Under the Sharia, *waqf* may be made for any purpose whatever which is recognized by Islam. Thus a Muslim cannot create a *waqf* for a church or synagogue. A *waqf*, being a form of *sadaqa* (the object being to acquire merit in the sight of God and a reward (*thawab*) in the next world)[9] cannot be used for purposes unpleasing to God.

The purposes recognized by Islam are the following:

(i) The man's duty to his family: The Quran approves of righteousness of him who spends "of his substance, out of love for Him, on kin, orphans, the needy, the wayfarer, those who ask and on the ransom of slaves ..." (2:177)

Waqf, in all systems, may be created for the support of the founder's own immediate descendants, and for collaterals with the remainder to go to the poor.

---

[6] *Ibid.* pp. 303–313.
[7] Minority under Muslim law terminates on completion of the 15th year. A Muslim who had attained the age of 15 is competent to make a will disposing of his property (Amir Ali, 4th edn, Vol. I, pp. 212–213).
[8] Abu Zahra, *op. cit.* pp. 53–54.
[9] *Minhaj, loc. cit.* p. 234.

It is to be noted that in Abadi Law if a man leaves property as *waqf* for his descendants, whether for one or two generations, or in perpetuity, his immediate children can either confirm the *waqf* or reject it, and deal with the property as their own property.[10]

(ii) The maintenance of mosques dedicated to God for worship according to the teachings of Islam.
(iii) Charities such as hospitals, schools, universities, pensions and other works of public utility.

3. Property Capable of Being Given as *Waqf*

The following items may be created as *waqf*:

(i) *Al-Mal al-Mutaqawwim* – i.e. property capable of legal ownership and legal transfer.
(ii) *Mulk* – i.e. in actual ownership – It must be in existence at the time of creation of the *waqf* and must be capable of immediate delivery.[11]

4. The Form of Creating a *Waqf*

This takes the following methods:

(i)   Divesting of ownership: The founder of the *waqf* must strip himself of all title in the property settled. According to all systems, a *waqf* that is recoverable is not valid.
(ii)   Formalities of *waqf*: A *waqf*, as explained above, may be made either verbally or in writing.
(iii) The formalities by a will: A *waqf* in death-illness is subject to the same restrictions as, and does not have any priority over, other gifts or legacies.
(iv)   It must not be subject to a condition that is not in existence at the time of the constitution of the *waqf*.
(v)   It shall not be timed to commence after death, otherwise it will be tantamount to a will.
(vi)   It shall not be subject to an option.
(vii) It shall not be subject to a condition that is inconsistent with the essence of the *waqf*.
(viii) It must indicate either explicitly or implicitly, the permanence of the *waqf*, and cannot be revoked after its dedication has been completed.[12]

5. Private *Waqf*

(i) The dedicator may assure the permanence of his family from generation to generation. This type of *waqf* is one for the settler's own family and his

---

[10] Anderson, *Islamic Law in Africa* (London, 1954), p. 77.
[11] Sabiq, *Sunna Jurisprudence*, p. 382.
[12] *Ibid.* pp. 381–382.

descendants, and is called *waqf ala al-awlad* and is in favour of unborn descendants.[13]

(ii) The dedicator may avoid the strict requirements of the Law of Inheritance. In the case of *waqf* in favour of descendants, the succession is contrary to the rule of the Hanafi Law of Inheritance. Males and females, in the absence of a contrary provision in the deed of *waqf*, take equal shares.

6. Power of the Founder (*Waqif*)

The founder has an unlimited power when laying down the succession of beneficiaries. However, Algerian courts hold, according to Algerian Law, that the founder shall not have the power to exclude from the *waqf* his own son and his own daughter from having a benefit in his estate.[14]

In the absence of any specific direction by the founder, the following principles shall be followed:

(a) male and female have the same share;
(b) agnate and cognate share alike;
(c) children of deceased beneficiaries represent their parents even during the lifetime of those beneficiaries nearer in degree.

But as explained, the founder has unrestricted power, and if he so wishes, may take steps that any or all of these rules be barred by specific direction.

(d) The founder may, during his lifetime, appoint, remove and control the *mutawali*, define the amount of remuneration and appoint a new *mutawali*.[15]

7. The Administrator (*Mutawali*)

The administration of the *waqf* is in the hands of a person known as the *mutawali* or *qaiyim*, who is merely a manager of the *waqf*. The first administrator is usually appointed by the founder and receives a salary for his services. Frequently, the first administrator is the founder himself, and he shall be deemed the *mutawali* if he does not appoint another person to act in that capacity. He may appoint one or more *mutawali* to act during his lifetime, or provide for their appointment to take place after his death. He may repeatedly dismiss any *mutawali* he has appointed on any grounds. On the death of the founder, the *mutawali* shall be dismissed unless otherwise previously directed by the founder. In the absence of

---

[13] *Ibid.*
[14] *Cf.* Art. 218 "The conditions laid down by the founder shall be fulfilled unless they contravene the Sharia requirements of the *waqf* in which case the condition shall be void and the waqf remain valid.".
[15] Abu Zahra, *op. cit.* pp. 130–153.

a *mutawali* appointed by the founder to act after his death, the judge may appoint a *mutawali* who shall preferably be a descendant or a relative of the founder, provided the appointee shall possess legal capability. Otherwise, the judge may appoint a person not a blood relation, until a member of the founder's family becomes eligible. The *mutawali* must be sane, adult, honest and capable of the administration of the *waqf*. The *mutawali* may be non-Muslim, blind, mute, male or female. In the event that two *mutawalis* are appointed by the founder to administer the *waqf* after his death, neither of them may act severally without the other's permission. If only one of them has accepted the administration, and the other has declined, the judge may appoint a second person to administer jointly the *waqf* or may empower the one *mutawali* to administer the *waqf* on his own if he is capable. The judge cannot dismiss a *mutawali* appointed by the founder, nor can the founder dismiss a *mutawali* appointed by the judge unless the *mutawali* ceases to be capable of performing his duties as a result of inability or betrayal of trust.

The *mutawali* represents the *waqf* in all legal actions related thereto, whether as a claimant or a defendant. He acts on behalf of the beneficiaries. Like inheritance, entitlement to the proceeds of a *waqf* cannot be disclaimed by the beneficiary.[16]

8. The Conditions of a *Waqf* Contract

The *waqf* is a Sharia contract to be formed at the founder's will, and the offer is subject to acceptance if it is temporary, or to a particular person. The founder must be in possession of legal capacity, that is to say, he must be sane, adult and not placed under interdiction for prodigality, imbecility or insolvency. If a debtor under no interdiction constitutes a *waqf* in his death-illness, and his debts exhaust his assets, the creditors shall be entitled to apply for the declaration of the *waqf* as void. If a debtor under no interdiction constitutes a *waqf* while in a state of health, the *waqf* shall be valid and effective, and creditors shall have no right to dispute it, even if the *waqf* was founded in order to escape debts. A Muslim may constitute a *waqf* for the non-Muslim poor, and *vice versa*.[17]

9. Comparison Between Trust and *Waqf*

(i)   The *waqf* requires a religious, pious, or charitable purpose.
(ii) The founder of a trust may be a beneficiary under such a trust. With the exception of Hanafi Law, the founder may not reserve to himself any benefit from such a *waqf*.
(iii) A trust may be made for any lawful object, but a *waqf* may only be created for a charitable, religious or pious motive, though as explained above, its object may be a family settlement to assure the permanence of his family.
(iv) Any transferable property may be the subject of a trust.
(v)   The *mutawali*, as explained, has fewer powers than the trustee.

---

[16] *Ibid.* pp. 303–339.
[17] *Ibid.* pp. 48–61.

(vi)   The *waqf* is perpetual.
(vii)   The *waqf* property is inalienable.
(viii) In the case of a trust incapable of execution, the benefit then returns to its founder.

CHAPTER 15

Gifts (*Hibat*)

The gift as a legal disposition has been treated extensively in the Sharia Law and in the modern Arab Civil Laws of Egypt, Jordan, Syria, Iraq, Kuwait, Libya and the Lebanon (the Law of Obligations and Contracts). The Tunisian, Algerian, Sudanese, and Yemeni legislators deal with gifts in the Personal Status Law.

In the sections below, we shall start with the general Sharia provisions on gifts, followed by those of the corresponding modern Arab legislations to show where they agree or differ.

1. Definition

According to the Sharia, a gift is a contract by which a person (the donor), disposes of property belonging to him during his lifetime to another person without consideration.[1] This definition is adopted in the modern Arab Civil Codes (Arts. 486/1, Egyptian; 475/1, Libyan; 200, Tunisian; 202, Algerian; 454/1, Syrian; 601/1, Iraqi; 524, Kuwaiti; 267(1), Sudanese; and 168, Yemeni). Jordanian Article 557 adds "the disposition of a property right."

All these Articles, except the Iraqi and Yemeni, add in a second paragraph that a donor, without being diverted of the intention of making a gift, may impose upon the donee the performance of a specific obligation. Iraqi Article 601/2 adds that a charity, that is a property given out of religious piety, is considered as a gift unless otherwise provided.

The disposition of a property distinguishes gift from *Aariya*, i.e. a loan for use, which is a contract whereby the lender hands over to the borrower, without consideration, a non-consumable thing for his use during a specific time, or for a specific purpose, to be returned after use.

The stipulation of making the gift during the lifetime of the donor distinguishes the gift from a bequest which takes effect after the death of the testator. By the "no consideration" component, the gift differs from sale.

According to the Sharia Law, neither the offer nor acceptance of a gift need be made in writing, whether the subject of the gift is movable or immovable, although delivery of the gift is a condition of validity.[2] Modern Arab legislation,

---

[1] Sabiq, *Sunna Jurisprudence*, p. 388.
[2] Badran, *Inheritance, Wills and Gift*, p. 222; Al-Hilli, *Jaafari Provisions*, p. 126.

however, makes a distinction. Egyptian Article 488/1 rules that: "The gift must be made by an authentic document under pain of nullity, unless it is made in the form of some other contract."

A gift of movables, however, may be completed by delivery to the donee, without an official instrument being necessary (same Art., para. 2). Similar provisions are to be found in Syrian Article 456, Libyan Article 477, Iraqi Article 602–603, Jordanian Article 566, Algerian Article 206 and the Lebanese Law of Obligations and Contrasts, Article 509–510. Kuwaiti Article 525/1 provides that a gift may be completed either by taking possession, or by an authentic document.

However, the Egyptian Law, Article 20, while ruling that contracts between persons are governed as regards their form by the law of the country in which the contracts are concluded, allow such contracts also to be governed by the law regulating basic provisions of a contract, by the law of domicile of the parties, or by their common National Law.

2. Essentials

It would seem that the gift, like any other contract, requires the two essentials of offer and acceptance. However, Islamic jurists differ here. Of the Hanafis, the Imam Abu Hanifa and the two Companions Muhammad and Abu Youssof, maintain that offer alone is the essential of a gift, since it is a contract for no consideration, acceptance being only a condition for confirmation of transferred ownership. Another Hanafi, Zufar, requires acceptance as well, even receipt, as further essentials of a gift. The Shias, Hanbalis, Shafiis and Malikis also insist on both offer and acceptance, on the ground that no ownership of property can be transferred to and become binding on another person without the latter's acceptance.[3]

Under the Sharia, offer and acceptance of the gift may be by word of mouth, in writing, by deed, and, according to the Malikis, by a gesture, even if the donor/donee is capable of speaking.[4] This ruling is adopted in Sudan (Art. 269) and Yemen (Art. 171).

Tunisian Article 204 does not acknowledge the validity of a gift unless it is made in a formal document, although movables can be the valid object of a gift through delivery.

Most modern Arab laws on gift stipulate that no gift shall be complete until it is accepted by the donee or by his representative (Arts. 487/1, Egyptian; 445/1, Syrian; 476/1, Libyan; 507, Lebanese; 558/1, Jordanian; and 206, Algerian).

Under the second paragraph of the same Articles, the representative of the donee is the natural or legal guardian of the donee if the latter is a minor.

Apart from that, offer and acceptance in respect of the gift are governed by the same Civil Code rules for other contracts.

Tunisian Article 201 rules that a gift shall not be effected without the delivery of the object. A gift is void if the donor or donee dies before delivery, even if the donee tried hard to have the gift delivered. However, the donee may claim the gift if the delivery thereof is not affected (Art. 203).

---

[3] Sanhouri, *Sources of Rights*, pp. 42–43; Al-Hilli, *loc. cit.*; see also Abul Naja, *Summary of Hanbali Jurisprudence*, p. 51.
[4] Al-Aqil, *The Gift Contract*, pp. 47–48.

3. Conditions of the Gift

The Islamic jurists set conditions for the validity of the gift in respect of the two parties, the object and the form.

The gift being a disposition of property for no consideration, the donor must possess legal capacity to that effect, i.e. he must be a major, of sound mind, acting on his own free will, and not subject to interdiction, and the owner of the object of the gift. No minor or insane person can make a valid gift, because it is a disposition of property wholly to his disadvantage. No father can make a gift of a property of his minor child without a consideration as this is an injury to the child.[5]

The majority of Islamic jurists rule that a healthy wife of age has the right to make a gift of all or any part of her property to whomsoever she chooses without her husband's permission. Only the Malikis set a limit of one third of her property.[6]

The Shias subscribe to these conditions, but add that a person who is not a prodigal may make a gift of his whole property if that does not render him needy. Some Shias allow a voluntary agent (*foudouli*) to make a gift of a property which is not his.[7] The Hanafis make such a gift subject to the approval of the owner.[8]

The draft Egyptian Civil Code included Article 665 to the effect that it would be a condition for the validity of the gift that the donor be the owner of the given property, and enjoy the legal capacity to make a gift. However, during the committee stage, this Article was omitted on the grounds that the general rules of the contract were sufficient. Instead, Article 491 of the Egyptian Civil Code rules that if a definite and specific thing does not belong to the donor, the rules of the sale of a thing belonging to another shall apply, namely that the purchaser may demand the annulment of the sale or the owner may ratify the sale and the gift.

This provision, which differs from the Sharia, is adopted in Articles 459, Syrian; 480, Libyan; 559, Jordanian; and 530, Kuwaiti. But the Sharia rule is maintained in Iraq, where Article 609 (1) requires that the gift be owned by the donor, and in the Lebanon where Article 513 prohibits making a gift of a property which the donor does not own at the time of the contract. The same provision is also implied in Algerian Personal Status Article 205 which allows the donor to make a gift of all or any part of the property, whether it is a thing, a usufruct or a debt on a third party.[9]

The bulk of Islamic jurists rule that the donee must be actually existent at the time of the gift. Only the Malikis allow a gift to an unborn child provided that it is born alive, otherwise it shall remain in the ownership of the donor. If it died after birth, the gift shall devolve on its heirs. However, if the donee is a minor or insane, his legal or natural guardian or his custodian may accept possession of the object or gift on his behalf.

---

[5] *Ibid.* pp. 53–54.
[6] Badran, *op. cit.* p. 228.
[7] Al-Hilli, *op. cit.* p. 126.
[8] Sanhouri, *Commentary on the Civil Code*, Vol. 5, p. 120.
[9] *Ibid.*

Modern legislations concur (Arts. 487, Egyptian; 455, Syrian; 476, Libyan; 558 (2), Jordanian; and 604, Iraqi). However, Article 12 of the Egyptian Act No. 119/1952 on guardianship of property forbids a guardian from accepting a gift or a bequest for a minor creating certain obligations, without the court's permission. Algerian Article 209 enacts that a gift may be made to an unborn child provided it is born alive, thereby following the Maliki opinion.

The object of the gift should be actually in existence and valuable. Tunisian Article 205 makes a gift of future property void. It must be an object of ownership, negotiable and transferable, e.g. no valid gift can be made of water in the river, fish in the sea, or a flying-bird or mosque. It must not be inseparable from other property retained by the donor like fruits, trees or buildings without land.

It should be divisible and not part of joint property in order for the donee to be able to take possession.[10]

The Hanafis maintain that the gift of joint property is not valid. The Malikis, Shafiis and Hanbalis rule that the gift of joint property is valid. The Malikis go even further to say that a gift may be made for what may not be the object of sale, such as a runaway camel, fruits before being ripe, and usurped property.[11]

The Shias allow a gift of a joint property, whether divisible or indivisible, on taking possession thereof, provided in the latter case that the gift is of known magnitude.[12]

Egyptian Article 826 provides that: "Every co-owner in common is the absolute owner of his share. He may alienate his share and collect the fruits thereof and make use of his share provided he does not injure the rights of the other co-owner. ..." The Iraqi Article 609/2 specifically provides that a gift of joint property is valid. Similarly, Kuwait Article 528. The form must denote the transfer of ownership forthwith. A gift is void if it is subject to a condition that does not actually exist, or if it is deferred to some time in the future. It cannot be in the interrogative as it then implies asking for offer or acceptance without asserting it.[13]

4. Death-Illness

According to the Sharia, if a sick person, during death-illness, makes a gift to another, it shall not exceed one third of the estate unless allowed by the heirs. But if the donor makes a gift to one of his heirs, and then dies, and the rest of his heirs claim that the gift was made during death-illness, and the donee claims that the gift was made by the donor during good health, the donee has to prove his case. If he fails to do so, the gift shall be considered to have taken place during death-illness, and shall be governed accordingly, i.e. it will not be valid unless approved by the heirs.[14] The Ismailis, on the authority of Imam Jaafar,

---

[10] Badran, *op. cit.* pp. 230–231.
[11] Sabiq, *op. cit.* p. 391.
[12] Al-Hilli, *op. cit.* p. 127.
[13] Al-Aqil, *op. cit.* p. 56.
[14] For the definition of the death-illness and its effects on repudiation and inheritance, refer to Chapter 12, 5 and Chapter 6, 2.B.vi respectively.

maintain that a healthy person can make a gift to a son or anyone if he owns it. But if he was ill and died because of his illness, the gift is not valid.[15]

If the donor makes a gift during death-illness and then recovers from his illness, the gift shall be deemed valid. Modern Arab legislation follows suit (Arts. 916, Egyptian; 565, Jordanian; 877, Syrian; 920, Libyan; 1109, Iraqi; 529, Kuwaiti).

5. Possession of a Gift

Some Sharia jurists take the view that a gift passes to the ownership of the donee on the completion of the contract, maintaining that taking possession thereof is not a condition of validity in contracts, such as in the case of sale. Imam Ahmad ibn-Hanbal, Malik and the Zahiris are of this opinion, as are the Ismailis, relying on a ruling by Imam Jaafar[16]. Accordingly, if the donor or donee dies before delivery, then the gift will not be void because once the contract has taken place, the gift becomes the property of the donee. Imams Abu Hanifa and ash-Shafii, however, are of the opinion that taking possession is a condition for the validity of the gift. Without it, the donor is not under any obligation. If the donee or donor dies before delivery, the gift becomes void.[17]

Modern Arab legislation follows the view of Abu Hanifa and Shafii, and requires that taking possession is a condition for the validity of the gift. Without it, the donor is not under any obligation. If the donee or donor dies before delivery, the gift becomes void[18] (Arts. 488/2, Egyptian; 456, Syrian; 477, Libyan; 603, Iraqi; 558/1, Jordanian; 509–510, Lebanese; 206, Algerian; and 525/1, Kuwaiti).

The emphasis on the need to deliver the gift and for the donee to take possession is further dealt with in Articles 493, Egyptian; 461, Syrian; 482, Libyan and 567, Jordanian.

6. Revocation of a Gift

Apart from the Hanafis and Shias, Islamic jurists are of the opinion that the revocation of a gift is not permissible, except if the gift is made by a father to his son. According to a Tradition of the Prophet, "It is not permissible for a person to make a gift or to revoke it except the father for what he gives to his son."[19] This ruling is held by the Hanbalis and the Shafiis who, by analogy, allow a mother to revoke a gift to her son provided that the father is alive. The Malikis make such a revocation subject to two conditions: that the donee has not married nor incurred a debt. The Zahiris rule out any revocation of a gift.[20] Notwithstanding this ruling, all jurists are unanimous that no revocation is possible for a gift made for charity.[21]

---

[15] Qadi an-Numan, *op. cit.* Vol. 2, pp. 264–265.
[16] *Loc. cit.*
[17] Sabiq, *op. cit.* pp. 391–392.
[18] *Ibid.* pp. 396–397.
[19] Al-Aqil, *op. cit.* pp. 216–217.
[20] *Ibid.*
[21] *Ibid.* pp. 220–228.

To this impediment the Hanafis add seven others in the absence of which the donor may wholly or in part revoke a gift, unless he has not dropped his right of revocation within a specified agreement or in the terms of the gift contract. The seven impediments are:

(i)   if there is an inherent increase of the thing given involving an increase in the value thereof, e.g. land on which the donee has constructed a building; if the obstacle disappears, it renews the right of revocation;
(ii)   if the donor or donee dies;
(iii) if the donee has definitely alienated the thing given; however, if such an alienation is only partial, the donor may revoke the gift as to the part remaining;
(iv)   if the gift is made by one spouse to another, even if the donor wishes to revoke the gift after the marriage dissolution;
(v)   if the gift is made for the benefit of a relative in a prohibited degree;
(vi)   if the object given has perished while in possession of the donee; again, if the loss is partial, the right of revocation remains for the part remaining;
(vii) if the donee has supplied valuable consideration for the gift.[22]

These seven impediments for the revocation of a gift, plus the impediment regarding a gift made for charity making eight in total, are held by the Ithna-Asharis, although some allow a spouse to revoke a gift made to the other unless there is another impediment.[23] Some modern Arab legislators adopt the eight above impediments (Arts. 502, Egyptian; 470, Syrian and 491, Libyan). Iraqi and Jordanian Articles 623 and 579 add a further impediment, namely, a gift made by a creditor of a debt to a debtor. Kuwaiti Article 539 follows the Shafiis, ruling out the revocation of a gift from a mother to her child who is an orphan. Sarakhsi adds yet another impediment, i.e. a gift made to a child.

The Algerian Law of Personal Status, while adopting these general rules which are not mentioned expressly, but referred to generally under Article 222, allows both parents to revoke a gift to their child of whatever age unless the gift is made for the marriage thereof, as a guarantee for a loan or in settlement of a debt or if the donee has disposed of the object or changed its nature (Art. 211).

The Tunisian Law rules that if the donor sets a condition preserving his right to revoke a gift if he so wishes, the gift is valid and the condition void (Art. 209). Nevertheless, the donor (Art. 210) may apply for the revocation of his gift, without prejudice to a third party's duly acquired rights, and in the absence of impediments stated under Article 212, on any of the following grounds:

(i)   If the donee fails to honour his obligations to the donor, provided such failure constitutes an act of gross ingratitude.
(ii)   If the donor becomes incapable of providing for himself a living standard befitting his social status or becomes unable to meet any maintenance he has to provide under the law.
(iii) If the donor begets a child who remains alive at the time of revocation.

Under Article 211 the right to apply for revocation on grounds of ingratitude

---

[22] Al-Hilli, *op. cit.* pp. 129–131.
[23] Al-Aqil, *op. cit.* p. 221.

lapses on the expiry of a year from the date of the fact of ingratitude or of becoming aware thereof and shall lapse in any event after ten years of the fact.

Article 212 enumerates the impediments to the revocation as follows:

(i)   If there is an inherent increase of the object involving an increase of the value thereof.
(ii) If the donee has alienated the object, but the donor may revoke the remaining part of the object, if any.
(iii) If the object has perished while in possession of the donee, whether through his own actions, through an event over which he has no control, or through usage. If only a part has perished, the donor may revoke the remaining part.

Bibliography

A. In Arabic

I. Arabic Religious Texts

The Holy Quran
Saheeh-ul-Bukhari, 8 vols. (Cairo).
Saheeh-u-Muslim, 19 vols. (Cairo).
Both are anthologies of authenticated Traditions of The Prophet.

II. Manuals and Epistles

ABDULLAH, Prof. Omar, *Ahkam-ush-Shariat-il-Islamiyya fil Ahwal-ish-Shakhsiyya* (Islamic Sharia Provisions on Personal Status), (6th ed., Alexandria, 1968).

ABDUL LATIF, Prof. Hassan Subhi Ahmad, *Ahkam-ul-Mawareeth Fish Sharia-til-Islamiyya* (The Inheritance Rules of the Islamic Sharia), (Alexandria).

ABIANI, Muhammad Zaid, Al-, *Mukhtasar Sharh il Ahkam ish Shariyya fil Ahwal ish Shakhsiyya* (A brief commentary on the Sharia Provisions on Personal Status by Muhammad Qadri Pasha), (Cairo, 1924 AD, 1342 AH).

ABUL NAJA, Shaikh Sharafuddin Musa Ibn Ahmad (died 960 AH), *Zaadul Mustaqni Fikhtisaar il Muqni* (A Summary of Hanbali Jurisprudence), (Cairo, 1398 AH).

ABU ZAHRA, Professor Muhammad, *Al Ahwal ush Shakhsiyya-Qism uz Zawaj* (Personal Status: On Marriage), (Cairo, 1950 AD, 1369 AH).
Sharh u Qanoon il Wasiyya (Commentary on the Wills Act), (2nd ed., Cairo, 1950 AD, 1369 AH).
Akham ut Tarikaat i wal Mawareeth (On Estates and Succession), (Cairo 1963 AD, 1383 AH).
Muhadaraat fit Waqf (Lectures on Waqf).
Al Wilayatu alan Nafs (Guardianship of the Person), (Cairo).
Al Mirath u Ind al Jaafariyya (Inheritance according to the Jaafaris), (Cairo).
Al Milkiyya wa Nathariyyatul Aqd Fish Sharia til Islamiyya (Ownership and the Theory of Contract in the Islamic Sharia), (Cairo, 1977).

ALAMGIR, *Al Fatawa Alamgiriyya Almaarufa bil Fatawal Hindiyya* (Alamgiri Legal Opinions known as The Indian Legal Opinions), 6 vols. (Cairo, 1310 AH).

257

AQIL, Dr. Jamaluddin Taha Al-, *Aqd ul Hiba bayn al Fiqhi-l-Islami wal Qanoon-il-Madani* (The Gift Contract according to the Islamic Jurisprudence and the Civil Law), (Cairo, 1978).

BADRAN, Prof. Badran Abul Ainain, *Huquq ul Awlad-fish-Shariat-il-Islamiyya wal Wanoon* (The Children's Rights under the Islamic Sharia and the Law), (Alexandria, 1981).

Al Mawareeth wal Wasiyya wal Hiba (Inheritance, Wills and Gifts), (Alexandria).

BARDISI, Professor Muhammad Zakariyya Al-, *Al Mirath u wal Wasiyya fil Islam* (Inheritance and Wills under Islam), (Cairo, 1964 AD, 1384 AH).

BAYLANI, Dr. Basheer Al-, *Qawaneen-ul-Ahwal-ish-Shaksiyya fi Lubnan* (The Personal Status Laws in the Lebanon), (Cairo, 1971).

GHANDOUR, Dr. Ahmad Al-, *Al Mirath fil Islam wal Qanoon* (Inheritance under Islam and the Law), (Cairo, 1966).

At-Talaq Fish-Sharia-l-Islarniyya wal Qanoon, Bahth Muqaran (Dissolution of Marriage under the Islamic Sharia and the Law – A Comparative Study), (1st ed., Cairo, 1967 AD, 1387 AH).

HAIDAR Ali, Commentary on Mijallat-el-Ahkaam.

HANAFI, Ibrahim, *Qanoon ul Wasiyya* (The Wills Act), (Cairo, 1950).

HILLI, Shaikh Abdul Kareem Rida Al-, *Al Ahkaam ul Jaafariyya fil Ahwall-ish Shakhsiyya* (Jaafari Provisions on Personal Status) (Baghdad Muthanna Library, Cairo, 1947 AD, 1366 AH).

IBN HISHAM, Abu Muhammad Abd-ul-Malik (died 761 AH), *Sirat-u-Rasul-il-Lah* (A biography of the Apostle of God), (Cairo, 1936).

IBN HAZM, Abu Muhammad Ali Ibn u Ahmad (died 456 AH), *Al Ihkam fi Usul-il-Ahkam* (The Definite Opinion on the Sources of Jurist Rulings), 8 vols. (Cairo, 1345 AH).

Al Muhalla (The Decorated Book), (Cairo).

IBN QAYYIM AL JOUZIA, Shamsuddin Abu Abdullah Muhammad Ibnu Abi (died 751 AH), *Zad ul Maad Fi Huda Khairil Ibaad* (On the Prophet's Traditions), 4 vols. 2nd ed., Cairo, 1369 AH).

Aalaam ul Muwaqqe'een An Rabb-il-Alameen (The Authoritative Expounders of Islam), 4 vols. (Beirut, 1973).

KASSANI, Alauddin Abi Bakr Masud Al- (died 587 AH), *Badaia As-Sanaie fi Tarteeb ish Sharaie* (On the Classification of Sharia Laws), (Cairo, 1910 AD, 1328 AH).

MADKOOR, Prof. Muhammad Sallaam, *Al Wasaaya fil Fiqh il Islami, Wassiyyat ul Laah (Al Mirath) wa Wassiyyat ul Insan (Al Wasiyya)*, (Testaments in Islamic Jurisprudence of God [Inheritance] and Man [The Will]), (2nd ed., Cairo, 1962).

Al Madkhal-ulilal-Fiqh-il-Islami, Tareekhuhu wa Masadiruhu wa Nazariyyatu-Hul-Amma (An Introduction to the Islamic Jurisprudence, its History, Sources and General Theories).

NAJI, Muhsin, *Sharh u Qanoon il Ahwal ish Shakhsiyya* (A Commentary on the [Iraqi] Personal Status Act), (Baghdad, 1979).

NAWAWI, Abu Zakariyya Yahya bin Sharaf An- (died 676 AH), *Minhaj ut-Talibeen* (The Method), (Cairo, 1357 AH).

NUMAN – Abu Hanifa an-, Daaim ul Islam.

QADI Khan – Fakhruddin Hassan ibn Mansur (died 592 AH), *Al Fatawa Al Khaniyya* (The Khaniyya Legal Opinions) (Published on the margin of Al Fatawa al Alamgiriyya, q.v.).

SABIQ, As SAYYID, *Fiqh us Sunnah* (The Sunni Jurisprudence), 3 vols. (Cairo, 1365 AH).

SABOONI, Dr. Abdur-Rahman As-, *Nizam ul Usra wa Hallu Mushkilatiha fi Dawa il Islam* (The Institution of the Family and the Solution of its Problems in the Light of Islam), (9th ed., enlarged and revised, Cairo, 1983 AD, 1403 AH).

SANHOURI, Prof. Abdur-Rassaq Ahmad As-, *Alwaseet ft Sharh il Qanoon il Madani-l-Gadeed* (Intermediate Commentary on the new [Egyptian] Civil Code), 10 vols. (Cairo, 1952).
Masadir ul Haqq fil Fiqh il Islami (Dirasa Muqarana) (Sources of Rights in Islamic Jurisprudence [A Comparative Study with Western Jursiprudence]), 6 vols. (Cairo, 1967).

SARAKHSI, Shamsul Aimma Abu Bakr Muhammad ibn Abi Sahl As- (died 438 AH), *Al Mabsut* (The Detailed Treatise), (Cairo, 1324 AH). (3 Vols.)

SHAFII, Abu Abdullah, Ash- Muhammad ibn Idris ash- (died 204 AH), *Al-Umm*, (The Main Source), 7 vols. (Cairo).

SHALABI, Muhammad M., Professor, al-Madkhal.

III. Statutes and Court Precedents

Algeria

The Civil Code, Prime Minister Order No. 75–58, of 26/9/1975 (20/9/1395 AH).
The Family Law No. 84-11, of 9/6/1984, 9/9/1404 AH.

Egypt

Act No. 25/1920, in respect of Maintenance and some questions of Personal Status.

Act No. 25/1929 in respect of Some Personal Status Provisions and the Explanatory Note thereof.

Major amendments to these two acts, especially on maintenance and divorce, were introduced under the Presidential Decree No. 44/1979. However, the said Decree, having been unduly promulgated by the President, was declared unconstitutional by the Egyptian Constitutional Court on 4 May 1985, but was adopted by the People's Assembly on 4 July 1985 under Law No. 100/1985.

Legislative Decree No. 78/1931, in respect of Regulations and Procedures of Sharia Courts. This Decree was extensively amended by:
Act No. 462/1955 on the Abolition of Sharia and Religious Courts.
Act No. 77/1943 on Inheritance.
Act No. 71/1946 on Wills.
Act No. 131/1952, on cases for Dismissal of Guardians of the Person.
Decree No. 119/1952 on Guardianship of Property.

Egyptian Court of Cassation

Majmouat-ul-Qawaid al Qanooniyya (Madani) (Compendium of Legal Rules [Civil]), vol. 1 (Cairo, 1940).
Al-Muhamaat (The Organ of the Egyptian Bar), year 15 (Cairo, 1934).

Mawsooat ul Ahwal ish Shakhsiyya (An Encyclopaedia of [Egyptian] Personal Status Laws), (Alexandria, 1985).

DIGWI, Muhammad Al-, a former President of the Egyptian Court of Appeal. *Al Ahwal ush Shakhsiyya Lil Misriyeen al Muslimeen fil Fiqh wal Qanoon* (Personal Status for the Muslim Egyptians, according to Jurisprudence and Court Precedents) (Cairo).

Iraq

The Civil Code under Act No. 40/1951.

The Personal Status Law No. 188/1959 as amended by Act No. 11/1963 and Act No. 21/1978.

KARAM, Dr. Abdul Wahid, *Al Ahwal ush Shakhsiyya fil Qanoon id Dowali l Khas il Iraqi* (Personal Status under the Iraqi Private International Law), (Baghdad, 1979).

Jordan

The Civil Code, Provisional Law No. 43/1976.

The Personal Status Law, Provisional Law No. 61/1976.

Kuwait

Law No. 51/1894, promulgated 7/7/1984.

Lebanon

The Law on Obligations and Contracts 1932 (The Civil Code).

The Ottoman Family Law 1917 was promulgated by the Ottoman Sultan Muhammad Rashad on 25 October 1917, shortly before the collapse of the Ottoman Empire and the independence of the Arab States therefrom. It was not put into effect until the promulgation of the Decree No. 241 on 4 November 1942 on the Sharia Courts, in which Article 111 reads as follows:

"The Sunni Judge shall rule according to the most authoritative opinion of the Hanafi Doctrine except in cases provided for in the Family Rights Law promulgated on 8 Muharram 1336 corresponding to 25 October 1917 in which cases the Sunni Judge shall apply the provisions of the said Law while the Jaafari Judge shall rule in accordance with the Jaafari Doctrine and the provisions in conformity with this Doctrine under the Family Law."

The said Decree was later abrogated by a new Law on 16 July 1962 which nevertheless has retained the above text of Article 111 under a new Article 242.

The Lebanese Druze Personal Status Act on 24/2/1948.

SAIGH, Nabeel Az-Zawahira As-, *Mausooat-ul-Ahwal-ish-Shakhsiyyati li Jamee-il Mazahib wal Adyan fi Surriyyat i wal Ordon wa Lubnan* (Personal

Status Encyclopaedia for all religions and Denominations in Syria, Jordan and the Lebanon), (Damascus, 1984).

Morocco

Royal Decrees Nos. 343/57/1 and 379/157 promulgating the Personal Status Law.

Sudan

Law No. 1991, published 24/7/1991.

Syria

The Civil Code, Decree No. 84/1949.
Decree No. 59/1953 on the Personal Status Law amended by Law No. 34/1975.

Tunisia

Personal Status Code Decree of 13/8/1956 AD, 6/1/1376 AH.
Decree of 18/7/1957 AD, 20/11/1376 on Guardianship.
Civil Status Act No. 3 of 1/8/1957 AD, 4/1/1377 AH.
  Act No. 27 of 4/3/1958 AD, 12/8/1377 AH on Public Guardianship and Adoption, Compiled by Muhammad At-Tahir As-Senoussi, in *Mejelle of Personal Status* (Tunis, 1958).

Yemen

Personal Status Code No. 20/1992 amended by Decrees No. 27/1998 and No. 24/1999.

B. In English

ANDERSON, Prof. J.N.D., *Islamic Law in Africa* (London, 1954).
BAILLIE, Neil B.E., *Digest of Muhammadan Law* (London, 1826).
BLACK, Henry Campbell, *Black's Law Dictionary* (5th ed., West Publishing Co., St. Paul Mimm, 1979).
FYZEE, Prof. Asaf A., *Outlines of Muhammadan Law* (Oxford, 1949).
GU, J., "Iranian Cultures" in *Encyclopaedia Britannica*, vol. 9 (USA, 1979).
JAFRI, S. Husain, M., *Origins and Early Development of Shia Islam* (London, 1979).
LEWICKI, T., "Al-Ibadiyya" in *Encyclopaedia of Islam*, vol. 3 (Leiden, 1971).
MANEK, Mohanlal Dayalji, *Handbook of Mahomedan Law (Muslim Personal Law)*, (Bombay, 1948).
M.S.M. "Islamic Theology and Philosophy" in *Encyclopaedia Britannica*, vol. 9 (USA, 1979).
MULLA, Sir Dinshah Fardunji, *Principles of Mahomedan Law* (3rd ed., Calcutta, 1933).
NASR, S.H., "Ithna Ashariyya" in *Encyclopaedia of Islam*, vol. 4, Fascicules 65–66 (Leiden, 1974).
F.R. "Islam" in *Encyclopaedia Britannica*, vol. 9 (USA, 1979).

SCHACHT, J., *An Introduction to Islamic Law* (Oxford, 1979).

TYABJI, Faiz Badruddin, *Muhammadan Law – The Personal Law of Muslims* (3rd ed., Bombay, 1940).

VESEY-FITZGERALD, Symour, *Muhammedan Law – An Abridgment According to its Various Schools* (London, 1931).

E.V. ZAMBOUR, "Dirham" in *Encyclopaedia of Islam.*

Glossary

Abadis. Named after Abad At-Tanimi, a sect mainly based in Oman, North and East Africa, who derive their doctrine from the Quran, Sunna of the Prophets and the first two Patriarchal Caliphs, Abu Bakr and Omar, and the consensus of the community of Islam. Usually referred to by Arabists and Orientalists as "Ibadis" and considered by them as a Khariji sect, which the Abadis deny.

ahliyyat. Legal capacity.

ahliyyatu adaa. Literally, the capacity of execution, i.e. the capacity to contract, dispose and validly fulfil one's obligations.

ahliyyatul wujub. Literally, the capacity of obligation, i.e. to acquire rights and duties.

ahli-ul-kitab. Literally, the people of the Book: non-Muslims who believe in some holy scriptures: usually Christians and Jews. The Shias add the magis.

ansar. Literally, the "helpers", those are the citizens of Medina who supported and helped the Prophet and the muhajireen.

asaba. Literally, the agnates: the sons or the relations on the father's side: in inheritance, those who have no prescribed shares in the estate but take the residue left over after the sharers receive their prescribed portions. To that effect, the *asaba* are of three classes – (a) **asaba-bin-nafs**, i.e. in their own right; (b) **asaba-bil-ghayr**, who become *asaba* through another; and (c) **asaba maal-ghayr**, who become *asabe* or residuaries with another.

as-hab-ul-furud. The sharers.

aul. Proportionate abatement, in the event of the totality of shares in terms of fractions exceeding the unity.

bain bainoon kubra. Major irrevocable repudiation of marriage when the wife becomes temporarily (and under Tunisian law, permanently) prohibited for the husband to remarry following three pronouncements of repudiation.

bain bainoon sughra. Minor irrevocable repudiation of marriage when the husband may remarry his repudiated wife under a new contract, following one or two pronouncements of repudiation and after the lapse of *iddat*.

batil. Of a contract: void without any effect.

dhawul-arham. (From **rahm**, womb; those related through females). In the Sunni law of inheritance, the relations who are neither *asaba* (q.v.) nor sharers, e.g. the brothers' sisters or female cousins.

dhul ghafla ("dh" has the sound of "th" in 'this'). The imbecile: a person who can be easily cheated in property transactions due to his naivete, legally considered of defective legal capacity.

fard. A prescribed share in the deceased's estate for the first category of heirs. pl. **faraid** or **furud**, hence **As-hab-ul-furud** q.v.

fasid. An irregular contract, which is defective but can have some legal effect under certain conditions.

hadana. Literally, caring. Custody by the mother or a woman, usually.

hadeeth. A saying. (See **Sunna**).

hadina. A female custodian of a child.

hadini. A male custodian of a child.

hajr. Interdiction: the status and act of imposing legal restrictions on the capacity to dispose of property.

hiba. Gift.

hijra (migration). The Islamic calendar, starting from the emigration of the Prophet from Mecca to Medina in AD 622. The hijra year is lunar.

iddat. (From **adda**, to count.) The period counted by a divorcee or a widow from the termination of marriage through divorce or death, during which she cannot re-marry.

ijmaa. Consensus: a source of Islamic jurisprudence.

ijtihaad. Independent, informed and reasoned opinion on legal or theological issues. Mujtahid: the Islamic thinker who gives such an opinion.

263

ilaq. Vow of continence.

imamat. The doctrine of the leadership of the Islamic community and the subject of controversy between the Kharijis who believe that the Imam (the leader) must be elected by all Muslims irrespective of race, and the Shias, especially the Imamis or Ithna-Asharis who consider the imamat as a prerogative of the House of Ali and his descendants, the Imam being the sole authoritative source of knowledge in legal and religious matters. (See also **Shia**.)

istihsan. (From **istahsana** meaning to find preferable or more convenient.) A discursive device used by some jurists whereby preference is given to a rule other than the one reached by the more obvious form of analogy.

istis-hab. (From **istas-haba** meaning to find a link.) A methodological principle whereby a state of affairs known to have once existed is regarded to have persisted unless the contrary can be proven.

istislah. (From **istaslaha** meaning to seek the interest [of the Islamic community]. A methodological principle whereby public interest is deemed paramount in reaching a legal judgment.

Ithna-Asharis. Literally, the Twelvers: the Shia sect which believes in twelve infallible Imams. (See "The Shia Position" under Chapter 1.)

khilwat-us-sahiha (al). Valid retirement: the event of the husband and the wife, under a valid marriage contract, being together by themselves in a place where they are secure from observation.

khula. Release or redemption. *Khul'* is a dissolution of the bonds of marriage by the use of this word or its derivatives and for consideration which the wife pays or promises to pay.

kitabi. A believer in the Jewish or Christian scriptures, or a *magi* (a fire worshipper).

lian. A form of irrevocable dissolution of marriage in which the husband affirms four times under oath that his wife has committed adultery and invokes the curse of God on him if he was telling a lie; the woman then affirms four times under oath that her husband is telling a lie, and invokes on herself the curse of God if he was telling the truth. Also called **mulaana**.

maatooh. A person mentally deranged and lacking legal capacity.

madh-hab. School of religious law.

madhoon. A clerk appointed by the court to conclude marriage contracts.

madhoosh. Literally, the stunned: a person who has lost discretion because of rage or otherwise, to the point of becoming unaware of his uttering.

mafqud. Missing person.

mahr (also called **sadaq** or **oqr**). The dower: a sum of money or other property which becomes payable by the husband to the wife as an effect of marriage.

majnoon. Insane: a person considered of void legal capacity.

mandub. A desirable cause.

marad ul-maut. Literally, death-illness. A person in *marad-ul-maut* is suffering from a terminal disease ending in death.

Mijalla (Magazine). The Ottoman Civil Code compiled in AD 1877, AH 1293, based mainly on the Hanafi juristic schools. It remained until the 1950s the Civil Code of Syria, Iraq and Jordan.

muallaq. Subject to a condition in the form of an oath or relegated to some event in the future.

mubah. A permissible cause.

mubaraat. Mutual discharge. (See **khula**).

muhajireen. The first Muslim who embraced Islam in Mecca and subsequently migrated with the Prophet to Medina.

mujtahidoon. These are Muslim scholars who are authorized to use reasoning to deduce legal opinions on the basis of the Quran, the Tradition of the Prophet and by analogical deduction.

mulaana. Literally, mutual cursing. (See **lian**).

munjaz. With immediate effect.

muta. Literally, pleasure. A form of temporary marriage recognized only by the Shia school, and considered as illegal by the Sunnis.

mutat. Compensation paid to a woman by the husband who has arbitrarily divorced her.

mutawali. The administrator of the *waqf* who is merely a manager of the *waqf*.

nashiz. The disobedient wife who refuses to submit to the authority of her husband.

nafith ("th" as in "this"). Of a contract: effective.

oqr. Dower. (See **mahr**).

qayyim (al) (in Arab North Africa). The curator: a guardian appointed by the court for the minor who has no guardian.

qiyas. Analogy: a discursive method used by Islamic jurists whereby a judgment is derived from similar cases ruled upon under the Quran, Sunna or previously established ruling by unanimity. In formal logic, *qiyas* is the translation of 'syllogism'.

ra-ay. Literally, personal opinion. **As-Haab-ur-Ra-ay**: a school of juristic thought which advocated the interpretation of the religious texts and analogy derived from precedents, as opposed to **As-Haab-ul-Hadeeth** who adhered to the Quran and the Prophet's traditions and refrained from judging any hypothetical question.

rud. Return: the converse of proportionate abatement (**aul** q.v.) when the total shares are less than a unity. The shares are then proportionately increased.

sadaq. Dower. (See **mahr**).

safeeh. The prodigal: a spendthrift who is unnecessarily wasteful or lavish, although endowed with sound mind. Considered of a defective legal capacity. (See also **dhul ghafla**).

Sahaba (from **sahib** meaning friend). The Prophet's Companions; singular, Sahabi.

sahih. For a contract: valid and effective.

Sharia (from **sharaa** meaning a path). The Divine Law of Islam.

Shia (sect). The Followers of Ali and the People of his house, as contradistinct from the Sunnis who represent the orthodox and mainstream sect of Islam. The largest Shia denomination is the Ithna-Ashari, the official doctrine of Iran and of the Shias of the Arab Middle East and Pakistan. Also known as Jaafaris, after the sixth Imam and the first to codify the Shia law.

Sunna (originally the trodden path). Traditions attributed to the Prophet. The Prophet's Sunna is usually divided into (a) verbal utterances (*sunna qawlia* or *hadeeth*); (b) acts of the Prophet (*sunna filia*); and (c) the tacit assent of the Prophet (*sunna taqririyya*).

sura. Chapter or section of the Quran.

talaq. The dissolution of a valid marriage contract forthwith or at a later date by the husband, his agent or his wife duly authorised by him to do so, using the word **talaq**, a derivative or a synonym thereof.

talaq ala mal. A divorce for a pecuniary consideration. (See **khula** and **mubaraat**).

tamleek. The passing of property.

Umma. "Community" – Community of Islam, a collective term to denote all Muslims, past and present, bonded together in faith, regardless of ethnic differences.

waqf. The *waqf* is the permanent dedication by a Muslim of any property in such a way that the appropriator's right is extinguished for charity or for religious objects or purposes. (Called **habous** in Algeria and Morocco).

waqif. Dedicator of the *waqf*.

wasey al-mukhtar (al). The testamentary guardian: a person appointed by the father in a testament to look after his children after his death.

wilaya. Guardianship: for marriage it can be with the right of compulsion (**wilayatul-ijbar**) or without such a right (**wilayatul-nadb**).

zihar. Injurious assimilation.

Index

267

1. *Islamic Law and Finance*, Chibli Mallat (ed.) (1988)
(ISBN 1-85333-121-X)

2. *The Islamic Laws of Personal Status* (2nd ed.), Jamal J. Nasir (1990)
(ISBN 1-85333-280-1)

3. *Islamic Family Law*, Chibli Mallat and Jane Connors (eds.) (1991)
(ISBN 1-85333-301-8)

4. *Mixed Courts of Egypt*, Mark S.W. Hoyle (1991)
(ISBN 1-85333-321-2)

5. *The Theory of Contracts in Islamic Law*, S.E. Rayner (1991)
(ISBN 1-85333-617-3)

6. *The Marriage Contract in Islamic Law*, Dawoud S. El Alami (1992)
(ISBN 1-85333-719-6)

7. *Unlawful Gain and Legitimate Profit in Islamic Law*, Nabil A. Saleh (1992)
(ISBN 1-85333-721-8)

8. *Islamic and Public Law*, Chibli Mallat (ed.) (1993)
(ISBN 1-85333-768-4)

9. *Finance of International Trade in the Gulf*, Dr. Ahmed A.M.S. Al-Suwaidi
(1994)
(ISBN 1-85333-947-4)

10. *The Law of Commercial Procedure of the United Arab Emirates*, Dawoud S.,
El Alami (1994)
(ISBN 1-85966-080-0)

11. *The Status of Women under Islamic Law* (2nd ed.), Jamal J. Nasir (1995)
(ISBN 1-85966-084-3)

12. *Business Laws of Yemen*, Abdulla M.A. Maktari and John McHugo (1995)
(ISBN 1-85966-112-2)

13. *Arab Islamic Banking and Renewal of Islamic Law*, Nicholas D. Ray (1995)
(ISBN 1-85966-104-1)

14. *The Law of Business Contracts in the Arab Middle East*,
Nayla Cornair-Obeid (1996)
(ISBN 90-411-0216-7)

KLUWER LAW INTERNATIONAL – THE HAGUE, LONDON, NEW YORK

15. *Islamic Institutions in Jerusalem*, Yitzhak Reiter (1997)
(ISBN 90-411-0382-1)

16. *Islamic Law and Finance: Religion, Risk and Return*, Frank E. Vogel and
Samuel L. Hayes III (1998)
(ISBN 90-411-0547-6)

17. *United Arab Emirates Court of Cassation Judgments 1989–1997*,
Richard Price and Essam Al Tamimi (1998)
(ISBN 90-411-1005-4)

18. *Legal Pluralism in the Arab World*, Baudouin Dupret, Maurits Berger, and
Laila al-Zwaini (eds.) (1999)
(ISBN 90-411-1005-0)

19. *Intellectual Property Laws of the Arab Countries*, Abu-Ghazaleh (2000)
(ISBN 90-411-8842-8)

20. *An Introduction to Islamic Finance*, Mohammad Taqi Usmani (2001)
(ISBN 90-411-1619-2)

21. *Studies in Modern Islamic Law and Jurisprudence*, O. Arabi (2001)
(ISBN 90-411-1660-5)

22. *Egypt and its Laws*, G. Alleaume, N. Bernard-Maugiron and B. Dupret (eds.)
(2001)
(ISBN 90-411-1639-7)

23. *The Islamic Law of Personal Status, Third Edition*, J. J. Nasir (2001)
(ISBN hb: 90-411-1661-3; pb: 90-411-1663-X)

KLUWER LAW INTERNATIONAL – THE HAGUE, LONDON, NEW YORK